THE LONG
GOLDEN
AFTERNOON

THE LONG GOLDEN AFTERNOON

GOLF'S AGE OF GLORY 1864–1914

STEPHEN PROCTOR

First published in 2022 by

ARENA SPORT
An imprint of Birlinn Limited
West Newington House
10 Newington Road
Edinburgh EH9 1QS

www.arenasportbooks.co.uk

ISBN: 978 1 913759049

British Library Cataloguing-in-Publication Data
A catalogue record for this book is available on request from the British Library.

Typeset by Biblichor Ltd, Edinburgh

Printed and bound by Clays Ltd, Elcograf S.p.A.

CONTENTS

One

'TERRIBLE THINGS'

⸺•◦●◉●◦•⸺

Horace Hutchinson, the famed English amateur, had just slogged in from his final round in the 1890 Open Championship when he heard the news that was spreading like wildfire around the links of Prestwick. The talk was about John Ball Jr, a gentleman golfer from Royal Liverpool. At that moment, Ball was playing his homeward nine and, as Hutchinson recalled, doing 'terrible things'.

Hutchinson, of course, meant 'terrible' in that peculiarly British sense of the word that defines an accomplishment so unexpected as to be unthinkable. Ball was playing with such machine-like precision that the unimaginable might well happen. Hutchinson and his friend, Dr William Laidlaw Purves, both influential leaders in the rapidly growing world of English golf, hurried off to catch up with Ball and follow the nation's rising star home.

By 1890 competitive golf had been played for a century and a half, and in nearly all that time the gentlemen who ran the game lagged far behind professional players, often laughably so. The best of the amateurs had come closer in recent years, but those watching the Open still must have raised an eyebrow when Ball started the Championship with twin nines of 41. His tidy 82 left him a stroke off the pace set by St Andrews professional Andra Kirkaldy, the heavy favourite. Ball's admirers would not have been surprised. He entered the Open in magnificent form.

Three months earlier he had won the Amateur Championship for the second time in its five-year existence.

In the afternoon round, as Kirkaldy struggled, Ball marched steadily along, making the proper figure on every hole. By the time he reached the 16th, it had become clear to Hutchinson, Purves and everyone else at Prestwick on that afternoon of 11 September 1890 that only an unforeseen calamity could prevent the Englishman from doing 'the most terrible thing that had ever yet been done in golf – he, as an amateur, was going to win the Open Championship.'

Exactly the sort of catastrophe that might yet derail Ball had befallen his playing partner, Willie Campbell, three years ago on this very hole. The ill-fated professional from Musselburgh had a two-stroke lead in the 1887 Open when he stepped up to the tee of the 16th. Playing boldly, Campbell tried to carry his shot over a fairway bunker. It fell short, ending up mired in gnarly grass that rimmed the hazard. He needed five shots to get out and tossed away his best chance to become Champion Golfer. Not long afterwards, Hutchinson had seen poor Campbell and his caddie sitting atop upturned buckets in the professional's shop, weeping uncontrollably. Ever after that sinister pot bunker would be known as Willie Campbell's grave.

No such disaster would befall John Ball. In the end, he would win the Open by three strokes with matching scores of 82, for a total of 164. As the inevitability of his victory dawned on the two pillars of English golf, Hutchinson remembered, Purves turned to speak to him. '"Horace," he said to me in a voice of much solemnity. "This is a great day for golf."'

Even those forward-thinking men had no idea just how great a day it was. Golf had been growing slowly but steadily in England since the institution of the Open Championship and the rise of the game's first superstar, Young Tom Morris of St Andrews. Ball's historic victory at Prestwick turned that smouldering fire into a conflagration.

The quarter century that followed would witness the game's coming of age. It would see golf's popularity explode – in England and Ireland, in the Americas and Europe, in Africa and India, and in Australia and New Zealand.

It would see the emergence of professional golf tours, and the anointing of the Royal and Ancient Golf Club of St Andrews as the game's governing authority and guiding light.

It would see the beginning of a relentless quest to make golf easier that has shaped the game from that day to this, as well as the blossoming of a literature that remains the envy of other sports.

And it would see, against all odds, the first period in history in which the gentlemen golfers who had ruled the game since time immemorial could actually compete against the professionals whose prowess had always humbled them, even as they sneered at the men as ruffians.

These revolutionary changes unfolded against the backdrop of something else Hutchinson sensed on the 18th green at Prestwick as he, Purves and the crowd lustily cheered John Ball as the first amateur to be hailed Champion Golfer of the Year.

'What interested me much at the moment,' Hutchinson wrote, 'was the attitude of the professionals towards the result. I had expected that they would feel rather injured by seeing the championship which they had regarded as their own going to an amateur. To my surprise that did not appear to disconcert them in the least. What they did resent, however, so far as resentment may be carried within the limits of perfectly good sportsmanship, was that it should be won by an Englishman.'

That autumn afternoon at Prestwick stoked a rivalry as passionate as any in sport. Scotland now had a genuine competitor at its national pastime. In the years leading up to the First World War, the battle between Scotland and England for supremacy on the links provided the dramatic backdrop for this transformative generation.

As one century ended and another began, Scottish stalwarts like John Laidlay, Freddie Tait, Willie Park Jr and James Braid fought bravely to turn back the rising English tide represented by John Ball, Harold Hilton, John Henry Taylor and Harry Vardon.

These golfers became childhood heroes of the writers who chronicled that glorious era, especially *The Times* correspondent Bernard Darwin. Their fierce skirmishes would produce an astonishing number of performances that will stand for the ages. By the time war was declared on 28 July 1914, the outlines of golf's future were well established. The struggle for superiority between England and Scotland had also been settled – and the most important result was that the game itself had won.

The heart-stopping drama of the championships and celebrated matches of that era – coupled with dramatic advances in balls, clubs and science – positioned a game that for centuries had been played only by Scots to become a worldwide obsession. In the aftermath of the Great War, that truth would be almost immediately revealed.

Two

GOLF MOVES SOUTH

—•◦●◦•—

Golf arrived in England the same way it would nearly everywhere else – through connections with a Scotsman.

In 1853 a British Army engineer named William Driscoll Gosset was stationed in Ayr, on Scotland's west coast, to work on drafting topographical maps of the nation. He arrived two years after the famous St Andrews golfer Tom Morris Sr had moved to neighbouring Prestwick to lay out a golf course and become keeper of the green. Captain Gosset came to know Morris, learning the game from him and drawing the first map of the dastardly links he had crafted along the shores of the Firth of Clyde.

Later that year the captain paid a visit to his cousin, Isaac Gosset, the Vicar of Northam, a small village in an area of southwest England known as North Devon. Isaac had also been bitten by the golf bug, having been introduced to the game while visiting his sister in St Andrews. She was married to General George Moncrieff, a prominent member of the Royal and Ancient Golf Club. While the captain was visiting the vicar in Devon, the two of them took a stroll along Northam Burrows, a vast sprawl of links land on the picturesque shores of Bideford Bay. Captain Gosset couldn't help but note what General Moncrieff would later observe on one of his visits to Northam: 'Providence obviously designed this for a golf links.'

Clubs and balls were promptly ordered from Tom Morris and the

Gossets began playing on the Burrows in the same way golfers in Scotland had done for centuries – by cutting holes in the ground with a knife every few hundred yards and hitting shots to them. Gosset's neighbours gradually began to take an interest in this curious new Scottish game. By 1860 – the same year the Open Championship made its debut at Prestwick – Tom was asked to pay a visit to North Devon. He stayed a month, teaching the locals how to play golf and helping Reverend Gosset improve his rudimentary course.

Four years later, on 18 May 1864, came a momentous occasion for the game – the formation of the first golf club that could fairly be described as English: the North Devon and West of England Golf Club. It was not, of course, the nation's oldest club. Golf had been played on English soil, although almost exclusively by Scotsmen, since King James I brought his royal court from Edinburgh to London in 1603. Golfers played at Blackheath, where the nation's first golf club was established in 1766. Expatriate Scots also played at Kersal Moor in Manchester as early as 1818.

North Devon was something different. It came to be acknowledged as the 'cradle of English golf' for the simple reason that fully three quarters of its original 51 members were Englishmen new to the game. In time the club would come to be better known as Westward Ho! That nickname was adopted from the title of an adventure novel Charles Kingsley had written in a hamlet next door to the Burrows not long before the captain and the vicar discovered its possibilities for golf.

His club now established, Reverend Gosset knew what to do next – invite Tom Morris for another visit. Tom arrived that August as a celebrity, having twice won the new Open Championship at Prestwick. He spent eight days at Northam, during which he designed a formal 18-hole golf course on the Burrows, the first seaside links outside Scotland. Tom also played a daily foursome, introducing southerners to the most popular form of the game in those days. It consisted of a match between two-man teams, with players on both sides alternating shots until the ball was holed, a sublime and volatile format.

When Tom returned home, he would begin an important new chapter in his own life. That year, he was persuaded to return to his birthplace in St Andrews and tend its famed links. He would stay in that ancient seaside town all his days, gradually emerging as the Grand Old Man of Golf.

Gosset's next step was to do what every club founder would do for decades to come, recruit a Scotsman to be North Devon's golf professional.

The club hired Johnny Allan, who had grown up in Prestwick as a childhood friend of Tom's precocious son, Young Tommy. It is a testament to how quickly golf took root in England that only three years passed before Gosset's venture received recognition deeply valued in a nobility-conscious nation. The Prince of Wales, later King Edward VII, became the club's patron and gave it a new name – The Royal North Devon Golf Club.

Among the club's founding members was Colonel William Nelson Hutchinson. He had a precocious son of his own named Horatio Gordon, after the famous British admiral. A tall, striking figure who preferred to be known as Horace, Hutchinson quickly emerged as one of the best golfers at Westward Ho! In 1875, aged 16, he was admitted as a club member. That autumn, Hutchinson recalled, he 'committed the blazing indiscretion' of winning the club medal, which made him captain of Royal North Devon. That meant he, a mere teenager, had to take the chair at the club's general meeting. 'I do not know that I made a much bigger hash of it than any other boy forced into the same unnatural position would have done,' he wrote.

Hutchinson wasn't one to make a hash of many things, despite a lifelong struggle with frail health. He would go on to study Classics at Oxford, flirt with taking up sculpture, see his hair turn prematurely white, become a leading amateur golfer, and emerge as an important voice on golf. Hutchinson's work inspired a generation of writers who grew up reading his books and magazine articles, chief among them future *Times* correspondent, Bernard Darwin.

On the links, Hutchinson was a flamboyant player, taking a long, loose swing with what he described as 'bombastic freedom' – a move that saw both his knees bending, his right elbow flying, and his body never quite catching up to his arms on the follow-through. With that swing and his fearless approach to the game, Hutchinson was inclined to find more than his share of trouble. Thankfully, as Darwin put it, 'Nobody was ever better at improvising a stroke for some difficult or, as it looked to the too confident adversary, impossible occasion.'

Important a figure as he was, Hutchinson would not turn out to be the most famous golfer in his household. That distinction would fall to a lad then working as a boot boy for the Hutchinsons – a small, thin, tow-headed young man named John Henry Taylor. Before the Great War drew the curtain on that formative era of golf, Taylor would emerge as a player for all time and an enormously influential figure in shaping the game's future.

Royal North Devon may have been the birthplace of English golf, but it was hardly the only place where the game was taking root south of the border. In 1865, a year after the founding of Westward Ho!, the London Scottish Volunteers formed a club on Wimbledon Common. It, too, attracted English neighbours eager to take up the game.

By 1873 the Englishmen had split off to form a club of their own, playing from the other end of the common. Eleven years later the Prince of Wales became patron of that club, too. It would be known ever after as the Royal Wimbledon Golf Club. Wimbledon had the disadvantage of not being a seaside course, but that was offset by proximity to London. It became an important power centre of the English game, home to such influential figures as Henry Lamb and Dr William Laidlaw Purves.

Turning point

The pivotal moment for English golf, however, came in 1869. That was the year a golf club was established in a small fishing village along the Dee Estuary known as Hoylake. The village is 12 miles west of Liverpool, a bustling trade centre and England's gateway to the world.

Being next door to Liverpool meant Hoylake was home to ambitious businessmen inclined to be bold in any endeavour they undertook. Its location by the seaside also meant that a club led by such forward-thinking men was far better positioned to be a dynamic force in the growth of English golf than one situated inland, as Royal Wimbledon was, or in a remote place like Westward Ho!

The centrepiece of Hoylake was the Royal Hotel, a resort founded in 1792 by Sir John Stanley as a way of capitalising on a fashion then sweeping the nation, bathing in the sea. The Royal stood on the edge of a vast rabbit warren that was also home to a racecourse. Since the mid-19th century the Liverpool Hunt Club had conducted race meetings there. By 1869 the hotel's lustre had faded, but its fortunes were soon to be revived because the rabbit warren also happened to be ideal for golf, a game whose popularity had been surging in Scotland and England for the past two decades.

Golf was spreading 'like Noah's flood', as golfer Andra Kirkaldy put it, because a genius known as Young Tom Morris had come along to take advantage of new technology – the arrival of the first hard-rubber golf ball in 1848. The ball was made of gutta-percha, a sticky substance drawn from trees in Malaysia. The 'gutty' replaced a ball made of leather stuffed with feathers. Those balls were extremely fragile and vastly more expensive than gutties, meaning that for centuries only wealthy men could afford to play proper golf. The arrival of the cheap, durable gutty opened golf to the masses and drew thousands of new players to the game.

A dozen years later, all those new players got a national championship to root for when the Open debuted at Prestwick. With the stars aligned for a golf revolution, along came Young Tom Morris to ignite the spark. The year before Hoylake was founded, aged 17, Tommy began his inexorable march to claim the Open's first trophy, The Challenge Belt, by winning three Championships in succession. Young Tom's prowess and star power attracted lavish attention from the London press. Not surprisingly, gentlemen reading about Tommy's exploits in English newspapers began to take an interest in this newfangled game emerging from Scotland.

Those newly curious Englishmen often had Scottish acquaintances more than happy to introduce them to the glories of golf, in the same way that Old Tom Morris helped his friend, Captain Gosset, bring the game to North Devon. That was especially true at Hoylake, which was teeming with Scottish merchants – men like John Muir Dowie of West Kirby. He was married to the daughter of Robert Chambers Jr, an Edinburgh publisher and skilled golfer. Chambers was famous for having won the second of the three Grand National Tournaments for amateur golfers conducted in St Andrews beginning in 1857. On Thursday 13 May 1869, at the urging of his father-in-law, Dowie sent a letter to 20 prominent Hoylake residents. It began: 'It has been suggested that Hoylake offers a suitable and convenient ground for playing Golf, and some friends have asked me to endeavour to organise a Golf Club.

'Your name has been mentioned as a probable member, and I take this liberty of asking you to join.'

Twenty-one men attended a meeting held two days later at the Royal Hotel. Together they resolved to form Liverpool Golf Club, with Dowie as its first captain and a room in the hotel serving as its clubhouse. Later that night, in the sky above Hoylake, villagers witnessed a sparkling celestial display we now know to be the Northern Lights. Back then people thought the sky had been set alight by the tail of a comet streaking overhead. They considered that a portent of good things to come. For golf, at least, it certainly was.

Chambers was in town for the occasion and had brought along his personal golf professional, Old Tom Morris's brother, George. The two of them laid out a crude nine-hole course in front of the Royal, and newly christened members celebrated the club's birth by playing a few matches even as horses raced around the oval next to their links. By 1876 the racecourse would be gone and the rabbit warren left to the golfers.

In August 1869, Hoylake's connections to the founding family of golf would deepen when George Morris returned with his son, Jack, to explore the possibility of his becoming Liverpool's golf professional. Hoylake still seemed a bit sleepy to George. He worried that his son might not thrive there and suggested they return home to St Andrews. Jack ignored his father's advice and decided to give it a go. He set up shop in a stable behind the hotel and stayed until his death 60 years later, becoming as much a fixture at Hoylake as the mighty winds that sweep over the links from the Dee Estuary.

From the start, the men of Liverpool Golf Club – which would receive its royal patronage from Queen Victoria in 1871 – proved themselves to be a forward-thinking lot determined to make a mark in the game. In the decades that followed, Royal Liverpool would become the English equivalent of St Andrews as an epicentre of the game. Unlike the Royal and Ancient, however, Hoylake would prove to be a dynamic agent of change, the club responsible for nearly every significant innovation in championship golf.

'The Englishman who golfs today,' Hutchinson wrote years later, 'may do well to think that, had it not been for the zeal and energy of the early members of the Royal Liverpool Golf Club, we, in the South, might never have come into our golfing heritage.'

The first sign of that zeal wasn't long in coming. In the spring of 1872, Royal Liverpool staged the Grand Tournament for Professionals, the first major golf competition held on English soil. Club members subscribed more than £100, an enormous sum, to finance lavish prizes. These included a payout of £15 to the winner, the largest prize ever offered. By comparison, the Open paid the winner £8 that year.

Just as remarkable, however, was that Royal Liverpool agreed to cover the railway expenses of every golfer who competed in the tournament and to provide them with dinner in the evening. That was an enormous gesture of respect, perhaps even a turning point for professional golfers, at a time when they were viewed by gentlemen like Hutchinson as 'feckless, reckless creatures'. The idea, of course, was to make certain Hoylake attracted the biggest stars in the golfing firmament – Young Tom and his St Andrews sidekick, Davie Strath.

The timing could not have been more perfect. Eighteen months earlier, Tommy had set the golf world aflame by winning his third consecutive

Open at the age of 19. That victory ended a decade-long quest to claim The Challenge Belt by making it Tommy's personal property. It also left the Open in limbo for a year, as its founding club, Prestwick, reached out to St Andrews and Musselburgh to subscribe for a new trophy and create a bigger, brighter future for the game's premier championship.

That made the Grand Tournament a marquee event, and it came off precisely as planned. Tommy, Davie and every other leading golfer turned up to compete at Royal Liverpool on Tuesday 25 April 1872. The only glitch was that it rained so torrentially that play occasionally had to be suspended. The nasty weather didn't stop a hardy crowd from following the action, among them a ten-year-old from Hoylake who was soon to make his own mark in golf – young Johnny Ball. True to form, Tommy and Davie staged a fierce battle for the largest purse ever offered in golf, with Davie taking the lead in round one and Tommy rallying on the second 18 to win by a single shot.

Bold stroke

If the Grand Tournament put English golf on the map, it was two amateur events launched over the next dozen years that secured the future of the game south of the River Tweed.

The first was the annual University Match between Oxford and Cambridge. That competition debuted on 6 March 1878 at the London Scottish Volunteers' course on Wimbledon Common. Both teams fielded four players, who faced off man to man. Oxford's team, led by the ever-present Hutchinson, won every match, a lopsided victory to begin a contest in which honours have been fairly even over the decades.

The University Match immediately became the only first-class amateur event in an age when the golf calendar contained just a single certain fixture, the Open. More important, however, was that it signalled the acceptance of the game by Oxford and Cambridge. Generations of students destined to become Britain's leaders and brightest minds would grow up steeped in golf. That was no small thing in the 1870s – a time when, 'you could not travel about with golf clubs . . . without exciting the wonder and, almost, the suspicions of all those who saw such strange things,' Hutchinson wrote.

Significant as the University Match was, however, the most transformative development in English golf unfolded half a dozen years later at Royal Liverpool. On 13 December 1884, during a meeting of the club's committee, Honourable Secretary Thomas Owen Potter proposed that Hoylake host a tournament open to all amateur golfers during its spring meeting the following year. His idea received near unanimous approval at an extraordinary general meeting of the club on 28 January 1885.

The notion of a national amateur championship was not a new one. At the instigation of Prestwick's James Ogilvie Fairlie, patron of Old Tom Morris, St Andrews had hosted three such championships beginning in 1857. That was the event in which Robert Chambers made his name a decade before he helped found Hoylake. The competition lapsed after its third year because it interfered with the Royal and Ancient's Autumn Meeting. In the years since, the idea had resurfaced. In 1884, an R&A member urged the club to host a championship open to all amateur golfers, but his suggestion was not taken up. Still, there continued to be agitation in the press, much of it coming from newly minted English players, for an amateur championship to rival the Open.

Those dreams were realised the following spring. Beginning on 20 April 1885, 44 players from 11 clubs in Scotland and England competed in the first Amateur Championship. The format was different from the one used in the Open, where the trophy went to the golfer with the lowest score over 36 holes. The Amateur featured a series of one-on-one battles in which the player who won the most holes prevailed. The last man standing won the title. With its thrust-and-parry drama, match play was everybody's favourite form of golf in that era. Scots considered it the only true test of a champion.

The competition could not begin, however, until the committee in charge of the event, Hutchinson among them, dealt with a ticklish situation – defining what constituted an amateur golfer. The issue arose because an entry was received from a Scotsman named Douglas Rolland. He had finished second in the 1884 Open, earning a modest prize. It would have been easy to bar Rolland as a professional, but for an awkward truth. Hoylake's favourite son, young Johnny Ball, had also pocketed a £1 prize when he competed in the 1878 Open, finishing fourth as a boy of 16.

In the end, the committee did what committees often do. It split hairs, deciding that any player who hadn't accepted a prize in five years remained an amateur. Hutchinson considered that grossly unfair. Ball's case and Rolland's were 'fundamentally on all fours', he wrote. Hutchinson resigned in protest before the vote was taken. The committee also barred any player who made clubs or balls for a living, worked as a caddie or gave lessons for money – the rough outlines of what would become the rules for amateur status.

Once that messy business was concluded, players set out for three days of match play in an event that quickly emerged as one of the major championships that golfers and fans looked forward to each season, a worthy companion to the Open. Every leading club in the kingdom was represented – from the Royal and Ancient and the Honourable Company of Edinburgh Golfers to Royal Blackheath, Royal North Devon, Royal Wimbledon and more. The gentlemen who had presided over golf since its earliest days now had a championship of their own, guaranteeing that English interest in the Scottish game would only redouble.

The first Amateur Championship did not come off perfectly – mostly because the committee running the competition decided that both players would advance to the next round if a match was halved, rather than having them play off until a winner was determined. The unfortunate result was that three players, not four, made it into the semi-finals. One of them, Allan Macfie, received a bye into the final, an absurd situation. Not surprisingly, that led to play-offs being adopted in future Amateurs.

The most compelling match of that inaugural Championship turned out to be the hotly contested 18-hole semi-final between Hutchinson and Ball, the up-and-coming 23-year-old from Hoylake. Hundreds of the faithful turned out to root for their young champion as he and Hutchinson waged a desperate battle on a lovely afternoon marred only by a boisterous south-west wind. The partisan crowd's hopes were raised as Ball played the outward nine flawlessly, displaying the exquisite long game that would be his hallmark.

By the time the players turned for home, Ball was leading by a hole. The tension reached boiling point when he pocketed the tenth to go 2 up. Hutchinson, however, was not one to wilt in a crisis. He won the next four holes, taking his own 2-up lead with four left to play. The young son of Hoylake fought valiantly through the finishing stretch at Liverpool, one of the toughest in golf. Ball won the 17th to give his fans a glimmer of hope as the tandem approached the final hole, with Hutchinson leading 1 up.

Alas, the home crowd's hopes were dashed when Hutchinson laid his approach to the 18th stone dead, winning the hole and the match 2 up. That battle with Ball clearly exhausted Hutchinson. He was a shadow of himself in the final, going down meekly to Macfie, who 'rested in peace while Horace and John went out to cut each other's throats', as Bernard Darwin put it.

A Scotsman born in Liverpool to a family of sugar merchants, Macfie belonged to both Hoylake and the Royal and Ancient, but always entered tournaments as a representative of St Andrews. He closed Hutchinson out on the 12th green, going seven holes up with just six left to play. Macfie became the first player – and the first Scotsman – to be crowned Champion Amateur of the Year.

What Hoylake did next would turn out to be pivotal to golf's future. The club decided that no new championship would be recognised as such unless it were conducted under the auspices of the institution revered wherever the game was played, the Royal and Ancient Golf Club. It was the earliest indication that England would make a choice one might consider unthinkable for a nation which had so often fought with its northern neighbour – that in golf, at least, it preferred to be ruled by Scotland.

In January of 1886 Hoylake sent the R&A a letter asking the club to take charge of the event going forward and invite other leading clubs to subscribe for a trophy. Never inclined to seek out leadership, the Royal and Ancient was reluctant at first, but by May it had agreed to organise a meeting of leading clubs to discuss the Amateur's future.

The meeting took place three months later in Edinburgh, where it was decided that the Championship would be administered by the R&A and played alternately at St Andrews, Hoylake and Prestwick. Twenty-three clubs contributed a total of £159 to buy one of the most handsome trophies in sport, an enormous silver cup topped by a likeness of Old Tom Morris.

That decision would, at least temporarily, erase Macfie from the record books. Thereafter the 1886 tournament would be viewed as the first official Amateur Championship. It would not be until nearly four decades later, in 1922, that the R&A recognised Macfie as the first champion, adding one more victory to Scotland's tally in that contest.

With the Amateur firmly established, and one of England's three Royal clubs at the centre of it all, golf was poised to grow in earnest south of the border. What English golf needed was a home-grown champion like Scotland's Young Tommy – a player capable of whipping the Scots at their own game. Nothing could do more to spark English interest in the Scottish game than taking the fight to their age-old enemy.

Three

A HERO FOR ENGLAND

———————————— •◦◉◦• ————————————

The boy who would grow up to be the first idol of English golf made his debut a few months after having watched in awe as Scotland's King of Clubs – Young Tom Morris – took down a stellar field in the Grand Tournament for Professionals at Royal Liverpool.

In the summer of 1872, still six months shy of his 11th birthday, Johnny Ball won the first Hoylake Boys' Medal, a competition for sons of members aged 15 or younger that is still contested today. The club's records include no score for Ball that year, although he won the medal a second time in 1875 with a score of 98.

It was the year after that second Boys' Medal that Ball began to play the kind of game that made Hoylake members realise they might be witnessing the emergence of the first truly consequential English golfer. That September a match was arranged between young Ball and the latest winner of Royal Liverpool's Gold Medal, a scratch player named John Dunn.

Given that Ball was 14 years old, it was decided that he should be given six strokes over the 18 holes. Ball humbled Dunn, closing the match out on the 12th green, taking a seven-hole lead with just six holes left to play. Dunn and Ball played three more matches after that with no strokes given. The precocious youngster won two of those and halved the third.

Not long afterwards, Ball was chosen to be a partner in a foursome match that may be among the saddest ever recorded. In early 1875, a challenge had been issued for Ball to team up with Young Tommy and take on Davie Strath and any amateur of his choosing. Davie picked Arthur Molesworth, a prominent gentleman golfer from Westward Ho!

How Ball must have looked forward to that match, a chance to play alongside his hero. It never came off because of Young Tommy's tragic death on Christmas Day in St Andrews. The following year, perhaps to honour his friend's memory, Strath took Tommy's place as Ball's partner in a match against Old Tom Morris and Molesworth. They played four rounds over the Liverpool links. Strath and Ball romped it by seven holes up with five left to play, having led in every round.

Those matches marked the beginning of a love affair between Hoylake and John Ball that would be as passionate as any golf would ever see. Over the next three decades, Ball would amass a record rivalled by few amateurs in history. The people of Hoylake, from the wealthiest merchant to the lowliest fisherman, responded with an outpouring of affection the reserved Ball often found too much to bear. Years later one of those who fell most deeply in love with England's rising star, *Times* golf correspondent Bernard Darwin, would reflect on the devotion of the Liverpool faithful.

'I am profoundly sorry for those who never watched Mr Ball playing a big match before a big crowd at Hoylake,' he wrote. 'The hero, himself, always with a buttonhole presented by some admirer, the bodyguard of rosetted stewards, the fishermen in their blue jerseys carrying the rope with the air of men performing a sacred rite, the tramp of the crowd behind the rope, the very errand boys on the road neglecting their work to hear how "John" was getting on – I have seen many scenes of enthusiasm in my wanderings over many links, but never one like that. It possessed some quality of its own – touching, exciting, bringing a lump to the throat – which no words can depict, and we shall never see its like again.'

It is, perhaps, not surprising that Ball fell in love with the Scottish game. He grew up literally on the Hoylake links, as his father was proprietor of the Royal Hotel, situated just off the links and headquarters of the golf club. When the day's chores were done, young Johnny could do what he loved best, slip out to a quiet corner of the golf course and practise this new game that had captured his imagination.

Ball's father turned out to be something of a natural athlete himself. Having taken up golf when Hoylake was founded in 1869, he reduced his handicap from 36 to scratch in a year and became a player to be feared. When he and his son were in top form, Ball's father was fond of issuing challenges in Hoylake's clubhouse that they would take on any two players in a foursome. Few were inclined to try.

A Christmas Eve baby – born in 1861 to the former Margaret Parry – Ball shared a name with his father and grandfather. Over the years, that created a bit of confusion as to how the young golfer ought to be known. As a boy, he was John Ball Tertius, a Latin word meaning the third. When his grandfather passed in 1887, he became John Ball Jr, the name he would be known by during his glory years on the links. Eighteen years later, when his father died, he would become, simply, John Ball.

Young Johnny grew up differently than most men who dominated amateur golf in his day. They attended fashionable public schools and went on to university. Ball took a simpler path. He learned the basics at the local primary school until he reached an age when he was old enough to work, typically twelve at the time. Work meant helping out at the hotel or on his grandfather's 55-acre farm nearby. The solitary life of working the land proved more appealing to Ball than the public business of running a hotel. When his grandfather became too old for such back-breaking work, young John would become the farmer in the family.

That life of rigorous labour showed in Ball's frame. He stood 5 feet 9 inches tall and weighed 154 pounds, all sinew and muscle. He could be recognised anywhere for his thick moustache and the way in which he always seemed to lean forward as he walked, a curious-looking gait that provided fodder for cartoonists. At golf, Ball wore the player's standard uniform, a tweed or Norfolk jacket and knickerbockers. On the right occasion, he was not afraid to adopt a bold look, sometimes wearing loud patterns of checks or pinstripes. He also displayed a fondness for red-topped stockings and, on occasion, white shoes.

Ball's most distinguishing characteristics, however, were shyness and modesty, traits that no doubt endeared him to his fellow Englishmen. He was a man of few words, although when he did speak it was usually something witty and memorable. One famous story about him concerns a medal competition at Hoylake played in the kind of merciless wind that so often blows off the Dee Estuary. Ball's score was so low it left mouths agape. With the subtlety of a knowing wink, he explained that he happened to be hitting the ball just the right height for that day.

Ball never could become comfortable with the attention lavished on him. At the peak of his powers, Royal Liverpool had his portrait painted and hung on a stairway in the clubhouse. Ball responded by doing everything he could to avoid walking up the stairs. The face that stares out from that portrait has none of the dash and fire in the eyes that characterises the iconic picture of Ball's boyhood hero, Young Tom Morris. It is, rather, the face of a brooding man with a faraway look – the image of the kind of player Ball was, 'a dour and bonny fighter', as Darwin described him.

Despite the nationwide fame that came with his exploits, Ball would be the least-known, most enigmatic player of his time. He was one of the few among his peers who never wrote about his own life, and he loathed speeches and interviews, once telling an inquisitive reporter that he couldn't think of anything to say that readers might find interesting.

A self-taught player – he never took a lesson even from Hoylake's resident professional Jack Morris – Ball had an odd-looking grip and an unusual stance but a gorgeous swing. He held the club with his right hand so far under the shaft that his knuckles pointed towards the target. He stood with his feet wide apart, his legs stiff, and the ball back almost as far as his right toe. Bobby Jones never could understand how Ball could make such a lovely move through the ball holding the club that way. But what a lovely move it was.

'I have never seen a player whose hitting was such a pleasure to watch.' wrote Horace Hutchinson, 'such a beautiful exhibition of grace and power, showing such ability to concentrate in a moment, and on a spot, all the muscular power that the human frame was master of. It was a beautiful sight.'

On the links, Ball's strengths were his driving and laser-like approach shots with a brassie or a cleek, the equivalents of a modern fairway wood and 2-iron. His shots started low then rose gradually and stopped nearly dead when they landed, building on the standard Young Tom had set for banging the ball right up to the flagstick.

'It was his business,' Darwin wrote, 'to go faultlessly down the middle and let the other man make the mistakes, and the more intense the crisis the more closely he stuck to his business.' Ball might have been invincible but for a weakness he shared with Old Tom Morris. 'He was,' Darwin wrote, 'not entirely trustworthy over the short putts.'

New challenges

Not long after Ball had trounced Hoylake's Gold Medal winner one on one and played so admirably alongside Davie Strath, it was decided that the time had come for the young man to try his hand at competition outside Hoylake.

In September 1878, escorted by Jack Morris and his assistant George Lowe, Ball took the journey north to Prestwick to compete in his first Open. What a grand adventure that must have been for a 16-year-old boy, travelling to the links where the Championship had been born and the heroes of this new era had been crowned. It was an exhausting trip, requiring more than ten hours of travel by horse-drawn tram, ferry and train.

Ball played better than one might have expected, finishing the first round three shots off the lead held by St Andrews legend Jamie Anderson, who would win the second of his three consecutive Opens that year. Ball's performance would not have been entirely unexpected. Given that Old Tom's nephew was the professional at Hoylake, the Prestwick crowd would no doubt have heard about the promising young Englishman coming to test his mettle against Scottish players on a Scottish green.

Ball fell out of contention afterwards, finishing with a respectable score of 165 that left him tied for fourth. He was eight strokes behind the winner, Anderson, but 14 in front of Hoylake professional Jack Morris and 16 ahead of George Lowe. The lad won the princely sum of £1. Morris suggested he slip it into his pocket, the advice that created an awkward situation later during the birth of the Amateur Championship.

Ball may not have been old enough yet to become a member at Royal Liverpool, but he was already one of the best players at that club or any other. In August of 1881, three months before he became a member, Ball played for the Hoylake team that travelled to North Berwick to take on Tantallon Golf Club in one of the home-and-home matches (inter-club fixtures) that were a staple in those days. Ball played against A. Mackenzie Ross, a first-class Scottish amateur. When Ball calmly took Ross's scalp, newspaper writers were deeply impressed.

'Better and more dashing (as well as careful) play than this exhibited by the Hoylake representative in the latter portion of the final round we never saw, and it was no disgrace to succumb to it,' *The Sporting and Dramatic News* reported. 'Nothing was missed, he could not do wrong and the most difficult shots were done with apparent unconscious ease.'

As soon as he became a Hoylake member, Ball pocketed the club's two most cherished trophies, the Dowie Cup and Kennard Gold Medal, then kept right on winning one title after another. He took four of the six club medals the following season and ended that year with an astonishingly low handicap of plus 6 at Royal Liverpool.

Hoylake's love affair with Ball was in full flower, further stoked by the game's Grand Old Man, Tom Morris, telling anyone who would listen that, 'Mr Ball is the best amateur player in the world.' Ball's backers at Royal Liverpool were hot to prove it. In the summer of 1883 – the year Robert Louis Stevenson published every British schoolboy's favourite, *Treasure Island* – they issued a challenge in *The Field* offering to back their man against any Scottish amateur.

The challenge was taken up by one of Old Tom's favourites, Douglas Rolland of Earlsferry. He was still considered an amateur in those days, two years before Hoylake's decision to bar him from the first Amateur Championship as a professional. Dougie, as his friends called him, was a dashing figure who stood 6 feet tall and weighed 170 pounds. Working as a stonemason, he had developed a thick chest and massive forearms. Not surprisingly, he was among the longest drivers of his day, fond of exclaiming as he bashed one off the tee, 'Awa' she sails with a dashing spray!'

The match was set for early December. It would feature 36 holes each at Rolland's home course in neighbouring Elie and Ball's at Hoylake. There were no stakes involved, except that the loser had to pay travel expenses for the players. That didn't stop golf fans across England and Scotland from placing a bob or two on their man. Among those who staked a shilling on the outcome was a young Liverpool golfer then away at boarding school. His name was Harold Hilton, and like every boy growing up in Hoylake he worshipped Ball and believed he knew no equal.

'I was at school in Norfolk,' Hilton recalled, 'and it so happened that there was another boy at the school who knew something about the game of golf. He was a native of Musselburgh, and occasionally we had little arguments about the game. He used to quote Bob Ferguson and other Scottish celebrities, and was quite impartial, but he could always find about six Scotsmen who could beat any Englishman. I had only one reply as to the prowess of his many celebrities, and that was that Johnnie Ball was quite good enough for me.'

One afternoon between classes the two of them noticed in *The Field* that the challenge issued by Ball's backers at Hoylake had been taken up by Rolland, a golfer who was then a mystery to Master Hilton. 'I had never even heard of his name before, and possibly spoke a little contemptuously of his chance, and scorned the idea of anyone beating Johnnie,' he wrote. 'Whatever it was I said, it evidently aroused the ire of the Scotch boy, as he promptly remarked – "I will bet you a shilling that Rolland wins." I didn't hesitate a moment in accepting the offer, only thinking at the time that I hoped he had an honest and good memory.'

Unfortunately for Hilton, Ball was not yet ready to live up to his billing. In the first 36 holes at Elie, he succumbed to his Achilles heel, timid putting. Rolland bombed away, establishing a nine-hole lead as a huge crowd followed the young stars around the course. Back at Hoylake, the faithful expected the real John Ball to show up and stage one of the furious rallies that would become his trademark. Young Ball apparently was too discouraged by events at Elie to deliver his best. He slogged in with rounds of 90 and 91 as Rolland ran away with the match.

A well-known yet beloved roustabout, Rolland decided to stay at Hoylake another day to avoid a court date back home involving what Ball's biographer referred to discreetly as 'an affair of gallantry'. It was, in fact, a paternity suit. The extra day left time for a rematch. Ball showed his typical mettle to start, taking a 4-up lead with five holes to play. Redemption seemed at hand. Down the stretch, however, Ball let the holes slip away, and Rolland prevailed again. Poor Master Hilton had to part with his shilling.

'I couldn't make it out at all,' Hilton wrote. 'I was simply dumbfounded at the result. I tried hard to forget the incident, but that boy Gibson would not let me. Eventually I had to recourse to the extreme measure of wilfully avoiding him – I was getting really tired of the subject.'

The true believers of Hoylake could not have known it then, but the next five seasons would be Ball's equivalent of Bobby Jones's famous 'lean years' – the desultory stretch between the Dixie Whiz Kid's first appearance as a prodigy in the US Amateur of 1916 and his first victory in a national open at Inwood Country Club in 1923.

Ball's drought would continue from the debacle against Rolland into that first Amateur Championship in 1885. Despite high hopes that he would prevail on his native green, Ball could not hold back Hutchinson. The remainder of that year would see one disappointment heaped upon another. That September Carnoustie hosted an event to rival Hoylake's Grand Tournament of 1872, a multi-day affair that featured a match-play event for amateurs and a tournament for professionals. It provided a perfect opportunity to travel north for that competition and stay for the Open the following week at St Andrews.

Ball entered the amateur event at Carnoustie, but was humiliatingly put out in the third round by a fellow Hoylake member to whom he would have conceded five strokes at home. The Open at St Andrews came to an even drearier end. Ball continued to be far off form, so much so that he never turned in his card – the same fate Jones would meet 36 years later in his first Open over the Old Course in 1921.

The story would not be much different in the 1886 Amateur – the first held under the auspices of the R&A at St Andrews. Ball had no trouble dispatching the middling players he faced in the first three rounds. In the fourth, with a berth in the semi-finals on the line, he came up against a competitor he would face many times in years to come – a Scottish amateur named John Laidlay. Both Johnnies played undistinguished golf, with Ball prevailing 3 and 2 as *The Field* noted with dismay that, 'the scoring was rather high'.

Ball's supporters had every right to expect he would make short work of the man he would face next, Henry Lamb of Royal Wimbledon. Unfortunately, 'Ball's play was wretched,' *The Field* wrote. 'His troubles seemed to be as many as Job's.' Ball made a horrifying 54 on his outward nine and went down meekly as Lamb closed him out by going 7 up with six to play. The following afternoon, Hutchinson demonstrated how easily Ball ought to have moved on to his first Amateur final. He trounced Lamb by the same 7 and 6 to claim his first Championship.

When the 1887 season opened, Ball put his admirers at ease by going right back to being all but invincible over his home links. That year he won all six of the scratch medals at Hoylake, an extraordinary feat, with an average score of 80, superb in those days over that treacherously narrow, rugged and difficult course. In the six years since he had been made a club member, Ball had won 28 of the 39 medals competed for at the club. Hopes naturally were running high when the Amateur returned to Royal Liverpool that August.

The opening rounds went according to Hoyle. Ball cruised through his early matches and, much to the joy of his followers, easily won his semi-final. Now, at long last, he would have a chance to realise the dreams that had been harboured for him by winning the Amateur before an adoring crowd at Hoylake.

In the other half of the bracket, meanwhile, an unexpected development was unfolding. Ball's father had made it to the semi-final. Along the way, he dispatched a rising Hoylake star making his Amateur debut, 16-year-old Harold Hilton. In the semi-final, to everyone's surprise, the elder Ball was leading Hutchinson by a hole as they approached the 17th. That's when Ball made a fatal mistake. Standing on the fairway, having just taken his second shot to that long hole, he said to Hutchinson, 'It would be a funny thing if father and son had to play it off together.'

Hutchinson, as Darwin noted, 'had a quick temper, and played all the better for it, sometimes in a cold anger that was rather alarming'. He turned to Ball and snapped, 'Wait a bit, Mr Ball, you haven't finished with me yet.' It clearly unnerved Ball, who slapped his next shot into a bunker short of the green to hand Hutchinson the hole. On the 18th, Ball watched in dismay as Hutchinson dropped his putt for a three to claim the match and take his spot in the final against the hotel proprietor's son.

The match between Hutchinson and Ball, a replay of their semi-final battle in 1885, proved to be an equally tense and dramatic affair. Both reached the turn in 42, and the match remained halved as they played the 14th. There young Ball displayed some of the magic that had earned him such a devoted following. On the green, Hutchinson laid Ball what was known as a stymie. That meant his putt stopped directly between his opponent's ball and the hole. Players were not allowed to touch the ball then, even on the green. Ball had to go around or over the obstacle in his path. When he calmly curved his putt past the blockade and saw the ball drop into the cup, the crowd erupted in cheers. Ball now had his first lead in the match with just four holes to play.

Those four holes, however, present a brutal test of golf, and in the heat of that moment neither player mastered them. They halved the 15th, but on the 16th Ball hit one on the heel of his club and it sailed out of bounds. Under penalty of a stroke, he calmly dropped another ball and played it with his favourite brassie. Tragically, the shaft broke during his swing. There went the club, the hole, and the lead. On 18, Ball found himself badly bunkered and, for the second time, lost to Hutchinson on the final hole.

What was it, exactly, that stood between the young Hoylake star and the realisation of his obvious talent? It may simply have been that Ball was still young, just 25 years old when he faltered on that final hole. Hutchinson had a different idea of what was holding the Hoylake star back. Ball, he concluded, had not yet convinced himself he was a great golfer. 'Possibly it was Mr Ball's modesty that prevented him from doing better,' Hutchinson wrote. 'It was a long while before he had a belief and a confidence in himself.'

Breaking through

Britain was enjoying those harbingers of spring, blooming snowdrops and a chorus of larks, when Ball signalled during an early April visit to Lytham and St Annes that the 1888 season might finally see him realise his vast potential.

The course required precise shot-making or all manner of trouble might ensue. Ball calmly marched around in a record score of 73, extraordinarily low in those days. That may have been the round he needed to convince himself he had what it took to win a championship. A month later Ball would have a chance to prove it at Prestwick. He had fond memories of success there as a boy, although with all the misfortunes he had suffered since that must have seemed ages ago. Ball was among 38 hopefuls who gathered during the second week of May to contest the fourth Amateur Championship over a course where desperate trouble was never more than a shot away.

With the links in mint condition and 'the meteorological deities smiling auspiciously', as *The Golfing Annual* reported, 'everything bade to go as merrily as the oft-quoted bridal bell.' Gorgeous as the days were, with the majestic Isle of Arran shimmering in the sun off the coast of the Firth of Clyde, the only complaint that could be mustered was that a brisk wind blew continuously across the links from the sea.

As he had done in his previous Championships, Ball breezed through his opening rounds with little trouble but for a brief scare in the fourth round when he needed all 18 holes to dispatch his rival. Shockingly, Hutchinson fell by the wayside in round three, a development Ball must have noted with relief. It was another familiar opponent who earned the right to face the rising English star in the final – Scotsman John Laidlay.

Laidlay was one of the most successful golfers of his day. A year older than Ball, Laidlay was born on 5 November 1860 to a well-to-do family in Seacliff, two miles east of North Berwick. His father, John Watson Laidlay, was a fellow of the Royal Society of Edinburgh, Scotland's national academy of science and letters. The elder Laidlay was a master of languages, specialising in those of India and the Middle East. His skills earned him opportunities overseas with the East India Company, where he made his fortune overseeing indigo factories and married an Edinburgh woman named Ellen Johnston Hope. By 1854, the couple were back in Britain and living in Seacliff.

Young John Ernest Laidlay attended Loretto School near Musselburgh, where he excelled at cricket and golf and became an acolyte of the Honest Toun's golfing hero Bob Ferguson. Laidlay did not go on to university, and with his family well situated was able to lead the life of a sporting gentleman. In his final years at Loretto, he earned a reputation as one of cricket's best slow bowlers, and in 1878 played for Scotland's national team. Beyond sports, Laidlay's principal passion was photography, a new art then. Years later he would produce photographs for the first instructional book ever written by a professional player, Willie Park Jr's *The Game of Golf.*

A trim man who sported a bushy moustache under his prominent, aquiline nose, Laidlay liked to spice up the classic, knickerbockered look with a flashy checked cap. His eyes were close together, which tended to give him a rather quizzical look. His approach to golf was quizzical, too.

'Mr Laidlay's style is indeed the despair of the golfing instructor,' Hutchinson wrote. 'Its special peculiarity is that the swing is entirely "off the left leg". The ball, when Mr Laidlay addresses it – whether with driver, approaching club or putter, and perhaps in this uniformity there is to be found some explanation of its success – is placed far to his left, very nearly, if not quite, opposite his left foot.'

His grip was also unusual. Laidlay did not hold the club in the palm of his hands, as most golfers did. He gripped it lightly in his fingers, using particularly thin shafts, with the pinkie finger of his right hand overlapping the knuckles of his left, the grip the vast majority of players use today.

Having grown up playing at North Berwick, which demands accurate approach shots, Laidlay excelled in that art, as well as putting. At the time he and Ball met in the final of the 1888 Amateur Championship – with Laidlay playing as a member of the Honourable Company of Edinburgh Golfers – he was ranked with S. Mure Fergusson and Leslie Balfour-Melville as one of the best golfers in Scotland.

The weather for their match was even more glorious than it had been all week, and an enormous crowd followed the two Johnnies around Prestwick. Unfortunately, the match did not turn out to be the kind of tense, thrust-and-parry battle that can make an Amateur final desperately exciting. Ball and Laidlay approached the match like wary prize-fighters, playing 'a cautious rather than a dashing game, each having too much respect for his opponent to throw a chance away', *The Annual* reported.

Ball's fans must have fretted when he sliced his opening drive onto the railway that runs alongside the first at Prestwick, which had been expanded to 18 holes since Ball's last visit in 1878. It now measured nearly 5,800 yards, a formidable test in those days. Never fear, however. Ball won the second to square the match, and 'thereafter held the trump card', *The Annual* wrote. 'He kept pressing Mr Laidlay in a way that can only be understood by those who have had the misfortune to play an uphill game in similar circumstances. It demoralises the best and takes the heart out of the pluckiest.'

By the time the players turned for home, it was obvious to *The Annual* and to everyone else that the lean season of the 26-year-old 'Hoylake marvel' was coming to an end. The moment of triumph arrived on the

14th green, where Ball won the hole, the match and the title by taking a 5-up lead with only four holes remaining. In addition to the gold medal proclaiming him the year's Champion, Ball was permitted to buy an item worth £8. Ever the practical man, he chose a double-barrelled shotgun, which would be helpful for keeping rabbits at bay back home.

Ball finished off the first of his glory years at a new course south-east of London known as St George's. It had been founded a year earlier on a dramatic stretch of undulating dunes land in Sandwich on the Kent coast. Within five years St George's would make a distinguished mark in golf. Like Hoylake, the club made its ambitions clear early by staging a tournament in the autumn of 1888 featuring competitions for amateur and professional golfers. Amateurs played in the inaugural Grand Challenge Cup, more popularly known as the St George's Vase. It became the annual stroke-play championship for amateurs and a staple of the calendar for players like Ball.

That first event was contested in a near gale blowing in from Pegwell Bay. Scoring was so difficult that only six of the 33 entrants bothered to turn in a card. Ball went around the first 18 in 94 strokes, on any other day a ruinous score. He shaved off eight strokes in the second round, coming in with 86. That was good enough to overtake first-round leader Arthur Molesworth and earn Ball a second consecutive victory in top-flight amateur competition. His final round becomes more impressive when compared to scores posted by professionals, who played the last round of their event that same day. Among them only Rolland broke 90.

A score of 86, even in brutal conditions, might not be expected to raise eyebrows. Yet one can't help but wonder if the professionals playing that week at Sandwich – golfers who had never before had anything to fear from mere amateurs – took note of how Ball had broken through that season. Did they have even the slightest notion, as reporters of the day were fond of saying, that the time had come for them to 'look to their laurels'?

Four

ROSE AND THISTLE

G iven the centuries-long history of war between England and Scotland, from Bannockburn to Flodden Field, it was perhaps predictable that as soon as golf took root in the south, the English became fixated on vanquishing their northern neighbour.

As early as August 1882 – when John Ball was just 20 years old and the Amateur still three years in the future – a man who styled himself 'St George' was writing to *The Field* to say that the time had come for an international match between the best golfers from England and Scotland, the rose against the thistle.

Clearly an Englishman feeling his oats, St George wrote: 'Where is the Scotch gentleman player who will beat John Ball, Tertius, or where can four Scotch amateurs be found who will meet the gentleman already named and Messrs A.H. Molesworth, F.P. Crowther and Horace Hutchinson?' St George was inclined to think they didn't exist. 'If this be so,' he added, 'then glory is departing from Scotland and England is taking the lead.'

St George's missive sparked a flurry of letters in *The Field* over the next three months, many of them supporting his call for an international match. The discussion was not confined to sporting publications. In September of that year, two members of the R&A proposed assembling a committee representing leading clubs on both sides of the border to discuss conducting a match between players from England and Scotland.

As was so often the case, the R&A decided not to move forward. When Hoylake staged the first Amateur Championship three years later, the clamour for an international match died down, at least for the moment. There is no record of what the brash St George had to say when Scotsman Dougie Rolland humbled Ball in their match a few months after his letter sparked such a lively discussion in *The Field*.

St George may not have got his wish for an international match, but he was right about one thing. In the years ahead, golf competitions large and small would be framed as battles between north and south, as Englishmen set out to conquer the country that introduced them to its national game. Their skirmishes would deliver unforgettable scenes that remain etched in golf lore on both sides of the border.

In the 1880s, with the game still in its infancy outside Scotland, the only place for this budding rivalry to gain traction was in amateur competitions. No other country had yet developed professional golfers who could challenge Scots in the Open, high-stakes matches, or the other professional tournaments that popped up during any given year.

The reason for that was obvious. England, Ireland and Wales had no cultural history of playing golf. Boys there did not grow up the way working-class Scottish children did, playing street golf with crude imitations of clubs and balls until they were old enough to take to the links. They tended to focus on football, cricket or rugby. It would be years before golf had the mass appeal in other nations that it enjoyed in Scotland.

In England and elsewhere, golf developed much as it had in Scotland – as a gentleman's game that revolved around life at the club, where the focus was as much on fellowship as winning matches. A foursome in the morning would be followed by lunch in the clubhouse – at Hoylake that meant the famed Cheshire cheese and potted shrimps – and another 18 holes in the afternoon. The day ended with a sumptuous dinner at which drinks would flow, new matches would be made, toasts would be raised to Queen and club, and songs would be sung.

Horace Hutchinson remembers travelling to Hoylake in the 1870s and the merry, well-lubricated evenings he and other members spent in the Bar Parlour at the Royal Hotel. R.W. Brown, whose clock-like swing earned him the nickname 'Pendulum', played the piano and sang as Honourable Secretary Thomas Owen Potter conducted with an ivory baton given to him in recognition of his service to the club. That baton is now the club captain's symbol of office, handed to his successor when he takes over.

'Bar Parlour sounds a little ominous,' Hutchinson mused, and one can see his eyes twinkling as he pens those words, 'but I never saw a man who could not talk straight or walk straight out of it.' It was, perhaps, in the afterglow of just such an evening that gentleman golfers like St George first set their sights on taking the fight to the Scots.

Ancient rivals

Golf's greatest rivalry had begun slowly, with matches like the home-and-home affair between Dougie Rolland and the young hero of Hoylake, but it took on a fierce intensity as the newly minted Amateur Championship produced three consecutive meetings between the leading gentlemen golfers from England and Scotland – the two Johnnies, Ball and Laidlay.

The final between them in the 1888 Amateur, which ended Ball's long drought in major competition, had not been especially riveting, with Ball taking a commanding lead early and never looking back. That would change the following year, when the two stalwarts found themselves in the same bracket – meaning only one of them would have the chance to be hailed as Champion Amateur of the Year. That issue would be decided in a stirring semi-final match over the links of St Andrews.

Played in early May, the 1889 Amateur drew a field of 44. Every round was played in lovely weather, 'there being an entire absence of wind, which, on the east coast of Scotland, so frequently tries the tempers and spoils the scores of even the best of players,' *The Golfing Annual* reported. The Amateur may be the toughest championship to win. Even in those early days, and much more would be required as fields grew over time, the winner had to survive at least four 18-hole matches to reach the final. Anything can happen over 18 holes, even to the best golfers in the world.

Ball's first match in the Championship came in the second round – he'd received a bye in the first – against his nemesis, Hutchinson, winner of two of the three official Amateurs played to that point. Fortunately for Ball, Hutchinson was off his feed and went down easily, succumbing on the 15th green. Years later Hutchinson acknowledged that, 'I never set out to play a match with Johnny Ball without the full consciousness that if we both played our game I was bound to be beaten.' Ball dispatched his third- and fourth-round foes with equal aplomb, beating one by seven holes and the other by four.

Laidlay's path was not quite so smooth. In his third round – after a bye and a romp to begin – the Scotsman came up against Harold Hilton, making his second Championship appearance. Laidlay barely survived, winning on the final hole after what *The Annual* described as 'a magnificent tussle'.

He and Hilton came to the 17th all square. Hilton's approach shot wound up on the road, a fatal mistake that saw him lose the hole and the match. Laidlay also had a tough time shaking off A.F. Macfie, winner of the inaugural, now-unrecognised Amateur, squeaking by 2 and 1.

That left the two Johnnies to face off in one semi-final as the St Andrews amateur Leslie Balfour-Melville made his way through the other half of the bracket. The battle between Laidlay and Ball was 'a sight for the gods to witness', as *The Annual* put it, easily the most thrilling match the young Championship had seen. Laidlay claimed the first hole with a three, and by the turn he was two holes up, much to the delight of the partisan Scottish crowd. He remained in front until Ball began a late charge by stealing a long putt on 14. When Laidlay found himself bunkered at 16, Ball squared the match with two to play, among them the deadly Road Hole.

Both men played gingerly at 17 and avoided disaster. They were on the green in three, each about two club lengths from the hole. Laidlay gave Ball an opening by missing his putt for four. Ball let the chance slip, leaving his answer agonisingly short. He made the same mistake on 18, and the hole was halved in fives.

It was back to the first hole for a sudden-death play-off, with the enormous crowd watching in breathless silence as the Johnnies teed off in the shadow of the Royal and Ancient clubhouse. This time it was Laidlay who missed a golden opportunity. He crossed the Swilcan Burn in two superb shots, while Ball stumbled and needed three to find the green. With the pressure wearing on both players, Laidlay three-putted to hand Ball a half.

The end came at the second hole, the twentieth played during that unforgettable semi-final. Ball hit his approach shot first, using one of his deadliest weapons, his cleek. It disappeared over the ridge that guards the front of that green and to all appearances had been perfectly played. While Laidlay was lining up his approach, however, signals came from the green that Ball's shot had run past the hole and into a pot bunker. That proved to be fatal. Laidlay made another perfect approach to win the hole and the match with a four.

His electrifying victory must have been a comfort to Scottish patriots after three seasons in which the Champion Amateur had hailed from England. It set up an all-Scottish final against Balfour-Melville. While not as riveting as the match between the two Johnnies, the final also became a tense affair as Balfour-Melville fought valiantly to whittle away Laidlay's early lead. Three holes down with four to play, Balfour-Melville narrowed the gap to one at 16, only to have his hopes dashed at the Road Hole, as so many have been before and since.

If Ball was disappointed by his heartbreaking loss at St Andrews – quiet as he was, it was never easy to tell what was on his mind – he would have taken solace in claiming his second consecutive St George's Vase later that season at Sandwich. He also would have had the comfort of knowing that when his chance for redemption came round the following spring, the battle would be joined over his beloved Royal Liverpool. In the Amateur Championship of 1890, Ball would be the overwhelming favourite, as he always was on his native green.

Home to Hoylake

An awful lot had occurred in the world since the Vicar of Northam brought the game to England in 1864. The Civil War that was raging in America as golfers began knocking balls around the Burrows had come to its bloody end. In 1880, Britain's ambitions in southern Africa, where it sought to gain control of diamond and gold mines, found the nation on the losing end of a war against the Boers, descendants of the area's original Dutch settlers. War with the Boers would flare up again at the end of the century, bringing with it one of the darkest days golf would ever know.

Around the world, the quest for modernisation that characterised the Victorian age continued unabated. The tradition of hosting a World's Fair to show off developments in technology, begun in 1851 with the Great Exhibition in London, played out again in May 1889 at the Exposition Universelle in Paris. The most talked-about guest was American inventor Thomas Edison. He'd crossed the Atlantic to introduce the world to his new creation, the phonograph. The Paris exposition, however, would be best remembered for the unveiling of the spectacular Eiffel Tower, at 300 metres then the tallest structure in the world.

That generation had also seen enormous growth in England and Scotland. When the Census was taken in 1861 – three years before the founding of Westward Ho! – England counted just over 18 million residents. By the time the Exposition Universelle closed in the autumn of 1889, that number was nearing 27 million. There had been similar growth in Scotland, although it had a much smaller population. Scots numbered three million in 1861 and just under four million 20 years later.

Not surprisingly, the number of golf courses was also growing, especially south of the border. When Old Tom Morris laid out England's first seaside links on the Northam Burrows in 1864, it was only the third golf course in the country. By 1889 that number had risen to 84, just one fewer than the number of courses in Scotland. By the end of the following golf season the tide would have turned. England would have more courses than Scotland – 124 in the south to 101 in the north.

The implications for golf ought to have been obvious. Ball, Hutchinson and Hilton would hardly be the only English golfers capable of trading blows with Scots. They were the tip of an emerging iceberg. But as the 1890 season dawned – with Laidlay having regained the Amateur title and no Englishman having ever seriously threatened at the Open – proud Scots may not have grasped the enormity of the threat developing south of their border.

As was usually the case, the Amateur was played that year in association with Royal Liverpool's Spring Meeting, highlighted by its competitions for the club's Gold Medal and Dowie Cup. The partisan Hoylake crowd must have been shocked when Ball turned out for those competitions far off his game. He lost the medal to Laidlay and the cup to Hutchinson. To make matters worse, the following day Ball and club captain Charles Hutchings played a foursome against Laidlay and Hutchinson and went down meekly.

If proof were ever needed that golf is a fickle game, it was provided the moment the Championship began. The real John Ball suddenly materialised. He drew a bye in the first round and cruised through the second and third rounds never needing more than 15 holes to put away his foe. It wasn't until the fourth round that Ball ran into any trouble. That came in the person of his admirer and fellow Liverpool star, Hilton. Now 21, Hilton was emerging as a player to be feared. He had humiliated his opponent in the previous round, romping by 9 and 7 as he went around in a sparkling 80.

When the titans of Hoylake met it was Ball's turn to go around in 80. Hilton hung with his hero most of the way – he was 1 down with four to play – but succumbed to the pressure over that brutal finishing stretch at Royal Liverpool, finally losing at the 16th. Ball went right back to easy victories in his next match. Despite playing indifferently, he dispatched Balfour-Melville on the 15th green and earned a chance to play for the title.

In the other half of the bracket, Laidlay was making his way to the final. He won his first two matches without playing more than 14 holes, and finished his third match at 17. His fourth-round bout against Hutchinson was a different matter. The Englishman was in far better form and gave Laidlay all he wanted. 'When players of the calibre of these come together a grand match may be looked for and a grand match it was,' *The Scotsman* wrote. The two golfers were neck and neck all the way, until Hutchinson lost by missing his putt on 18. Laidlay also struggled in his semi-final, trailing for most of the match before prevailing on the final green.

The Amateur final between Ball and Laidlay would be fought out over a course recognised as one of the most difficult tests in the game. Hoylake measured just over 5,400 yards for the 1890 Championship. That was on the short side, but the greens were frighteningly slick and the course was rugged and subject to punishing winds. The biggest challenge, however, may have been the sense of claustrophobia Hoylake created by having so many areas that were out of bounds. Scottish hero Jamie Anderson famously put five balls out of bounds on the first hole and exclaimed in frustration, 'Ma God! It's like playing up a spout.'

While the weather for the Amateur had been ideal in the early rounds – sunny and cool with a freshening breeze – it took a decided turn for the worse before the final began. 'In the forenoon it was pleasant, though the south-easterly wind was strong enough to bother the players some-what,' *The Scotsman* wrote, 'but the final between Mr Laidlay and Mr Ball had to be delayed half-an-hour in the afternoon in order to allow a thunderstorm to pass over the links, and even after that delay the match was not finished in comfort, for rain fell heavily for some time during its progress.'

The ugly weather did not stop a huge crowd from following the two combatants around the links. Ball wasted no time in demonstrating that this would be his day. He holed a long putt on the first to seize the lead, and never let up after that. 'From the outset, Mr Ball showed exceptionally brilliant form,' *The Golfing Annual* reported, 'and when he completed the first nine in the unprecedentedly low score of 37, he stood six holes to the good. The result was now, of course, a foregone conclusion.' The reigning champion fought back valiantly but vainly, winning two of the next five holes. The end came at the 15th, when Ball closed him out 4 and 3.

This was the moment all those blue-jerseyed fishermen towing the gallery rope and all the adoring fans tramping behind them had waited so long to witness – no doubt with lumps in their throats. Ball, at last, had claimed the laurels on his home green. Thunderous cheers echoed across the links as he was hoisted onto sturdy shoulders and borne in triumph to the Royal.

It would be hard to conceive of a victory that gave Ball more satisfaction than becoming Champion Amateur Golfer as every luminary of Liverpool looked on proudly, his father and Jack Morris among them. It would be equally hard to imagine anything that would make a shy, modest man more uncomfortable than the outpouring of affection that erupted in the aftermath of that victory. The celebration would go on into the night, but it is a safe bet that Ball slipped away at the first opportunity, content to savour his accomplishment on the quiet confines of his farm.

It was not simply Ball's fans who understood the significance of his second Amateur title in three years. *The Scotsman* did, too. 'The result of today's play is undoubtedly a feather in the cap of English golfers, who so long as they have a representative like Mr Ball in the field need have no fear of the honour passing from them without a struggle,' the newspaper concluded.

Classic battle

In the months between Ball's victory and the Open at Prestwick in September, the golf cognoscenti were consumed with one of the high-stakes challenge matches that so captivated the imagination in those days, a battle for £100 a side between players from those age-old rivals, St Andrews and Musselburgh.

St Andrews was represented by the lovable rogue Andra Kirkaldy. He had grown up in the 'Auld Grey Toon' as the son of a soldier who served in the Crimean War and later took to carrying clubs for gentlemen. Andra and his brothers, John and Hugh, also grew up to be caddies, although unlike their father, who never played a round in his life, they became professional golfers. At the age of 19 Andra followed in his father's footsteps by enlisting. He served six years in India and Egypt, where he was twice wounded in fighting at Tel-el-Kebir.

Back home in St Andrews, Andra quickly earned a reputation as a fearsome player and a man who loved sharing a colourful tale, often in unprintable language. Over the years he became one of the city's most beloved figures. In 1910, two years after the passing of Old Tom Morris, Andra was named the R&A's first Honorary Professional. Ever after he took Old Tom's place holding the flag on 18 as players completed their rounds.

Musselburgh's banner was carried by Willie Park Jr, son of the town's most famous family. His father, Willie Sr, won the Open four times, including the first in 1860. Young Park was one of Scotland's best golfers. He was not long off the tee, and inclined to be wild, but he was deadly on the green. His favourite saying was, 'The man who can putt is a match for anyone,' and he'd proved it over and over. The Parks were club makers by trade, and Willie would become the most accomplished among them, inventing improvements in balls, clubs and putters. In time he would take over his father's shop and transform it into a flourishing international business even as he emerged as one of the earliest golf architects.

Kirkaldy and Park had finished tied in the 1889 Open at Musselburgh with twin scores of 155. When Park won the play-off, claiming his second title in three years, the inevitable result was a challenge match. It took place the following season in late August, ending a week before the start of the 1890 Open. Just as Old Tom and Willie Sr had before them, Kirkaldy and Park Jr faced off over four courses, 36 holes each at Musselburgh, Prestwick, Troon and St Andrews.

Kirkaldy's short game was magical throughout, especially his ability to lay long, tricky putts absolutely dead. 'I shake every time I see him take his wooden putter in hand,' an awed spectator told *The Annual*. Kirkaldy came into the last leg of the match at St Andrews leading by three holes. Nearly 5,000 hyped-up fans gathered to watch history unfold, a staggering number in those days. The end proved to be an anti-climax. Kirkaldy destroyed Park, winning 8 and 7.

It is hardly surprising, given the excitement generated by the Park–Kirkaldy duel, that Ball's victory in the Amateur that spring was no longer top of mind by the time 39 players gathered at Prestwick for the Open Championship. Kirkaldy, naturally, was everybody's favourite to win, with Park, Willie Fernie of Troon and Archie Simpson of Carnoustie close behind. The top amateurs – Ball, Laidlay and Hutchinson – weren't exactly ignored, but were given only a modest chance. After all, no amateur had ever won the Open. Still, an astute observer of Championship trends would have noticed the improving prospects of gentlemen players.

In the first two decades of the Open, the closest any amateur had got to the winning score was eight strokes. That feat was first accomplished in 1867 by the legendary William Doleman, a baker from Glasgow. It was repeated 11 years later by Ball. In 1869, Scottish amateur Mure Fergusson finished third, 11 strokes back. Those were aberrations, however. Most years the closest amateur was 15 strokes behind or more. The gap narrowed perceptibly after the institution of the Amateur Championship. In every year since, a gentleman had finished within seven strokes. Laidlay did it three times, Hutchinson twice. Balfour-Melville came closest at four strokes off the lead.

The 1890 Open would be played over a Prestwick links whose dangerously fast and puzzling greens were hardly the only challenge the course presented. Its terrors also included the mammoth Cardinal bunker and blind shots over the Alps and Himalayas – gigantic dunes that provided panoramic views modern designers try to recreate at 'stadium' courses.

The morning of the Championship, 11 September 1890, dawned with a gale blowing from the north-west. Those who went off early were all but swept away in the wind. Willie Park, for instance, came in with a ruinous score of 90. By the time late starters began their rounds, Kirkaldy and Ball among them, the wind had died down considerably, a tremendous break in any championship.

In the opening round, Ball played with relentless precision, trudging calmly along in that forward-leaning way of his and repeating over and over the gorgeous swing that so mesmerised Hutchinson. It was a sight to behold. 'His play made a great impression on the cognoscenti, his driving being full of *fire* and straight as an arrow, while his uniformly good approach play never left him much to do on the putting green,' *The Annual* wrote.

Ball came in from the first 18 at Prestwick with twin nines of 41, a stroke behind the leader and favourite, Kirkaldy. While the St Andrews professional descended into mediocrity in his second round – reaching the turn in 44 and making a succession of ho-hum fives afterwards – Ball continued to play such impeccable golf that even the Scottish crowd abandoned its hero for the young amateur star from Hoylake.

'So much was the attention of the crowd taken up with the play of Mr Ball that Kirkaldy was allowed to proceed on his way after the first few holes practically unattended,' *The Scotsman* reported.

By the time Ball had turned for home, he was 'showing such form as made it quite certain that if he was not at the very top of the tree at the finish he would not be far from it,' the newspaper wrote. This, no doubt, was the word that filtered back to Hutchinson as he finished out of the running. By the time he and William Laidlaw Purves saw Ball finish playing the 16th, the Hoylake star had taken just 155 strokes. He had 11 left for the last two holes to defeat the leaders in the clubhouse, Fernie and Simpson. Both had come in with 167. Ball needed only nine strokes, again making twin 41s to become the first Englishman and the first amateur to win the Open. Even the partisan Scottish crowd erupted in thunderous applause as his final putt dropped.

Ball's momentous win that afternoon at Prestwick would be remembered as a turning point for the game reminiscent of Young Tom Morris's electrifying march to claim The Challenge Belt. Ball's victories in the Amateur and Open set off such a frenzy of passion for golf in England that within a decade Scotland's hegemony over its own national pastime would be in jeopardy.

Ball's sweep of The Double, as it came to be known, would also stand for all time as one of the game's greatest achievements. Only one other man would ever sweep both titles in a single season. That was Bobby Jones, who won the Amateur and the Open Championships of both Britain and the United States in 1930, on his way to completing what many believe to be the greatest feat in golf, the Grand Slam.

In its report on the Open Championship, *The Scotsman* got straight to the point Ball's victory had raised: 'Golfers on the north side of the Tweed will find food for reflection in the result of yesterday's meeting – in the fact that on a Scottish green and in a Scottish game an Englishman has proved himself more than their equal.' A challenge had been laid down. The battle between rose and thistle was now on in earnest.

Hutchinson also remembered that afternoon at Prestwick as a turning point, albeit for a different reason. 'It seemed at once to bring the Open Championship within the practical horizon of the amateur for all years to come,' he wrote. 'It had broken a spell.' Hutchinson had good reason to reach that conclusion. Ball's score would have won nearly half of the Opens played since Young Tom Morris raised the bar by winning The Challenge Belt.

Having endured being carried off the green after his Amateur victory earlier that year at Hoylake, one wonders if Ball fretted on the journey home about what kind of celebration might be in store when he pulled into town on the train. The scene that awaited would have made him want to disappear down a rabbit hole. Smoke signals were set off as the train pulled in. At the platform a cheering throng, backed by foghorns, waited for the champion to step off the train. A carriage was at the ready to bear him to a lavish party his father had arranged at the Royal Hotel. The carriage's horses had been replaced by those blue-jerseyed fishermen who so idolised Ball.

When that grand procession made its way back to the hotel, Ball unpacked the Claret Jug from his luggage – the first time that trophy had ever been seen on English soil. Another cherished reward would come in January, when Hoylake awarded him life membership. That night in the Bar Parlour at the Royal, as Pendulum Brown banged away on the keys, the crowd of Liverpool luminaries, as they had on so many other evenings, raised their voices in song. They belted out a version of the popular ditty, 'Do You Ken John Peel,' that had been rewritten in Ball's honour:

> *Yes we ken John Ball and his modesty too,*
> *His skilful play and his heart so true,*
> *And his champion score of twice eighty-two*
> *On Prestwick links in the morning.*

It was a scene to make one wonder if St George had been merely ahead of his time when he wrote his letter to *The Field* seven long years before. Maybe the glory was departing from Scotland, and England was taking the lead.

Five

MINDS AT WORK

———————•◦◉◦•———————

John Ball's Championship sweep was not the only development of lasting consequence that unfolded in 1890. It was also a year of milestones in a trend that would significantly influence the game's future – men of science and letters applying their brain power to golf.

Top men in every field, from agronomists and scientists to inventors and writers, had fallen under golf's spell and were feverishly applying their skills to enriching the game they loved. That reality would never change. Golf would always attract its share of well-situated and highly educated men and women anxious to put their minds to work.

Nowhere was the influence of golf's intelligentsia more evident than in science. In 1890, the journal *Nature* printed a dense article by Professor Peter Guthrie Tait, a world-renowned physicist at the University of Edinburgh, detailing his studies examining exactly what happens when a golf club meets a ball. Since the late 1880s, the golf-mad professor had been trying to determine how fast the ball was travelling when it left the face of the club. That information would make it theoretically possible to determine exactly how far a ball could be driven in the air from the tee.

In conducting his experiments, Professor Tait took measurements of the mammoth drives hit by son, Freddie, a promising young amateur who would soon make his own mark in the game, including hitting the longest drive ever recorded with a gutty ball. The *Nature* article, which was reprinted in the 1890–91 issue of *The Golfing Annual*, mentions a term every student of modern golf technology knows well – the coefficient of restitution, a way of measuring the speed at which a ball rebounds off the face of the club.

Professor Tait's discoveries represented an important step in the age-old quest to make a difficult game easier to play. In time, the ceaseless march of science would develop balls that flew vastly farther, clubs that were dramatically more forgiving, mowers that tamed once-rugged courses, grass strains that made greens as smooth as billiard tables and more. Every one of these advances would profoundly change the game John Ball and the other heroes of his era had grown up playing.

The quest to gain mastery over an unconquerable game had begun, naturally, with the ball itself. Not long after the gutta-percha ball replaced the feathery, golfers and ball makers realised that while it was far superior to the old ball, the gutty had flaws. The first gutty balls were smooth-faced and tended to duck sideways in the air. Players soon discovered that the ball flew straighter once it had been hacked up with an iron.

Ball makers responded by producing guttas that had been hand-hammered to control flight. By the 1870s moulds had been invented to add patterns that markedly improved aerodynamics. In 1890, Willie Park Jr, always at the forefront as an inventor, patented a diamond mesh pattern that represented a major step towards modern-day balls whose flight is aided by increasingly complex patterns of dimples.

More radical changes to the ball began in the late 1870s, when inventors began experimenting with combinations of gutta-percha and other materials to create a softer, more playable ball. The most successful of these, patented in 1877 by William Currie of the Caledonia Rubber Company in Edinburgh, was made of gutta-percha that was combined with ground cork, leather and other materials and then moulded and vulcanised. That process hardened the rubber while creating a pattern of indentations on its surface. The ball was marketed as the Eclipse and, perhaps because it was endorsed by Horace Hutchinson, was still going strong in 1888 when William Currie & Co. took out a full-page advertisement in the first *Golfing Annual*.

It went unnoticed at the time, but the most radical change in the golf ball – one that would not catch on until the next century – had already been discovered by Captain Duncan Stewart of St Andrews, a member of the Royal Navy. In 1871, having already created his own composite gutty, Stewart tried out an idea he considered vastly superior – a ball made of wound rubber threads encased in a cover of gutta-percha.

Stewart continued his experiments for a decade, although he never patented his invention. Problem was, he could not convince golfers of the ball's merit. It was so soft that it didn't make the same clicking sound as the gutty did when it was struck well. No click meant no sales. In 1879, Stewart moved to Campbeltown and gave up ball making. A generation later his early work on wound balls would come back to haunt Coburn Haskell, the American credited with inventing the ball that changed golf forever.

Those formative years also saw significant advances in the making of golf clubs, which had evolved rapidly from the moment Young Tom Morris started approaching greens with his rut iron, a club roughly equivalent to a modern sand wedge. Until then, golf had been played almost exclusively with wooden clubs, for the simple reason that a feather ball was likely to burst open when struck with an iron.

Before long, the number of irons a golfer typically carried expanded to include cleeks, mid-irons and mashies – clubs similar to the 3-, 5- and 7-irons in use today. When Young Tommy was in his prime, irons were smooth-faced. Club makers soon realised that boring holes in the face created spin that helped make the ball stop. By the dawn of the new century, ribbed irons like those golfers use today were the norm.

The 19th century also saw putters made of iron, and later aluminium, begin to outnumber the gorgeous, hand-crafted wooden putters of old. In 1892 Park patented his wry-necked putter, which got that name because its shaft was bent to get it behind the club face. That small change represented a major leap forward in putting technology. Even today most putters are built in a way similar to Park's original.

Another dramatic development in golf club design during those years was the move away from the long-nosed woods golfers had played with for centuries. Those slim, elegant-looking clubs had faces that appeared almost to be concave, with a slight hook at the toe. In 1885, the first so-called Bulger drivers appeared, with both Park and Henry Lamb of Royal Wimbledon claiming credit for the idea. Bulger drivers had a thicker, smaller head that looked much more like that of a modern driver or fairway wood. Players noticed immediately that they could hit the ball straight far more often with a Bulger. 'At once,' wrote prominent amateur Robert Harris, 'it became the prince of drivers.'

By the end of the decade, manufacturers had even begun making metal woods, the forerunners of modern clubs made of titanium or other composite materials. In 1896, Standard Golf Company of Sutherland, England, introduced brassies and spoons – the equivalent of today's fairway woods or hybrids – with heads made of aluminium. Within a decade, however, they had faded from view as club makers discovered a perfect new wood for manufacturing club heads – persimmon.

Along with the development of better balls and clubs came the introduction of gadgets for golfers, all those helpful aids modern players take for granted. These included golf bags and trolleys; tees made of wood, rubber or steel; early versions of shag bags; rubber grips for clubs; and various devices for practising at home. The number of patents issued during that generation demonstrates how quickly things were changing. Before 1893, only 97 had been issued. Between 1894 and the outbreak of war, another 711 patents would follow. Golf was well on the way to becoming a game Scotland's original King of Clubs – Allan Robertson of St Andrews – would barely have recognised.

Literature flourishes

The 1890 season also would be remembered as a watershed in the game's literary history. That year saw publication of volume 13 of The Badminton Library of Sports and Pastimes, a book called, simply, *Golf*.

The library was created in 1885 by Henry Somerset, the 8th Duke of Beaufort, a soldier and politician. The duke's goal was to fill a void in a rapidly changing society that increasingly valued leisure-time pursuits. 'There is no modern encyclopedia to which the inexperienced man, who seeks guidance in the practice of various British sports and pastimes, can turn for information,' he explained in Badminton's first volume.

By the 19th century sports had become an integral part of Victorian culture. They were believed to promote core values like 'fair play, gentlemanly behaviour, honest competition, modesty in victory, cheerfulness in defeat, manly courage and cooperation', as one scholar put it. In its first year, Badminton Library published three volumes, one on hunting and two on fishing. These were followed by books on racing and steeplechasing, shooting, boating, cycling, cricket, football and more.

Apparently it took a bit of persuasion to convince the duke that volume 13 should be devoted solely to golf. 'The publishers were in some doubt whether the game was of sufficient importance to justify its being accorded a full volume,' Hutchinson wrote. When the decision was made to give golf its own volume – and to make Hutchinson the editor – it was a powerful sign of how ingrained the Scottish game had become in English culture.

Hutchinson was the natural choice, and not simply because he had twice won the Amateur. In 1886 he had published one of the game's first instructional books, a thin, amusing volume called *Hints on the Game of Golf*. The book had but three chapters – 'Advice to Beginners', 'Hints to Golfers of Riper Years' and 'The Miseries of Golf' – each full of sound advice mixed with witty truisms.

'You should keep your eye fixedly on the ball from the moment that the club-head is lifted from the ground until the ball is actually struck,' beginners were told, advice as valuable now as it was then. Hutchinson also demonstrated a sense of humour about the golfer's travails. 'If your adversary is badly bunkered,' he wrote, tongue firmly in cheek, 'there is no rule against your standing over him and counting his strokes aloud, with an increasing gusto as their numbers mount up; but it will be a wise precaution to arm yourself with the niblick before doing so, so as to meet him on equal terms.'

Hutchinson took a more serious approach to his Badminton volume, perhaps the most influential book ever written about the game. *Golf* spanned more than 400 pages and 17 chapters, 15 erudite essays along with a list of the game's rules and a glossary of golf terms. The bulk of the book was devoted to instruction, but there were also essays on the evolution of the game, its most famous links and its most famous players.

Hutchinson wrote much of the book himself, but he also drew on leading figures of the day. Illustrations were done by St Andrews artist and photographer Thomas Hodge. Poet, novelist and literary critic Andrew Lang wrote an essay on how golf evolved from ancient stick-and-ball games, while writer and historian H.S.C. 'Harry' Everard handled a chapter on celebrated players.

By far the most influential contributor, however, was a man who would go on to become prime minister and whose social and political prominence played a major role in popularising golf – the Right Honourable Arthur James Balfour, a Member of Parliament representing Manchester East. He contributed a piece called 'The Humours of Golf', in which he explored the 'fatal fascination' the game exercises over its devotees.

Balfour was born in Scotland in 1848, the year the gutta-percha ball began overtaking the feathery. He was the eldest son of James Maitland Balfour and Lady Blanche Gascoyne-Cecil, who owned an East Lothian estate known as Whittingehame House. From the start, young Arthur seemed destined for a life in politics. His father and grandfather had been Members of Parliament, and his godfather, after whom he was named, was the first Duke of Wellington.

Balfour grew up a few miles from North Berwick, where his father and uncle were members, but did not take up golf seriously until his mid-thirties. He never became more than a middling player, counting himself among the 'unhappy beings, forever pursued by remorse, who are conscious that they threw away in their youth the opportunity of beginning golf at a time when the muscles can be attuned to the full perfection for that most difficult game.'

Three years before his essay appeared in *Golf*, Balfour was appointed Chief Secretary for Ireland, a high-profile and dangerous post because, as Hutchinson wrote, the country was 'seething with murderous discontent' over British rule. The calm, confident way Balfour handled the assignment made him a revered figure. That proved enormously influential when his admirers learned that the Chief Secretary had fallen in love with a game still new enough in England that it was mocked in major magazines.

'He was a very great figure in golf,' Hutchinson wrote, 'and just because it is very human to be influenced by an example, the effect of his example was to make many a man play golf, on the principle that "there must be something in a game if a man like Arthur Balfour plays it".'

While *Golf* would take its place as a seminal work on the game, it was not the first. That honour goes to *The Golfer's Manual*, a charming book of history, culture and instruction written in 1857 by 'A Keen Hand'. That was the nom de plume of Henry Brougham Farnie, the *Fifeshire Journal* editor who chronicled Young Tommy's march to claim The Belt even as he translated bawdy French operettas for the London stage.

A generation later Robert Clark published *Golf: A Royal and Ancient Game*, a lively compendium of poems, documents and other odds and ends related to golf's early history. In 1887, Sir Walter Simpson produced *The Art of Golf*, a beautifully written, often hilariously funny book of culture and instruction. The game's literature expanded rapidly over the rest of that decade, with volumes like Rev. John Kerr's *The Golf Book of East Lothian*, Willie Park's *The Game of Golf* and Hutchinson's own *British Golf Links* and *The Book of Golf and Golfers*.

The 1890 season also saw the debut of the first magazine devoted solely to the game – *Golf: A Weekly Record of 'Ye Royal and Ancient' Game*, which by the end of the decade would become *Golf Illustrated*. It was, of course, not the first magazine to cover golf. *The Field*, which was founded in 1853 and described itself as *The Country Gentleman's Newspaper*, wrote regularly about the game, as did national and local newspapers in England and Scotland.

No publication, however, did a better job of tracking the growth of golf through that transformative era than a book that debuted two years before the Duke of Beaufort published Badminton's 13th volume. It was known, prosaically, as *The Golfing Annual*. Introduced in 1888, primarily as a guide to the enormous number of new golf clubs forming in Britain and around the world, the series ran for 23 editions, each a green, leather-bound volume embossed with gold lettering and a stick-figure golfer on the cover. The last of the series appeared in 1910.

The Annual was the brainchild of Charles Robertson Bauchope, Scottish correspondent for *The Field*, from whose office the book was published. For years, Bauchope had been hearing from friends and readers that he was just the person to create a yearly guide that would help golfers keep track of the game's explosive growth. He promised readers a book that would be more than a dry compendium of new courses. The inaugural issue set the tone. The first hundred pages or so were devoted to thoughtful essays; reviews of famous courses, often with pull-out maps; poetry singing the game's praises, and accounts of the previous year's Amateur and Open, which grew to become in-depth reports detailing how the battles ebbed and flowed. Similar treatment would be given to new championships that emerged in Britain and around the globe.

The essays in that first edition provide a window into the evolution of the game. Walter Simpson, then captain of the Honourable Company of Edinburgh Golfers, wrote a lament about the rapidly growing game lacking a universal code of rules, an issue that would come to a head over the next decade. Hutchinson took readers on a rambling tour of English links, from his home in North Devon to Hoylake, Royal Wimbledon, Royal Blackheath and more. J.O.F. Morris, Young Tommy's brother, contributed a piece on the links at St Andrews. Bauchope added an essay about how the game was sprouting up around the world, as well as a poem in praise of the links life.

The heart of *The Annual*, however, was the Club Directory that comprised the bulk of the book. Each entry provided golfers with information about visiting or joining a club – entrance fees, annual subscriptions, names of secretaries, and details on trains and accommodations. These were supplemented by brief, lovely essays on the course over which the club played.

Sadly, Bauchope did not live to see what his *Annual* became. Before he'd completed the second edition, he took ill and died. His brother, John, finished that volume before becoming sick himself and handing the duties to David Scott Duncan, who edited the rest of the series. Duncan was also Scottish correspondent for *The Field*, as well as a superb runner who won the nation's mile championship five times.

The 1890s was not simply the decade that saw the emergence of lasting golf literature. It was also the decade of Oscar Wilde and Arthur Conan Doyle, of Henrik Ibsen and George Bernard Shaw. The '1890's was, indeed, the great decade of golf, and of so much else in English life!' wrote poet and golfer Patric Dickinson, whose book *A Round of Golf Courses: A Selection of the Best Eighteen* is itself a classic.

Challenge answered

Amid this intellectual ferment, one constant remained – the consuming interest in golf's major championships. The 1891 season presented an obvious question. How would Scotland's old guard respond to the challenge John Ball laid down the previous season by winning The Double?

The cards were stacked in Scotland's favour. Both the Amateur Championship and Open would be played that year over the links of St Andrews, which often presented an insoluble puzzle to golfers who played the course infrequently.

A field of 50 players gathered in that old grey town by the sea during the second week of May to contest the seventh Amateur Championship. That was the largest field yet assembled, although both Hutchinson and Leslie Balfour-Melville were absent. Ball was, of course, the favourite, but St Andrews had never been a course he played well. It wasn't that year, either, perhaps because he was fighting a cold and sore throat. Ball barely survived a first-round bout against a minor, much older player from Glasgow, and was put out in the second by a golfer from Dundee who was not on anyone's list of potential winners.

All was not lost for Hoylake and England, however. Harold Hilton had a bye and a walkover in the first two rounds. He had to win just three matches, only one of which went to the 18th, to make his way into the Championship final for the first time. The man he met there, predictably, was John Laidlay. The Scotsman had easily dispensed with all five opponents he faced en route to his encounter with Hilton.

The final was a dogfight throughout, with Laidlay always gaining a lead and Hilton always fighting gamely to close the gap. With five holes to play, the stalwart Scotsman was three holes up. Hilton was not about to quit, however. He took the 14th and 15th and just managed to sneak in a putt to win 18 and square the match.

For the first time in history, the final of the Amateur Championship had been left undecided in regulation, sending the competition into extra holes. The Scottish partisans following Laidlay and Hilton 'allowed the excitement to get so much the better of them that it was with difficulty that the course could be cleared', *The Scotsman* reported.

When order was finally restored, and both players had crossed the Swilcan Burn that winds across the opening hole at St Andrews, Hilton faced a makeable putt to claim his first Championship. Laidlay faced a testing approach from just off the green. Hilton's putt ran by. Laidlay laid another of his patented approaches stone dead and survived with a half.

On the second hole, both Laidlay and Hilton took a cautious route from the tee to steer clear of the bunkers. That meant the Championship came down to a short-game contest that Laidlay was always going to win. 'It was evident that Mr Hilton had not got his nerves under perfect control,' *The Scotsman* reported. 'He failed to be up in a putt of about two yards, and he thus gave his opponent a chance of being down in the like, and Laidlay was equal to the occasion.'

Joining Hutchinson and Ball before him, Laidlay was now a two-time Amateur Champion, his ears ringing with the cheers that must have seemed as if they came from all of Scotland.

When the Open came around four months later, it was clear that Hutchinson wasn't the only man who had concluded that Ball's victory the previous season brought the Championship 'within the practical horizon of the amateur'. A record field of 83 players turned out, and nearly half were amateurs. The field was so large that, for the first time in history, there was concern about whether daylight would last long enough to complete both rounds of the tournament in a single day.

'The question of a qualifying competition must, in view of the ever-increasing entry, be faced without delay, or a condition imposed that in the future, competitors whose scores were above a certain figure should then and there retire,' *The Annual* wrote, a suggestion that was a bit ahead of its time. A cut would not be imposed in the Open until 1898.

Players who teed off first – at nine o'clock, two hours earlier than normal – faced the kind of grim conditions that so often define an Open. 'The weather during the early morning was very unfavourable,' *The Annual* wrote, 'a strong southerly gale with heavy rain rendering matters very uncomfortable for players and spectators.' Conditions improved as the day wore on. Except for an hour-long downpour after lunch, the rain stayed away, but the wind continued to howl all day, making the homecoming nine a brute.

If Scotsmen were looking for their old guard to stand up to the English, their wish was granted. Hugh Kirkaldy, younger brother of everyone's favourite St Andrews caddie, brushed off the weather and raced to the turn in 39 strokes, marvellous under the circumstances. The home nine, playing into that gale, required 44. Still, the consensus was it would take some golf to do better than Kirkaldy's 83, and that turned out to be true. Only three players came within a stroke – Hugh's brother Andra, Willie Fernie and, unexpectedly, an English professional named Willie More of Chester.

In the afternoon, Hugh Kirkaldy, playing in the hour-long downpour that began at one o'clock, did one better than he had in the morning with 38 for the opening nine. Nine consecutive fives on the homeward half brought him to the clubhouse again with 83. He was the man to catch with a two-round total of 166, a new record for the Championship at St Andrews. The only two threatening to overhaul him were his older brother and Fernie, both of whom again came in with 84s to finish two strokes back. More held on for fifth, the best finish yet by an English professional.

On the 18th green, Andra Kirkaldy had a long putt to tie for the lead and force the first play-off between brothers in Open history. Anxious to hole it, he ran the putt far enough past that he needed two more to finish. The following afternoon, for the last time in Open history, the two men set out on a play-off for second place. From then on, purses would simply be split.

Andra Kirkaldy prevailed in the play-off, resulting in a one-two finish for the brothers, much to the delight of Old Tom Morris. He had pre-dicted before the first ball was struck that this would be Hugh Kirkaldy's year to be Champion Golfer. That prediction was understandable. Ear-lier that season, Kirkaldy had gone around St Andrews in 74, eclipsing the record of 77 held jointly by Young Tommy, J.O.F. Morris and Jamie Anderson.

Even with amateurs constituting half the field, gentleman golfers posed no threat in the first Open after Ball's breakthrough. Poor Ball was out of it after one round. His approach to 17 sailed over the road and into a ditch. He tried twice to hack it out, and finally took a drop that cost him two more strokes. When it was over Ball had run up a 94, and even a solid 83 in the afternoon was no help. The only positive he would take from that season was having won his fourth consecutive St George's Vase, a feat that would not be eclipsed for 85 years. Other leading amateurs didn't do much better in the Open. Laidlay came in with twin rounds of 90, while Hilton went around in 89 and 86. The only gentleman within shouting distance, at four strokes back, was the redoubtable Scotsman Mure Fergusson.

For 1891 at least, golfers north of the border had responded to *The Scotsman*'s challenge of the previous season to reflect on the reality that on the very green where the Open Championship was born an Englishman had defeated them at their own national game. Scottish golfers had carried off every medal on offer that season. They would not have long to savour those victories, however. In the year to come, the two heroes of Hoylake would give Scots plenty more to think about.

Six

GENTLEMAN'S DECADE

— • ● ● ● • —

The man who would prove that John Ball's breakthrough for amateurs in 1890 was no fluke was the same schoolboy who had lost a shilling betting on his childhood hero to beat Dougie Rolland. By the time Harold Hilton reached the pinnacle of his game, it would be obvious that a fundamental change was unfolding in gentlemen's golf.

Hilton was born on 14 January 1869 in West Kirby, near Hoylake. He was the son of Eliza Eleanor Pugh and Benjamin Holden Hilton, manager of Crown Assurance Company, which provided insurance to merchants of nearby Liverpool. As a boy, Hilton attended the same local primary school as Ball, but, unlike his idol, went on to boarding school at Norfolk County, some 100 miles north-east of London. Most boys who took that path continued on to university, but not Hilton. He returned home to work for his father.

Insurance, however, would never be his calling. Like most young boys in Victorian Britain, Hilton loved sports and excelled at several, including cricket, football, handball and running. Having grown up next door to Hoylake, however, it was golf that became his lifelong passion. Hilton learned the game from the man who finished fifth in the 1891 Open, Willie More, one of the earliest English professionals. More approached the game with a scientific frame of mind that captivated his pupil.

'I had five consecutive months' golf with him, and he certainly taught me much of the game,' Hilton recalled. 'I cannot say that I followed all of his little theoretical fads; he had far too many to take in all at once, and they had to be taken home, chewed and digested, but they taught me much.'

That early exposure to an analytical approach to golf would have a lifelong impact on Hilton. He would grow up to be one of the game's most respected thinkers and writers, eventually finding his niche as editor of *Golf Monthly* and *Golf Illustrated*. He would also write several books, a slim volume of history and instruction called *Modern Golf*; a limited edition collector's item titled *The Royal and Ancient Game of Golf*, done jointly with fellow magazine editor Garden Smith, and his memoir *My Golfing Reminiscences*. When Horace Hutchinson edited his *The Book of Golf and Golfers* in 1899, he chose Hilton to write a chapter titled 'Golf as a Game'.

'Even now I would say that no golfer, amateur or professional that has ever lived has *known* golf as he has,' wrote Bernard Darwin. 'To me he stands unrivalled in his power of observation and inference, in his understanding of how certain results follow from certain causes. Assuredly, too, because he is a highly strung man with the temperament of an artist, nobody has ever seen more deeply into the golfer's heart nor better understood his mental as well as his physical difficulties.'

As a golfer and a man, Hilton could not have been more different than Ball, eight years his senior. While Ball was painfully shy and quiet, Hilton was a jaunty extrovert who loved crowds and conversation. He played golf differently, too. While Ball went 'faultlessly down the middle', Hilton shaped his shots to suit the wind, fading some and drawing others as conditions demanded. His approach may have been different, but Hilton's results were the same – absolute precision. 'The stroke is repeated, time after time, with unvarying accuracy by Mr Hilton,' Hutchinson wrote, 'with accuracy perhaps more unvarying than anyone else has ever attained.'

Hilton never did have the lovely swing of Ball and was never as long off the tee. A smaller man at 5 feet 6 inches, Hilton took a loose-looking lash at the ball, sending his cap flying with every swing. 'Imagine a short man . . . with a long club placing his feet with meticulous care in regard to the line and then rather sitting down to the ball,' Darwin wrote. 'The waggle is careful and restrained; then suddenly all is changed; he seems almost to jump on his toes in the upswing and fairly to fling himself at the ball. There is no doubt he is on his toes at the moment of hitting and the follow-through of body, head and arms and all is of unrestrained and glorious freedom.'

The biggest difference between the games of Hilton and Ball, the place where Hilton had the edge, was putting. 'Fewer strokes are thrown away by him on the putting green, probably, than by any other living player,' Hutchinson said. How Ball would have loved to see those words written about him.

Hilton's sartorial style wasn't much different than that of other golfers, beyond a decided preference for white canvas shoes and a bow tie to accent his jacket and knickerbockers. He did cut a dashing figure on the links, however, as he was rarely seen without a cigarette dangling rakishly from his lips. Chain smoking was not Hilton's only distinguishing trait. The other was that he was nearly always clean-shaven, a rarity in Victorian Britain. Most men grew beards, mutton chops or moustaches as they aged, especially after marriage. Hilton stuck with the fresh-faced look, even after he married Frances Cooper.

Hilton came into golf in much the same way Ball had. He, too, made his debut in the Boy's Medal at Hoylake, having the temerity at the age of eight to enter in the senior division for boys 15 or younger. He was nowhere to be seen at the finish, but two years later he tried again and won. Hilton went on to win the medal three more times before turning 16, one of the first times he eclipsed his childhood hero, who won it only twice.

In those early years, Hilton was also matched against leading players from Hoylake, as Ball had been before him. He played Ball himself, receiving six strokes over 18 holes, and felt pleased when he won. Not long afterwards, playing even-up, Hilton beat one of the club's scratch players. While he also became a hero at Hoylake, Hilton never was as beloved as Ball. The fishermen who so adored Ball, a humble farmer, considered Hilton a toff, derisive slang for the upper classes. It was an unfair judgement. Hilton's family was hardly wealthy and he always scraped for his money.

Hilton's entrance onto golf's main stage would come in 1887, aged 18, when he entered his first Amateur at Hoylake. He survived only one round, being put out by Ball's father in the second. 'I must confess that my first experience of a Championship was not a happy one,' he recalled. 'I felt very subdued and chastened in spirit.'

Even then Hilton knew why he wasn't winning, a lesson driven home in the 1889 Amateur, where he first faced John Laidlay in his opening match. He hung with the Scotsman until the final green, and in the aftermath came to a realisation. 'I am afraid that I began that round with the idea that if I gave mine enemy a good run I should have done well, and when the match had finished I felt I had done well,' Hilton wrote.

'But that is not the spirit in which to approach a Championship. You must go out to win whatever your chance may be on paper.'

By the time the 1892 Championships came around, Hilton had more reason to be confident in his prospects. Two years earlier, he won his first tournament at North Berwick, defeating a man with whom his name would be forever linked, Freddie Tait. The young Scotsman had just entered the Royal Military Academy at Sandhurst with visions of becoming an officer in the Queen's army.

Unique spectacle

The 1892 season would prove to be a pivotal one for Hilton and the game, but it began in a state of turmoil caused by dissatisfaction among professional golfers that came to a head after the 1891 Open.

For years unrest had been brewing about the administration of the championship. Almost nothing had changed since its inception in 1860. The prize fund remained minuscule. The date of the event still wasn't announced more than a month in advance, and golfers still submitted entries by telling Old Tom Morris they wanted to play. The flaws of that system became obvious when, in a senior moment, Tom forgot to enter a player on one occasion and on another could not be sure if he had received entries or not. The unpleasant result was that some players competed under protest.

Adding salt to those wounds, at least from the perspective of professional golfers, was that more and more people were of the opinion that the relatively new Amateur Championship was a more significant event than the Open. After all, the Amateur usually drew a far larger field, and amateur golfers had lately proven themselves competitive for the first time in history. *Golf* magazine was unstinting in its criticism of the Royal and Ancient members who had overseen the 1891 Championship, describing them as 'ludicrously out of touch with the wider golfing world'.

Immediately after the Open, professionals called a meeting chaired by Old Tom himself. They agreed that something must be done to restore the lustre of the Open and made several far-reaching proposals for achieving that goal. Prize money should be sharply increased, especially the winner's share, and players should be charged an entry fee to fatten the purse. The tournament should be expanded from 36 to 72 holes and played over two days, not one as it had been for 30 years. And, finally, the Open should recognise the rapid growth of the game in England by staging a Championship in the south.

A document outlining their proposals was drafted and circulated to every leading club, including the R&A. Never before had professionals banded together to raise their voices about how the game ought to be run, and the significance of that meeting has not been lost on historians. 'It was without doubt the progenitor of all the Professional Golfers' Associations in the world today,' concluded David Malcolm and Peter Crabtree, authors of the definitive biography of Old Tom.

Before that meeting had taken place, the committee running the Amateur had already decided to include more English courses in its rota. Delegates voted to conduct the 1892 Championship at St George's, 80 miles south-east of London on the Kent coast. The course at Sandwich had been laid out five years earlier by William Laidlaw Purves, the same man who had followed along with Hutchinson as Ball marched into history at the 1890 Open in Prestwick.

Purves routed his course through an expanse of heaving sand dunes along Pegwell Bay. Measuring a full 6,100 yards, St George's had been designed to severely punish missed shots, especially those that were topped, a cardinal sin in the Victorian age. The course was famous for long, forced carries from the tee and blind shots. Its signature hole was the 176-yard Maiden, which required golfers to carry a massive dune of rough grass and sandy waste areas to an unseen two-tiered green.

In its earliest incarnation, St George's was hailed as a tremendous test of golf. 'A good many people say it is the best in the world,' wrote Hutchinson, 'and some really think so.' That last phrase suggests that he wasn't among those prepared to grant such lofty status to St George's, which received its royal patronage in 1902. Over the years, the penal style of design Purves admired would fall out of favour. Many holes at Sandwich, especially the Maiden, would be softened to suit evolving tastes.

Whatever golfers thought of the design, they adored playing at Sandwich, one of England's ancient Cinque Ports. A quaint town alongside the River Stour, it was there, in 1194, that King Richard the Lionheart first set foot in England again after the Third Crusade. Not far away are the famed Canterbury Cathedral and ancient Roman ruins. The centrepiece of the town, commanding a view of the quay, is the lovely old Bell Hotel. It served as the first headquarters for golfers at St George's and still caters to visiting pilgrims today.

'Sandwich has a charm that belongs to itself, and I frankly own myself under the spell,' wrote Darwin, who had grown up near the links in the home of his grandfather, Charles, the famous naturalist. 'The long strip of turf on the way to the seventh hole, that stretches between the sandhills and the sea; a fine spring day with the larks singing as they seem to sing nowhere else; the sun shining on the waters of Pegwell Bay and lighting up the white cliffs in the distance; this is as nearly my idea of heaven as is to be attained on any earthly links.'

A field of 45 gathered at Sandwich in the second week of May to contest the 1892 Amateur over three picture-perfect days. 'The only fly in the ointment being the excessive keenness of the putting greens, which occasionally disconcerted competitors on crucial putts,' *The Golfing Annual* wrote.

Ordinarily, an Amateur Championship is a slow-starting affair, with the favourites cruising through early rounds and the life-and-death battles coming towards the end. That was not true at Sandwich. Ball found himself up against the wall in his opening match. Alex Stuart, captain of the Honourable Company of Edinburgh Golfers, had taken a four-hole lead on Ball by the time the pair turned for home.

Stuart was a formidable golfer, but he was not expected to beat Ball. As he so often did when all hope seemed lost, Ball began hitting one perfect shot after another and clawed his way back to all square with two to play. When 17 was halved and Stuart could not get down his putt for four on the last, Ball had his chance. He calmly knocked in his putt to win by a hole.

'His plucky win, after being to all appearances out of the running, was loudly applauded and his reputation as a match player was greatly enhanced thereby,' *The Annual* wrote. From that day forward, Ball would be known as that most dangerous of opponents – the player who can reel his man in at will. Darwin tells a famous story about Ball playing a match at Hoylake, with a comfortable lead and half a dozen holes to go. Ball turned to a friend and said, 'I think we'll finish it at the Dun,' the 16th, the hole nearest the clubhouse. 'Sure enough,' Darwin wrote, 'the young gentleman was allowed to get a hole or two back. Then, when it came to the Dun, Mr Ball hit a great brassy shot right over the cross bunker and finished the match by 3 and 2.'

The second round of that 1892 Amateur saw a battle royal similar to the match between Ball and Stuart. Frank Fairlie, of the famed family of Prestwick golfers, rallied from three down with five to play to overtake up-and-coming star Tait. While Hilton, Laidlay and Leslie Balfour-Melville cruised through their early rounds, Ball again found himself fighting for his life in his third-round match against Hutchinson. This time it was Ball who marched out to a four-hole lead and Hutchinson who fought gamely back only to give way on 18.

Ball's brutal road to the finale of the Championship would continue in a see-saw semi-final against Balfour-Melville. Down three holes after five, Ball reeled off seven in a row to stand four holes up with six to play. Balfour-Melville responded with his own spurt of brilliance to square the match at 17. When his second to the home hole failed to reach the green, Ball survived again 'by his seemingly favourite margin of one hole'. Hilton, meanwhile, took sweet revenge on Laidlay in their semi-final, racing through the front nine in a brilliant 36 and dispensing with the Scotsman 5 and 4.

'Thus, we had the unique spectacle of the two Hoylake players fighting out the final,' *The Annual* wrote. An all-English final made another bold statement about the progress of the game south of the border, but alas the match between Ball and Hilton turned out to be a lacklustre affair. Both played undistinguished, if steady, golf. Ball never got more than a hole up over the first dozen that were played, but beginning on the 13th he shook Hilton off and claimed his third Amateur 3 and 1.

For the second consecutive season Hilton had the 'honourable but unsatisfactory' position of runner-up, but as *The Annual* noted Ball had 'much the harder task and his sterling play and indomitable pluck made his victory extremely popular'. Hilton may have lost, but his spirits were not dashed. He'd had tough luck on the home nine, while the bounces went Ball's way. 'I always consider that this was the only final I ever played in which fortune was a little unkind to me,' he wrote. Hilton walked away from that defeat confident that his day was coming – and soon.

Doubling up

In the months before hosting the 1892 Open, the Honourable Company adopted nearly every recommendation put forth at that contentious meeting of professionals the previous season.

They published the dates of the event early. They expanded the tournament to 72 holes over two days, charged an entry fee of ten shillings and added it to the £20 put up by the club. The purse increase was hardly as large as professionals wanted, but nearly all their suggestions had been followed. It was the Honourable Company's final announcement that ignited one of the most heated controversies in Open history.

In 1891, distressed by the deteriorating condition of the Musselburgh links and the constant overcrowding, the Honourable Company had moved eight miles east to Muirfield, where Old Tom Morris had laid out a new course for the private use of its members. That was the club's second move. In 1836 members abandoned their original home at Leith for similar reasons. What set the golf world reeling was the Honourable Company's announcement that the 1892 Open would move with the club and be contested at Muirfield.

That decision was a slap in the face of Musselburgh, which rivalled St Andrews as an epicentre of the game. By 1892 the town's nine-hole links had hosted six Opens, crowning such legendary champions as Jamie Anderson, Bob Ferguson, Willie Fernie, Mungo Park and his nephew Willie Jr. Only the most fervent Musselburgh loyalists would have disagreed with *The Annual's* conclusion that 'the Honourable Company were strictly within their rights in changing the venue'. But the majority in the world of golf agreed with *The Annual* when it wrote, 'We question the wisdom of the change.'

The objections to Muirfield were many. It was remote, four miles from the nearest train station, with almost no lodging nearby. That was no small matter for professional golfers, who already had trouble winning enough money to cover their travel expenses. Those costs would only be higher now that the competition would take place over two days. Crowds were certain to be thin for the same reason. The biggest objection to the move, however, concerned the new golf course at Muirfield.

'Muirfield is an excellent private course – in fact, we know of none better – and the putting greens are magnificent; but there is a sameness about the 18 holes, and they are not such a reliable test of golfing ability as the nine holes at Musselburgh,' *The Annual* wrote. That summed up the feelings of most golfers, and indeed the inadequacies of Muirfield's original layout were borne out by unusually low scoring throughout the Open that year. In the aftermath of that Championship, stung by the harsh criticism, the Honourable Company would make Muirfield longer and tougher.

A proud, rambunctious town, Musselburgh was in no way prepared to give up the Open without a fight. Leading businessmen got together and made an announcement of their own. Musselburgh would stage a championship on the same dates as the Open with a purse of £100, far more than the Honourable Company was offering. It was a bold ploy, but in the end the Musselburgh men had to back down, for two reasons. The Honourable Company matched the £100 purse, and professional golfers made it clear that they had no intention of skipping the Open Championship.

The controversy wound up benefiting professional golfers. Musselburgh moved its event a week earlier, giving players the unprecedented opportunity to compete for £100 purses in back-to-back weeks. Better still, going forward the Open would continue to pay £30 to the winner. Musselburgh's event drew every leading professional in the game, except Old Tom, who chose not to compete. It ended on a happy note when home-town hero Willie Park won by five strokes over Andra Kirkaldy and Tom Vardon, whose older brother, Harry, was just then starting his career as a club professional.

When the dust had settled, 66 players turned up at Muirfield to compete in the Open. The only big names missing were Laidlay, who did not always find time for professional events, and everyone's favourite rogue, Dougie Rolland. He hadn't competed in a championship north of the border since he left Scotland for England in the early 1880s. The Open was played over two lovely autumn days before a tiny crowd of fewer than 100.

Most fans followed either Ball or the previous week's winner, Park. Ball played his usual precision golf to set the pace with a stellar round of 75. Only Hutchinson did better, playing his irons brilliantly to come in with 74. Hilton and Park were four shots back. Both Hoylake men stumbled in the second round. Ball came in with 80 and Hilton with 81, as Park added a 77. Hutchinson, meanwhile, posted a 78 that gave him a two-round total of 152 and a three-shot lead over Ball and Park.

Hutchinson started his third round by yanking his tee shot into the woods that lined the first hole. Matters didn't improve for him over the rest of the round. He limped in with an 86 that dashed any hopes he may have harboured of winning. For the rest of his days, Hutchinson would regret that the Open had been expanded to 72 holes that year. While he was going into a funk, the two Hoylake men were catching fire. Ball marched around in 74 to seize the lead, but it was Hilton who stole the show.

'A grand tee shot to within a yard of the pin enabled him to get down in two at the first hole, and from here on to the home hole he showed the most brilliant golf, and holed out in 72 amidst general applause, thus taking second place to Mr Ball,' two strokes back, *The Annual* reported.

Ball was off early in the final round, with a chance to set a mark for others to match. His ball striking was brilliant, as always, but that old nemesis putting haunted him from start to finish. Again and again he left long putts woefully short and missed the second one. In the end, Ball posted a 79, a solid round but certainly one that could be beaten. Far behind him, his Hoylake mate Hilton was doing just that.

He caught Ball by the turn and continued to forge ahead as he marched through the home nine. With two holes to play Hilton was in the same position his idol had been at Prestwick in 1890. Only a catastrophe could keep him from winning. When Hilton's putt for three found the hole at the 17th, the Championship was all but over. He finished in 74 to become the second amateur to claim the Open. It was, *The Annual* wrote, 'a grand round played with the greatest confidence and dash, and amidst general cheering Mr Hilton was hailed as champion for the year.'

Hutchinson had come out to the 18th hole to watch Hilton finish, a scene that would be forever etched on his memory. 'I can see him now as he came up to the last hole . . . ,' Hutchinson wrote, 'walking along at top speed, chatting volubly with his friends, very pleased with himself, as well he might be, brimful of confidence and with the smoke trailing up from his cigarette even while he was playing the ball, so that it seemed impossible that he could see through it to hit the ball correctly. But he did hit it mighty correctly, for all that, and won the Championship.'

Hilton knew that fate seemed to have reserved that Championship for him. He almost hadn't come to Muirfield to compete, he recalled years later, 'chiefly for the reason that I did not think it was worth the financial outlay'. It was only when a friend offered him a free place to stay that Hilton changed his mind and hopped on the midnight train heading north. Luck also had been on his side during that final round. Twice he chipped in with his mashie, and the number of missable putts he holed was too many to count.

'Now when I look back on that round I cannot but realise that fortune was very much on my side,' Hilton concluded.

With Ball finishing tied for second, alongside Hugh Kirkaldy and a young Scottish professional named Sandy Herd, English golfers had again completed The Double, sweeping both the Amateur and Open in the same season. This time they'd done one better than 1890. Ball and Hilton had taken the top two places in both events. The significance of that accomplishment was not lost on either Hilton or the press.

When he was presented with the Claret Jug and the gold medal identifying him as Champion Golfer of the Year, Hilton made it a point to tell the crowd how proud he was to have won the Open as an amateur, following in the footsteps of his Hoylake compatriot. *The Annual* went even further, describing Hilton's victory as a wake-up call for Scottish golfers, amateur and professional alike.

'Within the short space of two years, we have seen the two distinguished Hoylake amateurs succeed, where all Scotch amateurs have failed, in vanquishing the pick of professional players, and so carrying the blue ribbon of golf south of the Tweed,' *The Annual* wrote. 'In them Hoylake has two sons of which she can feel justly proud, and, with English professionals . . . rapidly coming to the front to assist them, Scotland will indeed require to look to her laurels at her peculiar game.'

Seismic shift

What was unfolding in golf, however, was more than an English uprising. It was a tectonic shift in the competitive relationship between amateur and professional players.

Amateurs had ruled the game since it began, devoted all the while to the noble ideal of the sporting gentleman who plays for love and not for money. Only a generation before, no one would have dreamt of an amateur winning the Open. The closest amateur had been 29 strokes back the year Young Tom Morris claimed The Belt. Now amateurs had two wins in three seasons, with a fourth-place finish in between.

The trend that had been developing since the institution of the Amateur, which had seen gentlemen finish closer and closer in the Open, clearly was no happenstance. Amateur golf had reached an entirely new level. For the rest of that decade, amateurs would remain a force to be reckoned with in the championship. They would add another victory, another second and three third-place finishes during those seven years.

Between 1890 and 1899, seven different amateurs – Ball, Hilton, Hutchinson, Laidlay, Freddie Tait, Mure Fergusson and Arnold Blyth – would account for 18 top-ten finishes in the Open. Ten of those would be in the top five. The numbers are even more remarkable when one considers that amateurs rarely made up more than a third of the field, and usually a quarter or less.

Nor would that be the last great burst of amateur golf. When golf took root in the United States, the game developed much as it had in England. It was adopted first by wealthy gentlemen before becoming widely popular. Not surprisingly, the pattern of amateur success British golf was then experiencing would be replicated on the other side of the Atlantic. Between 1910 and 1920, three amateurs would win the US Open – Francis Ouimet, Jerome Travers and Chick Evans. Only nine Championships were staged over those 11 years, as two were cancelled during the First World War. In addition to winning a third of the Championships, amateurs would add six other top ten finishes.

In the decade that followed, a young man from Georgia would carry amateur golf to Olympian heights. Over those ten years, Bobby Jones would win three Open Championships and four US Opens – along the way securing the Grand Slam of amateur and open titles and earning a place among the immortals. Time and progress would catch up with amateur golf in the US after Jones, as it had long before in Britain. With exceptions like Johnny Goodman's 1933 US Open victory and Lawson Little's twin amateur slams in 1934 and 1935, the gentleman's game had seen its final days of glory.

It was, however, the English uprising and not the remarkable progress of amateurs that was on the minds of golf fans north and south of the border as the game's two most important championships returned for the 1893 season to the links at Prestwick. Scots responded precisely as they had to Ball's double in 1890. They swept both titles.

Peter Anderson, a divinity student at St Andrews University, won the Amateur in the biggest upset that Championship had yet seen. Willie Auchterlonie, whose family still operates a club-making shop a few blocks from the R&A, carried off the Claret Jug with a two-stroke victory in the Open. Best of all, Scotsman Laidlay finished second in both events. Englishmen were no threat in either. The amateur semi-finalists were all Scots, and the best the southerners could muster in the Open was a tie for eighth place between Ball and Hilton. 'The result was a complete triumph for Scottish, and particularly St Andrews, golf,' wrote *The Annual*.

Those Championships, however, would be remembered not so much for the winners as for performances in early rounds that gave hints of heroics to come. Easily the most exciting match in the 1893 Amateur was the semi-final between Laidlay and the young soldier Freddie Tait. It was a classic back-and-forth battle, with Laidlay forging ahead and Tait coming up with miraculous shots or putts to square accounts.

Neither man could finish off his opponent in regulation, forcing the pair to play on in front of a restless Scottish crowd that barely gave them room to breathe as they teed off again at the opening hole. Both men reached the green safely, where that hard-fought match came down to two putts of equal length. Laidlay moved on to the final when his putt fell in and Tait's didn't.

Despite the agonising loss, *The Scotsman* sang Tait's praises. 'Next to the actual champion, the most remarkable figure in the Championship was that of another young player, Mr F.G. Tait,' the newspaper wrote. 'In our opinion, the champion has Mr Tait in part to thank for his victory, for the keen contest which Mr Laidlay had to come through with the dashing young soldier-golfer before he reached the final gave the divinity student a better chance of beating him.'

In the Open, it was a single round of golf that turned the heads of every veteran at Prestwick when play began on the first day of August, one Old Tom himself described as the most miserable in Championship history. 'It rained in the most pitiless fashion from morn till eve,' *The Annual* wrote, 'and players and those whose business compelled them to be present, had a most unenviable outing, for, lovely spot as the far-famed Ayrshire green may be on a fine summer day when the sun glints on the peaks of Arran, we can conceive of no more dismal place when the rain drives in from the broad expanse of the Firth of Clyde.'

The most talked-about round of the tournament was delivered by John Henry Taylor, the young man who grew up as a houseboy for the Hutchinsons and had recently landed his first job as a professional at Burnham-on-Sea. He played as if the sun were shining and there wasn't a breath of wind. His cap tugged down on his head, his feet planted as if they were nailed to the ground, the man everyone knew simply by his initials, J.H., fought his way through the wind and rain in 75, a new record for the Prestwick course. *The Annual* described his performance as 'brilliant in the extreme'.

Before the tournament had begun, Taylor had taken on many of Scotland's crack players and beaten them all. He walked off the course after that round of 75 so confident that he made the classic mistake of a rookie playing in his first Open. 'I foolishly thought the Championship was mine,' Taylor wrote. He fell away in subsequent rounds, never breaking 80 again, and wound up in tenth place.

Far behind Taylor was another young English professional making his Open debut, Tom Vardon's brother, Harry, then the professional at Bury, north of Manchester. Harry Vardon would finish far back, 22 strokes off the lead, but he too had begun the Championship with a spurt of brilliance that caught the watchful eye of Hilton.

'He holed the first five holes in a very low total – something like 18 – and then went to pieces,' Hilton wrote, 'But it was at this meeting that one or two of us realised the possibilities of his game, and I always thought from that time that he had the makings of a very great player.'

Amateurs may have been experiencing their greatest innings in those early years of the 1890s, but the most astute observer among them already was getting an uneasy sense that it would not be long before gentlemen golfers were in for 'a rude awakening'.

Seven

HOME-GROWN PROFESSIONALS

—————•◦●◦•—————

arold Hilton may have been captivated by the brilliant spurts of golf he'd seen in 1893 from John Henry Taylor and Harry Vardon, but he was on to something far larger than that. Over the past decade, a fundamental change had been developing south of the Scottish border.

With new courses popping up in England every year – 87 were added between 1885 and 1890 alone – more and more local men took to caddying or making clubs for a living, just as Scots who became professionals had done in times past. New clubs no longer had to look north for a suitable golf professional. One of England's own could be hired instead.

Among the first of these new professionals was Tom Vardon, who, oddly, was not actually from England. He was born in the Channel Islands off the coast of France. The Islands are part of the age-old Duchy of Normandy, owned by a duke whose other title is King of Britain. While Jersey and the archipelago's other large island, Guernsey, are independently ruled countries, they are Crown Dependencies of the United Kingdom. In those days, that meant golfers from the islands were considered 'English' and competed under the St George's Cross just as players born on the mainland did.

When he reached the age of 16 in 1888, having learned golf as a caddie at Royal Jersey Golf Club, Tom Vardon was sent to the recently opened links at Lytham and St Annes to learn club-making from the course's professional, George Lowe. Naturally, as all club makers did, Tom eventually tried his hand in competition. When he won £12 in a tournament at Musselburgh, his older brother Harry took notice back in Jersey. Harry had planned to follow in his father's footsteps by becoming a gardener, but if his brother could win that kind of money there was no reason he couldn't, too. A life in professional golf suddenly seemed to be an option.

In 1890, Lowe was hired to lay out a nine-hole course at the private North Yorkshire estate of Frederick Samuel Robinson, better known as Lord Ripon. Tom saw an opportunity for his older brother and wrote to him in Jersey. Harry took the plunge and set out for a new life as the first professional of the Studley Royal Golf Club. Within a year, he'd moved on to Bury in Lancashire and was on his way to making an indelible mark in the game.

The year after Harry Vardon came north, John Henry Taylor moved to Burnham-on-Sea along the windswept Bristol Channel. Along with Hilton's mentor, Willie More, these men would form the first wave of English golf professionals. Many others would follow, gradually changing the balance of power in the game – men like Alfred Toogood, George Pulford and a Channel Islands contingent that included Ted Ray, Phil Gaudin, Tommy Renouf, Aubrey Boomer and his brother Percy, who would write a classic book of instruction called *On Learning Golf*.

The first among them to step to the fore was Taylor, the man who had so impressed Hilton with his sparkling 75 in the 1893 Open. He was born in Northam, a village in North Devon, on 19 March 1871 to Joshua Taylor and Susannah Heard, the second child in a family of five. Despite a back problem that left her hunched over all her life, Taylor's mother took in washing and worked as a midwife. His father was a day labourer, taking any job a tall, muscular man like him could handle, whether it was quarrying stone or digging wells.

Young Taylor was convinced that his father worked himself to death at the age of 46. He developed heart trouble after taking on the back-breaking job of blowing up and hauling away an iron pier built off the coast of Westward Ho! His recurrent bouts of illness left the family in dire financial straits. That may explain why his son was so committed to taking care of his own health and, unlike the vast majority of his fellow golfers, never drank or smoked.

As a boy, Taylor attended the local primary school, usually arriving hungry as working-class children so often did in that age. He proved to be a precocious student. Before he had turned 11, a year earlier than most, Taylor had worked his way through the Sixth Standard and was free to leave school and take a job to help his family. He never lost his love of learning, however. Taylor was a voracious reader all his life. Charles Dickens was a favourite, but he was most fond of James Boswell's *The Life of Samuel Johnson*. When the time came, Taylor would require no help in writing his own memoir.

In addition to intelligence, Taylor had all the qualities of a natural-born leader. He was a determined, focused man who was never shy about speaking his mind and comfortable in front of a crowd. By the time that transformative era of golf was in full swing, every professional in the game looked up to him as their leader and spokesman. 'No greater or more characteristic figure has ever appeared in the ranks of professional golf than John Henry Taylor,' wrote Bernard Darwin. 'Whatever work of life he had chosen, it is safe to say that he would have made his mark in it, for he possesses in remarkable degree enthusiasm, imagination and resolution.'

Even during his schooldays, golf was top of mind for Taylor. He spent every idle hour working as caddie, studying North Devon professional Johnny Allan and others to sharpen his game. When he left school, he took to carrying clubs full time, often for local star Horace Hutchinson. Soon afterwards he landed a side job shining shoes for the Hutchinson family. Caddies weren't allowed to work at North Devon beyond age 15 in those days. That meant Taylor eventually had to find another job. He worked as a gardener's boy and later as a hod carrier for a stonemason. Hauling bricks and mortar all day at 15 shillings a week turned that small, thin boy into a muscular, sturdy man who grew the requisite moustache and became a bit stockier as he aged.

Taylor's first ambition in life had been to join the army, but he was turned away six times, partly because at 5 feet 8 inches he was an inch short of the standard, but mostly because he had bad eyesight and flat feet. His disappointment was overcome in 1888 when he got his first break in the game that had developed into his consuming passion. A member of the ground staff at North Devon passed away, and Taylor was offered the job. Now he could spend every day on the links, learning the basics of greenkeeping, and every free moment with a golf club in his hands.

From the outset, Taylor developed a style all his own, a clipped three-quarter swing that ended with an audible grunt. It may have been the shortest swing in golf, but he used it on every shot, from drive to approach, without letting his feet budge. It wasn't a pretty by any means, but the result was uncanny accuracy and surprising length. Asked to describe his method, Taylor was fond of replying: 'Flat-footed golf, sir. Flat-footed golf.'

Darwin, who loved watching the pugnacious son of North Devon grind his way around the links, described his action this way. 'He was as firm as a rock, as if his feet were positively entrenched, and his swing was a marvel of compactness, with his elbows close to his body throughout. It needed a strong man to play in this style, and he was a very strong man.'

Not surprisingly, given his methods, Taylor was the master of the mashie pitch to the green, which he played with enough backspin to stop it close to the flag. He was not an especially noteworthy putter, but was fond of countering Willie Park's pet saying with his own: 'The man who can approach does not need to putt.' Still, as Darwin wrote, 'he could be relied upon to lay the ball dead, and he did not miss it when it was dead.'

When he edited his *Book of Golf and Golfers* in 1899, Hutchinson had Taylor write the chapter on 'Approaching', but his swing was not among those analysed in a lengthy 'Portrait Gallery' featuring the game's leading amateurs and professionals.

'There are points in certain men's styles which are commendable, even though they are arrived at by sacrifice of orthodoxy,' Hutchinson explained. 'J.H. Taylor, for example, plays all his strokes after a fashion that is only orthodox for approach shots. We believe this to be the secret of his wonderful straightness when in form; but that is not to say that all the world would do well, or would achieve his straightness or any of his success, by sacrificing the orthodox way of driving and imitating his manner.'

Taylor's first year on the job at Royal North Devon saw the formation of the Northam Working Men's Golf Club, one of the first artisans' clubs in England. The following season he showed his potential by winning the club medal at scratch. Inevitably, the Working Men's Club was challenged to pick a team to play against one from Royal North Devon. Taylor led his team into battle by taking on the club's most formidable player, Hutchinson.

'I am bound to confess that I viewed the match with some misgiving, as Horace was considered to be unbeatable,' Taylor recalled, 'but my work on the links had enabled me to put a polish on my game and I was not afraid. It may be that Mr Hutchinson treated me with some tolerance, but the truth must be told that once I had a grip on him I stuck in with a greater intensity and finished him off winning by three and two, successfully pitching a stymie with my one and only iron on the 16th green.'

Three years later came the offer that changed Taylor's life and the course of golf history. The new links in Somerset, Burnham-on-Sea, needed a professional, and Taylor was offered the post. He wasn't sure if moving was right for him. After all, a professional's job was a gruelling one in which making ends meet was easy only for the exalted few who won championships.

Golf clubs typically paid their professional between £35 and £50 a year to tend the green and serve the needs of members. He could supplement his income by giving lessons and operating a shop that sold and repaired equipment. The shop and lessons added at least another £70 to his pay. When it was all added up, a professional earned a salary somewhere between that of a police officer, at £72 a year, and a teacher at £133.

In the end, Taylor's mother made his mind up for him.

'With the usual optimism which had enabled her to face and overcome greater difficulties and with an abundant faith in her children, she had no doubt about the wisdom of my acceptance,' he wrote. 'So with £1 in my pocket borrowed from someone, or somewhere, by my mother, a big wooden box securely corded containing my scanty wardrobe, I left on January 1st, 1891, the home that had shielded and nurtured me for nineteen years, to face a new world that had yet to be explored.'

Burnham and beyond

Taylor thrived at Burnham, and before long his thoughts naturally turned to trying his hand against fellow professionals. His hopes no doubt were buoyed by having taken down Hutchinson again. Once Taylor had settled in at Burnham, Hutchinson paid a visit and offered a rematch of their encounter at Westward Ho! Taylor won, his second victory over the two-time Amateur Champion. As luck would have it, the ideal man for Taylor to test himself against Andra Kirkaldy, the professional at St Andrews, happened to be on temporary assignment at Winchester, a short train ride away.

The president of Burnham arranged a home-and-home match for £12 between Kirkaldy and Taylor. The first 36 holes were played at Winchester, which Kirkaldy had come to know like the back of his hand. Taylor considered himself lucky to leave the course down only one hole in the match. Back home at Burnham, where the wind can blow as mightily as it does at Westward Ho!, Kirkaldy found the going tougher.

The young upstart defeated him easily, 4 and 3, a rosy beginning to any budding professional's career. Not long afterwards, Winchester offered Taylor the job Kirkaldy was filling, and he moved there to be closer to the action in London.

'Walking off the last green together, Andra thrust his arm through mine and in a manner that showed no trace of rancour or disappointment said: "Well done, laddie, by God, you're a guid gowfer,"' Taylor recalled. 'It was a gesture which proved to me his bigness of heart towards a beginner, a young Englishman, who was desperately anxious, and I shall never forget its impression.' Kirkaldy and Taylor remained close friends all their lives.

Naturally, Kirkaldy got a raft of grief from his fellow caddies when he returned to St Andrews. How, they asked, could he allow a wee English-man 'to beat ye, Andra?' The old soldier's reply was, as usual, brutally frank. 'I'm telling ye,' he snapped, 'yon Taylor is a graun gowfer and would tak' the breeks off all of ye. You'll see when he comes ta' St Andrews.' Those would turn out to be prophetic words.

Two years after that victory over Kirkaldy, as he prepared to compete in his first Open at Prestwick, Taylor tested himself further by offering to take on any of the crack players on hand for the Championship. He played a match every day for a week, emerging unbeaten. The opponent who impressed Taylor most was Royal Liverpool's John Ball, and that impression was only reinforced when the 1894 golf season got under way with the tenth Amateur Championship, played that year at Hoylake.

Ball breezed into the final, only once having to play more than 14 holes to dispatch an opponent. He would play for the title against that old Scottish warrior, Mure Fergusson, the very man who had knocked Ball out the previous year after an especially dismal putting performance. Despite torrential rain that delayed the start of the match, nearly 4,000 fans came out to watch another classic face-off between an Englishman and a Scot.

The enormity of the crowd, and the difficulty in keeping it under control, clearly made Fergusson uncomfortable, as he would explain later in a letter to *Golf* magazine. Every shot had to be played to fairways even narrower than normal because they were hemmed in by spectators. Every green was surrounded by so many bodies that it was hard to judge the distance of an approach. Much to the delight of Hoylake fans, Ball reeled off the first four holes and appeared to be on his way to a dominant victory.

Slowly but surely, however, Fergusson put aside his anxieties and dragged Ball back. The match was all square again by the time they approached the 17th, and Scotsmen in the crowd were convinced their man had matters in hand. Harold Hilton heard one prominent Scottish golfer shout, 'Johnnie Ball's beaten. He's funking.' In all likelihood, Ball heard it too, and it was just the sort of comment to get his dander up.

'There,' Hilton writes, 'the man who was presumed to be funking brought off a shot that will live in the memory of all who saw it. It was one of those strokes which will be handed down to history.' Fergusson had played his second cautiously, well short of the green. Ball hesitated a moment, perhaps considering whether it was worth it to go for broke, then took out his brassie. 'He hit his ball as true as steel, and the ball in its flight hardly ever left the pin, and finished up just beyond the hole,' Hilton recalled. 'It was a really *big* shot played at a trying moment, and just when it was wanted.'

Ball took the hole, and with it the match, as the Hoylake crowd erupted in thunderous applause. Still in his early thirties, young for a golfer in those days, Ball had now won four Amateur Championships and one Open in seven seasons. It was far and away the greatest stretch of golf ever put together by an amateur – one that even now, 125 years later, knows few rivals. It is no wonder that when Taylor sat down to write his memoir, he had only the highest praise for that remarkable run by Ball.

'Even in those far-off days, when he was but a youth, Johnnie Ball's skill was legendary,' Taylor wrote. 'Hoylake people thought him unbeatable, so I was more than anxious to see him perform . . . I formed the impression, which long experience has tended to confirm, that in John Ball the world has seen its most brilliant amateur golf player . . . and when maintaining this opinion, I do not exclude the wonderful American amateur Bobbie Jones.'

The grand stage

Taylor's own chance to shine on golf's grandest stage – the Open – was considerably enhanced by a decision taken the previous June by the men who ran the Championship. They agreed to the final proposal put forward during that historic meeting of professional golfers back in 1891. The committee added two English courses to the Championship rota – Royal Liverpool and St George's. In 1894, the testing links at Sandwich would host the first Open conducted on English soil.

The Golfing Annual heartily endorsed the decision. 'The game has advanced in England during recent years by leaps and bounds, and it was only in keeping with the fitness of things that an English green of the highest class should at last be favoured.'

Players tended to be intimidated by their first view of St George's. Standing in front of the clubhouse, looking out towards Pegwell Bay, a golfer does not see the course stretch out before him as he would at St Andrews or Hoylake. The holes are mostly hidden by massive, undulating dunes, their faces scarred with sandy wastes. The view can't help but conjure up thoughts of the fearsomely long shots that will be required to carry those dunes from the tee. Taylor felt right at home. The place reminded him of Burnham and Westward Ho! The gales blowing in from the bay that rattled so many competitors seemed but a zephyr to a man who had learned his game over those windswept links.

The Open saw another permanent change in 1894. It moved from autumn to summertime, with the Championship conducted in the second week of June. It was now too big an event to be held in concert with a club's autumn meeting. The field that gathered at Sandwich was by far the largest in Open history. Ninety-two players signed up to compete, so many that the starting time was moved up to 9.45 a.m.

'The morning broke fine and bright at Sandwich yesterday,' *The Times* wrote, 'but a freshening wind from the north-west soon developed into a gale, and the auguries for low scoring were bad.' Among the first off was Ball. He set the early pace with his usual down-the-middle, on-the-green golf – 42 on both nines for an 84, perfectly respectable in fierce wind. Kirkaldy followed him with an 86.

Facing the worst of the weather, Taylor had to play his last two holes in slashing rain and howling wind. It didn't bother him a bit. He planted his feet, stuck out his chin, and slogged his way to an 84 and a tie for the lead. It wasn't until the last couple came in that a better score was posted. Sandy Herd, a Scottish professional then working at Huddersfield, turned in an 83 to seize the lead by a stroke.

The weather improved considerably in the afternoon, as the sun continued to shine and the wind died down. Kirkaldy and Dougie Rolland took advantage, racing around in twin 79s to tie the course record. Taylor had his own chance to match that mark, but he missed a short putt on 18 and settled for 80. Still, it was good enough to give him a one-stroke lead when the day ended. Ball, Herd and others fell out of the running with rounds in the mid-80s, not good enough in tamer weather.

Hilton and Hutchinson both dropped out after the round, having played so abysmally that they had not the slightest chance. A couple of weeks before the Open, Hilton had suffered a debilitating wrist injury that would haunt him for more than a year. Hutchinson may simply have been suffering one of his recurring bouts of poor health.

Taylor, meanwhile, was getting his first experience of having the overnight lead. 'I slept very badly,' he recalled. 'The mere possibility that I might win was a nightmare. The third round of a Championship is considered to be the most critical of the four, since one has to start afresh with the depressing knowledge that however good the previous day's score may have been, the whole nerve-wracking business has to be faced over again. And believe me, one requires a stout heart and heaps of confidence to do this successfully.'

If Taylor was quaking in his boots, it was not apparent as he began his third round in bright sun and light wind. He started with three consecutive fours and remained on an even keel all the way around that testing links, posting nines of 40 and 41 to increase his lead to three strokes. Kirkaldy and Rolland hung tough on the outward nine, but neither could do enough coming home. They wound up three and four strokes back, respectively.

When the final round began after lunch, Kirkaldy started so beautifully that he looked for all the world like the winner. He raced through the first six holes in 22 and reached the turn in 36, phenomenal scoring at Sandwich. Among those following the old soldier from St Andrews was an excited Hilton, who had backed Kirkaldy to win at odds of 10/1. Sadly, his hopes were dashed as Kirkaldy lost his swing and hacked his way home. 'Those last nine holes cost him no less than 48 strokes, and from what I saw of his play he deserved most of them,' Hilton wrote.

Playing steadily in the morning had clearly calmed Taylor's nerves. He played his opening nine nearly as spectacularly as Kirkaldy, finishing in 37. He hit the ball so straight 'that the guide flags were his only hazards, and his pitching was perfect', Hutchinson wrote. 'He was but twenty-three, and I feared all the while lest he should not be able to keep it up.' As it turned out, Hutchinson was right to be worried.

Taylor nearly tossed away his chance to win that Championship in the middle of the homeward nine. His third shot to the 13th – a mashie pitch of which he was usually the master – was a tad strong and ran off the green. It wound up in an area roped off to keep spectators away, sitting directly behind a wooden post. Taylor could have had the post removed, but instead tried to pitch over it. His shot landed on top of the post and bounced backwards, nearly hitting him. The result was an ugly 7 and a rising anxiety as Taylor approached one of the toughest holes on the course.

The second shot on the long 14th at Sandwich requires a carry over a stream known as the Suez Canal. Taylor briefly considered laying up short of the water, but in the end took out his brassie and gave it all he had. The ball landed on the far bank of the creek, and for a frightening moment he couldn't tell whether it had fallen in or not. Hilton, who had come out to see Taylor finish, gave him a signal that the shot had cleared the hazard by the smallest of margins.

'My sigh of relief when I received his assurance that it was over must have been heard by all the spectators,' Taylor recalled. 'I finished steadily and it was all over. I had achieved my life's ambition. I had won the Open Championship at the age of twenty-three, the first English professional to do so, and the first time it had been played on an English links.'

Rolland finished four strokes back, with Kirkaldy a shot behind him. Second fiddle was as close to a highlight as Scottish golf could muster in 1894 – except, perhaps, for the sight of the Right Hon. A.J. Balfour teeing off that October as the new Captain of the Royal and Ancient Golf Club.

England's day

Taylor's victory at Sandwich marked the turning point for English golf – and not simply because he won. Two newcomers from the south also finished in the top ten. Alfred Toogood of Eltham Warren took fourth, while Harry Vardon made his best showing yet, coming in seventh.

'It meant a great deal, that Championship,' Hutchinson wrote. 'It meant a great deal not only to Taylor personally, but also to all English professional golf. You see, Taylor was really the first English professional. Hitherto, when we wanted professionals, we had always been importing them from the North. It did not occur to the English caddie that he might become a professional, that there were possibilities, and money, in it. But all these possibilities the success of Taylor revealed to the English . . . It is not easy to overrate what that success of Taylor's meant for the professional golf of England.'

What that victory meant to Taylor personally, beyond pride in his accomplishment, was this: he could now tap into the real money in golf – playing in the exploding number of exhibition matches staged to mark the opening of new golf courses sprouting up across England and Scotland. Between 1894 and the Great War, he competed in 529 exhibitions. They added roughly £250 to his annual salary.

A player who reached that level – and very few did – entered a stratosphere beyond that of his fellow professionals. At his peak, Taylor was earning a salary about the same as an average engineer, some £380 a year. That was more than even his optimistic mother would have dreamed of when she packed him off to Burnham-on-Sea with £1 in his pocket.

Ever the astute observer, Hilton saw something else in Taylor's performance at Sandwich. He came away convinced that professionals would once again leave their amateur brethren behind. That was not the prevailing view at the time. Given that Hilton and Ball had won two of the past four Opens – and Laidlay had a second-place finish – most golf fans still thought the best amateurs were every bit as good as professionals.

'They certainly had some justification in this belief,' Hilton conceded. 'In fact, considering the disparity in the number of players taking part in the event, the leading amateurs had quite held their own with the professionals. There was a rude awakening at Sandwich in 1894, as there were nearly twenty strokes between the winner and Lieutenant Tait, the first of the amateurs.'

Hilton's notion was reinforced by a unique event that followed the Championship at St George's – a match between teams of amateurs and professionals, a tournament he considered 'one of the most interesting in the history of the game'.

Eight players were named to each side. The Gentlemen's team was chosen by the committee that hosted the Open. The Players' team was picked by veteran professionals Old Tom Morris and his protégé, Charlie Hunter. The Gentlemen were represented by John Ball, Harold Hilton, Horace Hutchinson, Freddie Tait, Mure Fergusson, Arnold Blyth, Charles Hutchings and Alex Stuart. The Players included Willie Park, John Henry Taylor, Sandy Herd, Andra Kirkaldy, Dougie Rolland, Willie Auchterlonie, Willie Fernie and Archie Simpson.

The tournament was a match-play affair spread over two picture-perfect days, using the same knockout format employed in the Amateur. 'The match created a lot of interest,' Taylor recalled, 'as it was thought, and openly stated, that the Gentlemen would require a lot of beating.'

That isn't how the match turned out. Only two amateurs survived the first round – Ball and Tait. Ball beat Park by a hole, while Tait cruised past Simpson 3 and 2. Two other gentlemen came close. Herd needed an extra hole to shake off Blyth, while Fergusson stuck doggedly to Auchterlonie, finally succumbing on 17. The other matches were one-sided, with the gentlemen losing by three holes or more. Hilton and

Hutchings suffered the worst beatings. Kirkaldy steamrolled Hutchings 7 and 6, while Hilton lost to Taylor 4 and 3. Hilton could, at least, take comfort in having won his second consecutive St George's Vase that year, even as he nursed his ailing wrist.

The only amateur to move beyond the second round was the soldier, Tait. He led nearly every step of the way in his second-round match against Fernie, winning easily, 3 and 1. The other remaining amateur, Ball, putted abysmally and was put out by Taylor after 15 holes. In the third round, facing fellow bomber Rolland, Tait came agonisingly close to carrying the banner of the Gentlemen's team into the final.

The two of them put on a driving display *par excellence*, with Rolland at last coming up against a man who could bash it as far as he did. Tait took a 2-up lead to start, only to see Rolland claw his way back. The match was all square when Tait hit a lovely shot to 17 that left him a makeable putt, while Rolland's approach was nowhere near the hole.

Rolland, however, laid Tait a dead stymie and escaped with a half. On the final hole, with Rolland on the green and Tait bunkered, it appeared the game was up. Tait, as he so often would, pulled off a magical up and down that sent the match into extra holes. Both golfers dropped marvellous putts for fours on the first extra hole, but when Tait's tee shot on the next found a brutal lie, Rolland lived to fight another day. Later that afternoon, he won the tournament by outlasting fellow professional Taylor 2 and 1.

The Annual wasn't nearly as discouraged by the outcome as Hilton was, saying, 'The play throughout was of a very high order. The draw furnished some grand matches, and on the whole the amateurs gave an excellent account of themselves.' The editor also strongly endorsed having the tournament played again the following season, when the Amateur and Open Championships were to be held at St Andrews.

'We are only echoing the sentiments of many enthusiasts north and south of the Tweed alike in expressing the hope that the Royal and Ancient golf club will repeat the experiment at St Andrews next June,' *The Annual* wrote. The R&A never took up the idea.

The Gentlemen may have been outclassed in that match at Sandwich – which turned out to be the last of its kind – but Hilton was premature in his gloomy assessment. Amateurs had by no means written the final chapter of that glorious decade, as Hilton himself would soon discover.

Eight

GOLF BOOM

·•●•·

Every club maker in Scotland took note whenever another Englishman won the Open, but not because they were smarting from defeat at their national game. They took note because orders came pouring in from southerners anxious to take up the Scottish game.

That trend emerged in the wake of John Ball's breakthrough at Prestwick. 'Within a few weeks of Mr Ball's success, one ex-champion, who is also a club maker, had to double his staff of workmen to compete with the orders he got from every part of England,' Dr Thomas Proudfoot explained in that season's *Golfing Annual*.

Taylor's victory as the first English professional to win – and on home soil to boot – only redoubled the interest of his countrymen. Golf had been growing steadily before Ball and Harold Hilton launched the south's uprising against the Scots, but that was child's play compared to the explosive expansion that would unfold over the next two decades.

When Ball stepped up to the first tee at Prestwick in September 1890, there were 246 golf courses in Great Britain and Ireland, almost exactly half of which were in England. By the time war was declared in the summer of 1914, there were 1,872, some 1,200 of them in England alone.

There was so much work to do that Scottish professional Willie Park – likely the ex-champion Proudfoot mentioned – couldn't find time to play golf. 'All my energies were demanded by my business,' he wrote. 'Not only was I launched on extensive club and ball trade, but I was simply overwhelmed with commissions to lay out or reconstruct golf links all over the country. Weeks and sometimes months elapsed and I never had a game.'

Golf was hardly alone in experiencing a growth spurt. Every sport was flourishing as the Industrial Revolution formed a new middle class; wages improved and social reforms created more leisure time, even for the lowliest. The vast expansion of the railway system, from a mere 1,500 miles of track in 1837 to 15 million by 1870, also made travelling to compete in or attend a sporting event financially feasible for most.

This period of massive growth in the game is often referred to as The English Golf Boom, but it might just as well be thought of as the result of the Scottish diaspora. Wherever Scots had gone as Britain assembled its vast empire – whether it was in war, in business or on holiday – they had planted the seed of their national pastime. Long before Ball's breakthrough, the game was sprouting up around the globe. It put down roots in Canada in 1823; in Calcutta in 1829; in South Africa in 1832; in Pau, France in 1856; in Ireland in 1881; in Australia in 1884, and in the United States in 1888.

Pau, a fashionable resort in the shadow of the Pyrenees mountains, turned out to be an especially effective incubator for the Scottish game. It was a favourite haunt of Britons and Americans, many of whom learned golf there and took the game home with them. The first serious history of American golf, for instance, credits a woman from Pau with introducing the game to friends in Boston when she visited there in 1892. Two decades later, it would be Boston native Francis Ouimet who ignited the flame of golf in the United States.

Everywhere golf went, it created jobs for Scotsmen – often better paying jobs than they could find at home, especially when golf began to grow in America. Scotsmen in great numbers left to seek their fortune and preach the gospel of their favourite game, some moving to new clubs in Britain and others overseas. Robert Harris, a prominent amateur who grew up in Carnoustie during the 1880s, watched the exodus from his home town to the United States. Among those he saw leave in what he described as 'a great emigration' were US Open winners Willie and Alex Smith, Archie Simpson, Geordie Low and Stewart Maiden, whose swing would be imitated by Bobby Jones.

Whether it was in Britain or abroad, men were by no means alone in falling in love with golf, especially not in England. Women there took to the game in droves. The first course built specifically for women was the ladies putting green Old Tom Morris created at St Andrews in 1867, known as the Himalayas and still home to an enormously popular club. Women had played long before then. In 1811 Musselburgh held a tournament for fishwives, and there are records from 1738 of women playing over Bruntsfield Links in Edinburgh.

It was in England, however, that women took up the game in earnest. When Ball made his breakthrough in 1890, the nation already had 30 women's golf clubs, nearly all affiliated with one for men. By 1914 the number of ladies clubs had risen to 479. The influence of women in the development of the game would far exceed those numbers, however.

From the outset, English golfers, men and women alike, argued that a game expanding as rapidly as golf needed a central governing authority. By 1893 leading English women, many of them from Royal Wimbledon, were calling for a Ladies Golf Union to oversee the game and conduct a national amateur championship. They turned for help to William Laidlaw Purves, among the most prominent and controversial men in the game.

Born in Edinburgh in 1842, Purves was orphaned as a boy. His father, William Brown Purves, was a doctor. He and his wife, the former Margaret Laidlaw, died of a disease the doctor caught from his patients. Young William was raised by two maiden aunts, whom he honoured by adding their family name to his. After graduating from Edinburgh High School, he worked his way through Edinburgh Medical School. By 1893 he was practising in London and devoting much of his considerable energy to golf.

Purves was more than happy to help women form a union. From his positions of prominence at Royal Wimbledon and St George's, he had long been agitating for a central authority in golf. His issue was the same one Walter Simpson had complained about in that first *Golfing Annual* – the lack of a uniform code of rules and a governing body to adjudicate them. Purves hadn't made much headway because his caustic, aggressive approach invariably alienated those whose help he needed.

He leapt at the chance to demonstrate how effective his ideas could be when put into practice. On 19 April 1893, 32 delegates from the 15 largest clubs for women attended a meeting presided over by Purves himself. They agreed to form the Ladies Golf Union and chose as its Honorary Secretary Issette Pearson, a woman so imposing that everyone, men included, tended to be intimidated by her. Purves and other golf luminaries served as vice presidents, among them writer and historian Harry Everard.

In the weeks before that final vote, one of the women involved, Blanche Martin, had written to Horace Hutchinson for advice on whether or not to form a union. Hutchinson responded with a misogynist diatribe. It began:

DON'T. My reasons? Well?
1) Women never have and never can unite to push any scheme to success. They are bound to fall out and quarrel on the smallest or no provocation; they are built that way!
2) They will never go through one Ladies Championship with credit. Tears will bedew, if wigs do not bestrew, the green.

Hutchinson could not have been more spectacularly wrong. With relentless determination, Pearson led the Union to accomplish the goals it laid out at that first meeting – to promote women's golf and host a championship; to establish a uniform set of rules; and to create a handicapping system that could accurately account for differences in difficulty from one course to the next. That had been another of Purves's pet projects. The Union's handicapping system would be among its most significant accomplishments. In time men would reluctantly follow suit, and the Union's creation became the foundation of handicapping systems used today.

Women golfers also demonstrated that they were fully capable of competing as rigorously and honourably as men. At its inaugural meeting, the Union had agreed to purchase a cup valued at £50 to be competed for that June in the first Ladies Championship. Like its counterpart in the men's game, the event would be contested at match play. It was held over the links at Lytham and St Annes, which, conveniently, had already planned to host a national competition for women. When St Annes joined the Ladies Golf Union it gladly allowed the new organisation to take over its event.

The winner that year, and for the next two years, was Lady Margaret Scott, the daughter of John Scott, third Earl of Eldon. She played a marvellous game that ought to have made Hutchinson hide his head in shame. In that first Championship she averaged 42 for every nine holes, a score nearly as low as a top man might make, though Scott competed over a shorter course.

Her sterling golf set a tone for a generation that would see such wonderful women golfers as May Hezlett, Rhona Adair, Dorothy Campbell and Charlotte Cecilia 'Cecil' Leitch. Years later, Leitch would play a ballyhooed match against Hilton, golf's version of the famed 1970s battle of the sexes between American tennis stars Billie Jean King and Bobby Riggs.

Within two years ladies amateur championships had been started in Ireland and the United States. It would be years, however, before women playing in those countries caught up with the standard set by their English counterparts. Lucy Barnes Brown, for example, won the first US Women's Amateur Championship in 1895 with a score of 132 for 18 holes. By the end of the decade *Golf Illustrated* was devoting multiple pages in every edition to ladies' golf. Women had secured their future in a game once all but exclusive to men.

'The pioneers of the Ladies Championship had to put up with a good many jibes from self-sufficient males who were sure that women would prove quite incompetent to run a championship or anything else,' wrote historian Robert Browning. 'The event was to prove these critics entirely wrong.'

Cultural changes

Not surprisingly, as the game spread from Scotland, its character began to change, a pattern that would be repeated wherever the game took root, especially in America. The farther the game spread from its birthplace, the farther it would drift from its ancient traditions.

'England, in assimilating Scotland's game, has somewhat altered it in the process,' Hutchinson admitted. 'There used to be something so grand and dignified about it when men used to play in swallow-tails and high hats; and in Scotland a portion of the high and noble brood over the game still. But the Englishmen did not accept the game as an inheritance with all its traditions.'

To begin with, English golf courses were nearly all private, unlike their counterparts in the north, where public access to the links was considered a birthright. Englishmen addressed that situation by forming artisans' clubs like the Northam Working Men's Golf Club. Royal North Devon's deal with the artisans was this: they received playing privileges in return for helping to keep the green. It became a popular arrangement and remains so today, with an Artisan Golfers' Association overseeing clubs from Aldeburgh to Woolton. Clubs for artisans had existed in Scotland for decades, of course, but their members had no need to trade labour for access to the links.

The English were also intent on keeping their score, even in match play, a habit Scots could not abide. Hutchinson defended his brethren. 'This last is regarded as his capital offence by the antiquaries,' he wrote.

'They say that match play by holes is the real game of golf – that score play is but a device for bringing together a number of competitors. Of course this is perfectly true, but why a man should not put down his strokes if he pleases, to give him added interest to the interest of the match, is hard to see.' Indeed it would be English professionals who turned the tide in favour of stroke play, as to a man they considered it a truer test of greatness than a match.

Another trait that offended Scottish sensibilities was the English obsession with handicap competitions that offered glittering cups as prizes. Scots thought serious competitions should be conducted at scratch. They dismissed these events contemptuously as 'pot-hunting'. Again, Hutchinson admitted the sin but defended the English as misunderstood.

'The Englishman has gone in for handicap competitions to an extent which is an abhorrence to the old school,' he wrote, adding that, 'People do not go to the competition meetings nearly as much for the sake of the prizes as because they know that they will meet a number of friends and get a number of pleasant matches. The objectionable spirit of "pot-hunting" enters into the business very little.'

The English innovation Scots disliked most, however, was the Bogey Competition. In 1890, Hugh Rotherham of Coventry Country Club came up with an idea that involved players competing not against one another or the field. Instead they would play a match against what he initially called the 'ground score' of the course – the score a first-rate club golfer was expected to make on a given hole. In time the 'ground score' came to be called the 'Bogey' score after a ditty popular in that age whose lyrics were, 'Hush! Hush! Hush! Here comes the Bogeyman.'

The first of these competitions against the unseen opponent 'Bogey' was conducted at Coventry in 1891. When this new form of competition spread to a military course, its leader decided that the foe needed a rank, and thereafter he came to be known as Colonel Bogey. Scots were appalled by the idea of playing against this imaginary rival. True golf was man against man, thrust and parry. No one would convince Scots that playing against an imaginary Colonel Bogey was anything like golf.

In the end, however, it would be another change insisted upon by the English that had the most lasting influence on golf as the game came of age during the 19th century – in particular the way the issue was resolved. From the outset, leaders of English clubs were adamant that a game growing as exponentially as golf needed a governing body and universal rules.

Even before Walter Simpson wrote his essay in the first *Golfing Annual* lamenting the reality that golf's rules were outdated and that the game had no acknowledged authority, there had been agitation in the press on that very topic. In March 1866, *The Field* began printing letters on the subject, a heated exchange involving William Laidlaw Purves, Simpson and others that would go on for two years.

The only code of rules in golf at the time was an ancient one that had evolved little in a century and a half. The original rules – 13 in all – had been written in 1744 by the Honourable Company of Edinburgh Golfers when the city gave them a silver club to award at their annual competition over Leith Links. Those rules were adopted, with few alterations, by the Royal and Ancient and had been revised only modestly since.

Most new clubs in England adopted some form of the R&A's rules, as St Andrews was fast earning a reputation as the unrivalled home of golf. Trouble was those rules were written for seaside links and did not account for difficulties encountered on parkland and heathland courses like those being built in England. With no formal authority overseeing their application, worrisome inconsistencies developed in the rules, most notably over how to handle lost balls and unplayable lies.

Beyond that, Englishmen thought the rules weren't clearly written, and they questioned the fairness of the stymie. When an opponent's ball blocked a player's path to the hole, they thought it should be marked and lifted, rather than requiring the golfer to putt around or chip over it. Stymies sometimes decided the outcome of tournaments and matches. Many golfers, especially the English, considered that unjust. Even Scots agonised over the stymie, which the Royal and Ancient had abolished for a year between 1833 and 1834.

The lengthy exchanges of letters in *The Field* prompted calls for the establishment of an English Golf Union – of precisely the sort women would form in 1893 – to govern the game south of the border and write a better code of rules. Purves and others at Royal Wimbledon had drafted a proposed set of rules they offered as an alternative to – and, in their minds, an improvement upon – the St Andrews rules.

All this unrest caught the attention of leading golfers – in particular those who believed the St Andrews rules ought to form the basis of any code, and that if golf was to have a central authority it ought to be the leading club in the nation that invented the game. The R&A, however, had never shown the slightest interest in leading the golfing world, the sole exceptions being reluctantly taking charge of the Amateur Championship and a willingness to address rules queries submitted to the club.

In his lament in *The Annual*, Simpson noted as much. 'We regret to say,' he wrote, 'that the St Andrews club seems indifferent to the position of guardian of the traditions of the game with which other clubs have shown their willingness to entrust it . . . Let us hope that St Andrews will awaken to a sense of its responsibility.'

That would take time. In 1890, the delegates who ran the Amateur proposed having their group draft a new code of rules that could be submitted to the R&A for consideration. That September the R&A responded by appointing a committee to take up the matter. It included such leading lights as Henry Lamb, Benjamin Hall Blyth, Hutchinson and, of course, Laidlaw Purves.

The code they drafted addressed the questions put on the table during that two-year debate in *The Field* – lost balls, unplayable lies and the stymie. It was presented to a general meeting of the R&A in May 1891. All the proposed changes were rejected, and the committee was asked simply to come up with a revision that would seek only to make the rules better organised and to clear up ambiguities in the language. That revision was adopted, but it satisfied no one.

Golf magazine responded with an editorial calling for the formation of 'A Golfers' Association' to run the game. 'Alone among high-class sports, golf stands out as a conspicuously difficult and intricate game played by thousands upon thousands of our educated classes absolutely without any organisation, with no cohesion among the body of players, with no code or rules made by duly accredited representatives of golf as a whole,' the editor wrote.

Nothing came of that editorial. The issue lay dormant until 1895, perhaps because Ball, Hilton and Taylor were generating enough excitement to keep *Golf* busy with reports of their conquests. That December, however, the magazine weighed in with another call for an association. By then *Golf* would have witnessed the early success of the Ladies Union, and one can't help but wonder if that helped rekindle its interest.

That editorial did get a response. Ernest Lehman, of Royal St George's, suggested that responsibility for the rules be permanently handed over to the committee that ran the Amateur – with the important proviso that it be always chaired by a member of the Royal and Ancient. That committee, Lehman reasoned, included sufficient representation from Scotland and England to make everyone happy.

That idea caught favour, and was taken up, with one substantive change insisted upon by members of the R&A. It was that this rules committee would consist *only* of members of the R&A. That was less a problem than it might appear, as so many golfers belonged to multiple clubs. The 15 men initially appointed to the committee represented an array of clubs from north and south broad enough to satisfy all parties.

It may have been a messy, divisive business, but the resolution, adopted on 28 September 1897, was among the most important decisions in the history of golf. No matter how far the game spread, no matter how much it evolved as it grew, golfers could rest assured that its guiding spirit would always be the Royal and Ancient Golf Club.

The committee's first full revision of the rules, released in early 1900, disappointed many by doing little beyond clearing up wording and definitions. The stymie remained intact. It would continue to bedevil golfers until it was abolished in 1952. The important point, however, was that rule 35, the last one in the new code, established that disputes could be submitted to the Rules Committee of the Royal and Ancient and its decisions would be final. It is a testament to how deeply St Andrews was revered that the outcome was the one even most Englishmen had wanted all along.

Familiar question

The happy resolution of the rules debate was still two years off in the spring of 1895, when the Amateur and Open Championships returned to St Andrews. The question on everyone's lips was whether Scots could reclaim glory, as they had in 1891 and 1893.

The situation was identical. Once again, England had swept The Double the previous season. Once again, Scots would have a chance to answer over their native green, which at 6,400 yards presented as thorough an examination of golf as any links in the kingdom.

Scottish hopes would be riding on Freddie Tait, now assigned to that mythic fighting force, the Black Watch, the regiment of Royal Highlanders that had played a leading role in every British conflict from Crimea to Egypt. Tait had shown great promise in recent years, and as Hilton described it, 'There can be little doubt that in St Andrews in 1895 the Scottish portion of the spectators were quite Tait mad. The majority would not listen to the possibility of his defeat.'

For Scots, the only thing better than an Amateur victory by Tait to start the season would be to see him vanquish one of the Englishmen who had so often carried the golfing laurels south. The semi-final of that year's Championship gave loyalists a chance to watch that dream unfold, as Tait faced off against that familiar nemesis of Scottish golf, John Ball of Hoylake.

'There was a delightful international flavour about the meeting of these two,' wrote Hilton, who was still fighting that wrist injury and nowhere to be seen competitively in 1895. 'They represented the respective hopes of Scotland and England, and moreover there was more than a little wagering on the result. The Scotsmen not only pinned their hopes to Freddie on account of his golfing ability; they argued to themselves that in the first place he was playing over his home green, to which he had always evinced a strong partiality, whilst in the second his enemy had never done well over the classic green, nor shown any strong liking for its peculiarities.'

That afternoon, however, it was Tait who could not solve the puzzle that is St Andrews. He missed easy putts for halves on the first two greens and never won a hole. The crowd of ardent fans following him endured the indignity of watching Ball cruise to victory by 5 and 3, despite having played merely steady golf. The bitterness of that loss would make an ugly appearance the following afternoon in the final.

Tait may have gone down ingloriously, but all was not yet lost for the Scots. Leslie Balfour-Melville, that paragon of amateur sport, remained to defend the honour of St Andrews. He and Ball teed off before a massive crowd of Scots partisans – nearly all of them with a bob or two riding on the outcome – at 11 o'clock the next morning, as Old Tom Morris looked on with the R&A clubhouse behind him.

Balfour-Melville had been lucky to reach that final. Both his previous matches had gone to extra holes. Both times his opponent handed him the match by dumping his second shot into the Swilcan Burn. Balfour-Melville's luck seemed to be running out early in that match against Ball, who claimed the first three holes, just as he'd done against Tait.

Balfour-Melville, a veteran of national competition in cricket, rugby and other sports, showed no sign of panicking. Gradually the holes came back to him. The match was all square again as the two competitors started the home nine. Things took an ugly turn when Ball missed a short putt to lose the tenth. The crowd burst into cheers, earning a stern rebuke from the captain of the R&A. Ball ran into more trouble on 13. His drive wound up in a pot bunker. When he tried to hack it out, the ball bounced off the face of the bunker and hit his club. Ball had to give up the hole.

When he and Balfour-Melville approached the 17th, Ball found himself in a position he'd faced many times before. His back was to the wall and it was time to reel his man in. It is a safe bet that the jeering on ten was ringing loudly in Ball's ears. He could be terrifyingly fierce if the crowd or an opponent made him mad, as one hapless golfer discovered in the Irish Amateur. Ball had been given an incorrect starting time, and showed up on the first tee to find his foe demanding that he be disqualified. Apparently, the man was intent on catching the last boat to Scotland that night. Ball tore him to shreds, winning 13 and 11, bowed and said, 'Now, sir, you can catch your boat.'

Grimly bearing down on Balfour-Melville, Ball took 17 and 18 to send the match to extra holes, a development that moved *The Annual* to describe that final 'as the most exciting yet decided'. Both men played their second shots on the first extra hole short of the Swilcan Burn, the prudent choice with the title on the line. Balfour-Melville played his approach first and it landed safely on the green. For reasons perhaps even he could not explain, Ball decided to play his third shot with a pitching club he seldom used rather than that mashie that had served him so well. Hilton was, of course, watching.

'There was a smothered groan when it was seen that Johnnie . . . had gone straight under his ball,' he remembered. 'To spectators some distance off it was a doubtful question as to whether it would clear the water or not, but quickly came the fatal splash, and the Championship was as good as over.' For the third time in three matches, Balfour-Melville had been saved by the burn.

The victory celebration in St Andrews capped off a glorious spring in the Auld Grey Toon, marked by the opening of a second course to handle the growing number of golfers. Ever after they would be known as the New Course and the Old Course. Thrilled as they were by Balfour-Melville's victory, Scotsmen knew their year would not be complete unless they reclaimed another title – Champion Golfer of the Year. That battle was a month away and the obstacle to overcome a formidable one – John Henry Taylor.

There were some in St Andrews who didn't fancy Taylor's chances on the Old Course, where slick, undulating greens would make it far more difficult for him to be effective with his cut-mashie approaches. Taylor scoffed at that notion, but he never got to test it in firm conditions. The lovely weather that had prevailed for weeks in St Andrews had taken a turn for the worse by the time a field of 76 turned out to contest the Open on 12 June.

'It was rather a disappointment to find the sky veiled by threatening clouds yesterday morning,' *The Times* wrote. 'The promised rain was not long in descending, and reminded golfers of the last Open Championship at St Andrews.' It took much of the starch out of the course.

Taylor was not his best in the opening round of his title defence, limping in with an 86. He was six shots behind surprise early leader, Harry Vardon, the professional at Bury. Close behind Vardon, at 82, was Sandy Herd, the Scotsman who had played so well in the opening rounds at Sandwich. Old reliable Andra Kirkaldy was just a stroke back of him, his spirits buoyed by having avenged his defeat by Taylor at Burnham in a match earlier that week.

Taylor returned to form in the afternoon round, in part because the rain had softened the greens enough that he could knock his mashie pitches to the hole with more than his usual confidence. 'Steadier play than his on the outward journey could scarcely be desired,' *The Times* wrote.

Taylor came in with a marvellous 78, but even that wasn't good enough to give him the lead. Playing 'golf of the most brilliant description', Herd had gone around in 77, which not long ago had been the record at St Andrews. He was five strokes in front of Taylor and Kirkaldy and looked every bit a winner, as Vardon and the others faded.

Not surprisingly, Herd took the lion's share of the Scottish crowd with him the next morning when he set off in search of his first Championship in lovely weather. 'He soon showed that he was in his best form,' *The Times* reported. 'Playing perfect golf, he did not make a single mistake on the outward half reaching the end hole in 39.' Herd slipped only once on the back, fluffing a chip into a bunker and recording a six at the 11th but finished with an 82 that would take some beating.

When Kirkaldy could do no better than 83, leaving him trailing Herd by seven strokes, all eyes turned to the one challenger remaining on the course – last year's winner, Taylor. He, too, played flawlessly, his one blemish also being a pitch dumped into a bunker at the second. A marvellous 80 left Taylor three shots to make up on the final 18. *The Times* believed no one else had a prayer. 'The play in the concluding round simply resolved itself into a match between Herd and Taylor,' the newspaper wrote.

Championships are often decided by a last-minute change in the weather, and as far as Hilton was concerned the rain that poured down that afternoon undid Herd. It made the course too soft for him. Herd 'likes a keen putting green,' Hilton wrote. 'He trickles his putts, and in the final round he could not get up to the hole, being short in his approach shots time after time. Sandy has never been very lucky in championships.'

At day's end those missed putts added up to an 85, keeping hope alive for Taylor. Herd's four-round total was 326. That meant Taylor needed

82 to tie and 81 to win. 'It was scarcely to be expected, in view of the weather conditions, that the Winchester professional would be able to perform this task,' *The Times* wrote.

Maybe to the *Times* correspondent, but not to Taylor. He played his best when conditions were the worst, and he put on an impressive show. 'It was a splendid exhibition of golf, the good points of which were heartily applauded by the crowd, who notwithstanding wind and rain, followed the champion over the course.' Taylor went around in twin scores of 39, for a mind-boggling 78 that easily could have been lower. He claimed his second consecutive Open with four strokes to spare.

It was another down year for amateurs. An injured Hilton withdrew again after the second round, and none of the leading gentlemen players scored much below the mid-80s. Tait was again best among them, finishing tied for 15th a full 19 strokes behind a joyously happy Taylor.

'It gave me a big thrill to win it on my first visit to St Andrews,' he wrote, 'and even greater satisfaction in proving that my high-pitched mashie shot was as effective there as anywhere else despite what the critics anticipated and had proclaimed with such certainty. I left St Andrews the following morning with more pride than ever before.'

Dispirited Scots were left to wonder what had gone wrong in their peculiar pastime. True, they had won the Amateur, but it was hardly a convincing victory, and even at St Andrews there was no one to stop an Englishman from carrying home the Claret Jug.

Nine

'COCK OF THE NORTH'

E ven the most optimistic English golfer – a man as bullish as the letter-writer 'St George' was when he prematurely declared that 'the glory is departing from Scotland' – could not have foreseen how quickly golfers in the north would be backed into a corner.

Since the institution of the Amateur Championship in 1886, the English had very nearly claimed dominion over the Scottish game. Englishmen had won six of the ten Amateurs played, and since John Ball's breakthrough at Prestwick in 1890 they had taken four of the next six Opens.

Losing hegemony over the Open was a deep wound for Scots after 30 seasons of unbroken glory. They had watched Young Tom Morris claim The Challenge Belt, and seen both Jamie Anderson and Bob Ferguson match the young superstar's feat with three consecutive Open victories. Now the Claret Jug was regularly being carried off by Englishmen – twice by a professional and twice by amateurs.

No wonder Scottish golfers lived in hope that a new 'Cock of the North' would arise to lead the forces of a beleaguered nation.

There was no mystery about the cause of this surging English tide. It was a manifestation of how quickly the game had been growing south of the border over the past five years. The new golf courses sprouting up every year brought with them waves of English professionals and amateurs dead set on dethroning the Scots.

Every one of these golfers, especially professionals; had more chances to sharpen his game in the crucible of competition. They had always been able to play in challenge matches and the growing number of tournaments, but by then exhibition matches had become so ubiquitous that they outnumbered traditional events by three to one.

New events were also being added to the Amateur and St George's Vase on the gentlemen's circuit, notably the Irish Open Amateur in 1892. Gentlemen also had more opportunities to enter medal competitions conducted at the meetings of all those new clubs. Ball's schedule in 1894 demonstrates how busy a first-class amateur's season had become. Between April and November, he competed in no fewer than 20 events, winning the Amateur, its Irish counterpart and a handful of club medals while setting five course records.

It was no surprise that gentlemen playing that much competitive golf had closed the age-old scoring gap against professionals. The galling truth for Scotland, however, was that none of its ancient clubs had seen a member cross the threshold and carry off the Claret Jug. That honour belonged solely to the prime mover of English golf, Hoylake, and its favourite sons Ball and Hilton. Newspapers never ceased to point that out, and it served as an unpleasant reminder to Scots that they were in danger of being overrun in the gentleman's game as they had already been in the Open.

Freddie's Year

Fortunately for Scots, their prayers that a new champion would step forward were about to be answered. Freddie Tait was, at last, ready to come into his kingdom.

Beyond being known ever after as 'Freddie's Year', the 1896 season would be remembered for two milestones outside golf. A month before the Amateur, the first modern Olympic Games were staged in Athens, and that autumn Queen Victoria would become Britain's longest-serving monarch to date, nearly 60 years after her coronation.

The Queen's memorable year got off to an embarrassing start with more misadventures in South Africa. In January news arrived of the Jameson Raid, a botched attempt to foment revolution against the Boers, who controlled the region's gold and diamond mines. Britain was disgraced, and tension with the Boers became worse than ever. Before that decade was out, it would reach boiling point.

There was no shortage of men in Britain, especially amongst amateur golfers, willing to join the Queen's army in pursuit of expanding its global empire, especially in amateur golf. Indeed the player who would become the new hero of Scottish golf was, at that moment, serving with the fabled Black Watch at Edinburgh Castle, not far from his family home.

One of seven children in a close-knit family, Freddie Tait was born in the Scottish capital on 11 January 1870 to the former Margaret Archer Porter and Peter Guthrie Tait, the world-famous scientist and Professor of Natural Philosophy at Edinburgh University. The professor was remembered as a forbidding presence by one of his students, J.M. Barrie, who would earn his own fame as the author of *Peter Pan*.

'I have seen a man fall back in alarm under Tait's eyes, though there were a dozen benches between them,' Barrie recalled. 'Those eyes could be as merry as a boy's, though, as when he turned a tube of water on students who would insist on crowding too near an experiment.'

Renowned for his work in mathematical physics and thermodynamics, Peter Tait was also a fanatic for golf – and not simply as another field to which he applied his passion for science. Professor Tait was known to play multiple rounds a day at St Andrews when he could find time away from his scholarly duties. His son John also was a skilled player, making it to the semi-finals of the 1887 Amateur. Young Freddie, the real golfer in the family, preferred to call both of them by nicknames. His father was 'The Governor', his older brother simply Jack.

Much as Freddie Tait loved and excelled at golf, a man born to a family as well situated as his would never have given a moment's thought to making it his profession. From a young age Tait's sights were set on becoming a soldier. He attended prep school and went on to Edinburgh Academy and Sedbergh School, where he excelled in cricket, rugby and golf. The goal was to prepare himself to enter the Royal Military Academy at Sandhurst. At Sedbergh, as he would all of his life, Tait emanated a *joie de vivre* that made him one of the most beloved boys in school.

'Freddie's nature was always affectionate, and this was probably the keynote of his subsequent popularity,' wrote his biographer, John Low. 'He seemed to like most people with whom he came into contact – to see the good in them, to understand the weaker side as well – and as a result of this amiable view of life, his acquaintances, as well as his friends, were irresistibly drawn to him.'

Nowhere was that affectionate nature more evident than in the letters Tait wrote to his family from Sedbergh and everywhere else he travelled. In March 1884, he wrote to 'My dear Aunt Jane' to thank her for sending him a batch of fresh eggs. The letter's breezy tone demonstrates how cheerfully Tait approached life and how deeply devoted he was to his family.

'I hope you are well,' he writes. 'I shall have grand breakfasts and teas now with your eggs. Did you get the postcard? It is a very nice day; I will have a jolly walk this afternoon from 2 till 4.30.' As nearly every letter would be, it was signed, 'Yours affectionately, F.G. Tait.'

Never the best of students, Tait ran into an obstacle when it came time to attend Sandhurst. He failed the entrance exam. That meant he had to enrol at Edinburgh University and enlist in its company of Queen's Volunteers before being admitted to military academy in September 1889. The following year his career got under way in the 2nd Battalion of the Leinster Regiment. Four years later, in June 1894, Tait got his dream assignment to the infantry division of Royal Highlanders known as the Black Watch.

Not surprisingly, given his father's passion for the game, Tait had been playing golf since he was a boy. He learned the game at Musselburgh and St Andrews, although the home of golf would always be first in his heart. Horace Hutchinson remembered watching Tait play when he was a wee lad. 'Freddie Tait was the very keenest golfer, as a boy, that I ever saw. I had watched him at St Andrews, growing up . . . and acquiring the mastery of his clubs as he grew. He was a favourite with everybody.'

When he was a 14-year-old at Sedbergh, Tait was involved in an incident that demonstrated the backbone he would display in golf and life. He and two schoolmates were taking a walk along a fast-flowing river in Yorkshire Fells when one boy slipped on a rock and went tumbling into the water, staying under for several frightening moments. Tait's other pal began screaming for help, but they were more than a mile from school and no one could hear. Tait described what happened next in a letter to his brother.

'I stood still and waited till he came up,' he wrote, 'and before I could get to him he went down again, but the next time when he came up I climbed down the rock to the side of the water . . . and when he came up the second time I caught hold of his hand and began to lug him out. But he was such a weight that he nearly dragged me in, but I got [my friend] to take my other hand, and with his help we lugged him out, quite insensible.'

That afternoon captures one of Tait's central qualities. In a moment of crisis, he could be counted upon to come through. Nowhere was that more evident than on the golf course, as everyone who faced him knew full well. 'You never had him beaten at any hole,' Hutchinson wrote.

As a grown man, Tait cut an imposing figure, standing 6 feet tall and weighing 175 pounds, chiselled like the soldier and rugby player he was.

He was among St Andrews golfers, men like Tom Kidd and Edward Black-well, who had grown up watching Young Tommy Morris take a furious lash at the ball and liked to give it a mighty swipe themselves. Tait was a prodigious driver, as long as any player of his day.

'There was a time, when Mr Tait was just emerging from boyhood, at which his great ambition seemed to be to drive all the holes at St Andrews in one,' Hutchinson mused. Those mammoth swipes could go dangerously awry, among them one hit so far off line that it pierced a man's top hat. Tait had to cough up five shillings to buy the man a new one, and bemoaned his fate to Old Tom Morris. 'Ah, Master Freddie,' Old Tom replied, 'ye may be very thankful that it's only a hat and no' an oak coffin ye had to pay for.'

In his heyday, Tait became famous for playing within himself and keeping his fearsome power in reserve for moments when it was absolutely necessary. The distinctive characteristic of his swing, beyond its notably upright finish, was that 'the club does not go very far back, nor is the turning of the body very much emphasised', Hutchinson wrote. Despite that his swing was as forceful as any in the game.

In January 1893, on a frosty morning at St Andrews with the wind howling behind him, Tait hit a drive that carried 250 yards and rolled out to 341 – the longest ever recorded with a gutty ball. His father, of course, had spent years before that trying to understand the science of what happens when a club meets a ball. He had once theorised that a gutty could not be carried farther than 190 yards – an idea Tait's wallop would have blown out of the water had the scientist not already discovered that back-spin could make a ball fly farther than other factors would have predicted.

Never one to brag about his accomplishments – beyond the letter home, he never told a soul about his heroic rescue of that boy at Sedbergh – Tait came to regret the attention that drive generated. Less than a month later, in a letter home from his army camp at Aldershot, he wrote: 'I wish I had never made that drive at St Andrews; everyone I meet here at once begins asking about it.' He'd even had a letter from a man in Ascot who claimed to have hit one 480 yards. 'This is the kind of chaff I've been getting lately,' he complained.

Long as Tait was, it was not his driving that crushed the spirit of his opponents. It was his short game and his seemingly miraculous ability to recover when in dire straits. 'The worse place you put him in, the better pleased did he seem to be,' wrote John Low. 'It was for him a chance to bring off one of the shots he had "up his sleeve".'

Tait also had an uncanny knack for sinking long putts when they desperately needed to find the cup. He was not one to trickle putts in or try to lay them dead. He went boldly for the hole every time. 'How clearly I can see him now, thrusting out his right foot in a most characteristic gesture as the ball hits the back of the tin and drops at the end of a long putt,' Bernard Darwin recalled.

In these ways, Tait called to mind the last great hero of Scottish golf, Young Tommy. Tait was easily the most swashbuckling figure the game had seen since that much-lamented superstar – a handsome, gallant soldier, always a brimful of confidence, a light heart and a merry twinkle in his eyes. Few players thrived on being in the arena more than he did, and the crowds responded with unbridled affection.

'In his day, in his own Scotland, he was a national hero,' Darwin wrote. 'I do not think I have ever seen any other golfer so adored by the crowd – no, not Harry Vardon or Bobby Jones in their primes. It was a tremendous, and to his adversaries, an almost terrifying popularity.'

Tait broke course records wherever he went, including setting the mark for both St Andrews and Carnoustie at the extraordinarily low score of 72. But it was not simply his brilliant golf or his sparkling presence that endeared him to the crowd. 'There was one thing about him that appealed intensely to the Scots,' Darwin wrote, 'namely, that Freddie was above everything else a Scottish golfer. Discussion simply ceased for him when any other course was compared to St Andrews. He stood by the Old Course and in the old ways . . . Moreover, he had, as it seemed to us, that almost parochial sort of patriotism which wants above everything else to see the Englishman beaten.'

True Scotsman that he was, Tait's constant companion was a shaggy, black terrier of uncertain pedigree called Nails. The name was well earned. Once when Tait and his family were staying in St Andrews, Nails jumped a neighbour's fence and nearly mauled their dog to death. Tait's father had to banish Nails to the family home in Edinburgh.

At the Black Watch, where the cups and medals Tait won carrying the regimental banner were displayed on a table in the mess tent, that 35-pound warrior was as popular as his master. In a letter home to his mother, Tait proudly explained how his mates had taken to his terrier.

'Nails is in great form, and has been made an honorary member of our mess, which means that he is allowed to come in whenever he likes,' he wrote. 'I may mention that this is a favour granted to very few dogs. He has made great friends with everyone.' Tait was so closely associated with Nails that the portrait of him later commissioned by the Royal and Ancient shows that faithful terrier by his side on the links.

Triumphal procession

As spring arrived in 1896, Tait signalled to the golf world that he was in far sharper form than he had been the previous year when he had fallen to John Ball in the semi-final of the Amateur at St Andrews. Neither Tait nor his admirers could understand how he had gone down almost without a fight at the course he loved most.

Tait put those thoughts out of their minds, and his, as he prepared for the Amateur at Sandwich by going around Muirfield that March in 73. He followed that up with an even more remarkable performance at North Berwick, which had just been extended beyond 6,000 yards and toughened in the process. Tait went out in 36 and came home in 38, for a 74 his admirers would rank with his greatest scoring feats. The next day he added the capstone to his visit in a match against North Berwick's professional, Ben Sayers. Tait crushed Ben so badly that he exclaimed afterwards, 'Beaten by eight holes on my own green; it's no' possible but it's a fac'.'

Tait never liked the course at St George's, even though it played to his strengths. He considered it a course that required but one shot, the drive. Tait had no fear of the long carries called for at Sandwich. Before the Amateur was played, he demonstrated his superiority over the links by winning his first St George's Vase.

It was a good thing Tait was razor-sharp and confident, as few players have faced a tougher road to the Championship final than the draw presented to him that season. He would face a murderers' row of golf's leading amateurs – among them Charles Hutchings, John Laidlay, John Ball, Horace Hutchinson and Harold Hilton.

That Amateur would be remembered for two reasons beyond the marvellous golf that was played. It would be the first to end with a 36-hole final 'thereby reducing that chance of a snatch victory to a minimum', as *The Golfing Annual* put it. It would also be remembered for a violent storm that wreaked havoc during the second afternoon of competition.

Hilton was playing a match against future golf architect Harry Colt when an otherwise lovely morning took an ominous turn, the sky suddenly becoming as black as ink. 'It was the most remarkable change of weather I have ever experienced,' Hilton recalled. 'Without a moment's notice, the wind swept down the course carrying everything before it and almost instantly flattening the press and other tents.'

Hilton and Colt were teeing off downwind on the tenth hole as the gale descended. Colt was nearly knocked down while swinging. Hilton barely got his ball airborne. Both balls went flying in the wind. The last Hilton saw of his 'was a white object careering over the mounds like a feather'. The two of them had to huddle under Colt's umbrella for half an hour before heading out to find their feeble drives some 300 yards from the tee. They finished the round with hands so cold they could barely feel their clubs. Having fallen behind in the melee, Hilton finally saved his bacon on the 20th hole.

Tait, meanwhile, was calmly dispatching that murderers' row. He finished off his first opponent in 13 holes, and breezed past both Hutchings and Laidlay. The game everyone was dying to see, however, was the rematch of the previous year's semi-final between Tait and Ball. The Englishman had injured his hand that spring, and wasn't a sure thing to enter the Championship, but apparently by May, Ball had recovered enough to give it a try.

'Keen interest was taken in the encounter between Mr Ball and Mr Tait,' *The Scotsman* wrote, 'and the contest between them was the more interesting because it was a pitched battle between two of the best-known English and Scottish amateurs. The meeting gave Mr Tait an opportunity of wiping out the defeat which he had suffered at the hands of Mr Ball a year ago at St Andrews.'

Tait was not about to blow that chance. Displaying brilliant form off the tee and around the green, he strode confidently through the opening nine in 36 and established a commanding lead as they turned for home. Ball seemed not to be himself, perhaps because of the injury, perhaps because he was simply stale, as even the best golfers can be from time to time. His putting, especially, was atrocious. By the time the pair reached the long and dangerous 14th, Tait was dormie, five holes up with five left to play. When Ball could do no better than match Tait's five, the Scotsman earned sweet revenge by 5 and 4.

Tait's procession into the final was very nearly interrupted in the fifth round by another Englishman, Hutchinson. He was in fine fettle, but Tait wasn't nearly as sharp as he had been against Ball. When he completed the front nine in a ho-hum 41, Tait found himself 2 down. He righted the ship on the homeward half, as Hutchinson became a bit wild and found one nasty lie after another. Tait finally poked his nose in front when he won the 12th, and from there he drew on his deep reserves of power and put Hutchinson away with a series of bombs from the tee, finally winning a hard-fought match 3 and 2.

The final of that Championship would be another battle between thistle and rose, as Tait faced that other Hoylake hero, Hilton. Whilst at army camp, Tait had learned to play the bagpipes, proudly writing home about the tunes he had learned. He was feeling so bullish about his match with Hilton that the night before he could be heard about town piping a melody he hadn't mentioned in that letter home: 'The Cock of the North'.

Hilton had been drawn in the bottom half of the bracket, mostly filled with outsiders, and had the far easier path to the title match. Only Colt and the weather had given him any trouble. The others he dismissed with ease. Still, Hilton can't have entered the final with an overabundance of confidence. He had faced Tait twice before in the Amateur, and lost both times, although once by a single hole. Not only that, as *Golf* reported, the word at Sandwich was that 'Freddie Tait is playing a great game'.

Tait came out playing even more brilliantly than he had all week. He dropped a ten-foot putt to win the first hole and didn't look back. He finished the outward nine in an astonishing 35 and the round in 76, a new record for Sandwich. By then he had seized a six-hole lead, as the Englishman could do no better than 84. The result was a foregone conclusion. Playing what Tait charitably described as a 'plucky uphill game', Hilton struggled in vain to make the match interesting. He won the first hole after the lunch break, but it was no use. Tait rolled over him 8 and 7.

'If it proved a disappointment in the fact that the game did not produce a close struggle,' *Golf* wrote, 'on the other hand it gave spectators an opportunity to witness as fine an exhibition of the game of golf, on the winner's part, as anyone could wish to see.'

Hilton acknowledged as much. Tait, he wrote, 'was in a most merciless mood, and I never had a chance . . . The truth was simply that I was outplayed in every department of the game.' That afternoon Tait proved he was the alpha male in any contest with Hilton. 'That great little man could not play against him,' Darwin wrote, 'and Freddie took perhaps some unchristian pleasure in crushing him.'

Sacred number

Scotland sorely needed Tait's victory. Nothing could have boosted the nation's wounded pride more than watching him vanquish their English conquerors one by one. All, of course, except John Henry Taylor. He remained to be confronted in the Open at Muirfield, just ten days away.

It is a safe bet that every Scotsman knew what another victory would mean for Taylor. It would mean he had won three consecutive Opens, and three was a sacred number in Scottish golf history. It was the number of wins in succession required to claim the tournament's original trophy, The Challenge Belt. Only Young Tom Morris, Jamie Anderson and Bob Ferguson had accomplished that feat. Dominant as they were, neither Old Tom nor Willie Park Sr managed it. As events turned out, no player would ever match the record Tommy set by winning his fourth straight in 1872.

Scotsmen were counting on Tait, or one of the nation's other stalwarts, to block Taylor's path to that sacred number. The soldier and his faithful fans had every reason to be confident. Hadn't Tait gone around in 73 just three months before at Muirfield, which had been lengthened and toughened since the 1892 Open? A score like that would be tough to beat in any Championship.

At the end of the first day's play, Scotland had reason to be both alarmed and hopeful. There stood Taylor, again in first place, having posted marvellous scores of 77 and 78. Close behind, however, were three Scotsmen. Sandy Herd had come in that morning with a 72 that 'took everyone's breath away', *The Golfing Annual* wrote. He hadn't been able to keep it up in the afternoon. An 84 left Herd trailing by a stroke, with fellow Scot Willie Fernie one behind him. Tait had started poorly with an 83, but a 75 in the afternoon brought him within three shots of the leader and renewed hopes of another triumph.

Neither Hutchinson nor Ball had bothered to enter the Open, Ball perhaps deciding that his injured hand had had enough. Hilton never managed to get below 82 all week, and wasn't a factor. No one seemed to notice another Englishman playing well enough to be just six strokes behind, a relatively unknown Harry Vardon, who had recently moved from Bury to take the professional's job at Ganton in Scarborough.

Every heart in Scotland had to be pounding when results came in from the third round, played in sweltering weather that made scoring tougher even on a windless day. Herd finished in 79, despite throwing away a few strokes on the green. When Taylor could do no better than 81, the Scotsman had a slender one-stroke lead with 18 holes to play that afternoon. Tait seemed to have thrown away his chance with an 84 that left him seven to make up. Vardon turned in a 78, again playing completely unnoticed. He was only four strokes behind with a live chance to win.

Taylor was out early that afternoon, playing his reliably consistent brand of golf. His score of 80 set the number to beat at 316. Every player on the links knew precisely what he had to do to win. Herd, who was starting out as Taylor came in, needed simply to match the English star's 80. Fernie and Vardon needed a 76. Tait needed a miracle. He would have to post a 74, and only one round all week had been lower.

Poor Herd never could seem to deliver his best golf in the clutch. When he stumbled home in 85, it seemed inevitable that Taylor would match Scotland's legends. Inevitable, at least, until the Jerseyman who had sailed under the radar all week reached the turn in 38. Vardon was paired that afternoon with Hilton, who had anticipated his partner becoming a great player ever since watching his Open debut in 1893. Hilton was astonished that no one thought Vardon had a shot.

'Now to give an idea as to what extent his chance was esteemed by the general run of the spectators, it may be mentioned that we started that last round without a single individual watching,' Hilton wrote. 'Eventually one casual spectator strolled up and followed us for a few holes, and finally asked me who I was playing with. When I told him, he didn't seem very much enlightened or impressed and eventually left us.' When Vardon holed out on 18 in 77 to tie Taylor, exactly ten people were there to watch. 'It seems absurd,' wrote Hilton, 'but it is true.'

Tait was the last player to tee off that afternoon, and as *The Annual* reported, he 'made a gallant effort to snatch a victory for Scotland'. Tait matched Vardon's front nine in 38, and when he raced through the first six holes on the homeward half in 23 strokes, the miracle he required to win did not seem out of reach. Tait needed to play the final three holes in 12 strokes, difficult but not impossible. When his third shot reached the green at the long 16th, Scotland held its collective breath.

Tait's ball lay 24 feet from the hole. About halfway home, his putt hit a rough spot on the green and pulled up six feet short. Tait missed his next, recording a six that took the wind out of his sails. He finished with two fives for a 77. That left him tied with Fernie at 319, three strokes behind the two southerners who would play off for the title.

Taylor knew he would have his hands full in the play-off. A month before the Open he had visited Ganton to play a match against Vardon. Taylor was so confident of victory he didn't bother to arrive in time for a practice round. Vardon handed him his head 8 and 6. He romped again in the Open play-off, beating Taylor by four strokes. It may have been some consolation to Scots that Vardon had preserved the sanctity of three consecutive Open victories. But that missed the larger point made so painfully obvious by the conclusion to *The Annual*'s report on the Championship.

'The result was a great triumph for English golf,' *The Annual* wrote. 'With the brothers Vardon and Taylor, not to mention other young and promising players, England bids fair to be gallantly represented in the Championship for many years to come, and Scotchmen, who are nothing if not patriotic, the fact, unpalatable though it be, has surely, by reason of England's three successive victories, been borne home that Scotland is in a fair way of being bested at her own royal and ancient game.'

Even that was a charitable assessment of where matters stood. In the professional game, the past six years had been dark ones indeed for Scottish golf, but it would become darker still north of the Tweed, even as a glimmer of hope arrived.

Ten

FINAL INNINGS

————— •◖◖●◗◗• —————

The past three Opens had been a demoralising blow to amateur golf, but Freddie Tait's valiant late charge at Muirfield gave believers hope that gentlemen still represented a serious threat to their professional brethren.

Just as he had three years earlier in the Amateur vs Professional match at Sandwich, when he nearly toppled the man who eventually won, Tait had come tantalisingly close to joining John Henry Taylor and Harry Vardon in that play-off for the Claret Jug. Many would have taken that wager as he was striding confidently up to the 16th green at Muirfield with that familiar light of triumph in his eyes.

It is true that Tait had carried the amateur banner nearly alone over the past three seasons, but that is deceptive. Harold Hilton and John Ball had both suffered injuries, and were unable to deliver their best. Hilton had recovered physically by the 1896 Championship, but still lacked confidence in a crisis. Ball apparently was hurting enough that he skipped the 1896 Open, the first he had missed since his victory at Prestwick.

Still, the amateur ranks clearly had thinned out. Leading gentlemen golfers like Englishman Horace Hutchinson and Scotsmen Mure Fergusson, John Laidlay and Leslie Balfour-Melville – all top-five finishers in the Open – had fallen by the wayside. Balfour-Melville hadn't entered the Championship since 1892; the others had simply stopped being a threat.

Hilton can hardly have been the only observer who believed that the halcyon days were nearing an end for amateurs, especially given the way Taylor and Vardon were playing. In the spring of 1897, however, there remained plenty of golf fans prepared to stake a half-crown on a gentleman to win the Open.

By the time that season rolled around, Hilton had given them reason to keep believing. He had rediscovered his game and his confidence in himself. He had also started out on the career in writing that would see him emerge as one of golf's leading voices. By then Hilton was the author of a popular weekly golf column in the *Sporting Chronicle*.

Hilton went into the Amateur at Muirfield that season with every expectation of winning. After all, he was in peak form and had broken through in the Open on that same course just five years before. Unfortunately for him and every other leading golfer, the 1897 Amateur turned out to be a series of unpleasant surprises. 'The big men went down like ninepins,' as Hilton explained it.

Laidlay succumbed in the second round, Tait in the third. Ball, at least, showed a bit of fire. He waged a desperate battle against a 21-year-old Scotsman making his Amateur debut, Robert Maxwell, or Bobbie as his friends knew him. Their match was not decided until the fifth extra hole, when Ball finally fell with a six to Maxwell's five.

Hilton was left to defend Hoylake's honour when he and Maxwell met in the fourth round. He got off to a fine start, winning the first hole, but did nothing after that, partly because his short game was feeble and partly because Maxwell laid him one stymie after another on the greens. 'It is true,' Hilton wrote, 'that I was accorded a very varied experience in the matter of manipulating stymies; but not by the most egotistical stretch of the imagination can I think that it made any difference to the result.' Maxwell won easily, 6 and 4.

The unlikely winner of that Championship turned out to be a University of Edinburgh medical student named Jack Allan. David Scott Duncan, editor of *The Golfing Annual*, had predicted to Hilton beforehand that Allan would win. Hilton had a hard time buying that when he saw the young student swing. 'His style was neither orthodox, nor elegant, and he seemed to lack the true golfer's methods and finish,' Hilton wrote.

The all-Scottish final between Allan and James Robb was a dispiriting affair marred by uninspired golf and a bizarre incident on the 11th hole. Allan hooked his drive so badly that it appeared to have sailed over a wall and out of bounds. When the players reached the spot, the ball was nowhere to be found. A spectator reported that Robb's caddie had picked it up.

The caddie admitted picking up a ball, but insisted it was a 'derelict' one. It was, in fact, Allan's ball. Robb lost the hole to go three down with seven to play. He never regained his equilibrium, and Allan went on to win, 4 and 2. Tragically, he did not live to see his victory immortalised in the next *Annual*. Allan died of tuberculosis early the following year.

Ugly as it was, the result of the 1897 Amateur gave Scots a streak in that Championship to rival the English run in the Open. Allan's victory was their third in succession, following those by Balfour-Melville and Tait. A dozen Amateurs had been conducted since the official start of the tournament in 1886. Scots had now evened the series at six wins apiece. That, at least, was some consolation for a nation demoralised by one humbling defeat after another in its own national championship.

Making history

Just three weeks would pass between that Amateur and another historic day for England – the first Open staged at the club that had done more than any other to promote golf south of the border, Royal Liverpool.

By then English courses were developing their own renowned history of championships – Ball's two Amateur victories at Hoylake, Taylor's breakthrough for English professionals at Sandwich, and that splendid performance by Tait over those same links in the 1896 Amateur. The 1897 Open would make history to top any of those.

That Championship gave Royal Liverpool its first opportunity to show off its impressive new clubhouse, built in 1895 for £6,500. Since 1869, when the club was founded, the Royal Hotel had been its head-quarters. When the lease came up for renewal in 1894, however, members decided they needed a more modern home of their own. The Royal may have been cosy, but it was never going to win any prizes for beauty. Hoy-lake wanted a home that reflected its exalted position in the game. It was a bitter pill to swallow for John Ball Sr, as it took away a big chunk of his business.

The new clubhouse was designed by a local firm, Woolfall and Eccles, in the Domestic Revival style popular at the time. Built with red brick and tile, it featured a roofline animated by gables, turrets and chimneys. The luxurious interior, with its timber-panelled rooms and dramatic staircase, spoke to the ambitions of the prosperous leader of English golf.

Moving the clubhouse necessitated changes to the links, which were lengthened in the process. For that Open, Hoylake played to 6,090 yards, still shorter than St Andrews but nearly as long as the brawny St George's.

Despite his lacklustre performance in the Amateur, Hilton was a decided favourite in the Championship, along with that other home-town hero, Ball. Hilton had played so beautifully coming into the Open that he caught the attention of the reporter covering the competition for *The Scotsman*. 'Mr Hilton,' the newspaper wrote, 'has exhibited such consistent form during the past week that great things were expected of him.' That was not the only reason he was on everyone's list of contenders. Hilton was always considered a bigger threat in a stroke-play event than he was in a match.

Hilton experienced the expectations of his admirers first hand. 'Time after time people came to me and remarked, "Johnnie and you ought to have a great chance this year,"' he recalled. 'Personally I thought there was a slight chance of one or the other of the twain making a good fight,' he wrote, 'but I had seen a good deal of professional golf, and the more I saw of it the more did I respect its many qualities.'

Eighty-eight players turned out for that Championship, so many that in a meeting beforehand the committee that ran the Open voted to institute a cut at next year's event. The 36 holes played on the final day in 1898 would be limited to players within 20 strokes of the lead. The only notable person missing from that first Open at Hoylake, beyond the ill-fated Allan, was Old Tom Morris. He had played in his final Championship in 1895 at St Andrews on the eve of his 74th birthday. He had attended in 1896 and wanted to again that year, but had to miss his first Open to tend to a sick relative.

The opening day of the Championship, 19 May 1897, was a tad warm, but ideal for scoring, sunny with a gentle breeze. Good weather or bad, players always had one obstacle to confront at Hoylake – its famously fast greens. *The Annual* considered them the only drawback in that Open, as their 'excessive keenness wrecked the chances of several of the best players'.

The amateur golf faithful had plenty to crow about after the first round. Their stalwarts Ball, Tait and Hilton occupied three of the top six places, each of them tied with professionals. Ball and Sandy Herd shared the lead at 78. Tait and David Brown of Musselburgh were a stroke behind. Hilton was tied for third at 80, with Englishman George Pulford and a relative newcomer named James Braid, a Scotsman working as the professional at Romford. The professionals everyone feared most,

Taylor and Vardon, seemed out of sorts, coming in with 82 and 84, respectively.

Ball was paired that morning with a fellow amateur, Scotsman John Laidlay. The two long-time rivals in the battle between rose and thistle were followed by a throng that created issues for the twosome playing behind them – Hilton and his partner, Joseph Dalgleish, a professional from Nairn.

'Time after time,' Hilton recalled, 'we had to wait until they cleared away from the greens, and going to the 16th hole we had to wait fully ten minutes.' That was hard on a high-strung player like Hilton, who admitted that he 'was very irritable about it'.

In the afternoon round Hilton tried a different strategy, purposely lagging behind Ball and Laidlay to avoid having his rhythm disrupted. It worked like a charm. Bouncing along in his jaunty way, leaving a trail of cigarette smoke behind him, Hilton played like a man possessed. He came to the final hole at Hoylake, a tough 350-yarder, needing a four for a magnificent 75. 'A four to this hole I did not expect, as it was played dead against the wind, and it was quite impossible to get home in two,' he wrote. 'A five would have quite satisfied me.'

Hilton's third shot to the hole was a beauty that stopped 12 feet from the pin. He was standing next to his ball, waiting for Dalgleish to putt, when Ryder Richardson, a fellow club member, turned to speak to him. Richardson tended the flag on the 18th at Hoylake to welcome players finishing their rounds, just as Old Tom Morris did at St Andrews.

'Did you hear what Braid has done?' Richardson asked. Hilton said he hadn't. 'Seventy-four,' Richardson replied. 'This took my breath away,' Hilton admitted, 'but at the same time it probably did me good, as I went boldly for the hole and holed the putt . . . In the end that putt meant much.'

Braid's flawless round gave him a one-stroke lead at 154, but the leading amateurs were right on his heels. Hilton was a stroke behind in second, followed by Tait at 158 and Ball at 159, tied with professionals Herd and Pulford. Neither Taylor nor Vardon had been able to solve the puzzle of Hoylake, coming in with 80s that left them well back.

Hilton knew how important his third trip around the links would be to the outcome of the Championship. In his Open victory at Muirfield, the 72 he posted in that crucial round clinched his victory. That knowledge put a lot of pressure on a fidgety player like him. It showed that afternoon.

'I did my best to throw the Championship into the gutter,' Hilton wrote, 'as whilst I was making no serious mistakes, I played the most weak-kneed golf. I cannot remember touching a single hazard, and still I took no less than 84; it was simply that I would not hit the ball up to the hole, with the result that at literally every other hole I dropped a stroke.'

Hilton's only consolation was that Braid also slipped, struggling with the treacherous greens and limping in with 82. That added up to 236, leaving him clinging to a slim lead. Tait remained in the thick of the battle, tied for second with Herd and Pulford. They had two strokes to make up. Hilton was three back and by no means out of it.

It was Ball who had thrown his Championship into the gutter. He came in with a disastrous 88. That was a shock, especially over his home green, but just as surprising was the uninspired golf of Taylor and Vardon. They played nothing like the men who struck fear in the hearts of Scottish golfers and were, as *The Annual* put it, 'completely out of court'.

Hilton headed into his lunch break as 'a very sick and peevish man'. While he was eating, a member of the inner circle at Hoylake came to Hilton's table and suggested that he top off his lunch with a bit of trifle, confidently asserting that it was 'the finest thing in the world on which to do a 75'. Hilton took the advice, and as he approached the tee for his afternoon round, his playing partner, an old friend named Peter Paxton, looked him squarely in the eye and said, 'Now, Mr Hilton, a 75 this afternoon, nothing more,' he remembered. 'That number 75 seemed to be in the air.'

It must have seemed entirely possible after Hilton stole a 45-foot putt on the first hole for an unlikely three. When he reached the sixth tee, he had taken just 18 strokes – a start as sensational as the one that had opened his eyes to Vardon's prospects in 1893 at Prestwick. Hilton was never likely to keep up that scorching pace, and when the final four holes required 20 strokes he reached the turn in 38.

He might have felt better about that score had it not been for an occurrence regrettably common in those days, when fans thought nothing of talking to players mid-round. While Hilton was waiting on the tenth tee, a man rushed up to him to report that Tait, out early that morning, also had taken 38 on the opening nine. That meant he was still leading Hilton by a stroke. Braid would be among the last out, so it wasn't possible to know where he stood. Maybe the news did Hilton good, just as it had the previous day when he learned of Braid's 74. Hilton bore down on the home nine, starting 4, 3, 4, 3 – perfect golf.

It is critical to get a good start homeward at Hoylake. The next four holes – famously known as Field, Lake, Dunn and Royal – provide a test as searching as any in the game. Hilton was happy to leave the Field with a five. At the Lake he had one of those lucky breaks that can win a Championship. His lengthy putt for four found the bottom of the cup.

Fives at the Dunn and Royal left him with four strokes to post the 75 that had been in the air all afternoon.

In his previous rounds, Hilton had concluded he had no chance of reaching the 18th in two shots. But as he stood on the tee he noticed that the wind had shifted. It was no longer in his face, but blowing across the hole. He decided to try and smash a drive far enough to give him a chance of reaching. 'I had a go, and fairly got hold of the ball, but when I came up to it I found that . . . there were still grave doubts as to whether I could get home,' Hilton remembered. It can't have helped that his caddie handed him a club to lay up short of the bunker guarding the green.

Hilton had plenty of time to consider his options, as it seemed to him that the couple in front were taking forever to finish. He decided, in the end, to take his spoon and go for broke. 'At last came the welcome signal, and without wasting any time over preliminaries, I let go. The ball went as true as steel off the club, but unfortunately I had the slightest bit of pull on the stroke, and I knew well that the farther you go to the left at this hole the longer is the carry.' No sooner had Hilton hit the shot than the Hoylake crowd burst into what he considered premature applause.

'I should not have been at all surprised had the ball plumped straight into the bunker,' he wrote, 'but it got over, by how much I cannot say; I have an idea that it must have been more a question of feet than yards, as by the way it jumped it must have landed on the banks just over the hazard.' The ball wound up fairly close to the hole, leaving Hilton two putts for his 75, a score always likely to carry the day in the tense final round of an Open.

Hilton was understandably nervous as he walked up to the green, with the massive crowd surrounding it and the Championship at stake. It showed when his chance came to play. 'Putt number one was not at all a bold one,' he confessed. 'One spectator called it a drunken effort, and he was not far wrong. Putt number two bobbled about, and eventually made its entry into the hole at the back door, but it got there and that was everything. I can see that ball now hesitating on the lip of the hole like a hopeless derelict.'

Even before Hilton had reached the 18th, he had learned that Tait had managed no better than 79, despite his tremendous start. Neither Herd nor Pulford had done enough either. Now it was a matter of whether the Scotsman Braid – the surprise player of the tournament – could deliver a 78 with everything on the line to tie Hilton and force a play-off.

The first thing Hilton heard when he walked into the clubhouse was that Braid had taken 40 strokes going out and would need 38 on that brutal finishing stretch to tie. He knew how tough that would be, so Hilton confidently went back out on the course to watch his adversary come in. What he saw made him queasy. As *The Scotsman* reported, Braid was 'making a magnificent struggle of it'. Two holes later Hilton was back at the clubhouse trying to interest himself in the newspaper or billiards. That didn't work either, and he eventually 'summoned up enough pluck to wander out again'.

At that moment, Braid was teeing off on the final hole. Hilton could hear a spectator shout that the Scotsman needed a three to tie. 'I felt a brave man again, as I knew that last hole at Hoylake. It is always a good four, and an exceptional three . . . In my own mind, I could not see Braid or anyone else doing that hole in three, and I felt that the Championship was in my pocket.'

Braid, however, was a fearsomely long driver. His tee shot was such a bomb that it was obvious the Scotsman would have no trouble reaching in two. Braid briefly considered using a wooden club, as Hilton had done, but decided he didn't need it. He approached with his cleek. 'In James Braid's long career, he has probably seldom played a finer stroke than that second of his to the last hole in 1897,' Hilton recalled. 'It was never off the pin.'

When it landed on that slick green, the ball kept rolling, passing within a foot of the flag, before trickling to a halt some 20 feet away. The tension was palpable as Braid stalked that putt for what seemed an eternity, trying to get a fix on the right-to-left break. Finally, the big Scotsman settled down over the ball and gave it what *Golf* magazine described as 'one of the manliest strokes ever made in a critical moment'. As the ball trundled towards the cup, it appeared as if Braid had holed it, but in the end it broke too sharply and slipped past on the left side. 'Thank heavens,' thought Hilton.

He would look back on that afternoon at Royal Liverpool as the signature moment of his career, especially because it came after a five-year dry spell that left some wondering if his victory in 1892 had been a fluke. 'It is easy to understand that an endorsement of the previous win was particularly gratifying to me, even though in this second success I had the advantage of playing over a course with which I was well acquainted,' Hilton wrote. In August, he topped off that glorious year by winning the Irish Open Amateur as easily as if he'd been playing a friendly game at Hoylake.

Faith undimmed

No one could blame true believers in amateur golf if they walked away from the 1897 Open convinced that the results vindicated their position that gentlemen were every bit the equal of professionals.

With only 14 amateurs in that massive field of 88 players, Hilton won, Tait tied for third, and Ball, Mure Fergusson and Hoylake's John Graham Jr finished in the top 20. Beyond that, the most feared professionals, Taylor and Vardon, had no say in the outcome. Braid was still so new on the scene that no one yet grasped what manner of golfer he would become, although he clearly represented a ray of hope for beleaguered Scots.

It was only natural that the leaders of amateur golf would have such abiding faith in the gentlemen who carried off their club medals year after year. These were men who devoted their energy to nurturing the game. These were men who put up the stakes for championships and took on the thankless job of running them. These were men who helped Britain assemble an empire that ruled the world in the Victorian age. It would have struck at the core of their beliefs to conclude that a gentleman was inferior to a working-class professional.

They were not alone in the admiration of gentlemen golfers. The press treated them as heroes, too. In the middle of that epochal decade for Amateurs, a magazine called *The Golfer* did a series of interviews with top players, featuring such prominent gentlemen as Laidlay and Tait. The interview with Tait opened with readers following along as the reporter meandered through the barracks of the Black Watch in search of the famous golfer's room. The picture it painted of a soldier's rugged life speaks to what romantic figures leading amateur players were in those days:

'It is not a light task to find one's way about the officer's quarters in Edinburgh's old Castle. And after *The Golfer* interviewer had wandered enquiringly along bare stone corridors and up flights of well-worn stone steps, arriving eventually at the flat nearest the sky, with the name Rookery painted over the door lintel, he had recourse to the guidance of a kindly disposed soldier-servant, and climbed downwards again.

'Cards, nailed to the prison-like array of doors, give information as to the names of the tenants; and in and around the quarters there is a true military avoidance of unnecessary ornamentation. In a room on the ground level, opening off a corridor that leads directly to the low terrace outside, Mr F.G. Tait has his regimental home. A room that has evidently seen generations of officers, simply furnished, lighted by one window set in thick walls, a rather gloomy apartment.'

There can't be much doubt that all summer long, at the dinners of clubs from St Andrews to St George's, there were bold predictions of future glory for gentlemen golfers. No doubt there were even a boastful few who believed that the outcome at Royal Liverpool proved that English professionals, Vardon and Taylor, were not as fearsome as they seemed.

Hoylake men, in particular, were busting their buttons over having one of their own back on top, especially with the Amateur returning to Royal Liverpool come spring. In the early months of the 1898 golf season, a rejuvenated Hilton was playing as well as ever. He racked up 13 holes for the Hoylake side in a home-and-home match with Royal North Devon and won both the club's Kashmir Cup and Gold Medal, the former by seven strokes. Surely this year, over his home links, Hilton would realise the dream that had eluded him – being hailed Champion Amateur of the Year.

The Amateur was played over four days in late May that *The Annual* described as 'rather too hot to be pleasant'. It brought a field of 77 to Royal Liverpool. There was some doubt whether Ball would be among them. He had suffered another injury, this time to his arm, in that team match at Westward Ho! In the end he did play, although Laidlay was sidelined with a bout of typhoid fever. That was not the biggest news when the draw for the tournament was released, however. Hoylake was buzzing because if the early matches went according to form, England's Hilton and Scotland's Tait would meet again in the fourth round of the Championship.

Hilton strolled through his opening rounds, displaying the same sharpness he'd shown all spring. Ball and Tait were nearly knocked out early. Ball needed an extra hole to shake off his third-round opponent, while Hoylake man Charles Hutchings nearly did Hilton the favour of dispensing with Tait, also taking him into extra holes. As he so often did, however, Tait came up with the heroic shot he needed to win on the 19th.

The Annual also took note of one other marathon match in the third round. H.A. Farrar, of the Liverpool golfing family, needed six extra holes to shake off a feisty Cambridge student making his Amateur debut, a 21-year-old named Bernard Darwin. He was reading law in those days, making his way towards being called to the bar. Less than a decade later, Darwin would toss off his wig and take up golf writing, becoming the greatest correspondent the game would ever know. He stayed to watch the rest of the matches, getting his first glimpse of Hilton, Ball and Tait.

The confrontation Darwin, and everyone else at Hoylake, wanted to see was the rematch between the reigning Champion Golfer and the swashbuckling soldier from the Black Watch. 'Our meeting was generally accorded the credit of being *the* match of the week, a species of battle royal,' Hilton recalled. 'People trooped out from Liverpool in hordes to witness it.'

The match got off to a ho-hum start, with the first hole halved in fives. Hilton began to wobble as early as the second. He had an easy putt for a half, but couldn't get it down. Hilton missed another tiny putt – less than three feet – to hand his foe the fourth. When Tait holed a 40-footer on the sixth, raising his putter aloft and thrusting his right foot forward as it rattled into the tin, the sky was looking dark indeed for the Englishman. Disaster struck for Hilton again at the eighth and ninth, the first time when he was snared by a bunker and the second when he found an impossible lie.

When Tait turned for home five holes up, not even the most optimistic Hoylake partisan held out much hope for Hilton. Puffing furiously on his cigarette, he looked, and was, a beaten man. The end of that 'inexpressibly sad procession', as Darwin described it, came at the 13th. There Hilton went down 6 and 5. His recollections of that match speak eloquently to the agony he endured by failing so miserably on his own green in front of his devoted fans, among them his wife, Frances.

'My opponent gradually increased his lead, and increased it without effort, until finally I was six holes in arrear, with only five to play, and in consequence was free to wend my sorrowful way to the clubhouse,' Hilton wrote. 'And sorrowful did I feel; it was akin to the sorrow of shame, and I really felt as if I dare not look anybody in the face. Freddie Tait was very sympathetic, but I am afraid I was past appreciating sympathy.'

Tait was ecstatic about the outcome. For years he had kept a diary of his games, with matter-of-fact comments in the margin about how he and his opponent played. His jottings after that Amateur were exuberant: 'The Open Champion quite demoralised, and totally incapable of playing any kind of shot. F.G.T. very steady. H.H.H. did not win a single hole!!!'

Tait went on to win that Championship, though it would be nothing like his glorious procession two years earlier at Sandwich. He squeaked past Hoylake's John Graham by a single hole. Graham played marvellously tee to green and ought to have won easily. But he missed one tiny putt after another, including a two-footer to hand Tait the match.

In that same round, any hope for Hoylake was extinguished when Ball, likely hampered by that arm injury, lost to James Robb, previous year's runner-up. Tait had another narrow escape in his semi-final match against St Andrews amateur John Low, who would soon be at the centre of perhaps the most important debate in golf history. Tait was wild off the tee, while Low was putting as brilliantly as ever. Their match was halved in regulation, and Tait survived only by pulling off one magic trick after another during the three extra holes required.

In the final, Tait faced a fellow Scotsman, the 43-year-old warrior Mure Fergusson. Whoever won, golfers in the north would be celebrating their fourth consecutive victory in the Amateur, matching the run southerners had mounted in the Open. Tait returned to his overpowering ways in that 36-hole final, romping home 7 and 5. While the match may not have been close, the first round included a moment that speaks volumes about the character of Freddie Tait.

At the 14th, the Long Hole, Fergusson's approach shot bounced off a spectator and rebounded onto the green. A local rule required the referee to take it off the putting surface and drop it. When he did that, the ball landed in a hole, leaving Fergusson an impossible lie. Tait would not have it. He strode across the green, lifted Fergusson's ball out of the hole, and gave it a perfect lie. The crowd roared its approval.

He may have swept past Fergusson with ease, but Tait agreed with Hilton that he had been extraordinarily lucky to survive so many close shaves en route to that title. He admitted as much when he was handed the trophy. 'Thank you for the way in which you have received my fluky win,' Tait told the crowd. 'I ought to have been beaten twice yesterday, but I got off. I played better today, but I really don't deserve the Championship.'

Tait celebrated his good fortune that evening by playing his bagpipes up and down Market Street for all of Hoylake to hear. That red-letter year would also see Scotland's national hero claim the second of his four victories in the St George's Vase. *The Scotsman*, naturally, was in a joyous mood, crowing about how Tait's victory had shifted the balance of power between Scotland and England in the Amateur Championship.

'Scotland, for the first time, has a balance in her favour in point of victories, having now seven, as against England's six,' the newspaper wrote. 'Thus, the sting has been taken from the reproach that Scotland has allowed itself to be outplayed in the great amateur event of the year.'

The humbling of amateur golf's best score-player did nothing to diminish enthusiasm for Hilton or another gentleman winning the Open two weeks hence at Prestwick. In wrapping its report on the previous year's Championship at Hoylake, *The Annual* had reminded professionals that 'a feature of this meeting has been the success that has attended the amateurs.'

Prestwick was a perfect course for Hilton and his trusty spoons, not to mention that Ball had enjoyed his greatest success there. Tait also had to be considered a threat, especially if he could produce anything like the magical form he had displayed in the 1896 Amateur. Leading up to the Open, one sportswriter, unmoved by Hilton's dismal showing at Royal Liverpool, picked him to win – a sentiment no doubt shared by many golf fans.

Hilton certainly was not ready to stake any money on himself. 'I cannot say that the confidence in my powers was sufficiently great to lead me to endorse this opinion,' he wrote, 'as I had not yet got over the terrible debacle at Hoylake.' It wasn't simply that, however. Despite his victory at Muirfield, Hilton could not shake the feeling that had nagged him since that dominant display by professionals at Sandwich in 1894 – the sense that he and his fellow amateurs were about to be left behind.

Hilton knew his golf. His victory in the 1897 Open would by no means be the last moment of glory for gentlemen golfers. It would, however, be the last time a British amateur carried off the Claret Jug. Scotland never would realise its dream of producing an amateur capable of defeating professionals. Hilton's twin Open victories would rank high among the very best performances achieved during that remarkable era, giving him another edge on his childhood idol, Ball. In all of history, as it turned out, only one player, Bobby Jones, would surpass Hilton's two Open wins as an amateur.

The generation that followed Hilton, Ball and Tait would carry the banner of amateur golf ably, but not as successfully, as their forebears. Although never pre-tournament favourites, golfers like Hoylake's John Graham and Tantallon's Robert Maxwell would lead amateurs to 13 more top ten finishes, including four in the top five, between 1900 and the outbreak of war. They managed that against increasingly tough odds, as the number of professionals grew exponentially. In only one of those years did amateurs make up more than a quarter of the field. Usually, they accounted for half that.

None of this was obvious as the golfing scene shifted to Prestwick for the 1898 Open. Nor would it be over the four thrilling days of that Championship. By year's end, however, it would be abundantly clear to everyone in golf that a new day had arrived.

Eleven

'RUTHLESS JUGGERNAUT'

————————•◗●◖•————————

Not one of the brightest minds in the game – not even Harold Hilton – would have predicted the mind-boggling stretch of golf the world witnessed beginning in the spring of 1898. Nor would they have guessed that before two seasons had passed, Harry Vardon would have established himself as the first transcendent player to arise since Young Tom Morris.

Vardon may have won the 1896 Open, but was still a relative unknown, and it would take more than one Championship to convince the golf world that he had surpassed the man who reigned supreme in professional golf – John Henry Taylor. 'In spite of this defeat by the great Harry, whose unique greatness even then we did not at all fully appreciate, the big man in golf was still Taylor,' wrote Horace Hutchinson. 'He was still at the very top of his game.'

The invincibility Vardon displayed over the next two seasons would leave no question as to who was the nation's true King of Clubs. The astonishing streak he put together, coupled with glorious performances that would follow in America and Britain, would elevate Vardon above even his gifted peers and secure his place among the game's immortals.

Henry William Vardon, who always went by Harry, was born in Grouville, Jersey on 9 May 1870 to Philippe George Vardon and Elizabeth Augustine Bouchard, both of whom had been born and raised on the island. Philippe worked as a gardener to support his eight children, and

Harry grew up the way every other working-class boy did. He attended the local school until age 12, when it was time for him to start earning money for his family.

In his memoir, Vardon described himself as the school's 'dunce'. He never wanted to be inside learning arithmetic or French and didn't apply himself in class. He preferred the outdoor life, especially sports, and with his sinewy 5 feet 9 inches frame he excelled at games, becoming especially fond of running, cricket and football. Vardon was seven years old when a sleepy Sabbath morning was disrupted by a group of surveyors who showed up on Grouville Common near his family's cottage to begin laying out a golf course – the event that would direct the future of his life.

Vardon was among the first generation of golfers from the south who grew up the way Scottish boys did, with golf clubs in their hands. From an early age, he began picking up a few shillings for his family by working as a caddie at Royal Jersey Golf Club. Naturally, it was only a matter of time before he and the other boys, his younger brother Tom among them, wanted to play golf themselves. Trouble was they could afford neither clubs nor balls. The Vardon boys and their mates solved that problem by using white marbles for balls and fashioning crude clubs from branches of Lady Oak and blackthorn trees.

Young Harry quickly demonstrated a gift for golf, but he didn't get many opportunities to play. In the Victorian age, every member of the family needed to add money to the till to help make ends meet. When Vardon wasn't carrying clubs for gentlemen, among them Arthur Molesworth and William Laidlaw Purves, he was at the beach gathering seaweed to sell.

As soon as he left school, Vardon went to work on a farm, churning butter and doing other odd jobs for a few years before taking work as a houseboy for a doctor. By age 17 he had decided to follow his father's path and become a gardener. Vardon went to work in that capacity for Major Spofforth, a keen golfer and member at Royal Jersey. Spofforth took a liking to the young man, gave him a few clubs, and often took him out to play a round.

By then Vardon had joined the new Working Men's Club at Royal Jersey, where he won his first trophy in competition. It would occupy pride of place on his mantelpiece all his days, even as he racked up the game's most venerated prizes. Major Spofforth could tell that Vardon, whom he preferred to call by his given name, had genuine talent for golf. He gave his young charge this piece of advice: 'Henry, my boy, never give up your golf. It may be useful to you one day.'

That day was coming sooner than either of them realised. Vardon was nearly 20 years old by then. His brother, Tom, was already working at Lytham and St Annes, where his experiences would give Harry reason to reconsider his plans for the future. The £12 Tom earned in a single afternoon by finishing second in the tournament at Musselburgh represented more than half of the annual salary Harry earned as an under-gardener for Major Spofforth. Harry knew he could take Tom's measure at will on the links. The life of a professional golfer suddenly seemed far more attractive to him than maintaining flower beds.

In the autumn of 1890, he left Jersey to take the job Tom had arranged for him as greenkeeper and professional at Studley Royal Golf Club on the estate of Lord Ripon in Yorkshire. The golfing life at Studley Royal was far too quiet for Harry, who needed competition to sharpen his game. Within a year he'd taken up a new post as professional at the nine-hole Bury Golf Club in Lancashire, where a game against a seasoned player was easily found.

About that same time Vardon's personal life took an unexpected turn. Before leaving Jersey, he had been courting a woman named Jessie Bryant, who ironed clothes for a living. The following year, Bryant sent Vardon a letter announcing she was pregnant with his child. They were married on 15 December 1891 at All Saints Church in St Helier, but Bryant couldn't be persuaded to return with Vardon to Lancashire. She stayed home with her family to await the birth.

The following summer, on 25 June, Vardon received a telegram informing him that he was the father of a son. He returned to Jersey three weeks later, but by then the child was gravely ill. That was tragically common in Victorian times, when the infant mortality rate was frighteningly high. Clarence Henry Vardon died on 5 August 1892.

Bryant was plunged into a depression from which she would never fully recover. She and Vardon remained married all their lives, but they would never have another child and their marriage would be an unhappy one. It would be years before Bryant joined Vardon in England, and even then she took no interest in his golfing life or his friends.

Vardon returned to Bury alone and channelled his grief into working feverishly at perfecting his game. He developed a swing far different than the long, sweeping move in vogue at the time. Vardon's swing was shorter and decidedly more upright, a style common to players from Jersey. He turned his upper body considerably farther than others did, and with effortless tempo swept through to a full finish that found him directly facing his target.

'The club does not come even so far round as to be horizontal behind the back,' Hutchinson noted. 'By way of compensation the turn of the body is great; the legs, the hips, the feet, all the lower half of the body, have taken a great share, an usually great share, in the movements.' Vardon's downswing was a mirror image of his backswing. 'The body has been allowed to follow on, and to follow the turn of the swing with wonderful freedom.'

In his earliest days, Vardon used the traditional palm grip. Later on, however, he stumbled on to the overlapping grip first used by leading Scottish amateur John Laidlay. Vardon's success would make that grip the one almost universally adopted. Sadly for Laidlay, it would be known ever after as 'the Vardon grip'.

Vardon's swing was so different that those who saw him play for the first time hardly knew what to make of it. 'It certainly seemed to me very strange and heterodox when I saw it,' admitted Bernard Darwin. Whatever one thought of Vardon's swing, the results were there for all to see. He was longer and straighter than most players of his generation, especially with a cleek or brassie. He needed only two shots to reach holes on which others required two and a pitch.

'He hit every ball perfectly cleanly, with his club head always travelling in the right direction,' Hutchinson wrote. 'This and the fact that such force as he did apply was applied precisely at the right moment – this it was that sent his ball flying so far and so straight.' One secret of Vardon's surprising length was that he used lighter clubs than his peers, increasing his swing speed. Lighter clubs would become all the rage once Vardon had reached the top of the game.

In the end, after years of watching Vardon hit one devastatingly accurate shot after another in moments of crisis, Darwin would overcome the initial shock of watching his new, oddly upright swing and come to this conclusion: 'I don't believe anyone ever had or ever will have a greater genius for hitting a golf ball than Harry Vardon.'

Vardon had one other trait that helped make him the player he became – a cheerful serenity on the course, where he seldom said a word, reacted to misfortune only with a wry smile, and could usually be found puffing calmly on his pipe between shots. 'There was a gay *insouciance* about his whole manner of addressing himself to the game which was very attractive,' Hutchinson wrote. Vardon remained enormously popular among his rivals, even as he beat them to smithereens.

It was only a year after the death of his son that Vardon decided he was ready to test himself in competition. He accompanied his brother

Tom to the 1893 Open at Prestwick, where that fabulous stretch of golf over the first six holes had convinced Hilton that he had seen a genuine golfer in the making.

Vardon didn't exactly take the golf world by storm after that. He slipped back to 23rd place after that promising start at Prestwick and finished fifth and ninth in the next two Opens. Even his victory against Taylor in 1896 at Muirfield seemed less impressive after his lacklustre showing the following year at Hoylake, where he was never a threat.

In early May of 1898 at a course on the south-east coast of England known as Hastings and St Leonards, Vardon began the scorched-earth march that would prove beyond doubt he reigned supreme in golf. In his first event of the season, an invitational, Vardon finished second. A month later, he won the open tournament at Musselburgh. The man who had humbled Taylor two years ago was finding his stride again.

It's hard to believe, given how large Vardon now looms in golf, that gamblers missed these clues as they placed their bets on the 1898 Open Championship at Prestwick. Bettors could not decide on a favourite. Hilton and Freddie Tait had their share of backers, as did half a dozen professionals, among them Taylor and James Braid, the surprise star of the previous year's Open at Hoylake.

On a Mission

Vardon and his compatriots south of the border would run into a man on a mission in that Championship: Willie Park Jr. Scots may have had something to brag about after Tait's victory in the Amateur, but their situation remained dire in the Open. The Claret Jug had been carried south in six of the past eight seasons. Every Scottish professional golfer felt the weight of a desperate nation on his shoulders – none more so than Park.

The pride of Musselburgh was the descendant of one of golf's first families, not to mention Scotland's only active two-time winner of the Championship. He knew full well that the country saw him as a link to the glorious past it hoped to recapture at the very links where the Open had been founded all those years ago when no one dreamed of Englishmen winning.

Since the onset of the golf boom in the late 1880s, however, Park had played hardly any golf. He was too busy laying out courses and managing Wm. Park and Son, the business he had taken over from his father, whose health had begun to fail. Park was nothing if not ambitious. By 1898 he had expanded the firm far beyond its home base in Musselburgh. The business now had 'emporiums' in London, Manchester and Edinburgh. It employed 60 club and ball makers at the generous salary of £3 a week. In 1895, the year the United States Golf Association was formed, Park saw new opportunities across the ocean and sailed to America to open a branch in New York City.

In 1896, after Taylor had won two consecutive Opens – the last of them, gallingly, at St Andrews – that Park decided that it was time to pick up his clubs, sharpen his game, and defend the honour of his homeland.

Scots, at that moment, were of the mind that the English might have the upper hand in stroke play, but would never be superior at the true game of golf – the thrust and parry of a match. Park set out to prove them right. He challenged Taylor to play for £50 a side over Musselburgh and a London course of Taylor's choosing. The Englishman picked Sudbrook Park in Richmond. It was narrow and tree-lined, a place where he knew an erratic driver like Park might have trouble finding the fairway.

Park putted like a demon at Musselburgh and seized a four-hole lead. Taylor fought back gamely at Richmond, where Park did, indeed, regularly find himself playing from the trees. Taylor had picked up three of the four holes he needed by the time they approached the 18th. There, as fate would have it, the match came down to a putt, the one part of the game where Park seemed infallible. It was a downhill six-footer. Park turned for advice to his caddie, a famous, weather-beaten character known as Fiery. 'Bolt it,' Fiery said, and Park did just that, knocking it firmly into the cup. Scots could, at least, take comfort in knowing that in a match their standard-bearers could still handle the best of the English.

Park was off to America again after that match, and didn't return in time for the 1897 Open. When Hilton rang up yet another victory for the seemingly unstoppable English, Park knew what he had to do. 'In the autumn of 1897,' he wrote, 'I made up my mind to put in a few months' solid practice, polish up my game to the old standard, and make a real try for the Open Championship at Prestwick in 1898.' He had fond memories of the course. Park won his first Open there in 1887, three years before the English onslaught began.

In preparation for Prestwick, Park placed an ad in the newspaper issuing his family's familiar 'Challenge to the World', a tradition his father started in 1854, when he was hoping to arouse the interest of the legendary Allan Robertson of St Andrews. Park offered to play any man alive in a high-stakes, home-and-home match. He was hoping an Englishman would bite, but the only response came from 1883 Open winner Willie Fernie, the professional at Troon. Park dispatched Fernie 13 and 11, a score Hilton described as 'absolutely silly against a man of Fernie's class. Park meant business that year, there was no doubt about it.'

He was not alone. Vardon and Hilton also were brimming with confidence. On the first day of competition, Wednesday 8 June, the miserable weather that had prevailed all month finally gave way, 'with the sun shining from a cloudless sky and glinting on the blue and peaceful waters of the Firth of Clyde', as *The Golfing Annual* described it. Nevertheless, the Championship began on a melancholy note. Old Tom Morris's daughter, Lizzie, had died of pneumonia that morning in St Andrews at the age of 46. With his family in mourning, the Grand Old Man would miss the Open again.

Eighty players entered for the Championship, the first that would feature a cut after 36 holes. Among the missing were Tom Vardon and the two Johnnies, Laidlay and Ball. Ball apparently opted to rest his injured arm, while Tom Vardon had been banged up in a bicycle accident.

It was far from clear after the first 18 holes what story that Open Championship would tell. With much of the crowd in tow, Park played every bit like a man who had got serious about his game. He made only two mistakes, hooking a tee shot on 14 into a nasty lie and finding a bunker on 17. Despite those slips, Park went around in 76 and shared the lead with Hilton, who might have done even better had three putts not cruelly 'rung the tin, but refused to go down', *The Annual* wrote.

Tait set out that morning followed by a horde nearly as large as Park's. 'Fresh from his victories in the Amateur Championship and the St George's Vase competition at Sandwich, Mr Tait was a marked man, and there was a general desire to ascertain in what form the day found him,' *The Scotsman* wrote. The outward nine found him in brilliant form, with 36. The inward nine not so much. Tait threw away one stroke after another and finished in 81, disappointing but hardly fatal.

The other big threats from the south appeared to be on their games, too. Vardon was last out that morning, again with almost no fans following him. He got off to an unsettling start, slicing his opening tee shot onto the railway that runs along the right side of the first hole. Vardon got down to business after that, and came in with 79, three strokes behind Park and Hilton. Taylor did even better. Playing almost flawlessly, he went out in 37 and came home in 41, a stroke fewer than Vardon.

The storyline took a decided turn after lunch. Hilton was playing brilliantly through the early holes of the second round. By the time he came to the fifth, the Himalayas, he had shaved two strokes from his spectacular morning round. One of the most famous blind par threes in golf, the Himalayas calls for a shot over a massive dune to a green some 200 yards away. For reasons he could never explain, Hilton made the same mistake John Ball had when he plopped his ball into the Swilcan Burn to lose that Amateur play-off in 1895 at St Andrews to Leslie Balfour-Melville.

'In the morning I had taken an iron club, and was a few yards short of the green,' Hilton recalled. 'In the afternoon round I came to the conclusion that a little more force was required.' Nine times out of ten in that situation, Hilton took his spoon. This time, he didn't. 'I took out a driving mashie, which I had not touched for over six months; it was quite a good club, but just a little long in the handle for me. The result was that I hit the ground and pulled the ball round into the sandhill on the left. I carefully watched the particular bunch of bent grass that it struck, and to this day I wish that I had not.'

Hilton trudged forlornly up that steep hill, drawing on his ever-present cigarette to calm his jittery nerves. 'Unhappily I found that ball and a pretty place it was in,' he wrote. 'For a moment, I hesitated whether I should take it out and tee it, losing two strokes, but there was literally no sound place on which to tee it, as the surroundings were one mass of sand.'

Hilton decided to play the ball, which turned out to be his second bad decision. It took him five more hacks to reach the green and two putts to hole out. The next words uttered, by his marker, were, 'I think that is eight,' Hilton recalled. 'He knew it was eight, and so did I, but I appreciated his kindly suggestion that he only *thought* it was eight.'

Hilton angrily tossed his putter at the box marking the tee of the sixth hole. Its name, Elysian Fields, must have seemed ironic to a steaming-hot Hilton at that moment. Having vented his anger, he began mentally working out what he might be able to do on the remaining holes. Hilton figured he could still post an 80 if he played perfectly. He came close, finishing just a stroke higher when the final putt dropped.

Meanwhile, Park was giving his countrymen every reason to believe their long days of darkness were coming to an end. 'The Musselburgh man did even more brilliantly than before,' *The Scotsman* wrote, 'and at his hands the spectators witnessed a grand exposition of golf. While he was in magnificent form both in driving and approaching, the outstanding part of his game was his putting, which was of the deadliest order.' He went out in an astounding 35, but cooled off coming home, finishing in 40 for a 75 that left him comfortably in the lead at 151 with two rounds remaining.

Vardon, again off last and playing nearly alone, started slowly, missing a makeable putt on the first and knocking his ball into the Pow Burn at the second. He found his stride on the third. 'From this point, he played in splendid style, and out in 38 he returned in 37,' wrote *The Scotsman*. That 75 left him alone in second place, three strokes behind Park. Taylor also played steadily that afternoon, matching his morning round with another tidy 78 that left him two strokes behind Vardon.

Despite the tragedy at the Himalayas, Hilton was not out of it. He was six strokes back, and still one ahead of Tait. The hero of the Black Watch improved substantially on his morning round with a 77 that left him in fifth. With two rounds to go, being seven back was a tough situation, but not an impossible one for a man capable of miraculous spurts of golf.

The big disappointment for Scots was the uninspired performance of Braid, who had played such sterling golf a year ago at Royal Liverpool. Scores of 80 and 82 left him out of the running. Braid would not play his best until the last round, when any hope had long since vanished. Scots would have a bit longer to wait before he developed into the golfer everyone expected him to become after that thrilling finish at Hoylake.

Fateful afternoon

Since the start of the Open, pairings had been drawn at random. Leaders didn't play together on the final day as they do now. If a player in contention went out early, he could post a number others would have to beat. If he went out later, he might learn during the round what score he needed to win. That information was not always trustworthy, however, and there were no leaderboards to check. Taking such rumours seriously was risky.

The draw for the second day set up two interesting situations. Park would play in the group directly behind Vardon, and Tait would follow Hilton. The contenders would be able to keep an eye on one another through those two crucial rounds. 'Delightful weather again prevailed,' *The Scotsman* reported. 'The links were bathed in bright sunshine, the air was very mild; but the heat was tempered by a refreshing westerly breeze.'

This time, as Vardon walked away from the first tee, he had a massive crowd trailing him. 'He began in magnificent fashion, taking the first three holes in 11 strokes,' marvelled *The Scotsman*. 'This fine form he maintained all the way out.' He reached the turn in 36, and started home with a bang by stealing a 30-foot putt on the tenth. Vardon stumbled twice after that, making a five at the short 11th and a seven at the 15th. He finished the homeward nine in 41, leaving him with a total of 231 – a score the newspaper thought 'promised well for his position at the close of play'.

Watching Vardon's torrid start may have spooked Park. He squandered his three-stroke lead by taking 15 shots on his first three holes, four more than Vardon. 'Pulling himself together, the Musselburgh professional settled down to his most powerful game, and despite the unpromising start, succeeded in doing the first half in 39, which means that he and Vardon at this point were on equal terms,' *The Scotsman* wrote. Park played steadily coming home, finishing in 39. His total for three rounds was 229, two better than Vardon's.

Playing later that morning, Hilton and Tait kept hope alive for the amateur loyalists in the crowd. 'They saw the famous Royal Liverpool representative in one of his formidable games, marred only by occasional weakness on the greens,' *The Scotsman* wrote. 'This was especially the case coming home, where he dropped at least a couple of strokes in putting, but he still managed to do the holes in the fine score of 77, which kept him well to the front.' Hilton's total was 234, five back of Park.

Playing right behind Hilton, Tait was in one of his all-conquering moods. 'He made a capital start with a four and a two, and maintaining a strong game, was out in an average of fours,' *The Scotsman* reported. 'On the way home, his long game was magnificent, but he had not the best of luck on the greens.' Nevertheless, he tied the low round of the tournament with 75. It left him a stroke in front of Hilton and four behind the leader.

The last contender out that morning was Taylor. 'He played sterling golf, with the exception that he failed occasionally on the greens, the strength of which he did not seem to have gauged in some cases,' *The Scotsman* wrote. Taylor's 77 left him at 233, tied with Tait in third.

This was shaping up to be the third consecutive Open with a neck-and-neck finish, following the play-off between Vardon and Taylor at Muirfield and Hilton's one-stroke victory over Braid at Hoylake. Thousands of people poured onto the links that afternoon to follow the final round, but despite how closely bunched the leaders were, the crowd thought only two golfers were truly in the mix.

'Looking to the exceptionally fine form of Park and Vardon, and to the fact that there were only two strokes between them, it was generally thought that the contest would resolve itself into a struggle for supremacy between these two – a pitched battle between professional golf north and south of the border,' *The Scotsman* wrote.

Just as he had that morning, Park had the unnerving experience of watching Vardon storm out of the gate, starting with the same 4, 3, 4 he had made before lunch. When Park repeated his 6, 3, 6 start of the morning, the tables had been turned. Now, instead of having a two-stroke lead, Park was trailing Vardon by two. Again, the Musselburgh man righted his foundering ship, and when he reached the turn in 39 to Vardon's 38, Park was still clinging to a one-hole lead.

'The issue was now narrowed greatly, and the excitement was keen among the spectators, the more because they were able from time to time to ascertain how the struggle went,' *The Scotsman* wrote. The first bit of news that spread around as the leaders made their way through the early holes of the final nine had nothing to do with Park or Vardon. Hilton, playing four groups behind Park, was making a spectacular charge.

'Additional zest was imparted to the play by the fact becoming known that Mr Hilton, by splendid golf, had done the first half in 35, which placed him at that point equal with Vardon and only one stroke worse than Park,' *The Scotsman* reported.

Both Park and Vardon continued to show excellent form through the home nine. 'Eventually, at the fourth last hole, a climax was reached for the couple were all even in strokes, and the round was rapidly nearing an end,' *The Scotsman* noted. Vardon finished superbly, but for a five at 17, the fearsome Alps. He made up for that by sinking an eight-footer on the last for a three. As the ball dropped, the fans packed around the green, with Prestwick's ancient stone clubhouse looming in the background, erupted in applause for Vardon's performance. His 76 left him with a total of 307.

Park played the first three of those holes identically, making the same five at the Alps. He came to the 18th needing a three to tie with Vardon and force a play-off. Two decades later Park would describe what unfolded on that green, a story that differs from reports in the press and memories of others who witnessed the drama. As he approached the last tee, Park wrote, he could hear the fans ahead cheer as Vardon holed out. 'I asked if anyone could tell me what Vardon had done the hole in,' Park recalled. 'I was told by several it was four, the par of the hole. I hit a beauty straight down the middle, and with my approach [putt] I laid the ball four feet off the hole.'

Vardon never left the 18th green. 'I finished very steadily, and stood amongst the huge crowd which surrounded the home green to see this famous Scotch player finish,' he remembered. 'His drive was a real good one, and finished on the corner of the green, and as he was renowned for his putting, it seemed to me that I was once again to be concerned in a tie for the Open Championship. Park's long putt stopped about a yard from the hole, which to my way of thinking was much too close.

'As the crowd pressed round the green to see him play his short putt,' Vardon continued, 'it so happened that I, the most concerned man standing around the green, was elbowed out. I stood at the edge of the crowd unable to see anything at all, and feeling more nervous than I had ever felt before. Never in the whole course of my playing career have I felt so uncomfortable as I did during those two or three minutes.'

Park wrote that when he walked up to his putt and examined it, he noticed something that troubled him. 'Halfway between my ball and the hole was a little bit of yarrow weed, like the top of a carrot, a sort of hard grub,' he recalled. 'It was on the exact line, and the only chance of holing the putt with the yarrow weed there was to skim over it with the putter laid back a little, and play firm at the back of the hole.'

This time he did not ask his caddie for advice, as he'd done on that winning putt in his match against Taylor. Instead Park turned to Fiery and announced his decision. 'I have two to tie for the Championship; I will make sure of the tie, and we will have a fine match for it in the morning.' Park wrote. 'I did not want to be second; it was a case of first or nowhere, so far as I was concerned, and I would have revelled in playing off a tie, I can assure you on that point, for I was playing as I wanted to play.'

Vardon never mentions having heard this exchange. Nor did he see Park's putt. 'At last, after what seemed an eternity, there rose from all around the ring a disappointed O-o-o-oh!' Vardon recalled. 'I made no attempt to look at his ball which was, of course, still outside the hole, for the crowd had told me in plain words that I had won the Championship, thus scoring my second win in the premier event.'

It was only after walking off the green, Park wrote, that he learned the truth. Vardon had made three on the last, and The Man Who Could Putt had tossed away his dream, and the dream of all Scotland, by shying away from one not much more than a yard long. That putt would haunt Park all his life. It struck at the very core of his identity.

Park was fond of telling stories about how he had grown up putting on the pavement outside his father's shop, honing the skill that would make him the deadliest putter in the kingdom. Not to mention that Park's most famous invention was the wry-necked putter – maddeningly, the very one Vardon used to hole that eight-footer to win. In 1920, when he published *The Art of Putting*, Park devoted much of the opening essay – titled, of course, 'The Man who Can Putt is a Match for Anyone' – to explaining why he had not gone boldly for the hole that afternoon at Prestwick.

The other contenders in the 1898 Championship never did quite enough to catch either Vardon or Park. Hilton put a 40 with his 35 to start. That was good enough to tie for the best round of the Championship, but it still left him in third, two strokes back. Taylor made another steady 79, placing him fourth, and Tait's 82 left him in fifth.

In his memoir, Taylor dismissed the idea that Park thought he needed a four on the final hole to tie Vardon. Neither *The Scotsman* nor *The Golfing Annual* mentioned anything about that in its coverage, either. *The Annual* said simply that Willie missed 'an easy putt', while *The Scotsman* wrote that 'grand putter as he is, he failed at the critical moment.' Taylor's description of what happened is about the same as those news reports.

'Park missed tying by failing to hole a three-foot putt on the seventy-second green,' Taylor wrote, 'which only proved that Willie, despite his expertness with the putter, was as human as an ordinary golfer in a crisis. Directly the unbelievable had happened, the rumour was started that Park, thinking that he had the putt to win, deliberately missed in order to have the satisfaction of playing the tie off the following day, but this can safely be ascribed as coming from a few disappointed Scottish caddies and not emanating from other more serious sections of responsible Scottish thought.'

Hilton walked away from that Open as disappointed as Park. He knew he had thrown away a chance to claim a third crown at the Himalayas in the second round. 'This Championship,' he wrote, 'is the one event in my career which I have always grudged another man winning. It was lost by one silly mistake – a mistake absolutely the result of overconfidence – and whilst it taught me a lesson it was a lesson learnt at a very big cost.'

Alone on top

It was not so much Vardon's victory in the Open, but what unfolded the rest of that year and into 1899 that made it unequivocally clear that professionals now stood alone astride the game, with Harry as first among them.

The day after outlasting Park, Vardon walked across the street to Prestwick St Nicholas and won another tournament, his third victory in four tries that season. Four days later, he won again at Windermere, and six days after that he finished second in an event at Sheringham. Vardon remained on an absolute tear for the next six months, winning at Norbury, Carnoustie, Elie, County Down, Barton-on-Sea and Lytham and St Annes before that unforgettable year came to a close.

In 1899, Vardon picked up where he left off. He won twice more before finishing second at Royal Eastbourne six weeks before it would be time to defend his title in the Open. Over the previous 12 months, Vardon had played in 15 events, winning a dozen and finishing second in the other three. 'He went up and down the country winning tournaments and matches and trampling down his adversaries like some ruthless juggernaut,' wrote Darwin. 'Nobody could touch him.'

Golf had not seen a streak like that since 1872, when that precocious son of Old Tom Morris played in 11 events and won nine of them. Inevitably Vardon was compared with the greatest golfer the game had yet known. 'When he was in his prime, the question was constantly debated whether or not he was better than the now-almost mythical Young Tom Morris had been,' Darwin recalled.

Players who had watched Tommy play – among them Andra Kirkaldy, Leslie Balfour-Melville, Bob Ferguson and amateur William Doleman – were of the mind that golf would never see his equal. Players of Vardon's own time thought differently, Taylor among them. He declared as much in his memoir, published in 1943 after he had witnessed the brilliance of Bobby Jones, Walter Hagen, Gene Sarazen and others.

'Little did I guess when playing him at Ganton that I was playing a man who was to make golfing history and develop into – what is in my solemn and considered judgement – the finest and most finished golfer the game has ever produced,' Taylor wrote. 'I have seen and watched every player of eminence during the past 50 years and taking into account everything they have done I still hold that my opinion is sound, and I am willing to uphold it even if the world should be against me . . . Harry Vardon stands alone in all the glory that his performances testify.'

Park no doubt watched Vardon's miraculous streak with clenched teeth. Less than a month after The Man Who Could Putt missed that short one in the Open, he had publicly challenged Vardon to a match for £100 a side at Musselburgh and Ganton. Vardon was happy to play a match, but he refused to play at Musselburgh. He believed the course was too small for the crowds a match of that magnitude would attract, and he was all too aware of its reputation for misbehaviour by rowdy fans.

The negotiations dragged on for so long that The Golfer felt compelled to chide Vardon, suggesting that he was more interested in raking in cash than defending his crown as Champion Golfer. 'Vardon is not eager to accept challenges and would rather play in invitational open tournaments and exhibition matches,' the magazine wrote.

All along Vardon had said he would be happy to play the match at Ganton and North Berwick, and that is how the matter was eventually settled. North Berwick also was something of a home course for Park. In 1897, following his second marriage to Margaret Inglis – his first wife died in childbirth – Park had purchased a home near the first tee of the West Links, reportedly for the extravagant sum of £3,000. That was a testament to how successful a businessman Park had become.

The match was scheduled for July 1899, just after Vardon would defend his title in the Open. From the outset, it would be viewed as one of history's 'Great Matches', a contest destined to be talked and written about as long as golf is played. It would rival The Great Foursome of 1849 that pitted Old Tom Morris and Allan Robertson against Willie and Jamie Dunn of Musselburgh; the mid-century battles between Old Tom Morris and Willie Park Sr, and the two 1873 clashes at St Andrews between Young Tom and Davie Strath. Indeed, the entire 1899 golf season would be remembered as one unforgettable battle between the thistle and the rose.

Twelve

THE TRUE GAME

————————— •◑◐• —————————

The notion Willie Park set out to prove when he picked up his clubs again and challenged John Henry Taylor to a match – that Scots were superior at what they considered the only true game, man against man – would undergo its ultimate test in 1899, in both amateur and professional golf.

The idea gained currency in part because in the only major championship contested at match play, the Amateur, Scots had the upper hand on their southern rivals. Not only did Scots have more wins, they also had nearly twice as many runner-up finishes. That wasn't the only reason the notion caught favour. Vardon's victory parade in 1898, coupled with English domination of the Open, seemed to have settled the question of who was better at stroke play, the game on its way to becoming the dominant form of golf. Match play was the one hill Scots had left to defend.

Scots had long ago realised they were outnumbered. In 1894, when he was interviewed by *The Golfer*, the first question amateur John Laidlay had been asked, on behalf of his fellow Scots, was: 'Are we afraid of the English?' His answer was that the best Scottish golfers were every bit as good as the cream of England's crop. 'I think we can hold our own, if you don't take too many,' Laidlay said. 'If you put the four best Scotchmen against the four best Englishmen? Yes, I think we would hold our own very well.'

When pairings were announced for the 1899 Amateur Championship, they raised a tantalising possibility. If the early rounds unfolded as expected, the question of who was superior at the true game would undergo the finest trial the gentlemen's game had to offer. In the 36-hole final, England's John Ball would face off against Scotland's Freddie Tait.

Bernard Darwin, who was at Prestwick that year to compete in the Championship, remembered his reaction to seeing where Ball and Tait landed in the draw. 'These two players were clearly the match-playing champions of their respective countries,' he wrote, 'and when their names appeared in opposite halves of the draw, there was from the beginning and growing daily brighter the hope of their meeting.'

Given the enormous field of 101 players, each man would have to win six consecutive 18-hole matches if the dream final were to materialise, never a guarantee in such a volatile format. In the fifth round, both Ball and Tait would face formidable obstacles. Ball would play Robert Maxwell, the Tantallon star who had put him out at Muirfield two years before after five extra holes. Tait would meet Harold Hilton. The Scotsman knew no fear of Hilton, but even he had to wonder how long he could continue to dominate such a gifted player.

Coming up to the Championship, the Ayrshire coast had been pounded by rain that had flooded portions of the links, especially the Sahara bunker that guards the green on the 17th hole, the Alps. It was half-full of water a foot deep in places. The rain stopped before the Championship began on 23 May, but lowering skies suggested Prestwick had not seen the last of troublesome weather. Ball made short work of his opponents on opening day, never playing beyond the 15th. Tait was fighting a hook, but managed to close out both of his opponents by the 16th.

The weather took a decided turn for the worse on the second day, which dawned raw and gloomy, with a biting wind blowing from the north-east. Before noon it was raining heavily, and it kept coming down for most of the afternoon. Ball was not as sharp as he had been on the first day of competition. Harry Colt stuck doggedly to him through the turn, before Ball drew away 4 and 3. In his second match, he fell behind an unheralded opponent before running him down at 16.

Tait got off to a strong start in his morning round against Sidney Fry of Mid-Surrey. He seized a four-hole lead through nine and was still up by four as they teed off on 14. Fry, however, was no pushover. He took the next three holes by making one astonishing putt after another, and was only 1 down as the players prepared to hit their approach shots at 17. One of the world's great par fours, the Alps presents golfers with a question. Do you dare try to cross that giant dune and the yawning Sahara bunker with your second shot? It was especially risky on a day when a ball that failed to carry would likely find that waterlogged hazard. Fry demurred, laying up. Tait went for it, as *The Scotsman*'s correspondent watched in awe.

'His magnificent second stroke at the Alps, which was played with the greatest of ease and soared grandly over everything till it dropped within four feet of the hole, by which grand stroke the match was ended, will never be forgotten by those who had the pleasure of seeing it,' the newspaper wrote. In his afternoon match, Tait finally had an easy time of things, winning 5 and 4.

As fate would have it, the two big threats to Ball and Tait – Maxwell and Hilton – also survived their first four matches. By lunchtime the following afternoon, Darwin and everyone else at Prestwick would know whether the battle royal they had been waiting all week to see was still on the cards.

It was gloomy, though no rain was falling, when Maxwell and Ball teed off the next morning. Maxwell got off to a miserable start, slicing his first onto the railway line, pitching weakly at the second and failing to negotiate a stymie at the third. He would have been four down after four had Ball not missed a tiny putt on that hole. Maxwell looked to be going down easily until the two men reached the 15th, with Ball 3 up. There Maxwell laid a lovely pitch stone dead, winning the hole. He also took the 16th to make it a match again, 1 down with two to go.

Ball and Maxwell halved the dangerous 17th in beautiful fours, leaving everything to play for on the last. The match was there for Ball to take, as he faced an easy putt to put Maxwell away. Again he failed to get it down, handing his opponent the hole. Back the players went to that narrow first, with an enormous mass of humanity swarming around them. Maxwell unleashed a bomb from the tee this time, but it found a horrible lie. He managed to force the ball out, but couldn't stop it, and it scampered across the green. Down-the-middle Ball made a tidy four and avenged his defeat at Muirfield.

Hilton and his familiar nemesis, Tait, met next, but this time it was no walkover for the Scotsman. Tait sprayed his tee shots all over the course, hooking some and slicing others, but somehow he always found a playable lie. Hilton struck the ball beautifully, but was timid on the greens. Holes he ought to have won or halved were allowed to slip away.

Tait was 2 up as he and Hilton teed up on the Alps. Again Tait missed his drive badly, but his lie was another manageable one. The Scotsman was not as lucky on his attempt to carry the Alps, however. He topped the shot badly and needed two more to reach the green. Taking his cue, Hilton made a safe five to win the hole and take the match to 18. When he could do no better than a half there, Tait had beaten him again, 1 up.

This time, however, Hilton had no reason to hang his head. 'Mr Hilton was extremely unlucky to lose,' *The Golfing Annual* wrote, 'for he played more consistently than Mr Tait, but the latter's tee shots seemed guarded by a special providence, and never once was he punished for leaving the line.'

Both Ball and Tait dispensed with their afternoon opponents, as expected, though again the Scotsman had the tougher time. Ball played the front nine in 35, never lost a hole and sent his man packing at 11. Tait started nearly as well, with a 36 that gave him a 4-up lead over J.M. Williamson of Royal Musselburgh. Williamson, however, would not fold.

Tait's lead was down to 2 up as he and Williamson faced the long shot over the Alps. Tait carried the trouble and landed safely on the green. Williamson just missed, his ball deflecting off the sleepers that shored up the bunker and rebounding into water a foot deep. He had no choice but to wade in and hope for a miracle. In those days, there was no relief from 'casual water'. Taking the ball out of the puddle would have cost Williamson two strokes. He flailed away, making three unsuccessful attempts to extricate his ball, before giving up the hole and the match. Tait prevailed 3 and 1.

Nearly divine

Mother Nature finally cooperated for the finale all of Scotland and England were anxiously awaiting. 'The sun shone brightly and the weather was altogether in its happiest mood this morning when before a large crowd the young Lieutenant of the Black Watch stepped forward to the first tee to defend the Amateur Championship Cup against John Ball, jun.,' *The Scotsman* wrote.

Some 2,000 souls turned out to watch the international 'contest between giants'. Nearly every player who competed in the Championship was there, along with a host of golf luminaries, proud soldiers and the Sheriff of Glasgow. 'The variegated costumes of the ladies, who formed a considerable part of the crowd, and the bright scarlet and tartan of a contingent of the 4th Battalion Princess Louise's Regiment, from their encampment in the neighbourhood, gave a lively aspect to the scene,' the newspaper wrote.

A crowd that size, particularly for a match in which the rivalry was so intense, could be problematic at Prestwick, given how tight the course was. Fans tended to swarm around players as they took their shots and to run helter-skelter after balls as soon as they had been struck. That made it hard to clear a path for the man playing second. Prestwick was notorious for its lack of crowd control, mostly because officials there believed a gallery rope was unmanageable on such a hilly golf course.

A.R. Robertson, who handled arrangements for the Amateur, had a dozen stewards on hand to restrain the crowd. On the first tee, he implored the assembled masses not to hem the golfers in or distract them with sudden movements. Old Tom Morris, who was back in attendance, thought Robertson also should have admonished the crowd not to erupt in cheers when their man holed a crucial putt or pulled off a miraculous recovery. *The Scotsman* was similarly critical of Prestwick's efforts to rein in fans, a subject in which its reporter admitted a vested interest.

'Might it not be better on future occasions to do something more for the regulation of the crowd?' the newspaper asked. 'It is said that a rope cannot be used on this green as on others, owing to the nature of the ground. This is all nonsense. Were the officials to show a strong hand, and confine spectators within bounds, giving some special facilities for viewing each stroke to those who have to give an account of the tournament to the large outside world interested in the game, they would deserve and receive thanks instead of being blamed for a looseness in control over the crowd.'

The 'contest between giants' looked to be no contest at all during the morning round. When he wasn't duffing a chip, Ball was handing Tait holes by missing putts any child could make. He managed that four times in the first 18 holes. Tait played brilliantly to start, reaching the turn in 36 and taking a 4-up lead, but he stumbled home in a mediocre 43. All morning long, Ball's admirers from Hoylake had been dispatching telegrams to the faithful back home about how their hero was getting on. The first, sent at 11.50, bore grim news. 'Tait 5 up at 14th hole.' The second, at 12.30, was only modestly better. 'Tait 3 up at end of first round.'

The lunch hour between rounds ordinarily was a matter of little interest, but not that afternoon. Ball spent much of his break on the 18th green getting a putting lesson from Hilton. Practising on the course was legal in those days. Dedicated practice areas of the sort golfers enjoy now were all but non-existent. If players needed practice, they headed out with the offending club to some remote corner of the links.

Tait, meanwhile, was doing something he almost never did, at least according to his friend John Low. 'I remember him lying down on the sofa before he had finished his lunch on that final day, and complaining that he felt tired, a most unusual thing for him to do,' Low wrote. Perhaps all those hard-fought duels had taken a toll.

Ball rallied quickly that afternoon. Tait sliced his second shot on the opening hole onto the railway line, handing the Englishman the first. At the third, both cleared the cavernous Cardinal bunker with their second shots, but this time it was Ball who displayed the crisp short game and narrowed the Scotsman's lead to 1 up. The two men traded mistakes over the next three holes, but by the sixth the match was all square again. It remained that way as Ball and Tait approached the tenth tee, with all 2,000 fans lining the fairway to watch the most thrilling finish in Amateur Championship history.

Ball stumbled only once on the homeward nine, missing a short putt on 11 to hand Tait the lead again. The Scotsman gave it right back by hitting a massive hook from the 12th tee, and lost the 13th the same way. For the first time all afternoon, the resolute Englishman had the lead. Another telegram, time-stamped 3.42 p.m., was dispatched to Hoylake: 'Ball 1 up at 32nd hole, playing splendidly.'

He remained 1 up as they came to the dangerous Alps. Rain may have stayed away all afternoon, but the Sahara bunker that guards the green was still more than half full of water at least ankle deep. Prestwick fans knew that the place to watch the action on the Alps is not the fairway, which is tucked in a dell below the dune. The place to be is on the knolls around that famous bunker and green. They provide an ideal view of the all-important effort to carry the Alps and the Sahara. All 2,000 souls at Prestwick – including Darwin, Hilton, Old Tom and Jack Morris – swarmed around that green, stacked 20 deep in places, as Ball and Tait prepared to play their seconds.

Both men had hit their tee shots well enough to give it a go. Tait played first, and despite the gravity of the situation he must have felt supremely confident. Only two days before, on this very hole, he'd hit that never-to-be-forgotten shot to four feet. Fate wasn't as kind that afternoon. Tait didn't strike the ball squarely, and it splashed into the puddle filling most of the bunker. Ball's answer looked for all the world as if it would carry, but it, too, was short. It landed on the bank above the bunker and rolled inexorably back into the hard-packed sand below, narrowly avoiding the water.

Who knows what thoughts raced through Tait's mind as he crossed the Alps and saw his ball floating in the water. It was only yesterday that he'd watched as Williamson flailed helplessly away from nearly the same spot. Tait, however, was not one to fail in a crisis, as he'd demonstrated since he was a boy at Sedbergh. He was in the same position Williamson had been. If he could not get the ball out and at least halve the hole, his Championship would be over. His only thought would have been of slashing his ball onto the green come what may.

Ball's situation was no picnic either. His ball lay a foot or two from the front of the bunker. A conjurer's trick would be required to get it up quickly enough from that hard-packed sand to avoid ricocheting off the sleepers. As he waited for Tait to play, Ball stood on the stairway players used to climb out of that deep pit and onto the green. His caddie stood in the sand below him, not far from his man's ball.

Darwin was watching with a friend when Tait stepped into the water to play his shot, as his caddie stood silently by. 'I can still see Freddie's ball rocking on the little waves he made in the puddle as he waded in,' Darwin recalled. 'I can hear a Scottish friend next to me crying out in agony, "Wait till it settles, Freddie; wait till it settles." I don't think he had the least notion that he was speaking above a whisper. Yes, that was a day of heroic emotions.'

Hilton was watching, too, as Tait took a ferocious swipe at the floating ball. 'The shot out could barely have been improved upon,' he wrote. 'He ploughed it out onto the green, and oh, the wild shouts that arose! I shall never forget them.'

While Tait waded out, Ball walked down the steps to attempt his escape. Hilton considered the shot Ball faced every bit as daunting as Tait's. That was especially true because Ball was so old-fashioned that he refused to carry a niblick, which he referred to disdainfully as 'another bloody spade'. He made all his close-up approach shots, even one from a spot as treacherous as this, with a relatively straight-faced iron.

'Johnnie Ball had, in my opinion, quite as difficult, if not a more difficult, stroke to play,' Hilton wrote. 'It is far from easy to raise a ball that quickly from a hard surface; but he did surmount it, as very few men could have done. I do not think that many appreciate what a difficult shot it was.'

Ball and Tait ended up halving that hole. The gallant soldier would need another miracle on 18 to keep hope alive. Uncharacteristically, Ball pulled his drive to the final hole, while Tait was safely on the fairway.

That was the opening he needed. Tait knocked his second close and boldly rattled the putt into the back of the tin to win the hole and square matters up – 'cheer after cheer being raised in acknowledgement of his pluck in saving the match at this stage', *The Scotsman* reported.

The multitude gathered around the 18th hole made a wild scramble for the first tee as the two warriors wended their way through the crowd to resume their battle. Darwin noticed a few defections. 'At this point some of the Hoylake stalwarts could bear it no more and retired to the club-house, where they waited for news, presumably groaning dismally like Mr Winkle with their heads under the sofa cushions,' he wrote, referring to a favourite character from Charles Dickens's *Pickwick Papers*.

As he so often did in critical moments, Ball dug deep and delivered a mighty blow into the fairway, outdriving the long-swatting Tait by nearly 20 yards. Hilton was waiting on the green to see what fate awaited their approach shots. Tait played first.

'What an excellent shot it was, never off the pin,' Hilton remembered. 'I was standing on the hill to the left of the hole when the ball pitched, and I have always considered that it was not at all well treated, as it seemed to get a shooting fall, the ground just short of the hole being very hummocky.' The ball raced out nearly 30 feet past the hole.

'Johnnie Ball's approach was also *ruled* on the pin,' Hilton wrote. 'What would it do? Skid over the green like the other or pull up? We were not long in doubt, as from the very first bounce it was evident that it was not going to travel far, and it gently trickled on until it passed the hole by about seven feet.'

Tait made his usual bold bid, but the putt never had a chance. The most electrifying final in the history of the Amateur Championship would come down to whether Ball, who had struggled so mightily with his putter that day, could find the hole from seven feet.

'A man standing beside me remarked, "These are just the ones he misses,"' Hilton recalled. 'I thought to myself, no, these are just the kind he holes. Had it been three or four feet I should have been more anxious. From where we stood we could not see the outline of the hole, and it was impossible to tell whether the ball was going in or not, but I liked the look of the striker as the ball was travelling. I knew his attitudes well, and was not at all surprised when the ball disappeared. I have seen some excitement at championship meetings, but never anything quite equal to that at Prestwick in 1899.'

The final telegram could now be dispatched to Hoylake, no doubt setting off a raucous party in that swanky clubhouse: 'Ball won at 37th hole, did hole in 3.' Even the Scotsmen in the crowd, heartbroken as they must have been to see their national hero vanquished, roared their approval of that hard-fought match. Rarely had there been a more exquisite display of the true Scottish game. Ball's fans swarmed the green, hoisted him onto their shoulders, and carried him in triumph to the clubhouse.

Darwin was still eight years from tossing off his barrister's wig and starting his career as a golf writer, a journey he would continue through the eras of Bobby Jones and Ben Hogan and nearly up to the debut of Arnold Palmer. Until his last day Darwin would insist he had never seen any match to rival the one that unfolded that afternoon at Prestwick.

'One must be allowed to be a little obstinate about the gods of one's youth,' he wrote, 'and I shall always maintain that this was the greatest golf match I ever saw, not by any means the most perfect in play, but the most nearly divine in terms of god-like thrusts by either side.'

Bitterly disappointed as he must have been, Tait was the picture of grace at the prize ceremony. He and Ball, while the fiercest of rivals, were also the best of friends. Later that summer they would room together, along with John Low, in the home of fellow amateur C.G. Broadwood near Ganton Golf Club while taking in the second half of the much-anticipated match between Harry Vardon and Willie Park Jr.

Tait admired Ball because he was, as far as any Englishman could be, a devotee of the old Scottish ways. Since he was a boy watching Young Tom Morris at Hoylake, Ball had been steeped in the ancient traditions by his connections to the Morris family and St Andrews. As a golfer, Tait could also appreciate that no player in history had accomplished as much as Ball had in the wake of that victory – five times the Amateur Champion and one of only two gentlemen golfers to win an Open. Later that season, Ball would add another Irish Amateur to his résumé, his third in seven years, while Tait would claim another St George's Vase, his third in the past four years.

When Ball was presented with the Amateur Championship trophy, Tait told the crowd, 'I would rather be beaten by Johnny Ball than any other man alive.' Ball was too shy to say so himself, but no doubt the feeling was mutual. Hoylake commemorated Ball's victory by raising £300 from members to commission the portrait of their hero that still adorns the clubhouse, along with the turret clock that to this day watches over players approaching the first tee at Royal Liverpool. Ball himself was given a gold watch.

The Great Match

It was not simply the exhilaration of that Amateur final or the eager anticipation of the Park–Vardon duel that put the 1899 Open in the rare position of being the year's least exciting major event. By then, Vardon had proven himself all but unconquerable in a stroke-play competition.

The only surprise was that a record field of 98 players bothered to turn up at Sandwich on 7 June to take Vardon on. Among them was Ted Ray, a newcomer from Jersey who would one day play a leading role in Vardon's story. In gloriously sunny weather, marred only by the stiff breeze that always seems to blow along Pegwell Bay, the tournament unfolded precisely as expected. Vardon set the pace and drew away from the field as easily as he pleased. He required just 310 strokes and won by five. Three of his four rounds were in the 70s, as most of the field was mired in the 80s. Twice Vardon began rounds with absurdly low scores on the outward nine, one of 33 and another of 34.

'Vardon's win was the easiest of recent years, and we are not alone in thinking that he could have won by more had he chosen,' *The Golfing Annual* marvelled. 'In the inward halves of his second and third rounds, he palpably "sat on" the lead he had established by his marvellous outgoing. The depths of this great golfer's capabilities have yet to be fathomed.' Vardon's winning score was 16 strokes lower than the one Taylor posted to win his first Championship at St George's just five years earlier.

There was some consolation for Scots in the outcome, as Jack White finished second, with Andra Kirkaldy third and Willie Fernie and James Braid tied for fifth behind Taylor. The two relatively new names in that line-up, White and Braid, gave hope of future glories. Braid especially had shown the same promise that so impressed fans in 1897 at Hoylake, beginning with two rounds of 78 before falling away in the later stages.

As Hilton had expected long ago, amateurs were left far behind. 'The result of the Championship was a triumph for England, but it was even a greater triumph for professionalism,' the newly christened *Golf Illustrated* wrote in its inaugural issue. 'The amateurs were not in it.'

The best among them, Tait, trailed by 14 strokes. In the years remaining before the Great War, gentlemen would present a serious threat on only four other occasions. Hilton would come close twice – agonisingly so in 1911 – while Tantallon's Robert Maxwell and Hoylake's John Graham each would challenge once.

Willie Park could not have come away from that Championship feeling bullish about his upcoming clash with the game's newest megastar. Like Braid, Park hung close to Vardon on the first day, finishing just four strokes back. He collapsed completely in the final two rounds, however, and was a full 21 strokes behind the leader when he finally stumbled home in 89 to finish.

Park's loss did nothing to diminish the enthusiasm of *Golf Illustrated* editor Garden Smith, himself a Scotsman and an unabashed supporter of the hero of Musselburgh. 'He is still the Achilles of Scottish golfers, and the brilliant young Jersey Hector will find Willie a very different nut to crack in a hand-to-hand-fight,' the magazine predicted.

In the three weeks between the Open and the Great Match with Park, Vardon did something he hadn't done in quite some time. He rested. He was keenly aware, as he wrote years later, that this would be 'one of the most important events of my life'.

No one reading golf coverage in 1899 would have disagreed. 'As a sporting event it created a partisan fervour and excitement which can be compared today only with the furore occasioned by a modern prize fight,' wrote the amateur Robert Harris. 'National feelings were aroused. Vardon had just arrived and was not as yet realised by the Scots. He was regarded as just an upstart interloper in Scotland's own game.'

While there may have been tension between the Vardon and Park camps during negotiations for the Great Match, the two respected one another in the same way Ball and Tait did. Park was the first to stop by and congratulate Vardon on his third Open win. It had always been that way, even in the most intense of rivalries. Park's father was fond of saying that he liked golf best when he played against his fiercest foe, Old Tom Morris.

The crowd that poured onto North Berwick on 12 July to witness the first leg of this ultimate test of the true Scottish game was unlike anything golf had ever seen. Some 8,000 fans swarmed the West Links, many arriving on special trains added for the occasion. Had the Prince of Wales not been visiting Edinburgh that same day, several thousand more might have turned out.

North Berwick, however, did a far better job than Prestwick in controlling that sea of humanity. When the match was over, neither Vardon nor Park had a bad word to say about the behaviour of the crowd. 'All of golfing Scotland appeared to have turned out to witness the contest,' Vardon wrote. 'Large as this crowd was, it was perfectly managed and never in any way interfered with the play of a single stroke of either my opponent or myself.'

The crowd was so enormous that officials realised fans would have trouble seeing the action unfold and figuring out which player had prevailed on a hole. They employed an ingenious system for spreading the word – holding aloft a red flag with a 'V' on it if Vardon won, a white one with a 'P' if Park prevailed, and both flags if the hole was halved. They also had gallery ropes stretched hundreds of yards along on both sides of the fairway to keep the masses at bay.

Park turned out for the match as if he intended to be the white knight coming to Scotland's rescue. He was dressed from head to toe in white – cap, shirt, jacket, slacks and shoes, offset only by a striped tie. As always, his bag was carried by the legendary Fiery, his sunburned, rugged face topped by his ever-present Scotch bonnet. Vardon wore his usual subdued Norfolk jacket, knickerbockers and flat cap. The one sign that he considered this an important occasion was that he had his younger brother, Tom, as his caddie. C.G. Broadwood served as Vardon's referee, while Tait did that job for Park.

The night before the match, Vardon nearly had an unfortunate accident. He and his brother were taking a walk when, suddenly, an iron horseshoe sailed over their heads and nearly hit Tom. It had been thrown by the most famous caddie in North Berwick, a giant with a booming voice named Big Crawford, who regularly carried for professional golfer Ben Sayers and politician A.J. Balfour. 'He explained that he was tossing the horseshoe over my head for luck, as he had backed me to win with every penny he possessed,' Vardon recalled. At least one Scotsman was prepared to concede that the reigning Open champion was the game's best.

The fans who turned out in such great numbers were treated to a dogfight featuring a classic clash of styles. The weather could not have been more glorious. It was cool, sunny and clear, with a slight easterly breeze, as Park struck the opening tee shot at Point Garry Out. From that first hole, it was clear that he could not keep pace with the relentless perfection of Vardon's ball-striking. Even Vardon, however, had to admit that Park's play demonstrated the proof of his maxim, 'The man who can putt is a match for anyone.'

'Although I was more accurate in the long game than my opponent, he splendidly upheld the reputation which he had earned for himself as a magnificent putter,' Vardon wrote. 'Time after time, when I appeared certain to gain the lead, his splendid holing-out saved him.'

The first ten holes were halved, both men finishing the outward nine in an excellent 38. First blood was not drawn until the 11th, and only then because of a rub of the green. Park still had the honour and hit his tee shot straight down the fairway. Vardon followed, but his shot landed on top of Park's ball, knocking it forward as his own ball deflected into a nasty lie. Vardon couldn't do enough with his second, and the white 'P' flag was raised as Park took the first lead in the match.

Vardon squared things up two holes later at The Pit, a classically Scottish par four. Its tiny green sits tucked behind one of the ancient stone dykes that add such charm to a round at North Berwick, along with spectacular views of the gargantuan Bass Rock in the distance. Vardon got his nose in front for the first time with a three at 15, the fearsome, oft-copied hole known as the Redan. He appeared poised to see the red 'V' flag raised again at 16, as his third landed on the green and Park's shot ran onto the beach.

When Park reached his ball, he made an unpleasant discovery. The only way he could hit a shot to the green was to play left-handed. He carried a left-handed iron for exactly that situation. Fiery was ready with the club, Park took it, and calmly knocked the shot onto the green – a miracle Vardon described as 'one of the finest strokes which I have ever seen'.

Adding insult to injury, Park holed his lengthy putt. Vardon had been a bit weak on the greens all morning, or his lead would have been larger. He took three putts this time to hand Park the hole. The Scotsman took the home hole, too, and had the satisfaction of heading into lunch 1 up.

The afternoon round began far differently than the morning had, with its long procession of halves. Vardon came out with a flourish and squared the match on the first. Park grabbed the lead back on the second, and Vardon promptly tied things up again by claiming the third. It was only then that the procession of halves began, bringing the combatants to the ninth hole with honours even and everything on the line.

Vardon could be forgiven if he thought he was about to see Park crack when, for the first time all afternoon, he took two holes in succession, the ninth and tenth, to seize a 2-up lead with eight to play. 'Park at this stage proved beyond any shadow of doubt what a fine match player he was,' Vardon admitted. 'Just when I thought I was in a secure position, he promptly dashed any hopes I had entertained of piling up a commanding lead by winning the next two holes from me.' While he admired Park's pluck, Vardon was not about to concede that the Scotsman was better at hand-to-hand combat.

'As if to prove that I too was a good match player, I followed up the loss of these two holes by winning the 15th and 16th to regain my advantage of two,' Vardon recalled. 'At the 18th I had a splendid opportunity to increase my lead to three, my putt for a win stopping on the very lip of the hole. A half in four was the result, and at the close of a memorable day's play, with the crowd cheering heartily, I was leading by two holes. It was a great match in every way.'

T.D. Miller, who wrote an essay about the match for *The Golfing Annual*, disagreed. 'It was not a first-class exhibition after all,' he said. 'From the first, indeed, it was seen that Vardon had the best of the game, for Park over and over again saved the half only by the consistent accuracy of his putting. He was called repeatedly to give the long odds, and while Vardon on several occasions failed to do himself justice, even to the foozling of putts, the local man was not able to seize the grand opportunity.'

Miller also dismissed the notion that Vardon was the Golfer of the Century: 'We cannot help, after the North Berwick display, calling to mind the St Andrews lad, whose career was cut short on Christmas Day of 1875, when he had seen but a couple of dozen summers, and who, in his time, played many big matches with exceptional success, whose powers were only called out in a higher degree the keener the contest, and who could have holed out with any player of more recent times. He is known in the annals of golf as "Young Tommy".' Scotland still loved its once-and-forever King of Clubs.

Golf Illustrated was thinking along similar lines. It was not prepared to acknowledge that Vardon's torrid streak of professional victories had established him as the greatest golfer of all time – a conclusion the magazine described as 'an exaggeration'. The magazine confidently wrote that 'a more dispassionate view of the present state of the Park–Vardon match has brought about considerable change in the attitude amongst Vardon's supporters. They begin to see that if Park drives, and above all approaches more in his best form, that Vardon will have his work cut out for him.'

Stunned and dumbfounded

Gordon Smith may have remained confident in Park, but losing to Vardon on his home green in front of a massive Scottish crowd seemed to have taken the starch out of the son of Musselburgh. That was evident when Park showed up ten days later for the second half of the match at Ganton. In his practice rounds, he looked nothing like the golfer who had battled so pluckily at North Berwick. He was far off form, hooking shots wildly on a course that would require his best.

Lest anyone had lost sight of the reality that this was a battle between England and Scotland, Ganton's rustic front gate bore a visible reminder. On the day of the match, one post was adorned with roses, the other with thistles. The crowd that assembled to watch the match was far smaller than the one that had swarmed North Berwick, numbering 2,000 or less.

Vardon came into that finale brimming with confidence. He knew that the back tees at his home course called for shots that soared high and carried a long way, exactly the sort of shot Park could not pull off. Like many old Scotsmen, he played a low-flying hook that compensated for his lack of power by allowing the ball to run when it landed. That would not do at Ganton, especially on the first three holes.

Vardon could not have been more prescient. Park failed to carry the hazards on all of those holes. Vardon pocketed two of them, and Park quickly found himself four down. By the seventh, Vardon was leading by six holes. From there it was a grim slog for Park and his admirers. Vardon humiliated that famous Scotsman, finishing him off on the eighth hole of the second round when he went 11 up with just ten holes left to play.

Even at the true game, a Great Match over two greens, Park could not compete. He never again issued his 'Challenge to the World'. The blow to his psyche was so severe that two decades later, when he wrote *The Art of Putting*, he explained away the loss in a way even his admirers knew was disingenuous. 'In the second half at Ganton, I took little interest,' Park wrote. 'No great stake match had ever been played prior to that time beyond the sound of the sea. Ganton was a moderate English inland links and local knowledge was invaluable. I only took a few days' practice for the final section and, developing a hook, I lost.'

Golf Illustrated seemed crestfallen. 'The big match between Park and Vardon came to a most lame and impotent conclusion,' the magazine wrote, describing the final as 'devoid of any interest or excitement from start to finish'. Park told editor Garden Smith afterwards that he had no chance with Vardon driving so powerfully. Robert Harris, the amateur from Carnoustie, described the loss as a crushing blow for his countrymen. 'Scotland was stunned and dumbfounded but stirred to great appreciation of a new young player of astonishing performance,' he wrote.

Vardon ended his season in style at Portmarnock in Ireland, competing in a tournament that featured a qualifying round at stroke play, followed by knockout matches to determine the winner. He won the qualifier by three, then torched the field, in the process lowering Portmarnock's course record to 70. In the 36-hole final, Vardon gave Taylor another pasting, closing him out with nine holes left as he again lowered the course record to 69.

Since that second-place finish at Hastings and St Leonards back in May 1898, Vardon had played in 17 tournaments, winning 14 and finishing second in the other three. That streak and his dismantling of Park left golf writers struggling for analogies capable of describing such invincibility. Harry Everard went furthest, declaring Vardon the 'Napoleon of the game'.

As if to prove he was equally dominant at the true game of match play, Vardon spent that summer and autumn on an exhibition tour of the nation, with a swing through Scotland to meet its leading professionals and amateurs in hand-to-hand combat. He trounced Willie Fernie at Troon; defeated A.H. Scott at Elie; whipped James Kinnell at Leven; Ben Sayers at New Luffness, and Joseph Dalgleish at Nairn. His only loss came at St Andrews, when he took on the best ball of Amateur Championship winners John Laidlay and Leslie Balfour-Melville. They prevailed, 2 and 1.

Vardon had now reached a level of fame surpassed only by one athlete in Britain – the grizzly-bearded lord of cricket W.G. Grace, a man revered in every corner of the kingdom. Golf manufacturers naturally sought to capitalise on the Vardon phenomenon. In 1899, A.G. Spalding & Bros. introduced the Vardon Flyer, a bramble-patterned gutty it heralded as 'the longest flying ball in the market'. Vardon was already raking in cash from exhibitions before Spalding offered him a chance to hit the jackpot.

Spalding was keen to market its Vardon Flyer, along with a line of clubs bearing the champion's name, in the United States, where the game was growing at a pace that would quickly eclipse the English golf boom. The company offered Vardon an exhibition tour of the nation that would last nearly all of 1900, with a break to return home and defend his Open title at St Andrews. Excited to see a new land, Vardon readily accepted. He spent the rest of the year making preparations to sail for the new world come January.

Back in June, while Vardon was racing to this third Open victory, unsettling news filtered into the country from South Africa, where Britain was still angling to seize diamond and gold mines in the Orange Free State and South African Republic, better known as the Transvaal. Boers controlled the mines, but had neither the technology nor manpower to capitalise on those resources. They reluctantly admitted immigrants – uitlanders, they called them – to help. The vast majority were British. Before long, there were so many uitlanders that the Boers were outnumbered.

In the wake of the bungled Jameson Raid, when uitlanders failed to rise up against the Boers, Britain tried a new strategy for gaining control of the mines. They sought full voting rights for uitlanders. Negotiations towards that end broke down just as Vardon was cruising to his third Open Championship. The Boers knew that if they relented they would lose control of their two states. Come September British Colonial Secretary Joseph Chamberlain issued an ultimatum: full voting rights or else. The following month, on 11 October, the Boers declared war.

The moment Freddie Tait sensed that war might be on the horizon, he began scrambling to get himself to the front. In May 1898, Tait had accepted a staff position as Inspector of Gymnasia, overseeing the training of British troops. Those billets were much sought after. Only the strongest, fittest soldiers – men like Tait – could get them. By July of 1899, however, he was asking to return to his regiment if fighting broke out in South Africa. He explained as much in a letter to his brother, Jack.

> I have just applied to be allowed to go out to the Transvaal in the event of my regiment being sent on active service. I think business is meant this time. This billet of mine suits me fine, but I don't want to miss a chance of active service. I suppose we shall see you early next year. Strive, etc.
>
> Yours ever,
> F.G. Tait.

By mid-October, Tait's wish had been granted. He returned to the Black Watch at Aldershot where he made ready to sail for South Africa on a steamer known as the *Orient*. One sad note amid all the anticipation was that Nails had to be sent home to Edinburgh. Tait would write home often from the battlefront to ask how Nails was getting along. His faithful terrier 'wrote' back, addressing his letters 'Dear Father'. On 24 October, Tait and his regiment left Tilbury Docks, south-east of London, and headed towards the fighting that had already broken out in the Transvaal.

John Ball was nine years older than Tait, but even as he approached his 38th birthday, the Englishman also was making plans to join the fighting in South Africa. Like most Victorians, Ball believed in the supremacy of the British Empire and stood ready to do his part. He enlisted in the Denbighshire Yeomanry. Ball's friends at Hoylake, Lytham and Leasowe subscribed to prepare him for battle, purchasing a charger, a Mauser pistol and field glasses for Ball to take with him to the Transvaal.

Just before Tait set sail, he and Ball had one final game together – a 36-hole match over the links at Lytham and St Annes. It was a hard-fought battle reminiscent of their glorious duel at Prestwick. Hilton was there to watch and provide an account to *Golf Illustrated*. The first 18 holes were halved. In the final round, Tait narrowly avenged his defeat in the Amateur, winning by a single hole.

Brothers in amateur golf, and soon to be in arms, neither Tait nor Ball knew, as they shook hands on the 18th at St Annes, that it would be the last time those two grand champions ever met.

Thirteen

HEARTACHE AND TRIUMPH

———————— •●◍●• ————————

Freddie Tait celebrated New Year's Eve on a cruise from Simon's Bay to Cape Town aboard the HMS *Niobe*, having just recovered from a battlefield wound. Harry Vardon was looking forward to his grand adventure in America, while John Ball was wrapping up his training at Aldershot. By early February he, too, would be sailing for South Africa.

The rest of the golf world greeted the new year with a sense of foreboding. It wasn't simply because every star who had made 1899 riveting was away and the coming season promised to be a desultory one. It was because so many days brought grim news of casualties in the South African War, many of them well-known figures in the game.

'A correspondent likens the consternation in Edinburgh over the recent losses of Scottish regiments to the state of Edinburgh after Flodden,' *Golf Illustrated* wrote.

Three days before Christmas, for instance, the magazine reported that Tait had been shot in his left thigh earlier that month during an ill-planned attack on Boer positions at Magersfontein. 'We had all dreaded it, for the gallant Highland Brigade has always had the post of honour and danger in these assaults, and Mr Tait is not the breed of man to shirk his work,' *Golf Illustrated* wrote.

Thankfully, Tait made a full recovery before the year was out and was fit enough to enjoy that holiday cruise before heading back to the battlefield. While he was recuperating, Tait wrote regularly to his mother, explaining in his letters what had happened at Magersfontein. In the dark of night, he and his men came under heavy fire from all sides when they discovered that the Boers had dug in far closer than they expected.

'Our brigade was simply thrown away,' Tait lamented. 'Hundreds of splendid fellows were killed and wounded and nothing gained in the end.' As he often did, Tait ended that letter by asking about his terrier. 'How is "Nails"? Give him plenty of food.'

By 11 January, his 30th birthday, Tait was ready to return to his regiment. He spent the day aboard a train headed for the Modder River, where the Black Watch was encamped, preparing to relieve a siege at Kimberley. Three weeks later, he and his men headed for Koodoosberg Drift. There, on the afternoon of 4 February, Tait would lead Company H in an assault on Boer positions. He snatched a few moments that morning to write home, letting his mother know he had arrived safely.

'The Boers seem to be in considerable force here as they have attacked us the last three days,' he wrote. 'Today they are making a more determined attack, but they have not attacked our section of the outpost line yet. We expect to be sent off to reinforce at any moment. No more time. I have to post this today to catch next Tuesday's mail. Yours affectionately, F.G. Tait.'

Tait and his men again came under heavy fire as they approached the Boer line. One of the men, Private Scott, later explained what unfolded. 'I got down beside our officer, Lieutenant Tait, on his right hand,' Scott recalled. 'He said, "Now, men, we will fight them at their own game." That meant that each man was to get behind a rock, and just pop up to fire and then down again.'

For half an hour, Company H gave as good as it got, until suddenly the Boers stopped firing. Tait and his men took advantage of the lull in the action to grab a bite. Tait shared his meal with Private Scott and another soldier, who had nothing of their own to eat. Soon afterwards, the lieutenant decided it was time for Company H to press ahead. 'I think we will advance another 50 yards, and perhaps we will be able to see them better, and be able to give it to them hot,' Tait told Private Scott and the others.

'We all got ready again,' the private said, 'and Lieutenant Tait shouted, "Now, boys!" We were after him like hares. The Boers had seen us, and they gave us a hot time of it. But on we went. Just as our officer shouted to get down, he was shot. I was just two yards behind him. He cried out, "Oh! They have done for me this time." I cried up to him, "Where are you shot, sir?" and he said, "I don't know." He had been shot through the heart and never spoke again.'

At about six o'clock, the Boers retreated into the woods. Tait's men spent the next few hours at the grim task of carrying the dead and wounded down the hill. The next morning, Tait was buried in a shady spot along the Reit River, a crude wooden cross with his name carved on it marking the spot. Only a day earlier, he and a fellow officer, T. Mowbray Berkeley, had bathed there together, when Tait 'was just like a school boy, larking in the water, and so thoroughly enjoying it'.

Eight days after his death, on Monday 12 February, Mowbray Berkeley sent a box of Tait's personal effects to his father. It contained, among other things, the soldier's watch, diary, knife, cufflinks, chequebook, pipe and tobacco pouch. The most poignant item was a letter from Nails. It was addressed 'Dear Father' and reassured Tait that he was fit and getting plenty to eat. The letter had been in Tait's breast pocket when he was shot through the heart.

On that same Monday morning, rumours of Tait's death first began to circulate back home, based on a telegram to London from a *Morning Post* reporter. No one wanted to believe it, *The Golfing Annual* recalled. '"Freddie Tait dead? It can't be possible. It would surely have been reported through the War Office along with the other Koodoosberg casualties." These were the remarks heard on every hand.'

Two agonising days passed with no official word, and 'hope sprang in every breast', *The Annual* wrote. 'But, alas! It was too true.' On 14 February, Professor Tait received a telegram from Wynberg Hospital. 'Freddie killed instantly,' it reported, a truth soon confirmed by the War Office.

'It is impossible to describe the universal feeling of sorrow which the intimation of Tait's death brought to the whole of Scotland, and to many who knew him elsewhere,' wrote John Low, who immediately began work on a biography of the soldier and golfer. 'But one name was on everyone's lips, but one thought in the hearts of all who knew him.' Scottish golf had not seen so dark a day since Christmas morning 1875, when Young Tom Morris was found dead in bed at his home in St Andrews.

Sadly missed

Three months passed between that fateful day and the Amateur Championship, conducted in mid-May at St George's. Having two of the game's brightest stars missing cast a pall over the tournament. 'Poor Tait, who won so brilliantly at Sandwich is no more, and Ball, also a Sandwich winner, is far away, and their absence will be sadly felt by competitors and spectators alike,' *Golf Illustrated* wrote.

Sixty-eight players turned out to compete at St George's. With Tait gone, Scotland desperately needed a new hero to carry its banner, especially given that stalwarts like John Laidlay, Leslie Balfour-Melville and Mure Fergusson were past their primes. All eyes focused on Robert Maxwell, of Tantallon Golf Club. In the St George's Vase, which preceded the Amateur, he put on an exhibition reminiscent of the nation's fallen hero. A long driver like Tait, Maxwell conquered Sandwich with equal aplomb, going around in 77 and 78 to tie the tournament record Tait had set the previous year.

The English contingent, of course, was hopeful that Harold Hilton would, at last, realise the ambition of a lifetime, while the Oxford and Cambridge Golfing Society had every reason to be enthusiastic about its leading light, young Joseph Bramston.

Now 31 years old, Hilton recognised he was 'arriving at an age when my game could hardly be expected to improve'. He also knew he would never have a better opportunity. This time he would not have to compete against the two best match players in Championship history. Ball had set sail for South Africa in early February, and would have heard of his friend Tait's death while en route to join the fighting in the Transvaal.

Hilton had good memories of Sandwich, having reached the final both times the Championship had been played there. Still, he did not exactly get a confidence boost from the St George's Vase. 'I made the most awful start in this event through sheer nervousness, as for the first few holes I could not hit the ball when near the hole,' he remembered. 'On the very first green, I took four to hole out.' Hilton eventually pulled himself together, playing well in the second round and finishing six shots behind Maxwell.

Still, Hilton knew that a repeat of his nervous start in the Amateur 'would, for a certainty, cause me to say goodbye to Championship honours at a very early date'. His anxiety was hardly eased when the draw revealed that, if all went well, he would face Maxwell in the third round. It would be only the second game for both men, as they received byes in the opening round. Hilton hadn't forgotten the way Maxwell had mauled him in 1897 at Muirfield, immediately after outlasting Ball in that five-hole play-off.

Hilton must have taken some comfort from the way he dismantled his second-round opponent, winning 8 and 7 in fierce wind and driving rain. Maxwell made equally short work of his man, cruising 6 and 4. That set up another clash between north and south, one many believed would settle the Championship before it was half over.

'I candidly acknowledge that I started feeling very nervous,' wrote Hilton, who had heard that Maxwell was driving the ball a fearsomely long way. 'I had a practical confirmation of this rumour at the very first hole,' he said. 'I hit a fair ball, but I found myself 60 or 70 yards behind, and, although this did not happen often, I generally found myself having to play the odd [shot] from some considerable distance behind.'

Maxwell took the early lead, going 1 up over the first three holes, but Hilton quickly settled down to his best game. By the seventh, the Englishman had seized a three-hole lead, and he never looked back. Maxwell struggled with his short game all morning, and Hilton finished him off on the 15th. That provided the jolt of confidence he needed. For the rest of the Championship Hilton showed no mercy, vanquishing every man he faced with consummate ease.

In the semi-final, he met fellow Hoylake star John Graham, who was expected to give Hilton more trouble than he'd faced thus far. Any hope of that happening was dashed at the second hole. Playing his approach into a headwind, Hilton hit a brassie, knowing it would take everything he had to clear a bunker guarding the green. The ball sailed on a rope for the flag, landing safely, although neither player could see where it stopped. Having sliced his tee shot, Graham had to play short and chip on with his third. When he and Hilton walked onto the green, only one ball could be seen, Graham's.

'I couldn't make it out, and was looking about in bewilderment when a reporter some 50 yards away called out something,' Hilton recalled. 'I couldn't exactly catch what he said, but one of the spectators did, as he remarked, "He says it's in the hole," and sure enough it was.' That shot effectively finished Graham. He never found his footing and Hilton sent him packing on the 13th green, winning 7 and 5.

Everyone at Sandwich expected that in the final Hilton would meet the rising English star, Bramston. Earlier that season, in a match at Royal North Devon, Bramston had taken out Hilton, John Low, Horace Hutchinson and Humphrey Ellis, all first-class golfers. He followed that up by finishing second in the St George's Vase and cruising into the semi-finals of the Amateur, his closest match along the way being a 4 and 2 victory. Bramston was heavily favoured in his semi-final match against James Robb of St Andrews.

Robb, however, stuck to his man doggedly. Bramston outplayed the Scotsman through the green, but over and over Robb saved himself with miraculous putts. That, apparently, was enough to make Bramston crack. It happened just as Hilton caught up with the match to size up his next opponent. A spectator filled Hilton in on the way Robb had been making one narrow escape after another.

'Whether these repeated recoveries on the part of the Scotsman had by degrees had an effect upon the temperament of his opponent is a question which could only be settled by the latter himself,' Hilton wrote, 'but I have seldom seen a man break down in a more complete fashion than Bramston did that afternoon at Sandwich.'

Bramston flailed mindlessly away in bunkers and knocked a ball carelessly into the water, seemingly unconcerned about the outcome of the match. It was obvious to everyone watching that Bramston had given up. 'It seemed impossible to believe that a man who had been playing with such sublime confidence would go to pieces so utterly,' Hilton marvelled, although it is worth noting that Bramston was only 19 years old.

Robb's putter had cooled off considerably by the time he and Hilton teed it up the following day. Without that weapon, he was no match for a player of Hilton's calibre. The English star turned out for the final wearing a sporty white jacket and white shoes accented by light-coloured knickerbockers. He gave Robb a thrashing as thorough as the one Hilton himself had received four years ago on this very green from the much-lamented Lieutenant Tait. Hilton won by precisely the same score, finishing Robb off 8 and 7.

'Needless to say his victory was very popular,' *The Annual* wrote, 'and he spoke from the very bottom of his heart when, in acknowledging the presentation of the Championship Cup and Gold Medal . . . he said that he had at last attained the height of his ambition.'

Even a dyed-in-the-wool St Andrews man like John Low could not help but applaud the Englishman's performance. 'Nothing could have been more satisfactory than the result of the Sandwich meeting,' he wrote, 'for the Amateur Championship has been won by probably the most scientific golfer, amateur or professional, who has ever played the royal and ancient game.'

Coming into Sandwich, Hilton had begun to wonder if his day as Amateur champion would ever come. 'I had struggled for it for 12 years, and in each succeeding year, it seemed to be going farther and farther away from me,' he wrote. 'I cannot say, even after the many failures that had been my lot, that I had yet arrived at a state of despair. Still, I knew well that every year I approached the competition with a gradually increasing feeling of anxiety, and I was beginning to realise that it would have been well had fate been a little more kind to me in 1891, when Laidlay beat me at the twentieth hole.'

Title defence

Three days before Hilton teed off at Sandwich, Harry Vardon pulled into Liverpool harbour aboard the RMS *Luciana*, taking a break from his grand tour of America to defend his title in the Open at St Andrews.

Vardon had been in the US for nearly four months. He had arrived on 3 February, just days before golfers across Britain were plunged into mourning by news of Tait's death. Since then Vardon had been travelling up and down the east coast of the States, playing one exhibition match after another before enormous, enthusiastic crowds, often over courses so rugged they were barely recognisable as golfing greens.

Before returning home, Vardon had competed in 32 matches, winning 28 of them. He lost only once playing man to man, going down 5 and 4 to an English expatriate named Bernard Nicholls. Vardon's other losses came in matches where he competed against the best ball of at least two golfers. Throughout the tour, he regularly posted eye-popping scores, often course records, including a phenomenal 69 at Allegheny Country Club in Pittsburgh. Americans loved him, especially Vardon's booming drives.

'When it is remembered that the gutty ball was in use at this period, the scores which I compiled must rank as some of the best performances during my career,' Vardon wrote.

Still, he wasn't brimming with confidence about his prospects at St Andrews. Succeeding on those rustic American courses had required him to adopt different methods than he used back home. He was concerned that he might not readjust to links golf quickly enough. Vardon also had been playing non-stop for months, often in searing heat, with gruelling travel between stops. He wasn't sure how he would recover from all those road trips and reacclimatise to chilly, Scottish weather.

Obstacles aside, Vardon desperately wanted another Open victory. 'I was particularly keen to win this Championship, as I had won the two previous ones and was anxious to make it three in a row.' He knew full well that three consecutive wins would make him the first southerner to enter the pantheon alongside Young Tom Morris, Jamie Anderson and Bob Ferguson.

John Henry Taylor, who had recently moved to a new job as professional at Mid-Surrey in Richmond, also came into that Open hungry for another Claret Jug. Vardon's win in 1899 had given him three victories to Taylor's two, and it was time to square accounts. Taylor had one advantage over his rival. He had played far better at St Andrews, a course Vardon never mastered. 'Remembering my success there five years previously, I had hopes that history might repeat itself,' Taylor wrote.

The Championship drew a field of 80 to the Auld Grey Toon in the first week of June. It would be played for the biggest purse in history – £125, with the winner's share rising to £50. Payouts had been increased in the wake of unrest at the previous year's Open. Players had circulated a petition demanding a higher purse. Word spread that they would strike if it wasn't forthcoming. That rumour turned out to be false, of course. Still, players eventually got a rise, although not nearly as much as they wanted.

The weather for the first day of the Championship was ideal for golf, overcast with an easterly breeze just strong enough to give players trouble on the homeward holes. Vardon was the heavy favourite to win, although Taylor, Hilton, Braid and Jack White all had their backers. Taylor was especially concerned about the lanky, long driver from Earlsferry. 'Both Vardon and myself were acutely sensitive to the possibility of Braid disputing our supremacy in the near future,' he wrote. A month earlier Braid had won the Musselburgh Open, defeating Taylor, White and Sandy Herd in the process.

Hilton's chances of winning may have been eliminated by the first day's pairings. He found himself drawn with Vardon again. With the leading amateur and professional in golf playing side by side, the pairing naturally was followed by the vast majority of the fans on hand to watch the Championship. That was never good for a nervous player like Hilton. It became worse when he learned that the committee in charge of the tournament had decided not to use a gallery rope to control the crowd.

'The explanation given for this extraordinary decision was that the committee had come to the conclusion that they could not possibly supply men with ropes for one individual couple in a *scoring* competition, as it would not be fair to the remainder of the competitors,' Hilton wrote. 'There may, on close analysis, be found a suspicion of logic in this argument; but considering that it was almost a foregone conclusion that fully 75 per cent of the gallery would follow Vardon and myself, it could hardly be said that we could be gaining any material advantage . . . even with the aid of ropes.'

The crowd did not seem to bother Hilton on the opening nine, which he completed in 36, three strokes better than the reigning Open champion. By the time he and Vardon turned for home, however, matters had descended into what Hilton described as a 'fiasco'. On every hole there was 'an absolute stampede after the tee shots were played, and one never got near one's ball without cleaving a way through a mass of humanity. You can stand that kind of thing for a certain period, but it requires a man with a very equable temperament to put up with that for two rounds in one day.'

Hilton was not that man. He fell to pieces on the homeward nine, coming in with a catastrophic 47 for an 83. He did, however, discover that there was a man who could calmly play his game amid the insanity, his partner. 'I shall never forget Harry Vardon that day,' Hilton marvelled. 'He stood it all like a saint. He seemed infinitely more amused than angry.'

Snaking his way through the masses, Vardon added a 40 to his outward nine to come in at 79, tied for first. His compatriots at the top of the leaderboard were no surprise. Taylor and Vardon's brother, Tom, had also gone around in 79, while White and Willie Park were lurking a stroke back. Braid was driving beautifully, but could not get the ball in the hole, coming in with 82. The best of the amateurs was Maxwell, just two off the lead at 81.

The outcome of the Championship was, more or less, decided by the second round. Taylor went storming around St Andrews, playing near-perfect golf. He needed just 36 strokes on the outward nine and finished with a 77 that tied the Championship record set in 1895 by Herd. When Vardon went round in 81, Taylor found himself sitting on a four-stroke lead. The other early leaders also failed to keep pace. Tom Vardon put himself out of it with 87, as did Hilton, while Braid and White posted twin 81s and Park fell back with an 83.

On the second day of the Championship, Taylor and the rest of the field awoke to a gloomy, misty morning that softened the greens enough to make pitching and putting easier, a prescription for Taylor's continued success if ever there was one. He did not have to wait long to see if the fates would be on his side that afternoon. Taylor's second shot to the opening hole was half-topped and ought to have found a watery grave in the Swilcan Burn. Somehow, it hopped over the stream, allowing him to record the unlikeliest of fours.

'The Deity that presides over the destiny of poor mortals was evidently on my side,' Taylor mused. His confidence now soaring, he cruised through the outward nine in a mere 37 and came home with 41 for a three-round total of 234 – a number that would be tough to beat, even in ideal weather.

Vardon, paired this time with Scottish favourite Herd, played solid, but unspectacular, golf. He came in with an 80 that left him with six strokes to make up in the final round that afternoon. Braid did the best of the rest, with an 80 that left him tied with White. Both sat nine strokes back. As far as *The Annual* was concerned, a Taylor victory was 'practically assured'.

Taylor made absolutely certain of that on his final trip around the links. 'The last round requires little description,' *The Annual* wrote. 'It saw Taylor excel at every point . . . Indeed, Taylor has never been seen to such advantage off the tee. Through the green he was equally good, and his approaching and putting were phenomenal. Every putt was played with refreshing confidence, and down they had to go, so to speak.'

It added up to a remarkable 75 – 38 out and 37 in – a new record for an Open at St Andrews. *The Annual* called it 'the grandest round ever played in a Championship'. Vardon came closest to Taylor's final tally of 309, posting a 77 that left him eight strokes back. Braid finally managed to come in under 80, with a 79 that left him in third at 322, a stroke ahead of White. The future continued to look bright for both of them.

The new Scottish hope, Maxwell, finished best of the amateurs. He came in seventh, although he was fully 20 strokes behind. Taylor's score was an astonishing 13 strokes lower than the one he'd made in winning the 1895 Open over the same links.

'Taylor's brilliant victory at St Andrews was immensely popular,' *Golf Illustrated* wrote. 'In the professional ranks no player is better liked or more highly respected and none is more fit, both as a golfer and a man, to wear the high honour he has now won for the third time.'

Taylor was as proud as a peacock. He now had as many Open victories as Vardon, the man hailed as the Golfer of the Century. 'A round of 75, even at St Andrews, is nothing much to boast about these days,' Taylor wrote four decades later, 'but in all humility I may put forward the claim that to get this figure in the last round of a Championship, playing with a gutty ball, is something which stirs the memory with pride.'

Later that year, members at Mid-Surrey held a dinner to honour Taylor and presented him with a gift of nearly £85. The champion wore all three of his gold medals to the ceremony, and in receiving the club's generous gift said, 'Gentlemen, if I had won a dozen Championships I could never have repaid the great kindness I have received from every member ever since I have had the honour to be your professional.'

Mid-Surrey members weren't the only ones thrilled to see Taylor on top again, after two seasons in which Vardon stood alone astride the game. 'A feeling gradually has been spreading that it would be in the interest of the game if someone could be found to place a spoke in the wheel of the Ganton man – probably a Scotsman, but if not a Scotsman an Englishman, provided he beat Vardon,' *Golf Illustrated* wrote. 'The question of nationality would readily be placed on the side, as the monopolisation of all the chief honours by one individual player was gradually assuming the nature of an abuse.'

Amid all the season's excitement, neither of the players whose absence had been so keenly felt at the Amateur and Open Championships had been forgotten by the golfing public. A week after Taylor's victory, *Golf Illustrated* published the first news of how Ball was getting on in South Africa. 'Golfers will be glad to hear that in a letter from Bloemfontein dated May 7, Mr John Ball, jun., reports himself "very fit",' the magazine reported.

In August, *Golf Illustrated* published a photograph of him and a fellow soldier chatting in front of their tent. Looking trim in his military khakis, Ball wears the same dour expression any opponent would have seen in the late stages of a match. The report sounded one sad note. The charger Ball's three golf clubs purchased for him before he left to join the war had died, apparently from drinking tainted water.

Tait's name also remained in the news all year. In the aftermath of his death, a memorial fund was established. *Golf Illustrated* supported the cause by selling portraits of the fallen soldier to raise money. Regrettably, throughout the year, the magazine's letters to the editor featured unseemly squabbling about how the money should be spent. In the end, more than £1,500 was raised. It was used to endow a bed in Tait's honour at St Andrews Hospital.

Tantallon, one of the many clubs to which Tait belonged, also memorialised Scotland's favourite son by commissioning a portrait of him to hang in its clubhouse. A year later, Tait would receive that same honour from the club he loved most, the Royal and Ancient. By December, Low's biography of Scotland's hero would be on sale, with all proceeds benefiting the widows and orphans fund of the Black Watch.

The turning point for English golf came in 1890, when John Ball became the first amateur to win the Open Championships. That epochal victory spurred enormous growth of the game south of the Scottish border. A painfully shy man, Ball never could become comfortable with the adulation showered on him by his passionate fans. *Reprinted with the kind permission of Royal Liverpool Golf Club*

Harold Hilton was never as beloved by the Hoylake faithful as his childhood idol, Ball, but his accomplishments were no less extraordinary. He remains even today the only British amateur to win two Open Championships, and is remembered as one of the brightest golf minds of his age or any other. *Reprinted with the kind permission of Royal Liverpool Golf Club*

One of the loveliest players of his era, John Graham was, sadly, destined to be remembered as the greatest amateur never to win a championship. He hated the crucible of competition, much preferring a quiet evening round with his faithful retriever and a few clubs under one arm.
Reprinted with the kind permission of Royal Liverpool Golf Club

The swashbuckling soldier Freddie Tait was, as Bernard Darwin described him, 'above everything else a Scottish golfer' – a trait that made him a national hero in his homeland. His constant companion was a scruffy black terrier with the well earned name of Nails. *Reprinted with the kind permission of the Royal and Ancient Golf Club of St Andrews.*

It was a high honour to have one's portrait painted in oil, but in class-conscious Victorian Britain one ordinarily reserved for gentlemen. It was a testament to the greatness of professional golfers John Henry Taylor, Harry Vardon and James Braid – and to the way they conducted themselves – that the men collectively known as the Triumvirate were immortalized in this painting. It now hangs in the clubhouse of the Royal and Ancient. *Reprinted with the kind permission of the Royal and Ancient Golf Club of St Andrews.*

The first great figure in English golf was Horace Hutchinson. Twice a winner of the Amateur Championship, he was the first player of distinction to write about golf with the elegance that would become a hallmark of the game's literature. As his acolyte, Bernard Darwin, put it, 'Horace was a personage; wonderfully striking in aspect, with this handsome face and white hair and an unquestioned air of being somebody.' *Reprinted with the kind permission of the Royal and Ancient Golf Club of St Andrews.*

No writer did more to preserve the memories of golf's pre-war Age of Glory than Bernard Darwin. He grew up worshipping players like John Ball and Freddie Tait, and later covered their exploits as the golf correspondent of *The Times*. In his memoir, John Henry Taylor expressed his wish to be remembered by posterity in the words of Darwin, a sentiment no doubt shared by the other luminaries of his era. *Reprinted with the kind permission of historian Dick Verinder.*

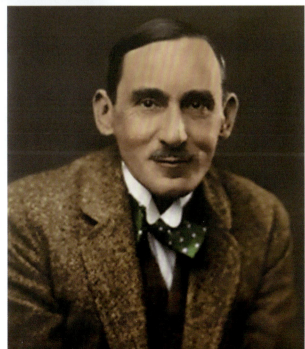

Few men were more influential in popularizing the Scottish game than politician Arthur James Balfour (above) and St Andrews legend Old Tom Morris (left). Balfour's interest encouraged Englishmen to take up golf because, as Horace Hutchinson put it, 'there must be something in the game if a fellow like Arthur Balfour plays it.' Old Tom Morris built the first seaside links outside Scotland, Royal North Devon, and helped spread the game around the globe by dispatching Scottish professionals to clubs in England, American and beyond.

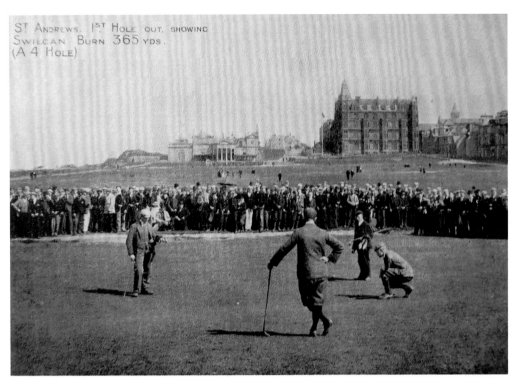

Any clash between John Ball and Freddie Tait, undisputed match-play champions of England and Scotland, drew an enormous, passionate crowd. Ball ordinarily got the best of Tait, as he did in the 1905 Amateur Championship, where the Scotsman is shown sizing up a putt.

Harold Hilton was better known for his exploits in stroke-play competitions, but his 1901 Amateur Championship battle against John Low (right) was remembered as one of the era's most brilliant exhibitions of match-play golf.

The International Amateur Matches that debuted at Hoylake in 1902 demonstrated one truth: Scotland's amateur bench was too deep for England. Scottish stalwarts included S. Mure Fergusson and John Laidlay (above left), as well as all-rounder Leslie Balfour-Melville, shown putting.

Before he became the first important voice in golf, Horace Hutchinson would emerge as one of the game's great gentleman golfers, winning two of the first three Amateur Championships. A free swinger, Hutchinson lashed at the ball with what he described as a 'bombastic freedom.'

In the aftermath of Freddie's Tait's tragic death, all eyes in Scotland turned to Robert Maxwell as the nation's answer to English legend John Ball. Maxwell generally got the best of Ball in international matches, but won only two Amateur Championships to Ball's eight.

In an age of great golfers, one man stood above them all – Harry Vardon. His exploits in Britain made him so famous that in 1900 he was recruited to tour the United States, a trip that launched the great American golf boom.

John Henry Taylor, golf's indispensable man, was the first English professional to win an Open, breaking through at Sandwich in 1894 and repeating the following year at St Andrews. He was also instrumental in founding the Professional Golfers Association, assuring a brighter future for his brethren.

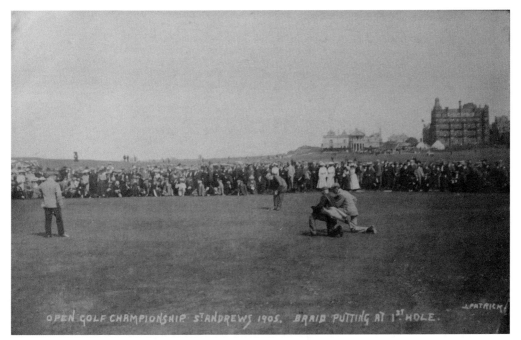

No Scotsman fought more valiantly than James Braid to stem the rising English tide.
He won five Open Championships – all on home soil – including this one
in 1905 at St Andrews, not far from his birthplace in Earlsferry.

Scotland's other stalwarts included Willie Park, Jr., a descendant of one of the game's legendary families,
and that old warhorse, Andra Kirkaldy. A beloved figure in St Andrews, Kirkaldy (looking on)
became the professional to the Royal and Ancient Golf Club.

Nothing stirred the soul of Scots like a Great Match, especially the International Foursome of 1905, pitting James Braid and Sandy Herd against Harry Vardon and John Henry Taylor. The first leg of the match drew 10,000, to the Old Course at St Andrews.

Eyes on America

By July, the golf world's focus had shifted back to the United States. Vardon returned to America after the Open, continuing a barnstorming tour that saw him compete up and down the east coast, through the Midwest, into Canada, and as far west as the Rocky Mountains of Colorado.

He remained all but invincible, playing 47 exhibition matches and winning 33 of them. Again he lost only once in a singles match, falling to the same man who'd beaten him earlier, Nicholls, this time by one hole. Vardon's goal all along had been to win the US Open, scheduled for the first week of October in Wheaton, Illinois. It would be played at the Chicago Golf Club, designed by one of the founders of the game in America, C.B. Macdonald.

'I was exceedingly keen to win the American Open Championship,' Vardon wrote, 'as I thought it would be a fitting climax to the successful tour which I had so far experienced.'

No sooner had the Open concluded at St Andrews than rumours began circulating in the British press that Taylor would soon be off to America himself, intent on confronting his fiercest rival again at Wheaton. Initially, Taylor denied the rumours, but by early August he, too, was steaming towards New York.

It wasn't simply the chance to become the first man to simultaneously hold the Open titles of both nations that lured Taylor to America. Five years earlier, he and a friend, George Cann, had formed a club-making business. Taylor had no illusions that he was a club maker, a skill required of all professionals. Teaming up with Cann solved that problem. By 1900, Cann had moved to the States, setting up a branch of their business in Pittsburgh. He persuaded Taylor to capitalise on his third Open victory with an exhibition tour of the country.

The passage across the Atlantic was tough for Taylor. He suffered a terrible bout of seasickness. During his three months in the US, *Golf Illustrated* reported, Taylor never felt his best, struggling with the heat and finding American food hard on his nervous digestive system. He didn't pursue a schedule as gruelling as Vardon's, partly because the minute he landed in New York he was offered a deal no man could have refused.

Colonel G.B.M. Harvey, chief executive of Harper & Brothers, publisher of *Golf* magazine in the US, learned that Taylor was a capable writer and asked him to become a correspondent. His job would be to cover important matches, write about how to play golf, and produce travel pieces on American courses. Harvey offered Taylor a staggering £2,000 a year to join the magazine's staff, and agreed to take on all of his expenses in the States.

'It was my first introduction to the possibility of earning big money in a very pleasant manner and I readily accepted such a tempting offer,' Taylor recalled. He started each morning by reporting to Harper's offices to get his assignment, and even bought himself a Stetson hat so he would look the part of a magazine correspondent.

Like Vardon, Taylor's principal goal for that trip was to take the US Open trophy back with him to England. He was stunned by the way the American press treated that coming confrontation, repeatedly publishing articles suggesting that there was bad blood between him and Vardon.

'It was a new experience for me, this endeavour to sow enmity between old friends,' Taylor recalled. 'It was amid this atmosphere of recrimination – from one side only, let me say – that Vardon and I met at Wheaton in October. The contest for the Championship was regarded as affording only two possible winners – Vardon and myself.' That was no surprise, as every winner of America's national open thus far had been English or Scottish. No American would win until Johnny McDermott broke through in 1911.

The weather was gorgeous in Chicago that autumn, and an enormous, fashionably dressed crowd turned out to follow the two British stars, the largest yet seen at an American tournament. They were neck and neck at the end of the first day, with Vardon leading by a stroke at 157. He began to pull away the next morning. Vardon took 76 to Taylor's 79, boosting his lead to four strokes with one round remaining.

That was too much ground to make up. Taylor could only narrow the gap to two, and Vardon claimed the prize he'd had his heart set on since he sailed from Liverpool in January – the sixth edition of United States Open Championship. He and Taylor were followed atop the leaderboard by eight Scotsmen. Not a single American finished anywhere close to being in the money.

'Needless to say, I was delighted to have won the title of American Open Champion,' Vardon wrote, 'and the reception which I received at the conclusion of the big event could not, in any way, have been more sincere if gained by an American player.'

The loss was a bitter one for Taylor after months of being hailed as the slayer of the great Vardon. 'I own to having been a little despondent at the result,' Taylor wrote. 'In congratulating my conqueror I hope I did so without any feeling of rancour or jealous envy.'

Before leaving the States, Taylor and Cann were presented with another tempting proposition by Colonel Harvey of Harper & Brothers and his business acquaintances. They offered to finance a greatly expanded club-making business to be known as J.H. Taylor & Cann. That would have removed the biggest obstacle the two men faced: lack of capital. It would likely have made both wealthier than they had ever dreamed of being.

Taylor was sufficiently interested that he wrote to his wife to ask whether she would consider bringing their family to America. He also asked Mid-Surrey if the club would give him a year's leave of absence to pursue this opportunity. Both turned him down, and Taylor professed to be happy they did: 'I admit that the temptation to make my home in America was a strong one, but overriding and above all other consider-ations, the thought of severing myself from British golf proved even stronger, and, looking back, I am glad I acted as I did.'

Speculation also abounded about how much money Vardon raked in from his American tour. Vardon himself never said. Based on the number of exhibitions he played, and the fee charged for each appearance, it is safe to say he earned something north of £1,000 and perhaps closer to £2,000 – an extravagant sum for a golfer in that era.

By the end of his long and tiring tour, Vardon was ready to go home. 'The weather here is something awful, and I can assure you that one does not feel like playing golf at all with heat so great,' he wrote to a friend in July. 'I shall be glad to get home again – it is not at all fun here.'

A month before Vardon left, a thief broke into his room at Apawamis Country Club in Rye, NY. *Golf Illustrated* said the burglar made off with cash, a watch presented to Vardon by Royal Jersey Golf Club, and several of his medals. Vardon never mentions the robbery in his memoir, and declares that he thoroughly enjoyed every minute of his grand adventure.

Whatever he thought of America, Vardon would remember that trip as, perhaps, the crowning achievement of his career. 'When I look back on this tour, it is with a feeling of the utmost satisfaction that I realise I was actually the means, through the medium of my visit there, of starting that which was to become in later years, the great golf craze of America,' he wrote.

Vardon had every right to be proud. That tour, and especially the two others he made in 1913 and 1920, did not simply stoke interest in golf in the States. His exploits were followed worldwide, and contributed significantly to the globalisation of the game.

Vardon's American adventure, however, would not be the only game-changing development of 1900. The true breakthrough would involve a package Taylor found waiting for him when he arrived in Chicago to face Vardon in the US Open. It came from a man named Coburn Haskell, of Akron, Ohio. 'A courteous note informed me that as the champion golfer of the world he was anxious to bring to my notice an entirely revolutionary type of golf ball that he had invented and asked that I should give it a trial with a report as to what I thought of it,' Taylor recalled.

He asked around, but no one could tell him anything definitive about this new rubber-cored ball. In the end, Taylor decided it was too risky to use a ball he had never played with in the US Open, a decision he would come to regret. Vardon, of course, would not have been offered the chance to play with Haskell's experimental ball as he was touring the US to promote the new gutty known as the Vardon Flyer.

Taylor did take the ball out for a test drive after he had returned to New York. He teed it up at a 240-yard hole where the group in front was on the green preparing to putt. 'Thinking they were well out of range, I put the new ball down and let fly,' Taylor remembered. 'The result astounded me. The ball pitched at their heels, and hurrying forward I offered my apologies, explaining that I was trying out a new ball, adding that I had never driven a golf ball so far before. My apologies were accepted with forgiving smiles, and then and there I knew that the gutty was doomed.'

News of the new ball would not reach Britain until the following year. The first report, a wildly exaggerated one, appeared in July in *The Field*. It suggested that even ordinary players could drive a Haskell ball 300 yards. *Golf Illustrated* first mentioned rumours of a rubber-cored ball that autumn, quoting a promoter of the Haskell as saying, 'the inevitable result of the use of our new ball will be that golf links must be lengthened.' If that proved to be true, the world of golf would be forever changed.

Fourteen

SCOTLAND RESURGENT

--------·•●◐●•·--------

W ith the triumphant return of Harry Vardon and John Henry Taylor, the focus in British golf returned to the question of whether Scots would mount a charge to defend their national game or succumb to English conquest.

It was now or never. The 1900 season had been the fifth in a decade when Englishmen swept both Championships. Scotland hadn't won an Open in seven years or an Amateur in two. Worst of all, the nation was still recovering from the deep psychic wound inflicted by Vardon's crushing defeat of Willie Park in their ballyhooed Great Match.

Still, even as they anticipated a renewed battle between thistle and rose, British golfers could not help looking over one shoulder at the United States. They fretted about the money Americans had lavished on Vardon and Taylor. They feared the Yankee dollar might lure their stars away for good. Throughout 1901 *Golf Illustrated* carried reports about English and Scottish professionals tempted to cash in. Vardon, the magazine wrote, might move to the States for good. Sandy Herd was being offered a job offer in New York. James Braid would tour the US immediately after the Open.

None of those golfers wound up leaving. In fact, 1901 would be the year Britain got the first taste of what the nation ought to have been worried about – Americans coming to test themselves against the world's best golfers, with an eye towards taking the game's most cherished trophies back across the Atlantic. In July and August, reigning US Amateur champion Walter Travis toured the nation to study the classic courses and size up the competition.

Travis played famous links from St Andrews to Sandwich, had games with British greats like Taylor and Harold Hilton, and was warmly received. 'The American Amateur champion, who is presently enjoying a golfing holiday in this country, has created a very favourable impression, both personally and as a golfer,' *Golf Illustrated* wrote. It would be an entirely different story when the feisty, cigar-chomping American returned three years later.

The year had barely begun when it became clear that the arrival of a new century would mark the end of an age for Britain. On 22 January, after years of failing health, Queen Victoria died peacefully, with her eldest son and successor, King Edward VII, at her bedside. Her 63-year reign had seen a great surge of progress – industrially, politically and socially – that continued to transform life in the kingdom. As the nation mourned her passing, golf and every other pastime came to a halt for weeks.

By springtime, when a sorrowful nation returned to business, Scots were bullish about reclaiming the nation's birthright as the home of Champion Golfers, none more so than *Golf Illustrated* editor Garden Smith. Everyone knew the odds were daunting. Nevertheless, Smith sensed that golfers in Fife and East Lothian, the ancient homelands of the Scottish game, were marshalling forces for a counter-attack against the English – and with good reason.

Robert Maxwell, the nation's brightest Amateur hope, was razor-sharp, as was up-and-coming professional Jack White. Even the demoralised Park seemed to be regaining form. It was, however, the long-driving son of Earlsferry who truly buoyed Scotland's hopes. James Braid had already come tantalisingly close to being the first Scottish professional since Willie Auchterlonie to win an Open, and in the previous season he had racked up eight wins against only four losses in matches against England's best.

'As the Championship again falls to be played north of the Tweed, it is to be hoped that the Scotchmen will do something to avenge the Flodden of last year, and a Scottish champion for the first year of the new century appears to be well within the bounds of probability,' Smith enthused.

Scotland's first opportunity to engage the English, the Amateur at St Andrews, began with a heartbreaking setback. The day the Championship was to begin, 7 May, word arrived that Maxwell's sister was gravely ill. He returned home to be by her side. 'On him, above all others, the old country relied, and now its expectations are almost extinguished,' *Golf Illustrated* wrote. Poor Maxwell had already endured his share of tragedy. The previous July his brother, Francis, had been killed in the South African War.

The weather reflected the gloomy mood, and not simply because of Maxwell's misfortune. St Andrews was hosting its first Amateur since the death of Freddie Tait. His loss was brought poignantly home by the presence in the field of his brother, Jack. Conditions on the first day of play were 'simply miserable, the air being cold, the wind keen, and the rain falling in torrents', *Golf Illustrated* wrote. Old Tom Morris, now in his 80th year, resolutely donned his waterproofs and stood stoically by as he sent off a record 116 players, among them his grandson, Bruce Hunter.

With Maxwell sidelined, Scotland desperately needed one of its stalwarts to step up. All eyes turned to John Laidlay, Mure Fergusson and Leslie Balfour-Melville, the heroes of earlier days. Instead, it was St Andrews man John Low who picked up the mantle for his homeland. A Cambridge 'Blue', Low was among the golfing elite – a leading writer on the game, member of the Rules Committee, unrepentant traditionalist and founder of the Oxford and Cambridge Golfing Society.

Sturdy and stern-looking, Low was the kind of golfer Scots referred to as 'pawky', a word that means cunning in wit or strategy. He hit his ball short but straight, managed his game beautifully and was deadly on the greens. Horace Hutchinson described him as a man of 'light-hearted and brave temperament' whose game was distinguished by his mastery of the classic wooden putter, which most players had long ago abandoned for newer models of iron or aluminium. Indeed, the Englishman went as far as to say that Low was as gifted on the greens as any player he knew.

Low was no stranger to success in the Amateur. Twice before he had made it to the semi-finals, both times losing in extra holes to miraculous recoveries by an opponent he had outplayed from tee to green. Still, Low would not have been on any shortlist of potential winners. He was not strong enough with his woods to pose a serious threat, or so it was thought.

Low played dogged, inspired golf throughout the Championship's early rounds. He had only two easy wins, defeating a fellow R&A member 4 and 2 and a college student 5 and 3. His other matches were desperately close. Three times he won on the last hole, including his semi-final match against Hoylake's John Graham. In the other match he squeaked by 2 and 1.

As expected, the man who cruised through the other half of the bracket was the reigning champion and pre-tournament favourite, Harold Hilton. He hadn't come into the tournament brimming with confidence, because he wasn't as sharp that season as he had been in 1900. Not only that, Hilton had never loved the Old Course. He tended to become vexed by the odd bounces that so often punish a well-struck shot. That spring, however, his chequered relationship with St Andrews would change.

Hilton broke a sweat only once en route to the final. He swept away John Laidlay 3 and 2 in a match that wasn't as close as the score suggests. Herbert Fowler, soon to be a famous golf architect, was so demoralised when Hilton won the first seven holes that he threw in the towel. Only Horace Hutchinson, recently recovered from a bout of illness, made Hilton earn his laurels. Hutchinson took the match to 18, where he three-putted to lose.

By the morning of the final, the ugly weather had finally blown out to sea. 'The sun shone brightly from a blue sky chequered with fleecy clouds which had no ill intention in their aspect,' *Golf Illustrated* wrote. All of St Andrews seemed to have gathered around the first tee, a crowd of 3,000 or more, to watch Hilton hit his opening tee shot with that ever-present cigarette dangling from his lips.

He was feeling plenty confident by then. 'I must candidly acknowledge that I thought I should beat my old friend John Low in that final round, even though it had to be played at St Andrews, over which green he is, no doubt, a more dangerous opponent than on any other course in the kingdom,' Hilton recalled. 'The fact was, I had not a very high opinion of his wooden club play, as I had never seen him play them really well.'

Low came out playing his woods beautifully that day. It was Hilton, who had recently switched to using the new Mills aluminium woods, who struggled to stay in the match. 'I was distinctly fortunate in being able to hold on to him for the first 12 holes,' he wrote. 'Indeed if the truth is to be told it was only by the aid of superior putting that I managed to do so.'

Hilton finally settled down to his best game on the closing holes. 'Towards the end of the round, I managed at last to get a little of the best of the long play, and taking advantage of the opportunity, finished with a three-hole advantage; but I cannot say that I quite deserved this lead, and I felt I had no reason to cavil at fortune.'

When Low and Hilton returned after lunch, elbowing their way through an even larger crowd, it appeared early on that the Englishman would run away with the match. Hilton won the first hole and added another at the fifth to take a five-hole lead with 13 to play. Low, however, was a true-blue Scotsman, and if men north of the Tweed shared one characteristic it was a steadfast refusal to surrender, no matter how desperate the situation.

Low had whittled Hilton's lead to two holes by the time they made the turn. At the 13th, his wooden putter finally delivered the magic that so impressed Hutchinson. Low holed one from what Hilton described as 'the far dim distance'– some 40 feet – as the wildly partisan crowd roared its approval. Low was within a hole now, and the horde following an increasingly tense match could not restrain its enthusiasm.

On the 15th Hilton faced a dangerous putt of 24 feet. It needed to crawl just over a hill and drift right as it approached the hole in order to stop close. As he lined it up, restive fans standing no more than six feet from Hilton kept up a running commentary about the dim prospect of him laying the ball dead. He asked them politely to be quiet. They paid no attention.

'I had to play conversation or no conversation,' Hilton remembered. 'From the time the ball left the club it appeared on the short side, and my friends behind did not fail to realise the fact, as they addressed the ball in all sorts of terms, many of which would barely stand reproduction, and truly fervent were the expressions when the ball failed to surmount the hill and remained some five or six feet short.' One fan predicted aloud that Hilton would not hole it. 'I was rather of his opinion,' he recalled wryly, 'but the audible endorsement of my thoughts seemed somewhat unnecessary.'

Low now faced an 18-footer of his own. If it went in, Hilton would have to make that tricky downhill putt to keep his lead. Low calmly knocked his in, and 'the cheering commenced in no half-hearted fashion,' Hilton wrote. 'I did not mind that: it was only natural as the effort was a great one.' Hilton nearly missed with his answer, misreading the line, though it managed to wobble in nonetheless. 'The only thing I heard was the remark of Johnnie Low, "Well putted, Harold," and that compensated for much.'

Both men played the 16th poorly. In the end Hilton had a three-footer to halve the hole in five. When his feeble effort failed to find the cup, the multitude following the match all but lost its mind. 'Youths were so overjoyed that they were kicking each other, and he that was kicked did not appear to feel or resent it, so overmastering and intoxicating was the national elation at Low's grand display,' *Golf Illustrated* wrote.

Having lost his commanding lead, Hilton trudged towards the 17th tee 'feeling in a semi-dejected, irritable frame of mind, possibly the worst state a man playing a serious game of golf can drift into.' At that moment, however, the partisan crowd stepped over the line and everything changed.

'An excited spectator, caring little and heeding less, made a beeline for the front place, and in his mad career charged full into me,' Hilton remembered. 'He nearly knocked me over, and as he travelled by on his hurricane passage I could not help hearing his remark: "We'll teach these bloody Englishmen!" This freely expressed opinion had a most salutary effect upon me: a modified form of anger took the place of the nervous hesitation which pervaded my system, and I said to myself: "Will you?" It was just the necessary antidote I required.'

Hilton hit a solid tee shot on 17, but hooked his second and faced a long, dangerous third. The shot had to avoid the world's most famous bunker without running across the green and onto the road beyond, from which recovery was a pipe dream. Low's third was well short, and he, too, faced a frightening approach with his fourth.

Hilton turned to his caddy and asked if he thought it was possible to carry the green from that distance, with a stiff breeze blowing in their faces. The caddy said he doubted it, and that was all Hilton needed. Using his driver, he took a mighty swipe at the ball.

'At this critical juncture, he played one of the most brilliant shots imaginable,' Harry Everard wrote in *Golf Illustrated*. 'Nobody thought that, at the best, he would be able to do more than reach the front of the green against the strong wind then blowing; yet he drove well onto the green, as straight as an arrow on the fly, and was only four or five yards short of the hole.'

Low must have been as stunned as the partisans desperately hoping for a Scottish victory. He knew he had no choice now but to take a bold risk of his own. His ball, however, ran onto the road. Low wound up giving up the hole and the lead.

Grimly, the Scotsman bore down, getting the best of the drives from the 18th tee. Hilton hooked his left again, and to his dismay found it in a divot. That meant another tough decision with everything on the line. Again Hilton reached for his driver, hoping that if he could knock the ball out of the divot he might get enough run on it to scamper up the Valley of Sin in front of the green – all that would be required for victory.

'The ball possibly did not carry more than 120 yards,' Hilton remembered, 'but I knew well from the strain on the shaft that it had plenty of steam behind it, and that once it landed it would run like a hare: my surmise was not wrong, as it mounted the hill short of the green without a falter, and toddled on until Old Tom, who held the flag, had to step aside to let it pass. Not a sound came forth from the crowd; their powers of articulation seemed suddenly to have deserted them.' The ball stopped a few feet past the hole.

Low made a brave bid for a three, but it was never going to be enough. Even if he had holed it, Hilton would have faced a short putt to win. As it turned out, the Englishman carefully laid his third dead and tapped in to claim his second consecutive Amateur. Hilton became the first player since Hutchinson in 1887 to win back-to-back Championships. Once again England poked its nose in front in the Amateur race, with eight wins to Scotland's seven.

Bitterly disappointed as they must have been by Low's defeat, the St Andrews faithful could not help but celebrate such a marvellous display of match-play golf. Many believed it surpassed even the exhilarating final in the 1899 Amateur between John Ball and Freddie Tait. With its series of heroic recoveries, that match may have stirred more emotion, but this ferocious duel had seen better golf.

Indeed, so brilliant was the final that a long-time member of St Andrews concluded that both men had emerged as winners. As he put it, 'Mr Hilton is the winner of the Amateur Championship Cup, and Mr Low is the winner of the Amateur Championship.' Every golfer in Scotland surely would have agreed, as they had in 1899 when both Tait and Ball were hailed as heroes for their gallant display.

Son of Earlsferry

Inspiring as Low's performance had been, the true test of Scotland's renewed hopes would unfold a month hence in the Open at Muirfield, where even the titans of English golf were keeping one eye on the Earls-ferry man who had been closing in on them over the past few seasons.

In the aftermath of his third Open victory the previous season, Taylor had been interviewed by the *St Andrews Courier and Advertiser*. His friend and roommate during that tournament, James Braid, was standing beside him. Taylor patted Braid on the shoulder and confidently told the reporter: 'This is next year's champion.'

Taylor was not the first man to pat Braid on the shoulder and predict he would one day become Champion Golfer. Braid's favourite story about growing up in Earlsferry – where he was born on 6 February 1870 – was about meeting an early hero of Scottish golf, Jamie Anderson. Braid was nine years old when Anderson came to Elie to play in a match. Every boy in Earlsferry idolised the St Andrews legend, who would win his third consecutive Open that autumn. Braid followed his hero around like a puppy dog. Noticing the adoration, Anderson asked the lad to pick up a club and take a swing.

'I hit a shot or two myself to show him what I could do, and he took particular notice of the way that I played them, and asked me to do one or two over again, so that he might make another examination of my style, if such it was to be called,' Braid recalled proudly. 'He seemed really to mean what he said, when at last he patted me on the shoulder and told me to go in for as much golf as I could, and practise as thoroughly as possible, and that if I did that I should be Open Champion myself one day.'

That moment sold Braid on a life in golf. There was, however, a significant obstacle in his path – his parents. His father, also named James, was a ploughman and forester who didn't play golf. He was dead set against his son pursuing a life in the game, as was Braid's mother, Mary. Nothing could have been more unusual in Earlsferry, which was as golf-mad as St Andrews. The town had produced its own line of famous golfers, among them Jack and Archie Simpson and Braid's first cousin, that dashing dog Dougie Rolland.

Ignoring his son's pleas, Braid arranged for young James to be apprenticed as a joiner – a highly skilled craftsman who did the fine detail work of carpentry, such as staircases, windows, doors and furniture. James continued to play golf wherever he could, winning a host of local medals and working himself down to scratch by age 15. Four years later, he moved to St Andrews to pursue his craft, and by 1891 he was living and working in Edinburgh. There his opportunity came to move into professional golf.

Braid's best friend, Charles Smith, worked at the Army and Navy Store in London as the foreman of club makers. He offered Braid a job. He had never made a club in his life, but Braid knew golf and how to work with wood. He accepted the offer in late 1893, deciding that aged 23 he no longer had to bend to the will of his parents.

The following season Braid entered the 1894 Open, finishing in the top ten. That same year he played his first professional match against a man who would become a lifelong friend, Taylor. Braid won the final two holes to earn a hard-fought half and the respect of golfers everywhere.

By 1896, Braid had left the Army and Navy job to become the golf professional at Romford outside London.

Among the tallest golfers of his day, Braid stood nearly 6 feet 2 inches and weighed 195 pounds. His most distinguishing traits, however, were a sly sense of humour and a face that seemed to convey serene wisdom, a trait he shared with Old Tom Morris. Not surprisingly, given his height, Braid developed into one of the longest drivers of his day. His swing was shorter than most, but he lashed at the ball with what Horace Hutchinson described as a 'divine fury'. Braid also was phenomenally accurate with his irons. It was on the green that the strokes melted away. 'His short putts at St Andrews in the 1900 Open were enough to make the angels weep,' Harry Everard wrote in the wake of that tournament.

That changed in 1901. Braid took up one of the New Year's resolutions *Golf Illustrated* listed in its first issue that season. He switched to the Mills aluminium putter, and with dedicated practice replaced the stabby stroke that so often failed him with a smooth one that enabled him to lay long putts dead and hole short ones with confidence. If he could do that in an Open, Braid would be a tough man indeed.

The week before the Championship, Braid made himself the hot favourite at Muirfield by winning a tournament at Musselburgh in spectacular fashion. He played 36 holes in 140, lowering Willie Park's record by seven strokes. It convinced fellow Scottish professional Ben Sayers. He told anyone looking to bet on the Open that Braid would 'win and win easily'.

Braid's opportunity to realise the dream he had harboured since Anderson asked him to take a few swings came on a gorgeous morning in early June. Lovely as the day was, a brisk westerly breeze dimmed prospects of low scores. Braid certainly did not look like a winner on his opening hole. He hooked his tee shot out of bounds, and his second appeared to be headed in the same direction before it bounced off the boundary wall and back into play. That rattled Braid, and he needed 43 shots to reach the turn. He settled down coming home, finishing in a marvellous 36.

Braid's 79 was the third-best score of the morning. Park had turned in a 78 to take the early lead, but Vardon later nipped him by a stroke. Taylor matched Braid's 79, but the other early favourites left themselves too much to do over the final three rounds. Hilton finished in 89 and Sandy Herd did only two strokes better. Most other scores were in the mid-to-high 80s.

By the end of the afternoon round, with the wind blowing even more fiercely, the Open appeared to have come down to another battle of thistle and rose between Braid and Vardon. Braid started slowly again, going out in 40, but another 36 coming in gave him the lowest score yet posted, a 76. Vardon played his usual machine-like golf, coming in with a tidy 78 that left him tied with Braid at 155.

The next closest man, Taylor, was seven strokes back at 162. The first-round leader, Park, fell apart, driving poorly and failing to hole putts. His 87 left him out of it, as were Hilton, Herd and Jack White, all in the 80s again. Only 34 golfers made the cut and nearly two dozen didn't bother to turn in a card. Tom Vardon played well enough to survive, but was so far behind that he withdrew to caddie for his brother, Harry.

The weather for the second day of the Open was even more gorgeous than it had been on the first, with the sun shining brilliantly and the breeze having died down. Every Scotsman in the crowd – and it numbered nearly 4,000 now that a train had been added to nearby Gullane – was praying that Braid would not be undone by his putter, as he had been in the past.

'The greater brilliancy shown by Braid flattered the hopes widely entertained that he was destined to bring back to Scotland the cup which England has held since 1893,' *Golf Illustrated* wrote. Bookmakers weren't convinced. Vardon started the final two rounds as the 3/1 favourite to win his fourth Open.

Hilton was out early, determined to improve upon his first two rounds. He played 'without the semblance of a slip', as *The Golfing Annual* put it, going out in 38 and coming home in 37 for a magnificent 75. Even Hilton would have known, however, that 244 for three rounds was not going to be close enough unless the leaders collapsed.

Braid was next out among the leaders. His play 'was practically faultless, and a brilliant round of 74 put him in a seemingly impregnable position,' *The Annual* wrote. That became even truer when Vardon set out on his round with the other hero of the south, Taylor.

'It was soon apparent that Vardon was by no means in his usual form,' *Golf Illustrated* wrote. He was slicing his tee shots, and he needed 40 strokes to reach the turn, two more than his playing partner. On their homeward nine, it was Taylor who sparkled, playing brilliantly to finish in 36 and match Braid's low round of the week at 74. Vardon needed 39 and posted his highest score yet, a 79. Braid now led by five with one round remaining. He stood at 229, with Vardon at 234 and Taylor at 236.

Braid played that final 18 holes like a man protecting a lead. He showed none of his usual 'divine fury', and his putting was shaky. He seemed content to record a succession of fours and fives. Braid went out in 40 and came home with precisely the same score to become the leader in the clubhouse at 309. That meant Vardon would need a 74 to tie with Braid and force a play-off, while Taylor would have to equal Herd's course record of 72. Even nervous Scots considered it unlikely that either man could post a score that low.

Vardon apparently didn't. He came to the 16th tee needing only three fours to send the Open into a play-off. As fate would have it, his approach to that hole was decidedly un-Vardon-like. He topped the shot into a bunker and could do no better than six. Not even a golfer as great as Vardon was going to make threes on the last two holes of a Championship. Scotland's long nightmare had finally come to an end, as Vardon posted 78 to finish three strokes back at 312 and Taylor's 77 left him at 313. With another brilliant 76, Hilton was best among the Amateurs, although his 320 left him 11 strokes behind.

The prize ceremony was a victory party for an exultant nation. Henry Cook, captain of the Honourable Company of Edinburgh Golfers, told an elated crowd that Scotland had entered that Open with hopes of winning, although they knew the English were formidable foes. It was, Cook said, among the happiest moments of his life to present a Scotsman as Champion Golfer of the Year. The crowd erupted in delirious applause. For years, Cook said, Scotland had its eyes on Braid and believed he would be 'big enough' to do it, a crack on his height that elicited uproarious laughter.

Reserved by nature, Braid was a man of few words. What he had to say as he accepted the Claret Jug has not been recorded. Even years later, as he reflected on the victory, Braid said merely that he became anxious in that final round and missed more putts than he should have because so many friends were slapping him on the back assuring him he was destined to win. The depth of his feelings about ending Scotland's long drought was revealed later in 1901 when he and his wife, Minnie, celebrated the birth of their second son. He was named Harry Muirfield Braid.

Not long after the Championship, word arrived that John Ball was sailing home from South Africa aboard the *Rosslyn Castle*. He'd been away 18 months and taken part in his share of the brutal guerrilla warfare and scorched-earth tactics which characterised that bloody conflict. Ball, of course, was not one to talk about what he had done in South Africa. A fellow Yeoman, however, wrote home about one of Ball's acts of bravery, which occurred as the men were riding away from a Boer farm they had just torched.

'In the gallop from the breakwater one man's horse came down, and John Ball immediately pulled up and went to his assistance, getting the horse up from the poor beggar's legs – all this of course under very heavy crossfire . . . Ball is too modest to speak about himself in any such connection, and won't have his name in the papers if he can possibly help it,' his fellow soldier wrote.

No doubt to Ball's chagrin, the story was reported in *Golf Illustrated*, which added, 'whether the deed will be considered sufficiently distinctive to gain the recognition of the authorities the future alone can decide – but his many friends, and they are legion, sincerely trust and hope that it will.'

Ball arrived in Hoylake in early July 1901. The scene was as it always had been – fog signals exploding, horns blaring, and 600 loyal fans crowding around the platform to welcome their hero home. His skin bronzed by the sun, his hair greying at the temples, Ball stepped off the train dressed in his army khakis amid a full-throated chorus of cheers.

His father and his sister Elisabeth were among those waiting to greet him. Ball and his sister walked arm in arm off the platform, their father behind them, and stepped into the waiting carriage. As always, its horses had been replaced by blue-jerseyed fishermen who would tow the family back to the Royal Hotel. It was a sombre procession on that occasion. A week earlier, Ball's mother, Margaret, had passed away even as her son made his way home. Later that year, Ball was among 2,000 Imperial Yeomen who received the South Africa War Medal from King Edward VII.

Momentous changes

The rest of that golf season and the year that followed would witness a series of revolutionary changes in the game – the first emerging at a meeting that took place in early September. It grew out of a debate that had raged since March, when *Golf Illustrated* ran an editorial condemning a practice that threatened the livelihood of every golf professional.

The right to operate a golf shop had always been part of a professional's deal with his club. Recently, however, clubs had taken to selling that right to the highest bidder, a competition few professionals could win. Without income from their shop, most professionals simply could not survive. 'The worst thing a club can do for golf is to be inconsiderate or shabby to their golf professional,' *Golf Illustrated* wrote.

Predictably, Taylor responded first. 'As you have pointed out,' he wrote in a letter to the magazine, 'the amount of money to be made by the average professional in matches, tournaments and by teaching is very small, and if the possibility of increasing his income by club and ball making is to be taken away from him and the business given to the highest bidder, the professional golfer will soon return to the state of poverty common not a great many years ago.'

Nearly every leading professional wrote to express agreement with Taylor – among them Braid, Herd, Vardon and White. Not long after their letters appeared, a prominent ball maker named Peter Paxton got to the point. 'Let Taylor then, if he is really in earnest, take this matter up, and I am sure he will have the hearty cooperation . . . and the deep gratitude of all connected with our noble profession,' he wrote.

Taylor needed no more encouragement than that. With Braid's help, the Englishman arranged a meeting of professional golfers on 9 September in London. This coming together of professionals had been brewing since 1891, the year Old Tom Morris chaired the meeting at which golfers laid out their proposals for restoring the lustre of the Open. It was inevitable, even then, that professionals would one day band together.

The result of the meeting was the formation of the London and Counties Golf Professionals Association, with Taylor as its chairman and Braid as its captain. It began with three goals: to establish an employment agency, create a benevolent fund to help golfers who fell on hard times, and stage tournaments that would create more opportunities for professionals, especially those in the middle ranks, to earn money.

Soon afterwards, with Vardon as its chair, came the Northern Counties Professional Golfers' Association and a similar organisation for the Midlands. Within weeks, all three had banded together under a new name – The Professional Golfers' Association – with Old Tom as honorary vice-chair. In the year ahead, the PGA would transform golf by launching the forerunner of the professional tours that dominate the game today.

While the formation of the PGA had more long-term significance than any other development in the 1901 season, it was not treated as major news by *Golf Illustrated*. It was back-of-the-book material, although the magazine contributed to the benevolent fund and encouraged readers to do the same. The wealthy men who ran golf would not have welcomed the news. Their dominion over the game had never been questioned. Employment agencies and benevolent funds were all well and good, but it would be a different story if the PGA sought to insert itself into the governance of the game – as time would soon demonstrate.

The news that truly stirred the blood of gentlemen golfers appeared in *Golf Illustrated* in January 1902, in a letter from Harold Janion, honourable secretary at Royal Liverpool. He announced that the club, responding to pleas from across the kingdom, would host an international match between gentlemen golfers from Scotland and England on 26 April in advance of the Championship at Hoylake. Each team would feature ten amateurs selected by a panel of top-flight golfers.

The golf world had been longing for this moment since 1882, when St George wrote to *The Field* daring Scotland to produce a team that could match with the likes of Ball and Hutchinson. Every gentleman understood that the Open was the Blue Riband, and most knew professionals were in a class by themselves. Still, since the game's earliest days their hearts and souls had been devoted to amateur golf, with a fervour modern players may have trouble appreciating.

The timing of Janion's announcement could not have been more ideal for Scotsmen. Emotions were riding high north of the border after a season in which Low had nearly dethroned Hilton and Braid had, at long last, carried the Claret Jug home. Surely, in this International Amateur Match, Scots would reclaim the field in golf.

The truest of believers was *Golf Illustrated*'s editor, Garden Smith. He had long argued that Scotland could produce a deeper side than England in a battle of amateurs. Smith's point was that all of England's glories in the Amateur had been achieved by only three men – Ball, Hilton and Hutchinson. Scotland, on the other hand, had eight golfers who had won or finished second in the Championship. This match, Smith insisted, would demonstrate the superiority of the amateur game in the birthplace of golf.

Given the excitement Janion's announcement generated one might be surprised to learn what happened next. *Golf Illustrated*'s letters were filled with bickering about the arrangements, especially the scoring system Hoylake chose. Janion had announced that the club would use the same system employed in the first University Match between Oxford and Cambridge. Players would face off into two 18-hole singles matches – one in the morning, one after lunch – and the team that took the most holes over the course of the competition would win.

Golf Illustrated and most players in Scotland felt strongly that scoring should be by matches alone. That wasn't the only complaint. There was wrangling over how teams were picked, how many players should compete, and whether foursomes would be a truer test than singles.

Hoylake listened, but stuck to its plans as the debate raged on in the letters to the editor long after the match had been played.

Scotland's side was chosen by Benjamin Hall Blyth, John Laidlay and John Low, who, regrettably, was unable to compete himself. They picked Robert Maxwell, John Laidlay, John Graham, Leslie Balfour-Melville, James Robb, Mure Fergusson, Fred McKenzie, J.R. Gairdner, Edward Blackwell and Charles Dick. England's selectors were Charles Hutchings, Hilton and Hutchinson. They chose Ball, Hilton, Hutchinson, Hutchings, Joseph Bramston, H.C. Ellis, the Hon. Osmund Scott, Bernard Darwin, G.F. Smith and Sidney Fry.

Despite the whining about arrangements, the first International Amateur Match emerged as the highlight of the 1902 season, overshadowing both major championships. The largest crowd ever seen at Hoylake, well into the thousands, assembled for the match. The only blemish was bitterly cold weather made worse by a stiff easterly breeze.

The match unfolded as if it were a scene from Garden Smith's dreams. Scotland's leader, Maxwell, surrendered only a single hole to England's Ball, making his first appearance on the main stage since returning from the war. Laidlay dominated Hilton, and Graham demolished his fellow Hoylake member Hutchinson. Scotland also picked up holes from Fergusson, Balfour-Melville, Robb, McKenzie and Gairdner.

Scotland won both sessions. Its side prevailed narrowly in the morning, winning 14 holes to England's 13. The failure of the tail end of Scotland's line-up in the opening round caused consternation over lunch, but Scots did even better in the afternoon. They took 14 holes to England's 8, for a final score of 28 to 21 for Scotland. It did nothing to diminish insistence on scoring by matches, but the result would have been the same either way. Scotland would have prevailed 11 matches to 8, with one match halved.

Englishmen could not help but note that Scotland's entire margin of victory came from one man, Graham. He took nine holes from Hutchinson. It had created a bit of awkward tension when Graham, who had grown up at Hoylake, chose to play for his nation, rather than his club. Scotland, of course, could reply that it had won without Low, the man who had fought so bravely in the Amateur.

Royal Liverpool celebrated the successful inauguration of the International Amateur Match with a lavish six-course dinner for players on both sides, which Low was able to attend. He gave a typically amusing speech following a toast to Hoylake for its innovative spirit and hospitality, saying that he did not want these matches between Scotland and England to 'perpetuate Bannockburn, but still it was as well to avenge Flodden'.

The Haskell

The two major championships that followed that historic match would be remembered not so much for the winners as for a development that would forever shape the future of the game.

Darwin caught wind of the change as he was making his way to Hoylake by train for the International. He ran into a friend who had a question for him. Did he intend to play with a Haskell? 'I said, "What is it?"' Darwin recalled. He and the rest of the golf world would soon find out.

The Haskell, of course, was the new rubber-cored ball from America dubbed the 'Bounding Billy' because it ran so far when it landed. It was just then making its way to Britain in serious numbers, although when Darwin arrived at Hoylake he quickly learned that 'no more were to be had for love or money, and I gave up the attempt in despair.'

Walter Travis had already used a Haskell to win the 1901 US Amateur, conducted after he had returned from his voyage of discovery in Scotland and England. The first salvo for the ball on Britain's side of the Atlantic was fired in the 1902 Amateur, in which the new ball was used by both Charles Hutchings and Sidney Fry.

Rumours had been circulating that Haskells went so far that inferior golfers were suddenly a match for their betters. They seemed to be verified by the way Fry and Hutchings cruised into the final of that Amateur. Hutchings had only one close call, beating James Robb 2 and 1 after easily sweeping aside such luminaries as Joseph Bramston and Horace Hutchinson.

Fry brushed off John Laidlay and Harold Hilton before outlasting Robert Maxwell by a hole. That match presented the most telling evidence of the new ball's advantages. Maxwell, among the longest hitters in golf, also used a Haskell, but the ball helped him far less than Fry.

The final was played on another grimly cold day with robust north-west winds. Midway through the first round the heavens opened up and play was temporarily halted. When the downpour stubbornly refused to stop, Hutchings and Fry trudged on as rain continued coming down in sheets. Hutchings drove the ball like a champion and putted even better, amassing a seemingly insurmountable lead of 8 up over the first 18 holes.

With a lead that large, no one at Hoylake figured that the match would last past the turn for home in the afternoon. After lunch, however, Hutchings began to look like the 53-year-old man he was, and Fry gave proof of *Golf Illustrated*'s description of him as 'a man who does not know defeat'. In the teeth of 'another terrific squall with pitiless rain and hail', Fry narrowed Hutchings' lead to five holes with eight remaining to play.

Hutchings, as *Golf Illustrated* described it, 'was palpably tired now' and hanging on for dear life. He was dormie two as they approached the 17th hole. A weary Hutchings left his second shot to the Royal well short, and Fry bagged another hole to take a match that had seemed a foregone conclusion to the final green.

The end in sight now, Hutchings dug deep, outdriving Fry on the last and leaving his third eight yards from the hole. Fry's approach was wide right, but he laid his fourth dead. Hutchings had two putts for the match. His first trickled to a halt agonisingly short, but he bravely holed the next to become the oldest man yet to win the Amateur. In the prize ceremony, Hutchings described himself as 'the proudest grandfather in England today'.

A few weeks after that Championship, the nation celebrated the end of the South African War, as the Boers surrendered and the Treaty of Vereeniging was signed on 31 May. The British Empire had, at last, realised its ambition of dominion over South Africa and its vast riches of diamonds and gold. Conquest came at a steep price – the lives of 22,000 British soldiers and 7,000 Boers. The long-term damage would include a legacy of brutal racism that affected every aspect of South African life, golf included. Even as late as the 1960s, the legendary Sewsunker 'Papwa' Sewgolum – the first non-white to take part in the South African Open – was prevented from realising his enormous potential as a golfer by the colour of his skin.

When the nation's attention returned to golf, the discussion in every quarter concerned the backlash against the new American ball. The debate unfolded even as golfers across the kingdom scrambled to shell out two shillings – twice the price of a gutty – for one of these rubber-cored marvels. 'As for the Haskell ball,' *Golf Illustrated* wrote some weeks afterwards, 'a perfect babel of controversy surrounds it. It is at least clear that a strong revulsion of feeling has taken place since the ball first made its debut in this country.'

Professional golfers, in particular, united in opposition to the Haskell ball, much as Allan Robertson had done in the late 1840s when the gutty ousted his beloved feathery. Like Robertson, professionals feared it would hurt business. Gutties often needed to be heated and remoulded, a lucrative trade, and their hardness took a toll on clubs, keeping professionals busy with repairs. Their chief complaint, however, was that this new American ball did not separate the wheat from the chaff the way the gutty did. It was so much easier to get airborne and it rolled so much farther that even moderate players could produce shots to rival those of a far better golfer.

One by one, professionals answered a query by *Golf Illustrated* with letters opposing the new ball – chief among them Braid and Vardon, who confidently predicted, 'I don't think they will be much used after a little while.' The most passionate argument came from Sandy Herd. 'I hope all the professionals play with it at Hoylake except myself,' he wrote.

Less than two weeks after writing those words Herd arrived at Hoylake early to get in a few practice rounds before the Open. He arranged to play the first of them with John Ball. Surprisingly, that stalwart traditionalist, the man who would not even deign to carry a niblick, was playing with the new American invention.

'He was using the Haskell ball, and doing such wonders with it that I found myself envying him,' Herd wrote. 'When we reached the 15th hole, Mr Ball, smiling at my comments regarding his drives, gave me a Haskell to try. That was the end of the gutta ball for me. The first drive I made with the Haskell was longer than any drive I had ever made with the gutta, and what impressed me chiefly was that the Haskell could be driven without any effort.'

When the two of them walked off the 18th green, Herd went directly to Jack Morris's shop, where he bought four of the rare and precious new balls. Before Herd left for Hoylake, his wife had given him a kiss and told him she'd prayed this would be his year to win the Championship. Perhaps at that moment in Morris's shop, her prayers were answered. With a supply of the new balls, 'My joy was unbounded,' Herd wrote.

In the first round, the new ball did not appear to have any revolutionary effect on Herd's play. He went around in a respectable 77. It was Vardon, playing with a gutty, who stunned the Hoylake crowd. He came in with a record-setting 72, despite having sent his first two shots out of bounds. No one else came close to that score. Willie Fernie bested Herd by a stroke at 76, while Braid came in with 78, Hilton and Maxwell 79, and Taylor 81. The surprise of the first round was a new player from France, Arnaud Massy, who matched Herd's score and was tied for third place.

Hilton bumped into Herd after that round. He noticed something markedly different about the Scottish professional's demeanour, despite his so-so score. 'I was so struck by his appearance of satisfaction that I at once came to the conclusion that the new toy was much to his liking, and proceeded to back him to win outright,' Hilton wrote.

Herd played steadily in the afternoon as well, shaving a stroke off his score from the morning. Vardon came in with the same 77 Herd posted in round one. Vardon's two-round total of 149 left him four strokes in front. The big move that afternoon was made by Vardon's fellow Jerseyman, Ted Ray. He bombed his way around Hoylake in 74 to sit tied for second with Herd at 153. Everyone else simply kept pace. Chief among them was Braid, whose 76 left him on Ray's and Herd's heels at 154.

In the critical third round, played in a boisterous wind, Herd had the good fortune to be drawn with Ball. 'Mr Ball was much more desirous that I should win than that he should beat me,' Herd marvelled years later. 'He played his best, to be sure, but in many quiet ways – all within the rules, of course – he gave me every encouragement that one man could give another.' Whether it was playing with Ball or playing with a Haskell can never be known, but Herd delivered the round of his life that morning.

'I played like one inspired against a very troublesome wind and returned a score of 73,' he wrote proudly, noting that both Vardon and Braid needed 80 shots that morning. 'At the end of the third round I led by three strokes from Vardon and eight from Braid,' Herd remembered. 'Could I hold on to my advantage?'

That was the question on the mind of every Scotsman. They had seen Herd in this position before, and simply did not trust him to come through. Even Herd could not shake memories of chances he'd thrown away in the past as he and Ball set off on the final round. Herd started beautifully, playing the first seven holes in level fours, but as nerves set in strokes slipped away.

'All the bogeys of the past, when championships have slipped through my fingers, seemed to troop alongside of me in that last round,' Herd admitted, 'and I finished with a score of 81 – distinctly below my form.'

Vardon was the only player considered a serious threat to Herd. The next closest was Braid, and he started eight strokes behind. Vardon needed 78 to tie and 77 to win, well within his range. Herd would have to sweat it out in the clubhouse, as the other contenders were playing behind him. Vardon was not showing his best form. He was thrown off by his partner using a Haskell ball and playing every shot to account for the run that followed. Vardon did the same thing, but his gutty simply stopped, and he threw precious strokes away by being short.

Still, Vardon walked up to the 18th green and the sea of people surrounding it facing a six-foot putt to send the Open into a play-off. Herd was among those watching as Vardon stalked the putt, dropping down on his right knee to survey the line before sending it rolling towards the cup. 'I should not have cared to be photographed as I watched that putt come up straight for the hole and then stop on the lip,' he admitted. Vardon, as was his way, accepted his misfortune with a wistful smile.

Herd's agonies weren't over, however. His fellow Scotsman, Braid was storming around Hoylake. The hero of Earlsferry began the day needing a 73 to tie, a score no golfer could be expected to produce in a Championship final. Yet, there Braid stood on the last green, brooding over a 24-foot-putt that would accomplish the unthinkable. Again Herd stood by, and again he watched the putt narrowly miss.

'I breathed again, and knew now that the goal of my ambition was reached, for I feared none else,' Herd wrote. He was right about that. His lead was never threatened, although the Frenchman Massy finished a respectable tenth in his debut. Another Scot, Maxwell, did amateur golf proud, finishing two strokes off the lead in fourth.

'Not in all my golfing career can I think of a red-letter day like that, when all my young dreams came true,' Herd recalled joyfully. 'For did I not, as a young boy frequently go as early as four in the morning to the first hole at St Andrews and say to myself as I practised putting, "You have this to win the Championship".' He was not the only one thrilled by the outcome. Hilton cashed in on the wager he'd placed on Herd after that first round.

The Scottish counter-attack was now in full gallop, with a second consecutive Open following that dominant victory in the International Match. Those triumphs made it easy to forget that four seasons had passed since Scotland won an Amateur, especially given how Tait and Low fought so bravely in two of those defeats. *Golf Illustrated* boldly proclaimed that Herd had 'followed James Braid in reasserting the ancient prowess of Scottish golfers'.

Everyone else in golf, however, was focused on something else – that both Championships had been won by players using the new Haskell ball, and one of them had been a 53-year-old man. A furious debate erupted among the golfing elite over how the game should respond to this leap forward in technology, one that still rages a century later.

It broke down into two camps. Traditionalists believed the R&A's Rules Committee needed to ban the Haskell ball and its many imitators to protect the integrity of the game. Their passionate leader was John Low, who railed against the new ball in his column in the *Athletic News*, with many of his comments reprinted in *Golf Illustrated*.

'I think that balls of this character will spoil first-class courses and make the weaker player with luck equal to the stronger,' Low wrote. In that single sentence he summed up the arguments against rubber-cored balls. They took the skill out of the game, robbing superior golfers of their advantage, and if they survived every course would have to be lengthened to keep its hazards relevant.

On the other side were luminaries like Benjamin Hall Blyth, Horace Hutchinson and Garden Smith. They focused on the reality that the new ball made the game far more pleasant to play for most golfers. 'So far as I am able to judge at present, the sole effect of the new balls is to make the game a little easier for everybody,' Smith wrote in *Golf Illustrated*.

From his perch on the Rules Committee, with the help of Scottish amateur Mure Fergusson, Low muscled the issue onto the agenda. By September, however, the Royal and Ancient had announced that any judgement would be postponed until spring. A divided golf world would have to wait to learn whether the renewed battle between England and Scotland would be waged with the old, reliable British gutty or the new American 'Bounding Billy'.

Fifteen

TWO ROADS

—•◦◉◦•—

T he choice golf faced in 1903 was not simply one between solid balls and balls with a rubber core. It was a decision about which path the game would pursue at that critical juncture, when it was growing rapidly around the world.

Would golf continue to be the game that had evolved over centuries on the windswept links of Scotland, one whose principal attraction was that it remained unconquerable, even for the most gifted players? Or would golf welcome the ceaseless quest to make an exceedingly difficult game easier with a ball that flies farther and straighter?

Truth be told, the evolution of golf clubs had already begun making golf easier before rubber-cored balls arrived. Innovations came so frequently that *Golf Illustrated* ran a standing feature on new patents. Every one of them, from the Bulger driver to the aluminium spoon, reduced the difficulty of getting the ball airborne and the likelihood that shots would go astray.

Those advances, however, had not yet tipped the scales in favour of making the game too easy, as John Low, Mure Fergusson and professional golfers were convinced rubber-cored balls would do. They believed nothing less was at stake in the debate over the Haskell than the soul of the game.

Low and Fergusson advocated making the gutty golf's standard ball, preserving for all time the classic links and the traditional Scottish game.

Others, angling for compromise, proposed restricting championships to gutties and allowing recreational players to use any ball they chose, an option modern golfers refer to as bifurcation.

In November 1902, the PGA wrote to the committee in charge of the Open opposing the use of rubber-cored balls in the Championship. A month later the fledgling organisation took a bolder step, voting 33-9 to ban rubber-cored balls in the tournaments it had begun staging soon after being founded. That was the first time the PGA asserted itself into the governance of golf, a notion that would have been unthinkable in an earlier age.

The reaction of the amateur establishment was swift and hostile. Gentlemen golfers generally favoured the new ball. They could not help but be seduced by the way it improved their games. Garden Smith lashed out at the PGA in *Golf Illustrated*, saying he had repeatedly warned members 'that their interests were indissolubly bound up with the good will of the amateurs and that if any friction arose it could only be to their disadvantage.'

The issue came to a head in March 1903, when the Rules Committee took up a motion submitted the previous autumn by Fergusson and seconded by Low. The motion asserted 'that the new rubber-filled balls are calculated to spoil the game of golf as now played over links laid out for the gutty ball and that it would be advisable to bring in a new rule for the regulation of balls and clubs to be used in playing the game.'

Long before the vote was taken, the writing was on the wall. The most influential man in golf – A.J. Balfour, now prime minister – had cast his vote for the Haskell ball when *Golf Illustrated* sought his opinion. 'Standardisation cannot logically be restricted to the balls,' Balfour responded, 'and it would be a pity, I think, to destroy the practically unlimited freedom of selection which among all games belongs, so far as I know, to golf.'

In the end, the fans of the new, easier-to-hit balls carried the day. The Rules Committee voted 10-5 against Fergusson and Low's motion – the no votes including Chairman Benjamin Hall Blyth, Horace Hutchinson and future architect Harry Colt.

Even before the vote, professional golfers could see which way the wind was blowing, and their solidarity began to crack. In a tournament at Bournemouth two days before the ruling, several broke ranks and used the Haskell, among them John Henry Taylor. By May he had been joined by Harry Vardon and James Braid, the two other leading professionals in what *Golf Illustrated* had recently begun to describe as The Triumvirate, a nickname that would stick. The gutty was gone forever.

Since its formation in 1897, the Rules Committee had been subject to withering criticism of the way it did its job. Nearly every issue of *Golf Illustrated* featured letters taking the committee to task for one perceived sin or another – none more unforgivable, at least south of the border, than its steadfast refusal to write rules for that unwelcome English invention, the Bogey Competition. This time, however, Smith led the chorus of praise for the vote against banning the new ball.

'There can be no doubt that the Royal and Ancient Golf Club . . . has correctly voiced the almost universal opinion of golfers in regard to this question,' he wrote in *Golf Illustrated*. 'There is a general consensus of opinion that they have done the game no harm, while they have added considerably to the enjoyment of those who play golf purely for pleasure and recreation.'

Sensitive to his amateur brethren, Smith added a few conciliatory words for traditionalists: 'At the same time, reflective golfers will be grateful to Mr Fergusson, Mr Low and their supporters for the zeal they have shown to safeguard what they believe to be the game's best interests; and it is quite conceivable that it may be necessary in the future to draw some definite line beyond which mechanical improvements in clubs and balls must not be allowed to go. All that can be said, however, is that time is not yet.'

More than a century later, when the 300-yard drive so feared by *The Field*, is commonplace, indeed a tad short, that time may finally have arrived. As this was written, golf's governing bodies seemed poised to reign in technology amid cries for limits on balls and clubs that remain as prevalent as they were when Low and Fergusson fretted about the future of the game.

Professional golfers never ceased to mourn the death of the gutty, especially as they watched the way rubber-cored balls revolutionised the game they had grown up with. Scoring in the Open at St Andrews provides some insight into the extent of the change. In the last Championship before the introduction of the Haskell ball, Taylor won with a score of 309. By 1910, Braid had shaved ten strokes from that total – and that after the links had been lengthened and toughened in response to the new ball. Vardon made the case as plainly as anyone in his memoir. 'I personally shall always regret the passing of the gutty,' he wrote. 'In my own mind, I am firmly convinced that with its passing much of the real skill had gone forever.'

The final drama involving the Haskell ball would unfold in court. In 1903 B.F. Goodrich sued British makers of rubber-cored balls, claiming infringement of its patent. In the end, even though the company pursued the case through appeals courts and up to the House of Lords, Goodrich did not prevail.

The court ruled that, in Britain at least, the idea was not a novel one. Captain Duncan Stewart had come up with it first, back in the 1870s, when he made wound rubber balls he couldn't sell because they didn't produce that confidence-inducing 'click' the way gutty balls did.

Battle rejoined

When the golf world's focus returned to championships, newly confident Scots were intent on reversing their run of losses in the Amateur, the one championship that had eluded them in the new century. This time, at least, there would be no chance that the new rubber-cored ball would help an inferior man win. Every leading player would be using one.

The biggest obstacle in Scotland's path was a familiar one. John Ball had returned to the form that made him the game's most feared matchplay golfer. His score of 77 to win the medal at Hoylake that spring brought this from Hilton: 'It is possible that finer golf has never been exhibited at Hoylake than by Mr Ball last week, particularly from the tee through the green.'

Even Scottish loyalist Garden Smith conceded that Ball had to be considered the favourite in the Amateur, which would be conducted that year in advance of the second International Match. Still, with the competition set for Muirfield, Scotland's new hope, Robert Maxwell, also represented a serious threat. He belonged to the Honourable Company and knew every blade of grass on its links at Muirfield. He also had been sharp that spring, taking the club's medal by coming in with 80 in a gale of wind.

A record field of 142 players entered the Amateur, forcing Muirfield to extend play over five days and raising anew the need to do something to limit the size of the field. The pairings for 1903 produced a Championship far different than last season's, when all the favourites faced one another early. This time the heavy hitters were spread out enough to produce a competition as wide open as any in memory.

'There were so many dark horses, and the rubber-filled ball has so modified the possibilities that the cognoscenti were chary of committing themselves to prophesy,' *Golf Illustrated* wrote.

Scotland's hopes of winning the Amateur got a giant boost in the third round. Despite leading 1 up on 17, Hilton fell to an unheralded player by fluffing an easy bunker shot and collapsing on the first play-off hole. England suffered an even more devastating blow in the sixth round, when Ball was nipped on 18. The good news for southerners was that the old warrior Horace Hutchinson, having just celebrated his 44th birthday, showed renewed vigour, surviving one close match after another to make it to the final for the sixth time in his career.

While all that was going on, Maxwell was making his way to the final nearly unchallenged. He had only one close encounter, a match that went 17 holes, before nearly giving Scotland a heart attack in his semi-final against Englishman Herman de Zoete of Royal St George's. Maxwell drove beautifully, while de Zoete sprayed his tee shots all over the course. One impossible recovery after another kept him alive, however, and the match ended all square in regulation.

On the first play-off hole, it appeared as if Scotland was fated to watch an all-English final. Maxwell pulled that all-important tee shot, and it wound up near the stone wall that runs along the first hole. He got it back in play, but not close to the green. De Zoete, meanwhile, finally found a fairway and reached the green with his second. Maxwell's third left himself a testing putt for a four.

At that critical moment, de Zoete later told Hutchinson, his nerves failed him. Knowing two putts would likely win, de Zoete could barely focus. 'He was unable, he said, to see the ball with any distinctness,' Hutchinson wrote. 'It looked all in a fog; and in playing at it through this obscuring atmosphere he sent it about a foot.' De Zoete's second was better, but didn't go in. It did, however, lay Maxwell a partial stymie. The Scotsman bravely holed his putt, narrowly missing de Zoete's ball, and moved on to his first Championship final.

The morning of the final dawned rather gloomily. By midday, however, the sun peeked out, the breeze picked up, and conditions were ideal for another battle between the thistle and the rose. Thousands of fans, mostly diehard Scotsmen from the East Lothian locality, turned out to follow the final, and the crowd only grew larger as the afternoon wore on.

Championship nerves being what they are, the morning round began sloppily. Hutchinson missed an easy putt to hand Maxwell the first, and the Scotsman returned the favour on the second with a weak approach. The game went back and forth until the turn, with Maxwell making 41 to Hutchinson's 43 and taking a 1-up lead.

During the opening holes of the homeward nine, Hutchinson squared the match, but the tide began turning on the 14th. There, improbably, Maxwell drained an enormously long putt to reclaim his lead. That rattled Hutchinson. He lost three of the next five holes to send Scotland's favourite son into lunch 4 up. 'I hardly know how it happened,' the Englishman wrote, 'for I do not remember that I played those holes extraordinarily badly, but I do know that I did not have nearly as good an appetite when we went in for luncheon.'

Hutchinson may have been dispirited, but he hadn't given up. 'I had a vision of bringing him down to quite a reasonable number of holes up, and making a close match of it,' he wrote. For the first few holes, Hutchinson did just that, closing the gap by a hole before they reached the seventh. It was there, however, that Maxwell broke his spirit.

'He made a great recovery out of the rough and won the hole which I had looked forward to winning,' Hutchinson remembered. 'I took three on the green and he only took one. That was the final touch.' Hutchinson could manage nothing better than a few halves after that, and Maxwell dispatched him on the 13th, winning 7 and 5.

Scotsmen were beside themselves with joy, having now added an Amateur to their back-to-back Opens and that resounding victory in the first International Match. Fans swarmed the green to carry their hero shoulder-high to the clubhouse. Maxwell, however, was every bit as shy and reserved a man as Ball, and he was having none of it.

'The new-fledged champion modestly bolted for the clubhouse and left the crowd far behind,' *Golf Illustrated* reported. Garden Smith must have been feeling a bit giddy himself, boasting that 'there was no finer golfer living' than Robert Maxwell.

The battle between Scotland and England would be rejoined the following morning in the second International Match, contested on a 'bright, beautiful and breezy' day that *Golf Illustrated* described as, 'a fitting climax to a splendid week'. In the face of last year's criticism, a few changes had been made in the format. Each team featured nine players this time, and they would face off in 36-hole matches.

The sides included many who had played the previous season, but this time the match was a close-run affair. It hardly started out that way. Maxwell, riding high after his Amateur victory, made mincemeat of Ball, going 4 up in the morning and finishing the hero of Hoylake off 8 and 6 in the afternoon. Hilton did the same thing to Scotsman John Laidlay, winning four holes in the morning and prevailing by 9 and 7 after the lunch break.

That trend continued through the remaining matches, with one side or the other romping, until the final match of the afternoon between England's G. F. Smith and Scotland's Charles Dick. They were approaching the 12th tee when the last of the early matches concluded, with the score tied at four wins apiece. Everything was riding on the seven holes that remained.

Dick started the afternoon round three holes behind, but had wiped out Smith's lead and forged ahead by a hole just as his fellow competitors turned up en masse to follow the match in. Dick lost his lead twice more on that final stretch, before making a marvellous putt at 17 to take the game to the home hole.

Both players hit splendid drives and reached the green in two, although neither was close to the hole. Dick played first, but with the weight of the nation on his shoulders anxiety overtook him. He left his first putt nine feet short. When Smith rolled his answer to within three feet, it was over. Dick missed and Smith holed to give England the victory 5 to 4.

Despite that agonising loss, *Golf Illustrated* was in a magnanimous mood. 'Honours are easy between Scotland and England,' Smith wrote, 'for if Scotland won the Championship, England has won the International. No result could have been better from the point of view of keeping alive the healthy spirit of international rivalry, for it was high time the Championship came north, and last year England lost the international.'

The tremendous excitement generated by these matches between Scotland and England was not lost on professional golfers. In January 1903, the PGA took a cue from the amateurs and voted to host an international match of its own two days before the Open that June at Prestwick. They chose a different format, 12 men a side with singles matches in the morning and foursomes in the afternoon.

The first professional International Match turned out to be every bit as thrilling as the amateur battles between north and south. James Braid and Willie Park led off for Scotland and set the tone with resounding victories. Braid dusted Harry Vardon 5 and 4, while Park demolished Rowland Jones 6 and 5. The morning session ended with six victories for each side.

The highlight of the afternoon foursomes was the lead match pitting Braid and Sandy Herd against Vardon and John Henry Taylor. Unbeknownst to those involved, this was a preview of an epic battle to be waged two years hence. Braid and Herd squeaked by 1 up, carrying their side to victory as England lost two of the other five matches and halved one.

'That the fixture has come to stay hardly needs to be argued with anyone who was fortunate enough to see the game on Monday,' *Golf Illustrated* enthused. 'The play was most interesting, and it was a treat to see the sportsmanlike spirit in which the match was played.'

Scotland's 9-8 victory, with one match halved, was its second in three international match-play competitions. That bolstered the nation's claim of superiority at the true game. The case was made stronger by the reality that Scotland did not field its strongest side, as players like Andra Kirkaldy and Archie Simpson were not PGA members and thus ineligible to compete. The issues that kept them from joining, however, were resolved in a meeting Taylor hosted the night after the match, and all was well for the future.

High hopes

Given Braid's resounding victory over Vardon in the International Match, Scotland carried high hopes that its run of glory would continue in the Open. The largest crowd ever seen at Prestwick, 6,000 or more, crammed the links to follow the nation's leading lights – Braid, Herd and Jack White – on a near-perfect June morning in Ayrshire.

The opening round did nothing to diminish Scotland's optimism. Herd matched Vardon stroke for stroke, as both came in with sparkling 73s to share a three-stroke lead. Braid and White remained close with 77s. It was in the second round, with the wind freshening and scores rising, that the truth about the 1903 Open began to be revealed. Vardon posted a 77, and extended his lead to four. His score might have been lower but for a sloppy seven at the Alps. Scotsmen occupied the next six spots, but the three given the best chance to win were well back. White had five strokes to make up. Herd and Braid were a stroke behind him.

What the Prestwick crowd did not know was that Vardon was putting on this display of golf despite being desperately ill. Earlier that year, he had suffered a nasal haemorrhage, the tell-tale sign of tuberculosis. Vardon recovered from that incident, but not fully. He was so worn down after his opening round that, for the first time in his life, he spent the lunch break lying down to gather strength for the afternoon.

'I had for some months been far from well, and had as a matter of fact been under the care of a doctor,' Vardon admitted afterwards. 'I was told it would be very unwise for me to take part in the big event. However, I made up my mind I would play.'

Vardon's 77 in the second round – four strokes higher than his score in the morning, with that ugly seven at the 17th – gave Scots slender hope that he might not resume his all-conquering ways in round three the next day. Despite feeling weak and ill again, Vardon 'set about resolving doubts of this nature in no uncertain fashion', *Golf Illustrated* wrote. Playing as well as he had in his life, he reached the turn in 34. When he came home in 38, 'his total of 72 placed him in practically an unassailable position.'

White made a valiant effort to close the gap, posting a superb 74. Even that performance left him with seven strokes to make up in the final round. No golfer alive was going to gain that much ground on Vardon over 18 holes unless he failed to finish. Herd and Braid were even farther back at ten and 13 strokes, respectively.

There was no guarantee that Vardon would make it through that final round. He spent the lunch break lying down again, his meal consisting of a bottle of Guinness. He headed to the first tee feeling 'so faint that I thought it would be impossible for me to finish'. He clung to the hope that with such a large lead he would simply need to survive to win.

Vardon played solidly through the outward nine, finishing in 37, but by then he was in desperate straits. 'On the homeward journey I must say that my fears of being unable to finish gave me a great deal of anxiety as I felt so faint on several occasions. It seemed to me more than once that I would have to give in.' Vardon staggered home in 41, but 'when I had holed out on the last green, I knew I had won the Championship.'

He had lost only a stroke of his lead, finishing six shots ahead of his brother, Tom, who turned in excellent scores of 75 and 74 over the last two rounds to nip White by two strokes. Herd and Braid followed White, claiming the other spots in the top five for Scotland.

Golf Illustrated tipped its cap to the champion. 'Harry Vardon scored the greatest triumph of his career, demonstrating his supremacy in unmistakable fashion,' the magazine wrote. Vardon agreed. 'My success in this Championship must rank as the finest achievement which I have ever accomplished,' he wrote. The toll it took on the now four-time Open champion would soon become apparent.

In January of that year, Vardon left his professional's post at Ganton and moved to South Herts Golf Club in Totteridge, near London, where he would remain for the rest of his career. Vardon returned to Totteridge after the Open, but not before ignoring his own best judgement by keeping a commitment to play in a tournament the morning after the Championship at Western Gailes, which he won by five shots over Taylor and Herd. Vardon took a few days of badly needed rest after that, then did what Open champions had always done. He cashed in on his victory with an exhibition tour of Yorkshire, where he continued to display exquisite form.

It was soon after he had returned to Totteridge, hoping his illness had passed, that Vardon experienced one of the most traumatic events of his life. He was on the links at South Herts when he suffered a major haemorrhage. Vardon had to be carried from the course. The next morning, he felt strong enough to get out of bed, and intended to return to the club. But as he bent over to tie his shoes, he endured another serious haemorrhage.

'It was now apparent that I was in a real bad state of health,' Vardon recalled in his classically understated way, 'and I was ordered to go to a sanatorium.' He would spend months recuperating at Mundesley Sanatorium in Norfolk, forbidden to play golf or enjoy his beloved pipe.

Taking control

A week after news of Vardon's illness surfaced in *Golf Illustrated*'s final edition of July, the fledgling PGA made a blockbuster announcement. The *News of the World*, a widely popular Sunday tabloid, had agreed to put up £200 to sponsor an annual match-play tournament.

The goals were to stimulate the growth of professional golf and promote the classic Scottish game of man-to-man combat. Entry would be restricted to PGA members, who would earn their way into the event through qualifying tournaments conducted by the association's various sections in Scotland, England, Ireland and, eventually, Wales.

These qualifiers added nine new annual tournaments to the schedule, a giant leap forward for professional golfers, especially those struggling financially. The top 32 players would make the News of the World, which instantly became recognised as a major championship on a par with the Open and the Amateur.

The tournament would consist of 18-hole elimination matches followed by a 36-hole final. The prize money dwarfed anything in golf. The winner would receive £100, twice what the Open paid. Every player in the top eight would earn money, in amounts ranging from £30 for second to £10 for eighth. Payouts would only increase as the years passed.

Even more important, for the first time in history professional golfers were in control of their own schedule, supported by their own sponsor.

In years past, they could rely on only one regularly scheduled championship, the Open, and its purse was at the whim of private clubs that had hosted the event since its inception. Beyond that, professionals had to rely on other clubs or promoters hosting the occasional event.

This bold step forward would be reinforced eight years later with the advent of the Sphere and Tatler Cup, also sponsored by a newspaper. It, too, would create a series of nine qualifying tournaments leading up to the main event. That would feature 32 finalists paired in two-man teams to compete in another classic Scottish game, foursomes. Prizes offered in the Sphere and Tatler Cup amounted to £350, a shade below the £400 paid out by the *News of the World* at its pre-war peak.

The advent of these competitions represented the birth of the modern professional golf tour. Numbers tell the story. Before the PGA was founded, an average of only 13 tournaments were staged annually. In the years between the association's formation and the outbreak of war, that number nearly tripled to 31. The pattern for the future was set. The tournament season, including one major, would be run by and for professional golfers, with the age-old clubs controlling only the Open. In time that formula would be repeated in the United States and elsewhere.

The first News of the World was played in October 1903 at Sunningdale near London, where Jack White was the golf professional. White surprised everyone by falling in the first round to Englishman Tom Williamson. The semi-finalists included Braid, Irish professional George Coburn, Taylor and Ted Ray, Vardon's mate from the Isle of Jersey.

In the first semi-final, Braid and Taylor faced off. Taylor was stiff and sore from a rainstorm he'd played through earlier. Braid took the first two holes and went on to win 4 and 2. The match between Coburn and Ray was close through seven, but Ray claimed the next four holes and prevailed 4 and 3.

The opening round of the 36-hole final between Braid and Ray was a dogfight between two of the game's longest hitters. Braid led by a hole before lunch. In the afternoon, however, he demonstrated his superiority, winning three of the first five holes to take a commanding lead and eventually finishing Ray off 4 and 3.

What a year it had been for golf – and especially for Scotland. The ancient home of the game had taken three of the year's five major events, prevailing in all but one of the four contested at match play. Scotland had, at last, produced heroes capable of stemming the southern tide, and the future looked as bright as it had been before the dark days that followed Ball's breakthrough Open victory for the English back in 1890.

It was clear, also, that the game had reached a turning point. The R&A had embraced technology that would shape golf for decades to come. The PGA, with its new events and its own major championship, was poised to eclipse the amateur game for good. *Golf Illustrated*'s circulation had expanded dramatically around the world – in Europe and Asia, Africa and Australia, North America and South America.

No one knew where these changes would lead, of course, but the following season would provide the first hint.

Sixteen

AMERICAN INVADERS

———— ·•◉•· ————

The biggest news in British golf in 1904 came not from Scotland or England, but from Garden City Golf Club in Long Island, New York. Walter Travis, now the three-time winner of the US Amateur, had decided he was ready to take on the greatest golfers in the world. He was coming to compete in the Amateur at Sandwich.

Travis was no stranger to British golf. Three years earlier, he had sailed across the Atlantic to tour the great links of Scotland and England, writing upon his return that golf architecture in the States had a long way to go to match what he found in the United Kingdom. During his trip, Travis had played matches against many of the nation's best, Harold Hilton among them, and usually been soundly beaten. Afterwards, *Golf Illustrated* carried regular reports on Travis's exploits stateside.

The previous season, Travis had been one of the American hosts for the Oxford and Cambridge Golf Society's triumphal tour of the eastern United States. The Society, led by John Low, lost only one match in America – and that by a single point. Britain's experiences with Travis convinced English and Scottish golfers that they had no reason to fear him, or any of the other five Americans who entered that year to compete at Sandwich.

Travis, however, was not a man to be underestimated. Part of the reason he had come to Britain in 1901 was to discover the weaknesses in his game by competing against the best. He had spent the past three years doggedly addressing those issues. Originally from Australia, Travis had lived in the States for a decade, married, and become a naturalised citizen before he took up golf at the age of 34. He'd never been tempted by the game, but his friends in Long Island were forming a golf club, and he decided he ought to join.

Travis was instantly hooked on golf, and taught himself to play by reading classic works of instruction, especially Horace Hutchinson's essays in Badminton's *Golf* and Willie Park's *The Game of Golf*. Travis applied that same relentless self-discipline to fixing the flaws he uncovered on his grand tour of Britain. By 1904, Travis was convinced his game could stand up to the best the old country had to offer.

He was encouraged by his friend, Devereux Emmet, who wrote to him from England, where he was, among other things, scouting classic courses for American architect C.B. Macdonald. 'If the weather is calm, I think you will win the thing,' Emmet wrote. 'They don't begin to know how good you are over here, and that will be greatly to your advantage.'

Travis had a game plan for his assault on the Amateur. He would arrive weeks ahead of time to practise at St Andrews and North Berwick, leaving plenty of time to explore the intricacies of Sandwich, a course that 'wants a lot of knowing', as Emmet put it. Travis had been so graciously received during his 1901 tour that he assumed he would be even more warmly welcomed this time after having hosted players from Oxford and Cambridge.

His plans went awry from the outset. When he arrived in St Andrews in early May, Travis discovered, to his dismay, that leading amateurs were no longer interested in a game with him. Apparently, it was one thing to take an admiring tour of British links, and another to visit with the intent of carrying the Amateur Championship trophy back to America. Worse still, Travis's game had deserted him. His play was embarrassingly bad, boosting the confidence of British golfers who saw him hopelessly flailing away.

Travis was so desperate that he bought a new set of clubs to see if that would change his luck. It didn't. During his trip, Travis said, professional golfers were the only men who welcomed him unreservedly, especially John Henry Taylor and Harry Vardon, whom he'd met during their 1900 tour of America.

North Berwick's professional, Ben Sayers, saw how Travis was struggling and loaned him a favourite spoon, a club similar to a modern 5- or 7-wood. The spoon was Travis's go-to club. At 5 feet 7 inches and less than 140 pounds, he was a short-but-straight hitter. He needed a wood to approach most greens. Sayers's spoon, it turned out, would play a pivotal role in the Amateur.

If the trip had begun badly for Travis, it reached its nadir when he arrived at Sandwich, the course he'd singled out as his favourite after the 1901 tour. He and the men running the Open clashed from the outset. At the age of 42, with his black cigar, intense stare and brusque manner, Travis was a forbidding presence. Whether it was that or, as he believed, resentment of his assault on the Amateur, Travis found himself in constant conflict with his hosts.

Relations began badly when Travis arrived to learn that no room had been reserved for him at Royal St George's Hotel, where the other competitors were staying. He'd have to find his own quarters in town at the Bell Hotel. Worse still, no locker had been reserved for him in the clubhouse. Travis would have to change clothes in the hallway and store his clubs in the professional's shop. He was so incensed that he turned down an invitation to dinner, which the British took as an insult.

Travis had come to Sandwich far later than planned, fearing that his awful play would prejudice his previously favourable view of the course. On his first trip around the links, he played only with a cleek he had picked up in North Berwick. That proved to be the antidote his game needed. 'From the first ball I struck, I knew I was on the road to recovery,' Travis wrote. 'For the first time in two weeks, I could "feel" the ball . . . I was at once transported into the golfer's seventh heaven of delight.' Except for one thing. Travis still could not hole a putt – ordinarily the strongest part of his game – and he knew that without his putter to compensate for his lack of length, he was doomed.

In desperation, one of the friends who had accompanied Travis on the trip suggested that he try a putter invented in Schenectady, New York. It was an unusual-looking weapon, with the shaft attached to the centre of the club head. Travis took his first putt with it the day before his opening match. It worked like magic. He felt his confidence return as putt after putt found the cup.

By then Travis had also decided to use what he perceived as mistreatment by Sandwich officials, including being assigned an incompetent caddie, as fuel for his competitive fire. Years later, Travis would write that he had arrived in Britain fiercely determined to win the Amateur, 'but that was as nothing to the now steel-clad resolution to do so'.

Bookmakers did not fancy Travis's chances. The favourites were John Graham, Robert Maxwell and, of course, Harold Hilton. Graham had begun the week with a commanding victory in the St George's Vase; Maxwell had led Scotland to another 6-3 romp in the International Match, with a gruelling play-off victory over John Ball.

From the outset, Travis played like a man who had won three national titles. His opening match unfolded in driving rain and fierce wind. Travis holed one long putt after another to take an early lead, and went on to win 4 and 3, causing a stir when he claimed the seventh hole after calling his opponent for grounding his club in a hazard.

Travis was soaked to the skin when he returned to the clubhouse, with only 20 minutes to go before his afternoon match. His request for a brief delay to give him time to change into dry clothes was denied, so Travis irately towelled himself off and headed to the tee to try his luck against two-time Amateur runner-up James Robb. Their match was a ding-dong battle that would come down to the final green, with Travis clinging to a one-hole lead. He narrowly survived by halving the 18th.

It might have been different had Robb not made a sporting gesture on the 11th. Travis had laid his putt dead, and his ill-trained caddie was holding the flag as his opponent prepared to putt from the edge of the green. Robb asked the caddie to remove the flag. Instead the young man picked up Travis's ball, infuriating the already angry American. Robb told Travis to replace his ball and play on, although he had every right to claim that hole.

The next day Travis resumed his winning ways, dispatching his first opponent 3 and 1 and surviving a cliffhanger in the afternoon against the former Irish Amateur Champion, H.E. Reade of County Down. Travis never led before 17, but prevailed 2 up. That victory awakened British fears that Travis might do the unthinkable.

'We had begun by not being at all frightened of Mr Travis,' wrote Bernard Darwin, 'and then gradually, as he got further and further through, a deadly terror had seized us by the throat.' Still, Brits could take comfort in knowing that on the morrow Travis would encounter Hilton and the winner of the match between Hutchinson and Maxwell, who had already knocked out Graham. Surely, one of them would give the American his comeuppance.

Genuine panic began to set in when Hilton, twice a winner of the Open and Amateur, showed up far off form on a windswept, drizzly morning. Travis won the first three holes on the strength of brilliant approaches with Sayers's spoon and even better putts with his new Schenectady. Hilton didn't take a hole until the 11th. Travis responded by reeling off three holes in succession, winning the match by 5 and 4.

British plans did not go according to Hoyle in the Maxwell–Hutchinson duel, either. Hutchinson was 45 years old by then, his best days behind him, and the partisan crowd expected that it would be Maxwell who showed the upstart American the door. Hutchinson was in a fighting mood, however, and stubbornly held on to the man who had trounced him 7 and 5 the previous year. The match was halved in regulation, and Hutchinson slipped past Maxwell on the first extra hole.

Hutchinson never had been a robust man, and the battle with Maxwell left him spent that afternoon. 'I started out . . . without the smallest idea in life that I was to be beaten by "that American", but I had not played two shots before I knew that all the best of the fight had been taken out of me by that stiff morning match,' Hutchinson wrote. Travis dispatched Hutchinson as easily as he had Hilton, strolling home 5 and 4.

The man upon whose shoulders the weight of the nation now descended was 38-year-old Edward 'Ted' Blackwell, a St Andrews man who would go on to be a captain of the Royal and Ancient. Blackwell was a giant of a man, standing more than 6 feet tall and weighing nearly 200 pounds. Not surprisingly, he was famous for his long driving. Blackwell was as long as any player, even Dougie Rolland or the lamented Freddie Tait.

Everyone at Royal St George's, Travis included, knew Blackwell would outdrive the American from every tee, often by 50 yards or more. Anxious Brits convinced themselves that Blackwell's length would unmask the short-hitting Travis. Those who knew Blackwell's game best, Hutchinson among them, weren't as sure. They worried that he was simply not good enough on the greens, putting with his razor-thin cleek, however far he drove the ball.

Fortunately for Travis, the morning of the final was a lovely one, with the sun shining and barely a whisper of wind. Even his friend Devereux Emmet believed Travis would be hard-pressed to show his best in the face of a stiff breeze off Pegwell Bay, especially against a bomber. It was evident from the first tee shot, even with a mere 300 fans looking on, that Blackwell was uneasy playing the role of Britain's last line of defence.

He pushed his opening drive into the deep rough, while Travis punched his down the middle. The American's next shot, with Sayers's spoon, was carefully placed shy of the bunker guarding the green, all but guaranteeing a five. Blackwell overreached with his second, yanking it into the left rough. The six that followed allowed Travis to seize the lead immediately. When he holed a putt of fully 40 feet to claim the second, the pattern for the day was set. Armed with a deadly putter, short-but-steady David was more than a match for Goliath.

Before the pair reached the sixth hole, Blackwell found himself four down. Travis made one of his few poor putts on that green, missing a short one to hand his opponent the hole. British partisans cheered his failure. That embarrassed Blackwell, who held his hand aloft to silence the crowd. He fought back valiantly after that, and had a chance to cut the lead to one hole as he and Travis stood on the 13th fairway. Blackwell couldn't capitalise, however, and when Travis won that hole and another on the way in, he headed into the lunch break sitting on a 4-up lead.

Terror had, indeed, seized Britain by the throat now. The forlorn, partisan crowd was searching for something, anything, to convince them that the American was about to crack. Travis gave them that moment of hope on the opening hole of the final 18. He played terribly, racking up his worst score of the day, an ugly seven that allowed Blackwell to cut the lead to three.

Travis did not wait long to disabuse Brits of any notion that he might, at last, be about to falter. He came right back to win the second hole, and added three more before he and Blackwell reached the sixth. Travis stood six up with only a dozen holes remaining. The rest of the round unfolded precisely as the morning had. Blackwell drove wildly. Travis poked one shot after another down the middle and holed seemingly every putt he faced. Ted could do no better than to whittle the lead to four holes, and the match ended on the 15th. Travis won 4 and 3, having led every step of the way.

It is impossible to overestimate the shock Travis's victory caused in Britain, especially in amateur golf. 'It was known that some Americans had come over and entered for the Championship,' Hutchinson wrote, 'but if anyone had prophesied that one of them was likely to give trouble or get into the final heats he would have been looked on as a lunatic.'

Ever since Vardon returned from the US in 1900, setting off a golf boom that would dwarf Britain's, there had been talk of the looming threat writers described as the 'American menace'. The recent run of triumphant British stateside tours, however, convinced most that any threat from across the Atlantic was a long way off.

'It was freely recognised that American golf was bound to improve,' wrote Taylor, 'but it was never anticipated that British superiority was to be so soon challenged and vanquished.' In just three years, British golfers would get another lesson about how the enormous growth of golf worldwide would shape the future of the game.

The final unpleasantness of an ugly week unfolded at the prize ceremony, where Lord Northbourne rambled on about the Roman occupation and the history of Kent before adding, as he handed over the trophy, 'Never, never, since the days of Caesar has the British nation been subjected to such humiliation, and we fervently hope that history may not repeat itself.' Travis hardly knew what to say. He acknowledged the fine play of his competitors, and said: 'I am hopelessly bunkered. I pick up my ball.'

Years later, in his magazine *The American Golfer*, Travis wrote bitterly about his experiences in Britain. His hosts, and many others, believed his complaints arose from a lack of understanding about how golf worked in Britain and that he only had himself to blame. Bernard Darwin, however, concluded that he and his countrymen could not fully be excused.

'I always have an uneasy feeling that we in England did not treat Mr Travis very well,' Darwin wrote. 'We are not, I am afraid, very good at welcoming our visitors or making a fuss of them, and then, Mr Travis did not give the impression that he wanted any welcoming; he seemed a silent and rather dour man who wanted to play his golf and be left alone. Still, when we have made all the excuses possible for ourselves, I am afraid that we were not very friendly to him either before or after he won.'

Travis would not return to defend his title.

Thrilling finish

The deep psychic wound caused by Travis's victory received just the salve it needed five days later at Sandwich with an Open, featuring an exhilaratingly close battle between thistle and rose.

The stage for that duel was set in the second International Match for professionals, which ended in an 8-8 tie. Scotland forged ahead in the morning singles, only to see England turn the tide in foursomes and lead 8-7 with one match still under way – the south's Rowland Jones and James Sherlock vs northerners Andra Kirkaldy and Ben Sayers. The old Scots pulled the match out of the fire for their nation to end the contest with honours even.

Four days later the largest field in history, 144 players, gathered for the Open. For the first time ever, play had to be extended over three days. The first two days would consist of 18-hole rounds, followed by a 36-hole final among those who made the cut. The now demonised Travis, showing no interest beyond honouring his commitment to compete, would not be among the 52 survivors.

The opening round was played in cold, windy weather, but that did not stop players from dismantling Sandwich. Scotsman Robert Thompson, an unheralded golfer from North Berwick, went around in 75 to take the lead. His countryman John Graham was a stroke back, along with Vardon. Just behind them at 77 were Taylor, Braid and Vardon's brother, Tom.

The wind died down for the second day's play. Harry Vardon took advantage by going around in 73 and moving into first with a two-round total of 149. Thompson posted 76 to finish second at 151, with Graham again a stroke back and Tom Vardon trailing in fourth at 154. Scotland's principal hope, Braid, faded to ninth with an 80, but Jack White compensated by turning in a 75 that moved him into a tie for sixth with Taylor at 155.

The highlight of that afternoon, however, came from Oxford University's James Sherlock. He went around in an astonishing 71, a new record for Sandwich, and the clearest sign yet that Royal St George's was a much less imposing test in the age of rubber-cored balls. Sherlock's round of a lifetime left him tied with Tom Vardon in fourth.

The stage was set for a finale full of fireworks, with six Scotsmen and four southerners within striking distance. Even the weather seemed to have been ordered up for an afternoon of heart-stopping drama. 'There had been much rain during the night,' *The Times* wrote, 'and this took the fire out of the putting greens, while the strong wind of Wednesday and Thursday was absent, and the light being even, it was just the day for perfect golf.'

Perfect golf is precisely what unfolded. Braid raised the hopes of his nation – and every eyebrow at Sandwich – by scorching the outward nine in an absurdly low 31. He played nearly as brilliantly coming home, taking only 38 strokes to eclipse Sherlock's day-old record with a 69. That put Braid in the lead, with a total of 226. Fellow Scotsman White, displaying his sterling short game, capitalised on the soft conditions with a 72 of his own. That left him in second, a stroke behind Braid.

Scotland's hopes only brightened when Harry Vardon's form suddenly deserted him. He went around in 79, ten strokes worse than Braid, and fell back to third place, with two strokes to make up. Taylor, who had been off his best all week, finally found his footing with a 74 that put him back in the race at 229, tied fourth with Tom Vardon.

The ideal weather on that windless day only got better and brighter as the afternoon wore on, and the crowd was eagerly anticipating more sensational scores. Out first among the contenders, White was in the enviable position of being able to post a low number for others to match. Truth be told, however, not many expected him to do that. Deadly as he was with his putter, and accurate as he was from the tee, the consensus was that White's long game was not powerful enough to hold off the likes of Braid or Vardon. Not only that, White was prone to collapsing under pressure.

This time White did not wilt. He reached the turn in 32, nearly as brilliant a performance as the far longer Braid had turned in that morning. He kept on playing flawlessly on the way home. White didn't make a misstep until the 16th, when his tee shot found the rough. He played out brilliantly, however, and saved his four. White wobbled again on 18, sending that drive into the rough, too, but again he scraped out his four to equal the low round of the tournament with a 69.

White's total of 296 was itself a record – the first time an Open had been completed in fewer than 300 strokes, a further testament to the influence of the rubber-cored ball. It set a fearful mark to beat, even under perfect conditions. Braid would need a 70 to tie, while Harry Vardon would need a 68 and Taylor a 67. Vardon came in first, and his 74, excellent on any other occasion, was not good enough that day. He finished with 302, a stroke behind his brother, Tom, who turned in a beautiful 72.

Hilton was standing on the ninth tee when Braid arrived there shortly after White made the turn for home. Braid had played beautifully on the opening holes, requiring just 34 strokes.

'How is Jack White doing?' he asked Hilton.

'Pretty well,' Hilton replied, cautiously.

'What's he out in?' Braid continued.

'Thirty-two,' Hilton answered. 'That made Jimmy look very serious, and when, to a further query, I replied that as far as I could gather, White had started home with three fours, he looked more serious than ever.'

Braid dug deep, playing flawless golf on his way in. His only slip came on 13, where he made five instead of the expected four, but he quickly made up for the mistake. He reached the long 15th in two and stole a 24-foot putt for a brilliant three. Before he teed off on that hole, Braid had run into another man he knew and asked him how White had finished. He was told his fellow Scotsman had come in with 70 – the sort of tragic misinformation commonplace before the advent of scoreboards.

'According to my reckoning,' Braid wrote, 'I had three fours left to tie – not by any means a difficult task, though one that left no margin for error or missed putts. In the circumstances, I was naturally inclined to play the cautious game.' Next came the 160-yard 16th, where the hole was tucked precariously on the back of the green. Braid faced a long approach putt and decided not to risk going boldly for the hole. His second stopped six feet short. Braid missed his third, but it was still the four he thought he needed.

Braid duly recorded his four on 17 and sent his approach on 18 eight yards past the hole. He carefully laid his first putt dead, and holed out for four. Hilton and the fans surrounding the green were baffled. 'The spectators, who were aware of his position, could not understand why he did not hit the approach putt sufficiently hard to reach the hole,' Hilton wrote.

'I thought I had tied,' Braid remembered, 'and not until then was I made aware, to my great disappointment, that White had finished his last round, not in 70, but in 69, and therefore I had lost the Championship by one stroke . . . This made the third time that I had a putt to tie for the Championship when on the last green, and each time the ball stayed out of the hole.'

In the excitement over Braid's finish, everyone at Sandwich seemed to have forgotten that there was still one contender on the course – Taylor, playing without a single fan following him. Even before White posted his marvellous 69, Taylor knew he had his work cut out for him that afternoon.

'I started out with the hope that a period of inspiration would come to my aid, and after playing three holes it looked as if it had arrived.' Taylor started his final 18 with a scintillating 3-3-2 and had played a mere 28 strokes as he stood in the ninth fairway preparing to approach the green. Just then he heard an enormous roar echoing across the dunes – a sound that could mean only one thing. Some other competitor was being hailed as champion. Taylor assumed it must be Vardon or Braid.

It was at that moment that he bumped into prominent amateur Sidney Fry, who asked how Taylor was getting on. He replied with a question of his own. Who was the crowd cheering? Was it Vardon or Braid? Fry shared the astonishing news that White had nipped Braid by a stroke and that Vardon had faded from the picture.

'I further demanded to know White's score, which Mr Fry was reluctant to give, and again he enquired as to my progress,' Taylor remembered. 'I replied that if I did the hole in four I should be out in 32, but again I insisted on knowing what White had done. "Well, John," said

Mr Fry in that calm voice of his, "if you insist, White was round in 69, which means that you need a 67 to tie." I got my four, and was faced with the almost impossible task of doing the long, inward half in 35 to force a play-off.

Taylor played brilliantly, lipping the hole on both 16 and 17 with putts that might have dropped. He came to 18 needing a three to tie. His tee shot found the fairway, and Taylor took out his mashie, with the idea of working the ball along a slope that would carry it towards the hole. The shot didn't come off, and he was left with a 30-footer to take the Championship to a play-off the following morning.

'I can see that putt as I write,' Taylor recalled. 'It was a dusty, dry, dropper with a yard borrow from the right. I gave it a firm chance and a few feet from the hole it looked in, but again touching the rim on the left side it slipped a foot past, finishing on the left side. I had failed by the lowest possible margin.'

White may have been an unexpected winner but no one begrudged the Scotsman's victory in one of the most sensational Championships golf had ever seen. 'He had plenty of dash, and the fast ground helped him, and when it came to putting there was no one to teach him anything,' Darwin wrote. 'He was a genuine artist on the greens.'

Disturbing signs

Two patterns emerged from the 1904 championships. More than ever, the outcome of both the Amateur and Open was determined on the greens. It had also become clear that even once fearsome courses like Royal St George's had been tamed by that other American invader, the rubber-cored ball.

Travis and White putted so magnificently at Sandwich that they were invited to team up on an instructional booklet called *The Art of Putting*, published later that year. It consisted of essays by the men on their methods and photographs of their style by George Beldam. He had previously published a similar book, *Great Golfers: Their Methods at a Glance*, featuring action photos of Vardon, Taylor, Braid, Herd and Hilton.

White was shown demonstrating his classically Scottish style, his stance open, his body nearly doubled over as he bent down to his work. Travis was pictured using his Schenectady putter, which initially became a hot item in professionals' shops, but was later banned by the Royal and Ancient as nonconforming because it was centre-shafted.

Far more discussion, however, focused on the reality that on one of the nation's most brutish courses, the winners were two of the shortest hitters in golf. In the gutty days, no one would have bet a halfpenny on Travis or White to win at Sandwich. The carries from its back tees favoured bombers like Maxwell or Braid. If the great courses of Scotland and England were to retain their teeth, something would have to be done.

Even before the Haskell ball came along, leading minds in British golf – nearly all of them connected with the Oxford and Cambridge Golf Society – had turned their attention to improving golf course architecture. With golf booming in England, more and more courses were being built on inland sites not nearly as suitable for the game as traditional links land.

Inland sites did not have hazards that had developed naturally over the ages, as links land did, leaving the men who designed these new courses to devise their own methods of testing golfers. They tended to follow ideas then in vogue in Victorian golf course design. The essence of that philosophy was that poor shots must be punished, with the severity of the punishment equivalent to the extent of the crime.

Most inland courses featured hazards that were placed where a ball that was topped, sliced or pulled would end up. Victorian-style courses tended to require forced carries from the tees, have bunkers lining fairways to capture stray shots, and ask golfers to cross another hazard to reach the green. This approach troubled new thinkers about architecture in two ways. The courses looked as if they had been imposed on the landscape, and the challenges they presented were not particularly interesting.

In 1897 Hutchinson had become golf editor of *Country Life* magazine. A disciple of Old Tom Morris, Hutchinson had been thinking about golf courses and their design for a long time. In Badminton's *Golf* he had written a seminal essay titled 'Some Celebrated Links', and a year later he published another study of classic courses, *Famous Golf Links*.

Hutchinson used *Country Life*'s weekly column 'On the Green' to promote a new brand of design. It emphasised making hazards appear natural, as if they had been part of the landscape all along, rather than creations of an architect. He also advocated making their placement more strategic than penal.

Hutchinson invited other forward-thinking men to join the call for a new style of architecture – people like Bernard Darwin, Herbert Fowler and Harry Colt. It was another member of the Oxford and Cambridge Golf Society, however, who would produce the manifesto of this emerging movement, the same man who had led the fight to bar rubber-cored golf balls – John Low.

The question Low and his compatriots explored was why classic courses like Prestwick and St Andrews were regarded as the greatest tests in the game. The answer, he concluded, was that they required more of golfers than simply a clean strike and a decent carry. Links like Prestwick and the Old Course could only be mastered by placing the tee shot in a spot that set up the most advantageous approach to the green. Golfers had to think about the challenge posed by each hole and develop a strategy for overcoming it.

In the autumn of 1903, Low spelled out his ideas in *Concerning Golf*. Most of the book was devoted to instruction, but two chapters came to be regarded as a manifesto representing the views of those who believed rubber-cored balls were ruining golf. The opening chapter on the character of the game argued passionately that the Haskell ball and its descendants had taken the skill out of playing golf. The gutty rewarded 'scientific' players – men who had learned to strike the ball properly and to shape its flight to suit the wind and the demands of the hole being played.

'Not only had the old ball to be hit hard, but it had to be hit accurately, or it would not go at all,' Low wrote. 'An India-rubber ball hit right off the nose of the club will go very nearly as far as a truly hit shot; this fact alone stamps their introduction as detrimental to scientific play.'

Low was remorselessly critical of the Rules Committee for failing to take action to preserve the essence of the Scottish game, which to his mind was quickly being replaced by distance-driven golf of an entirely different sort. 'The reason for this change is not far to seek; nor could it have been prevented except by prompt and decisive legislation,' he wrote. 'But the legislators were neither prompt nor brave enough to carry out their convictions, and thus, an irredeemable opportunity was lost.'

It was, however, a chapter titled 'The Links' that would have the most lasting impact on golf. It spelled out Low's ideas about what makes a golf course interesting and challenging. He flatly rejected Victorian notions about punishing errant shots. Low called for designs that require golfers to develop and execute a strategy for every hole, weighing up from both the tee and the fairway the risks of playing boldly or cautiously. That would hold true for both scratch players and high handicappers, but in seeking safety weaker players would lose strokes to more daring and able men.

In this way, Low wrote, 'Each stroke has to be played in relation to the following one, and the hole mastered by a preconceived plan of action.' His idea of punishment was not to trap the errant ball in the bunker, but to leave the player who made the mistake so out of position that making par became difficult, if not impossible. The true role of hazards, Low concluded, was not to punish bad shots, but to tempt the best golfers to go as near them as they dare to obtain the best angle for attacking the green.

'On many courses,' Low explained, 'the hazards are laid out only to catch really bad shots; this kind of difficulty has little interest for the good player ... What tests good golf is the hazard which may or may not be risked; the bunker which takes charge of the long but not truly hit shot.'

Low had begun to put his ideas into practice two years before he published *Concerning Golf.* He and a friend named Stuart Paton, who were members at Woking Golf Club near London, sought to mimic at that course the principles of St Andrews. They added two pot bunkers in the middle of the fourth fairway 180 yards from the tee, exactly where a good player's tee shot might land.

The idea was that these bunkers would function in the same way as the famous Principal's Nose on the 16th hole of the Old Course. That deep pit, with two others nearby, forces players to make a strategic choice from the tee. They can play safely to the left, or take on the challenge of gaining a more advantageous position by landing in the narrow strip of ground between the bunkers and the railway that, in those days, ran along the right side of the fairway. That area is now out of bounds.

Club members were outraged. Tom Simpson, then a barrister, walked in on their heated discussion of the issue one rainy morning at Woking and found himself agreeing with every word he heard. That is until he went out and looked at the fourth hole. It was only then that it dawned on him what Low and Paton were trying to achieve – a moment that would turn out to be an awakening for him and for golf.

'I can speak feelingly on this point, and may perhaps be forgiven for recalling the occasion when I realised, for the first time, what were the real possibilities which lay in golf course architecture,' Simpson wrote of that morning when he listened to members vent about the despised new bunker. 'Everyone agreed that such an innovation was a criminal outrage, and an insult as well, to the intelligence of the members.

'In the afternoon,' he continued, 'I went out fully prepared to find myself in complete agreement with the views that had been so eloquently expressed. So far, however, from agreeing, I realised for the first time, as soon as I saw this much-maligned hazard, that the true line to the hole should not always be the centre of the fairway, and that the placing of a bunker had a far more serious and useful purpose than merely the punishing of a bad shot. This led me to see the importance of golf architecture as an art as well as a science. I made up my mind on the spot to make a close study of the subject and to examine the great Scottish courses purely from this point of view.'

It is not much of a stretch to point to that afternoon at Woking as the dawn of the Golden Age of Golf Course Architecture. Soon after his revelatory moment on the fourth hole, Simpson would toss off his barrister's wig and devote himself to this new art of strategic design. He would join a circle of Low and Paton's friends who would also make a mark in golf architecture – prominent amateurs like Colt, Fowler and John Abercromby.

Simpson declared that these men and others who pursued this new path – Alister MacKenzie, Hugh Alison, Donald Ross, C.B. Macdonald, Albert W. Tillinghast and others – rescued the game from 'fatal deterioration' with the magnificent design work they did in both Britain and North America as the 20th century unfolded.

'It was due to their efforts that the practice of golf architecture is today recognised as having an artistic as well as a scientific bearing,' Simpson wrote. 'They were the pioneers in a movement which had done much towards restoring the ancient glories of the game.'

These architects not only realised the possibilities of existing courses, as Colt did at Willie Park's Sunningdale and Fowler at Old Tom Morris's Westward Ho!, but they also created masterpieces of their own, from Rye, Walton Heath and Addington in the old country to National Golf Links, Cypress Point and Pinehurst No. 2 in America. Even today the work these men left behind sets the standard for golf design.

In Simpson's own time, it would be decades before existing courses caught up with the new ideas in design. Indeed, the final major championship of 1904 unfolded in early October at Mid-Surrey in Richmond, a course designed by a man who espoused the very principles Low and his compatriots were rebelling against – John Henry Taylor. Like many professionals, he was loath to let go of the Victorian notion that hazards existed to punish the guilty.

The second News of the World Championship was the season's final engagement in what was becoming an increasingly tight battle for supremacy between the Scots and the English. Scotland's chances diminished when two of its champions failed to qualify – Andra Kirkaldy and White, who had fallen ill after his Open victory. Matters looked even worse when defending champion Braid went down in the second round, even though his conqueror was fellow Scotsman Herd. He went on to eliminate Vardon, but was knocked out himself in the semis by Taylor. That set up an all-English final against Alfred Toogood. Taylor won that easily, 5 and 3.

Before 1901, Scotland had been hopelessly outgunned by its southern neighbour. But over the past four years, Scots had claimed three of the four Opens and two of the three Amateur International Matches, while honours were even in the News of the World and Professional International Match. Scotland had been bested only in the Amateur. England won two of the three, with the fourth taken by the American invader, Travis. Scotland was assembling a decade of dominance to rival England's performance in the 1890s. It was no longer clear which nation reigned supreme in golf.

In the earliest days of competitive golf, there would have been but one response to the situation the game faced as 1904 drew to a close. Money men would have arranged a Great Match between thistle and rose to determine, once and for all, who ruled the field. It seemed inevitable that sooner or later some enterprising patriot in Scotland or England would harken back to those ancient ways.

Seventeen

SHOWDOWN AT TROON

———•◦◉◉◉◦•———

The resurgence Scottish golf was enjoying in the early years of the new century had, ironically, received its biggest boost from the latest innovation of the English – the Amateur International Match.

Since it was introduced by Hoylake in 1902, the match had, with one exception, become the opening act of every season. The roaring success Scotland enjoyed – and it would only become more dominant as the years passed – set a winning tone for the upcoming Championships.

Scotland romped in two of the first three matches, the inaugural and the third edition in 1904, and in both seasons a native son went on to claim one of the major Championships. That commanding victory in 1902 was especially inspiring, coming so soon after James Braid ended the nation's seven-year Open drought at Muirfield.

Even when Scotland narrowly lost the second match 5-4, the blow was softened by the success of Robert Maxwell. He humiliated English hero John Ball in the International, winning their match 8 and 6, and carried his momentum into the Amateur, scoring Scotland's first victory in that competition since Freddie Tait played his bagpipes through downtown Hoylake in 1898.

It would be hard to overestimate the uplifting effect of those victories for Scotland. Passion for the amateur game ran especially deep there. After all, Scottish gentlemen had conducted golf's first competition at

Leith in 1744, and ever since prizes awarded by the Royal and Ancient, the Honourable Company and other clubs had been among the game's most cherished. Defeating England in the International Match raised the spirits of every golfer north of the border, amateur and professional alike.

The 1905 International Match was a near replay of the previous season, a contest that had been overshadowed by Walter Travis's appearance in the Amateur Championship. Again, Maxwell and Ball played the opening match for their sides, and again Maxwell won easily, by 4 and 3. An emboldened Scotland slaughtered the rest of England's line-up, on the strength of masterful performances by Edward Blackwell, John Graham and Robert Andrew to a 6-3 victory, the same score they had racked up in 1904.

This time, that convincing win did not translate into success in the Amateur, even though the winner turned out to be a golfer who learned the game in the heart of Scotland. That year's Championship produced the most unexpected outcome since 1893, when St Andrews University student Peter Anderson shocked everyone by winning. The draw in 1905 pitted leading lights against one another early, and by the third round many were out of it, including Horace Hutchinson, Harold Hilton, John Laidlay and John Ball. Scotland, however, still had Maxwell and Graham to carry its banner into the late rounds.

Both of them, it turned out, would fall to Gordon Barry, another St Andrews University student. Just 20 years old, Barry had been born in Cornwall, England, but his family moved to St Andrews when he was a boy and he learned the game on its famed links. Barry was to Scotland what Graham was to England – a man who had been raised north of the Tweed and learned all his golf there, but played under the enemy's flag.

After dispatching Maxwell and Graham, Barry entered an all-English final against the Hon. Osmund Scott. Playing in torrential rain, Barry took the lead from the outset and won by 3 and 2, becoming the youngest Amateur champion. The significance of his victory as a sign of emerging English talent tended to be swept aside by controversy that erupted in advance of the Open two weeks hence over the Old Course at St Andrews.

The Royal and Ancient, having seen the way rubber-cored balls had neutered once-mighty Sandwich, decided that it simply could not allow that to happen to the most storied links in the kingdom. Towards the end of 1904, the club formed a committee to decide how to toughen the Old Course in advance of the 1905 Open.

John Low was not a member of the committee, but the spirit of the ideas he had outlined in his newspaper columns and in *Concerning Golf* hovered over the proceedings. Not only that, his friend Herbert Fowler was involved and they surely discussed the strategies required for meeting the challenge presented by a longer ball.

The result was extensive changes to the course. It was lengthened by some 200 yards, as nearly every course in the kingdom would be before that generation was out. The Old Course played more than 6,600 yards for the Open. Most of the length was added by moving tees back on the outward nine. The most dramatic change, however, was the addition of 13 bunkers on the right side of the second, third, fourth, sixth and seventh fairways.

The changes brought withering criticism, especially from professional golfers. 'They have ruined St Andrews,' declared Willie Anderson, a native Scot who had moved to the States and twice won the US Open. His fellow professionals mostly agreed.

The hostile reaction was directed squarely at Low. *Golf Illustrated* editor Garden Smith conceded that the changes were proof that his ideas had 'superseded the old doctrine of the obstacle hazard which the crooked and the straight alike had to surmount before winning the green.' Still, he was in no way prepared to admit that what Low and his admirers believed was good for golf.

Smith and the professionals entirely missed the point that these new bunkers would require players to think, to develop a strategy for attacking holes. They simply could not abide the idea that 'a shot which is all but perfect is trapped, with the certain loss of at least one stroke, while the opponent, who has gone ten yards wider, goes scot-free.'

If the scoring in the Open is any measure, the steps the committee took to defend the Old Course worked brilliantly. There would be no sub-70 scores at St Andrews, as there had been at Sandwich. Indeed only a handful of the best golfers in the world were able to post a score below 80.

Another record field of 152 entered for the Open in the first week of June, and again the tournament had to extend over three days. The first 18 holes were played in a fierce wind blowing from the north-east, which only grew stronger as the day wore on. That round set the tone for the Championship. Not a single score in the 70s was returned.

Four men managed to come in with 80 to take the early lead – Sandy Herd, John Henry Taylor, Harry Vardon and an unheralded Englishman named Walter Toogood. Another nine players were lurking a stroke back, among them James Braid, Rowland Jones and the Frenchman who had surprised everyone with his top-ten finish in 1902, Arnaud Massy.

By the next morning, when the second 18 was played, the wind had died down considerably. Taylor was first out among the leaders, but he showed none of the sharpness he displayed the previous day. He simply could not steer clear of trouble, finding one bunker after another, and limped home in 85 to fade from contention.

Braid was the first man to take the measure of the newly toughened Old Course. He started slowly, reaching the turn in 40, but played brilliantly on the homeward holes to post the first sub-80 round of the tournament, a 78 that gave him the lead. It didn't last long. Soon afterwards, Jones reeled off nines of 39 and 38 to nip Braid by a stroke and move into first place at 158.

Massy, Herd and Vardon did the best of the others. The Frenchman's 80 left him in third, three strokes behind. Herd and Vardon both posted 82. They would have four strokes to make up over the last 36 holes. Given the huge field, the cut line had been reduced. Only those within 15 strokes could continue, and a mere 45 players lived to fight another day.

In his book, *Advanced Golf*, Braid spelled out his strategy for winning championships: be well in front before facing the agonising pressure of that final round. His performance in the third round put him in precisely that position. Braid stormed through his outward nine in 36, the lowest score over the holes that had been toughened most. He couldn't maintain that torrid pace coming home, however. He finished in 42 for another 78 and a total of 237, a formidable score to beat.

The other contenders followed along with Braid's game plan. Jones racked up an eight and a six before reaching the turn and wound up with an unfortunate 87 that dropped him into seventh. The lightning-quick greens undid Vardon, who hadn't putted nearly as confidently since his illness. He had developed a twitch in his hand that bedevilled him, mostly on short putts. His 84 left him tenth. Taylor managed to find his game and match Braid's 78, but even that left him with six strokes to make up in the final round. Joining him in second, at 243, were Massy and Scottish professional James Kinnell.

As far as *The Golfing Annual* was concerned, another Open victory for Braid and Scotland was 'a foregone conclusion unless he sadly fell away'. Braid showed no sign of slacking off as he began his final trip around the links. He reached the turn in 38 and continued to play flawlessly until the 15th, a long, dangerous par four. Braid found a bunker from the tee and sliced his second onto the railway running along the right side of the fairway.

He described what happened next as an experience he would not easily forget. 'Playing off it, I hit a man and the ball rebounded from him and went into a nasty place, where it was tucked under a bush,' Braid wrote. 'The hole cost me six strokes.' The man he hit was uninjured, and given his comfortable lead, dropping two strokes wasn't much to worry about, as long as Braid returned to form over his final three holes.

Instead, as *The Annual* put it, he 'piled sensation upon sensation'. From the 16th tee, Braid drove his ball over the treacherous Principal's Nose bunker, but failed to clear the pit beyond it. Finding his ball lying nicely, Braid decided to go for the green – a risky play with the railway again stretching along the right side of the fairway.

'I became too venturesome,' he admitted. 'Instead of putting it on the green I got it on the railway and when I went up to it I found it lying in a horrible place, being tucked up against one of the iron chairs in which the rails rest.' The railway was in play, so there was nothing to do but drop and lose two strokes, or try to hack it out to safety.

'I took my niblick and tried to hook it out, but did not succeed, the ball moving only a few yards and being in much the same position against the rail,' Braid wrote. Braid flailed away a second time and got the ball out, but it went screaming past the hole and wound up near a bunker guarding the second green. Now he was in desperate trouble. The only way Braid could get the ball close to the hole and escape with another six was to try a daring run-up shot that would wind up in more trouble if it wasn't played perfectly.

'It was a bold and risky shot to play; but I played it and it came off, the ball running dead, so that I got my six,' Braid remembered, and one can almost hear the sigh of relief in his words. 'In all the four rounds of that Championship, I think that was the best shot that I played, because it was a good shot and it was played at a time when I was excusably very anxious, and knew that everything depended upon it, for it had to be remembered that there was the dreaded 17th hole waiting after that one.'

Pulling off that shot was just the medicine the Scotsman needed. He played the Road Hole in a comfortable five, made his four on the last, and came in with 81 for a total of 318. No one would get close to that number. Jones righted his ship with a superb 78 to finish tied second with Taylor, who came in with 80. Still, they were five shots behind.

James Kinnell took fourth, with Massy and another English newcomer, Ernest Gray of Littlehampton, a stroke back in fifth. For the first time in what seemed like ages Vardon finished out of the money. He wound up tied for ninth at 329, 11 shots behind Braid.

When Braid's final putt dropped, the partisan crowd that had followed his every step swarmed the green, hoisted the lanky Scotsman on its shoulders, and bore him off in glory. It would be hard to imagine a moment more meaningful for Braid than winning the Open at St Andrews, in the heart of Fife, where he had been born and raised and learned to play the game.

Who could say now that Scotland had not turned back the English tide? Scotsmen had carried home the Claret Jug in four of the five Championships conducted since 1901. The professional who led the English uprising, Taylor, hadn't won an Open in five years, and Vardon's best days seemed to be behind him. England continued to win more Amateur Championships, but when teams of gentlemen competed, it was clear there was a far greater depth of talent north of the Tweed. Even in the Professional International Match, Scotland was holding its own, losing one and halving two of the competitions conducted since the inaugural in 1903.

Barely two weeks after Braid's victory, a man named Frank Kinloch wrote to *Golf Illustrated* suggesting that the question of who reigned supreme in golf be decided the old-fashioned way. He proposed a Great Foursome between Scotland and England in which the two best professionals from north and south would fight it out in a match over multiple greens.

That was all the encouragement money men needed. Two 'anonymous' backers stepped up to provide the stakes, although their identities would quickly become known. Edward Hulton put up the money for England, while George Riddell backed Scotland. Both, as it happened, were newspaper proprietors. Hulton owned the *Sporting Chronicle* and *Athletic News*; Riddell ran the *News of the World*.

The stakes chosen were hardly accidental. Each side put up £200 – the same stake as the most famous foursome in history. In 1849, Tom Morris and Allan Robertson of St Andrews defeated Willie and Jamie Dunn of Musselburgh in a Great Match over three greens, with one round each at their home courses and the deciding round at North Berwick.

Staging another £400 foursome clearly was intended as a signal that this would be the Great Match of the new century – Scotland's chance to prove it had vanquished the English and reclaimed glory in its national pastime. The match would be played over four greens: St Andrews and Troon in the north, and St Annes and Deal in the south.

England's side was clear from the outset: Vardon and Taylor. Scotland, of course, would be led by Braid, but initially there was indecision about his partner. Scots looked first to their only other two-time Open Champion, Willie Park Jr. He'd had his fill of Vardon, however, and declared himself too busy and too out of form to play. In the end, Scots turned to the man Taylor thought they should have picked from the outset, Sandy Herd.

Braid and Herd had already proven themselves to be a formidable duo in a foursome. They had faced off against Vardon and Taylor 14 times since 1898, winning six and losing three, with the rest halved. Scotland's chances were also boosted by the reality that the first two matches would be played on home soil, giving them a chance to build up a daunting lead. Not surprisingly, Braid and Herd were favoured to win.

The International Foursome

Throughout history, Great Matches had aroused the passion of the golfing public in a way championships seldom did. Even in 1849, special trains to North Berwick had to be arranged to ferry all the fans desperate to see the finale of the foursome between St Andrews and Musselburgh. The mid-19th century clashes between Old Tom and Willie Park Sr became so heated that their match in 1870 had to be halted by the umpire when rowdy Musselburgh fans simply would not let Tom take a free swing.

Even those matches, however, did not generate the interest that surrounded two epic battles in the summer of 1873 between golf's brightest stars – Young Tom Morris and Davie Strath. Their 108-hole matches were breathlessly promoted, and the excitement they generated represented a turning point in the transformation of the Scottish game into a spectator sport that would soon be popular throughout Britain.

The anticipation for The International Foursome of 1905 equalled, if not exceeded, the hype for duels between Tommy and Davie. From the moment the match was announced, *Golf Illustrated*'s coverage exceeded anything it had done for an Open or an Amateur. In reporting on the match itself, the magazine even created graphics demonstrating how holes had been won or lost. *The Times* described the contest 'as possibly the greatest match in the history of golf'.

The stakes were not lost on the competitors. The Scotsmen, in particular, understood what was on the line. Their nation was counting on them to prove its superiority at the royal and ancient game. Between 1890 and 1900, England had stolen Scotland's crown. Scotland had rallied since, but nothing other than victory in this match could restore the nation's pride of place in golf.

When the battle began on 23 August at St Andrews, the rabid interest in the outcome was evident. Herd would never forget the scene that greeted him at the links. 'At least ten thousand people formed themselves into a great oval that stretched from behind the first tee away across the Swilcan Burn to the first green and back again,' he marvelled. 'I had never golfed before such a gathering of enthusiasts.'

John Low served as referee, aided by two umpires, 40 stewards, and a phalanx of policemen recruited to keep spectators in line. Stewards used the same flag system employed in the Vardon–Park match. A blue flag was hoisted when England won, a yellow one if Scotland prevailed, and both if a hole was halved.

If anything became clear during the first 18 holes, it was that the pressure of the match – and the enormity of the hostile, partisan crowd – weighed on Taylor and Vardon. Curiously, that was especially true of Vardon, who had never before seemed ruffled by spectators, or anything else. His long game was nothing like the crisp, precision golf that had won him four Opens. Vardon was occasionally outdriven by Herd and often wild, pulling one shot so badly that it hit a fan. Vardon was even worse on the greens, where he joined Taylor in frittering away one stroke after another to halve holes they ought to have won and lose holes they might have halved. By the time they reached the turn that morning, the English side was two holes down.

Vardon and Taylor continued to play nervous golf on the homeward nine, allowing Braid and Herd to add another hole to their lead, much to the delight of that rowdy horde of Scotsmen. The low point came at 17, where Braid and Herd managed a half after finding both the bunker and the road. Their lead after the opening round easily could have been 4 up had Herd not missed a short putt on 18. Vardon was becoming increasingly downcast.

'As the match proceeded it became more and more apparent that the sympathies of the crowd were not on our side,' Taylor remembered. 'Vardon became more discouraged at the partiality shown to the Scottish pair. More than once he declared to me his intention to chuck it and walk in, but I persuaded him otherwise, pointing out that the match was only beginning and that our turn would come.'

Things began looking up for the English side during the afternoon round. Braid missed a three-foot putt at the second, reducing Scotland's lead to two. Vardon and Taylor squared the match at the eighth, but immediately began letting holes slip away again. They had fallen 4 down before pulling themselves together to take 14 and 15. That was all they had that afternoon. The first leg of the match ended with Scotland 2 up, a result greeted with an outpouring of patriotic enthusiasm.

'Excited Scots rushed onto the last green and hoisted Braid and Herd onto several pairs of hefty shoulders and bore them triumphantly off towards Forgan's shop, Vardon and I dejectedly following,' Taylor wrote. 'I could not help remarking to my partner as we fell in at the tail of the procession that one would think the match was already over.'

Every Great Match has its ebbs and flows, but few see a turnabout as dramatic as the one that unfolded a week later at Troon, just north of Prestwick along the scenic Firth of Clyde. The second leg of the foursome was set for 30 August, a noteworthy day for science. A total eclipse of the sun would occur that Friday afternoon. As with all eclipses, complete darkness would only descend along a narrow path. In this case, they are stretched from Canada through Spain, where thousands of scientists had gathered to witness the celestial event.

Another massive crowd, estimated at 8,000 or more, showed up at Troon, with hopes for Scotland soaring sky high as Braid and Herd carried their 2-up lead from St Andrews into the match. *The Times* described the weather that afternoon as 'brilliantly fine' and reported that the green was in perfect condition for the big match.

Nothing seemed amiss for Scotland to start. Braid and Herd took the first with a tidy four to go 3 up, and were still holding that lead as they teed off on the sixth. From that point forward, however, 'misfortune began to dog their footsteps', as *The Times* put it. Braid became alternately erratic and feeble from the tee and the fairway, as he and Herd missed one easy putt after another. Vardon and Taylor, on the other hand, played as if they had a score to settle. They won the next four holes to take a 1-up lead in the match.

The story didn't change much on the homeward nine. Mishit shots and timid putts cost Braid and Herd three more holes by the time they reached the 15th. There, at least, they stopped the bleeding and headed into lunch 4 down, having surrendered six holes that morning. *The Times* stated the obvious: 'Matters were looking very black for the Scotchmen.' They had taken 80 shots, while the English side needed only 73.

If Scotland had hopes of rallying in the afternoon, they were dashed at the first hole. Braid and Herd played beautifully, reaching the green in two and making a tidy four. Taylor, however, ran down a long putt for three and England went 5 up. That seemed to take the fight out of the Scots, especially Herd. By the time the foursome reached the turn,

England's lead had soared to 8 up. On the homeward nine, as Bernard Darwin put it, 'The slaughter went on without rest and without mercy.'

The Scotsmen had dropped three more holes by the time they arrived at the 18th, where Herd capped off the most miserable afternoon of his life with a weak run-up that handed the English yet another victory. Vardon and Taylor finished 12 up in the match, having taken 14 holes that day.

Their score for the second round was even better than the one they had posted in the morning, a sparkling 72. That was nine better than the 81 taken by Braid and Herd. Taylor and Vardon agreed that they had never played better in a foursome. 'I personally have never seen such a brilliant exhibition of the game as we produced on this occasion,' Vardon wrote.

Scotland had played so horribly that rumours circulated of nefarious misdeeds. The night before the match, Braid and Herd had joined Taylor and Vardon for a dinner hosted by Fred Billington, a popular opera star and keen golfer from London. He was appearing in Glasgow and had come to Troon to watch the big foursome. It was whispered that Billington had drugged the drinks of the Scotsmen to guarantee an English win.

Taylor laughed off that notion. 'To suggest that he doped the drinks of Jimmy and Sandy was a farcical situation that not even W.S. Gilbert himself could have conceived,' he wrote, making reference to the popular West End shows of Gilbert and Sullivan.

There was, in fact, a reason Herd and Braid weren't at their best, but they would never have dreamed of talking about it at the time. Golfers simply did not make excuses. It was only years later in his memoir that Herd revealed the truth. Braid was fighting the flu all week at Troon, and Herd had injured his knee at an intervening event at Montrose. 'Every shot I played at Troon made me wince,' he wrote.

Still, Herd would never forgive himself for his performance that afternoon, especially on and around the greens. 'If anybody wanted to raise my dander afterwards,' he wrote, 'they had only to ask, "What sort o' course is Troon, Sandy, that ye made sich a hash o' it there?"'

Denouement

One week later, on 5 September, the match moved south to Lytham and St Annes on England's golf-rich west coast, 66-70 miles north of its more famous neighbour, Hoylake.

The weather for the third round of The International Foursome was ideal for golf – clear skies with a gentle breeze. Only 3,000 spectators were on hand this time, because promoters charged a half-crown entry fee to make the crowd more manageable. After the debacle at Troon – known in Scotland ever after as Black Friday – Braid and Herd needed to come roaring out of the gate if they hoped to make a match of it.

Unfortunately for the Scots, the day began as if it were going to be a replay of the disaster in Ayrshire. Taylor barely hit his drive off the first tee, but Scotland still managed to blow the hole when Herd hit a shaky approach and Braid's putt jumped the cup. The second hole was even more depressing. Herd hit his tee shot into a bunker, Braid got safely out, Herd hacked it into the rough, and just like that Scotland was 14 down.

It wasn't until the tenth that Scotland showed any sign of life. Herd knocked in a 45-footer there to win the hole, and after that he began to wield his putter like a man determined to slay the demon of Troon. By the lunch break, he and Braid had whittled England's lead to 11 up. This time they had played better golf, coming in with 74 to England's 75.

England came out firing in the second round, making a three at the first and returning to 12 up. From there, however, it was all Herd and Braid. Herd holed winning putts on seven and nine, Braid made brilliant approach shots and miraculous recoveries, and by the time the second leg of the match ended the English side's lead had been trimmed to 7 up. Scotland had outplayed England again, 71 to 74, and won five holes over the two rounds. The performance by Braid and Herd, *The Times* wrote, 'infused renewed interest in the contest. There was a general feeling that the Scotsmen would make a good fight to the finish of the match.'

Their chance would come four days later at windswept Deal, on the Kent coast just south of Sandwich. The weather for the final day was the worst encountered so far – bleak and fiercely windy with bursts of heavy rain. Barely 1,000 fans turned out to witness the finale of the much-ballyhooed International Foursome.

It may have been terrible weather for spectators, but it brought out the best in Taylor. He belted the first drive straight down the middle, while Braid sent his sailing into the rough. When Vardon's second found the green, an easy four put the Englishmen 8 up. Braid compounded his error by missing a putt from three feet on the second to lose that hole, too.

As far as *The Times* was concerned, that sealed Scotland's fate. Braid and Herd's 'only chance of success was to secure a hole or two at the start, but instead of doing this they lost the first two holes and practically gave away the match,' the newspaper wrote.

Over the rest of the round, Scotland fell victim to wayward drives, lame approaches and timid putts, with too few moments of glory between. Braid and Herd headed into lunch in the hopeless position of 13 down. They had played horribly, 86 to England's 79.

In the afternoon, the shellacking of Scotland was over before the players reached the turn. Braid and Herd won only a single hole, and when Vardon's putt to win the sixth found the cup, The International Foursome of 1905 ended, with England winning 13 and 12.

Indeed, the only drama that unfolded at Deal occurred the night before the match, and only the English side knew about it. Vardon had not been entirely well since 1903, when he spent six months recovering from tuberculosis at Mundesley Sanatorium. He'd had one or two relapses, but thought his health was improving before arriving at Deal.

'Unfortunately,' he wrote, 'I was to experience a serious relapse during the night prior to the match. My attack of haemorrhage was so bad that Taylor did not think I would be fit enough to play the following morning. Happily, when morning arrived I was feeling much better.' Vardon's play under the circumstances makes the overpowering English victory all the more impressive.

It is impossible to overstate how soul-crushing the outcome of that match was for Scotland. On that glorious afternoon at St Andrews, when Braid and Herd were carried shoulder high from the links, golfers north of the border confidently looked forward to a victory that would prove they had reclaimed supremacy in their national pastime. Instead, for the second time in succession – at their own 'true game' of match play – Scots had not simply been beaten. They had been humiliated.

In his memoir, Vardon told a story that captured the sentiment of every Scottish golfer on that afternoon at Troon when it became painfully obvious how The International Foursome would end. A reporter covering the event asked an elderly woman in the crowd if she had noticed the eclipse of the sun that unfolded as the match was played, which was not nearly as visible that far north as it was in Spain.

'I don't know about the eclipse of the sun,' the woman responded glumly, 'but I have seen this day the eclipse of Scotland.'

Eighteen

HUMBLED BUT UNBOWED

———— •◦●◉●◦• ————

J ames Braid responded to that crushing defeat in The International
Foursome the way any dour Scotsman would have done. He picked
up his sword and his shield and charged back into the battle against
the southern invaders. And what a charge it would be.

Braid's biographer considered the response typical of the man. 'It had
been a bad beating,' Bernard Darwin wrote, 'and I suppose that a little
something of bitterness always arose in the remembrance, but James
was of a disposition at once too placid and too determined to let it affect
his game.'

A month after the match Braid, along with the rest of the golfing
world, turned his attention to the 1905 season's final major championship,
the News of the World. It was played at Walton Heath, Herbert Fowler's
acclaimed new heathland course south-west of London. By then Braid
had become the club's professional, a post he would occupy for the rest
of his days.

Curiously, in the first match, Braid found himself facing his partner
in the big foursome. He and Sandy Herd waged a grand duel that went
into a play-off. On the first extra hole, Braid's deciding putt lingered
agonisingly on the lip before toppling in to give him the victory.

He cruised into the final after that, never requiring more than 15 holes
to win. In the deciding match, Braid found himself in another battle of
north versus south against Tom Vardon. By the fifth, Vardon had a 2-hole

lead, but, as Darwin put it, 'to play thirty-six holes against James at Walton was like playing Zeus on his home course on Olympus.' Braid squared the match before lunch, and loped home 4 and 3 in the afternoon.

With that victory Braid at least finished the season on a cheery note. The International Foursome aside, 1905 had been a year of tremendous personal accomplishments for Braid, highlighted by winning his second Open at St Andrews and his second News of the World tournament in three tries. Walton Heath added the finishing touch by presenting Braid with a £90 testimonial and his wife, Minnie, with a silver tea set.

The 1906 golf season began with a subtle but important sign that the game had reached another turning point. The change had been unfolding since the Professional Golfers' Association was founded five years earlier and launched its series of qualifying tournaments leading up to the News of the World Championship.

That year a record field of 183 players entered the Open at Muirfield, convincing the tournament committee that steps had to be taken to reduce the field. Instead of deciding for themselves, as gentlemen had always done, they sought the opinion of the PGA – a step that would have been unimaginable a decade before. In the end, the two groups agreed to institute qualifying rounds in advance of the 1907 Championship.

The decision to consult the PGA was a powerful symbol of the increasing ascendancy of professional golf. Since the game's earliest days, golf had been run by and for amateurs, who paid far more attention to the games gentlemen played than to those of the professionals their clubs employed, even as they acknowledged their superiority on the links.

But as golf became more popular in Britain, it was the professional game that captured the attention of fans. How could it be otherwise with The Triumvirate of Harry Vardon, John Henry Taylor and Braid setting a standard of play that eclipsed the best amateur golfers? It was not simply that, however. Before the PGA was born, every tournament professionals competed in was financed and managed by amateur patrons. Now professionals were fending for themselves and had their own power base, as evidenced by the committee's decision not to change the Open without consulting the PGA.

In addition to their series of qualifiers for the News of the World – and later the Sphere and Tatler Cup – British professionals were competing regularly on the continent, especially France, where the game was growing rapidly. Leading golfers travelled to play in the French, Belgian and German Opens, not to mention a host of smaller, well-financed invitationals.

Professional golf was on its way to becoming the lucrative, worldwide game we know today. Gentlemen would always control the game's rules and its greatest championships – the Open and its US counterpart – but the more the professional game grew, the more amateur golf faded into the shadows. Over time, the riches offered by professional golf would make it the only game that mattered.

Before the Open Championship committee had settled down to the business of figuring out how to manage progressively larger fields, the new season began in a manner that had become predictable by then. The Amateur, contested at Hoylake in late May, was preceded, as always, by the International Match. The result could not have been a better palliative for a nation trying to purge the dark memory of Braid and Herd's debacle at Troon. Scotland scored its most dominant victory yet, winning 7-2.

There were but two bright spots for England. John Ball avenged his previous defeats by Robert Maxwell, demolishing the Scotsman 8 and 6. F.H. Mitchell, whose selection for the side was questioned, got the only other point in a 7 and 6 romp over Scotsman James Robb. In the Championship that followed, however, Robb would have the last laugh.

With all the principal contenders – Ball, Maxwell, Harold Hilton, John Laidlay, Horace Hutchinson and defending champion Gordon Barry – ousted in the early rounds, Robb had only one serious competitor blocking his path to the final: John Graham of Hoylake. They met in the fifth round and Graham appeared poised to win until the last three holes. Under pressure, however, Graham did what he always seemed to do. He missed one tiny putt after another and Robb lived to fight another day, winning 1 up.

Poor Graham. He was one of the loveliest players of his age, and his record in medal competitions and matches rivals anyone's, but he never could deliver in the heat of an Amateur or Open. 'I think he hated championships,' wrote Hoylake historian Guy Farrar, 'the long drawn-out struggle, the clamour and the shouting, and all the other ordeals that a champion must face were repugnant to his rather shy and reserved nature.'

Once he was past Graham, it was smooth sailing for Robb. He easily tossed aside his three remaining opponents and defeated Sunningdale's C.C. Lingen 4 and 3 in a poorly played final. Fighting through gale force winds and showers of rain, neither man broke 50 going out that morning, and one hole was halved in nine. Still, Scotland moved on to the Open with its hopes restored after back-to-back wins to start the season.

Three weeks later, when the action moved to Muirfield, Scotland appeared poised to continue its run in the Professional International Match. Scots started with two critical victories. Braid outlasted Taylor, and Herd turned back Vardon. Sadly for Scotland, the rest of the line-up crumbled, with only Ben Sayers and Robert Thompson winning, allowing England to end the morning session with a four-point lead. When Vardon and Taylor revived painful memories by trouncing Braid and Herd 5 and 3 in the afternoon foursomes, England rolled to another easy victory, 12-6.

A pattern was developing in these International Matches that would continue until the Great War brought that era to a close. Year after year, they were one-sided affairs. In the amateur game, Scotland, with its array of ancient clubs, had a bench too deep for England to match. The opposite was true in the professional ranks, in part because so many Scottish professionals sought their fortune abroad. The amateur match was discontinued after 1912 for lack of interest. Scotland had won nine of the 11 contests, nearly always in a romp.

The professional match suffered a similar fate. After its opening victory in 1903, Scotland never did better than a tie, with England winning easily most years. By 1911, interest had waned so much that the match was abandoned in favour of an amateur vs professional foursomes event featuring nine pairings a side. It was billed as a 'coronation match' to celebrate the crowning of King George V, whose father, King Edward VII, had died the previous May.

That competition, alas, was even less exciting. Professionals proved again that they had outdistanced amateurs, winning 8-1. The original format returned in 1912, when Scotland managed its third tie, but in 1913 England romped again 13-4. That turned out to be the final match of the series. In a last-ditch effort to revive interest, the PGA moved the 1914 match to October. It was cancelled after war was declared.

The Great Triumvirate

In the 1906 Open, gamblers looking to take a flyer on up-and-coming talent would have had any number of choices. Scotland's George Duncan had shown promise, as had Englishman Charlie Mayo and Jerseyman Ted Ray. The smart money, however, would not have looked past Vardon, Taylor and Braid. One of those men had carried off the Claret Jug in eight of the past 11 seasons.

The opening round began with gloomy skies and a brisk wind suggesting difficult weather ahead. As the day progressed, however, 'the sky cleared, and the afternoon's play was carried through in genial sunshine,' *The Glasgow Herald* reported. Punters must have been flummoxed by results from that round. It seemed as if the clock had been turned back to 1890, when amateurs were beginning their decade of glory.

Not a single member of the Triumvirate was in the top ten after 18 holes. Instead, the leaderboard was crowded with amateurs – seven in all with four of them in the top five. Graham led the pack with a sterling 71, beating the record for Muirfield. Behind him at 73 was Maxwell, and a stroke further back in fourth were two other Scottish amateurs, Robert Whitecross and Hugh Watt.

The second day's play, in brilliant sunshine, saw a 180-degree turnaround. This time, the professionals posted low scores and the amateurs stumbled. Taylor seemed to have ruined his chances by going out in 41, but a searing 31 coming home put him in the lead at 149. Despite several missteps, Vardon posted a 73, leaving him only a stroke to make up.

Both Graham and Maxwell tailed off, with 79 and 78, respectively. That left Graham tied with Vardon in second, and Maxwell tied for fourth with Duncan at 151. Defending champion Braid finally sneaked into the top ten, four strokes behind, by adding a 76 to the 77 he had posted to begin.

In the third round, as the weather again progressed from disagreeable to charming, it became clear that if Braid was to defend his title he would not be doing it from the front, as he preferred. He played better than he had all week, going around in 74, but his three-round total of 227 was not enough to overtake Taylor. The Englishman put up a tidy 75 to remain right where he had begun the morning, in first place at 224.

Rowland Jones moved into second with a 73 that left him a stroke back; Vardon struggled with his putter again and posted a 77 to tie Braid for third. Graham and Maxwell remained unable to recapture the magic of their opening rounds, with 78 and 77, respectively. That dropped them into a tie for fifth, four strokes off the lead.

Every one of the leading contenders started the final round far earlier than Braid – so much so that only Taylor was still on the course when the long-striding Scotsman walked onto the first tee late in the afternoon. Vardon had come in with a ho-hum 78, while Maxwell and Jones had gone to pieces with 83s. Taylor had been paired with Graham for the final two rounds, and such was his feisty nature that he lost focus on the task at hand.

Taylor could not bear the thought of being beaten by an amateur, and became flustered as Graham matched him shot for shot. 'I still retain a vivid recollection of the way that Johnnie hunted and worried me for the whole thirty-six holes,' Taylor wrote. He beat Graham over those two rounds by a stroke, but the 80 he posted in the afternoon left Braid perfectly positioned for a come-from-behind win.

The Manchester Guardian was extraordinarily impressed with what it saw from Braid that afternoon. 'His nerve in the last round yesterday was wonderful,' the newspaper wrote. 'He knew absolutely what he had to do. To defeat Taylor and win the Championship he required a 76 – a score he had accomplished but once in the three previous rounds. Yet before he set out his brother professionals were fairly confident that Braid would win.'

Playing steady golf, Braid reached the turn in 38. That was excellent under Championship pressure, but as Darwin noted, 'It did not leave much margin against a rainy day.' Braid would need another 38 coming home to win this third Open. He did better than that, playing flawlessly through the opening holes and making brilliant threes at 14 and 17 that left him with seven strokes to spare as he approached the final hole.

Braid's homecoming nine of 35 added up to 73. He had found a new way to win a Championship – by posting a lower score every time he stepped onto the links. His total of 300 was four better than Taylor and five better than Vardon, whose second- and third-place finishes gave the game's leading golfers a clean sweep of the honours. Graham did best among the amateurs, finishing six shots back in fourth.

'Of all the Championships in which the Triumvirate showed their quality,' Darwin wrote, 'I think none was more notable than this one, for they were left well behind to start, but the audacious leaders all "came back to their horses", leaving the last round to again be a battle between the three inevitables.'

Over the past six seasons, Braid had been on a juggernaut of his own, with five major championships to his credit: three Opens and two News of the Worlds. He couldn't sustain his run in the 1906 match-play tournament at Hollinwell. Braid did, however, enjoy seeing Herd win his second major by 8 and 7 over England's Charles Mayo. Braid was back in the winner's circle the following autumn when the event returned to Sunningdale. He vanquished Ray 4 and 3 in the semi-final and went on to whip his old pal Taylor 4 and 2 to claim his third News of the World in five attempts.

Braid's game had reached a frightful peak by the summer of 1908, when the Open was played at Prestwick. That Championship would be conducted under a dark cloud, as weeks earlier Old Tom Morris, the game's most beloved figure, had fallen down a stairwell at The New Club in St Andrews and passed away at the age of 86. The weather mirrored the mood as the week began. The International Professional Match was washed out by a deluge of rain, which at least had the beneficial effect of taking the fire out of the famously fast Prestwick greens.

The Championship itself began on a lovely morning featuring a gentle breeze and grey skies. Braid came storming out of the gate with a three at the first hole, where the railway looms on the right, and another at the short second. He reached the turn in a scintillating 33, and despite two dropped shots coming home finished his round in 70 strokes, a new record for Prestwick.

Surprisingly, that record did not survive the round. Englishman Ernest Gray of Littlehampton torched the outward nine in 31, and dropped only a shot coming home to post an absurdly low 68. The men Braid feared most – Vardon and Taylor – had nearly played themselves out of the Championship, turning in twin 79s as the rest of the field capitalised on perfect scoring conditions.

With the newly instituted qualifying rounds, the Championship had returned to its roots, 36 holes played over each of two days. In the afternoon, followed by a massive crowd, Braid continued to play marvellous golf, reeling off 3s and 4s so often it appeared he might post a lower score than he had in the morning. In the end, his 72 left him holding a formidable five-stroke lead.

The new correspondent for *The Times* was deeply impressed by what he'd seen from Braid. 'His total for the two rounds was thus the wonderful one of 142, and finer golf than he played is hardly conceivable,' Bernard Darwin wrote. When Vardon and Taylor posted 77 and 78, and Gray fell from grace with 79, Darwin was inclined to go out on a limb even as he covered his first Open. 'Prophecy is, of course, rash,' he wrote, 'but chances are overwhelmingly in favour of a victory for Braid.'

Early in the third round, on a far windier day marred by occasional rain, there came a moment when Darwin must have regretted writing those words. Braid started slowly, dropping a shot at the first with a five, but followed it with a routine three. Disaster struck at the third hole, the dangerous 'Cardinal'. Braid played his cleek from the tee for safety, but still wound up in the rough. Instead of laying up short of the cavernous bunker that gives the hole its name, he tried to carry the hazard. He hit a low cleek shot that crashed into the sleepers shoring up that deep pit and rebounded into the sand.

Again, Braid tried the ambitious play, taking his mashie for distance rather than digging the ball out with a niblick. His first attempt ricocheted off the sleepers and landed out of bounds across the Pow Burn. His second met precisely the same fate, and when he finally did dig the ball out with a niblick the result was a disastrous eight that 'nearly brought him back to his nearest rivals at one fell swoop', as Darwin put it.

Imperturbable as always, Braid showed no sign of distress as he walked in that long, loping stride of his to the next tee. Years later, as he recalled that fateful moment, Darwin would marvel that there was 'not the slightest mark of emotion on his face'. Braid clearly was feeling the pressure, however, because he made matters worse with three weak putts on the fourth green to let yet another shot slip away.

Next came the dangerous Himalayas, a par three requiring a carry over a fearsomely tall dune. When Braid holed his putt there for a two – eliciting a deafening roar from the partisan crowd – it was as if the catastrophe at the Cardinal had never happened. Braid went serenely on his way and reached the turn in 39. Coming home with a 38 gave him a 77 for the round, rather pedestrian golf for him. None of the other contenders, however, played well enough to close the gap. In fact, Braid had actually increased his lead to six strokes with one round to go. He was among the last groups out that afternoon, needing only a 79 to win his fourth Open.

'From the start,' Darwin wrote, 'he looked certain to do it. He began with four and three, and hit a good tee shot to the "Cardinal", which had been so destructive to him in the morning. There was a long and tantalising wait before his second shot, but Braid finally hit a magnificent brassie shot onto the green. The crowd were obviously relieved. Braid was safely over the "Cardinal" and the Championship was to all intents over.'

Braid came to the final hole needing a four to finish with 72, and the scene that greeted him at the tee was one to behold. 'The home hole is 249 yards long, and the people stretched from the tee to the clubhouse on both sides of the course,' *The Guardian* wrote. 'When he had holed out there was a frantic outburst of joy by the enthusiastic Scots, who carried him shoulder high to the clubhouse.'

That 72 gave Braid a final score of 291 – only three over an average of four shots per hole for the entire Championship. No one had come that close to level fours in an Open since 1870, when Young Tom Morris set the mark at five over fours with his immortal 149 to claim The Challenge Belt. Braid's score was, by four strokes, the lowest made in an Open since the Championship moved to 72 holes in 1892. It would not be surpassed until after the war, when Bobby Jones turned in a 285 at St Andrews in 1927.

'To win the Championship by eight clear strokes nowadays is truly an astonishing performance,' Darwin wrote, 'and very possibly Braid might have been a stroke or two less in his last round if he had not obviously been putting for safety throughout. The rest of his game was, probably, better than in any of his other rounds, and he gave himself chances of threes with his approaches time after time. No doubt the weather for the two days was more favourable than usual to low scoring, while Prestwick was in the most perfect order; but even so, a total of 291 is amazing.'

Pinnacle

It was only fitting that the high point of what was emerging as the Decade of Braid would come two years later in his own Kingdom of Fife, where the Open Championship would celebrate its 50th anniversary in St Andrews. The Royal and Ancient marked the Jubilee by striking a commemorative medal featuring a likeness of the late Old Tom Morris on the front, with the winner's name to be inscribed on the back.

By the 1910 Open, qualifying rounds had been abandoned. All 210 entrants would play the first 36 holes over two days, with the lowest 60 scores and ties moving on to the final rounds of the Championship. That set the stage for two extraordinarily long days of golf, with play beginning at 7.30 in the morning and not finishing until 7.30 at night.

To complicate matters, the Championship hardly got off to the start the R&A wanted. Midway through the first round, the heavens opened. The downpour was so intense that the Old Course became unplayable. The round had to be abandoned, although Braid either didn't know that or didn't trust the news when it came to him on the links. 'In order to make sure,' wrote his biographer, Darwin, 'he ploughed his way home through the floods and finished in 76. It was a sad waste, enough to have discouraged most men.'

Braid was not like most men, however. He went out the next morning, in a raw mist and boisterous wind, and turned in the same 76, a sound start in any championship. It was young George Duncan who electrified the Scottish crowd by going around in a magnificent 73 to take the lead. Braid, Taylor and Ray were lurking three strokes back, with Vardon another stroke behind them.

The following afternoon it was Braid's turn to light up the links at St Andrews. This time it was he who posted a 73, while Duncan's lustre faded a bit with a 77. The young Scotsman's two-round total of 150 was one worse than Braid's. The other two members of the Triumvirate had fallen far behind and ceased to be a threat, with Taylor at 156 and Vardon 158.

Nearly everyone at St Andrews, *Times* correspondent Darwin among them, left the course that evening believing that was how the leaderboard would look come morning. But at about half-past seven, Willie Smith, a Carnoustie man who had emigrated to America, straggled with a remarkable score of 71 to sneak into the lead at 148.

The next day, with a massive crowd following him, 'Smith's meteoric light had disappeared as suddenly as it had arisen,' as *The Guardian* put it. The putts stopped dropping, Smith's tee shots kept finding trouble, and he was quickly out of the hunt. It was Duncan who again dazzled the St Andrews faithful. He matched Smith's 71 of the previous afternoon to retake the lead at 221.

For the first 16 holes of his round, Braid looked as if he might match Duncan shot for shot, but he stumbled late. A weak pitch found the Road Hole bunker at 17, and he finished in 74. He would have two strokes to make up on his Scottish compatriot in the final round.

Duncan had never carried a lead into the final round of an Open, and it was obvious to everyone watching that afternoon that the pressure of playing from the front weighed on him. 'He showed signs of very palpable, if natural, anxiety, and never looked at all comfortable,' Darwin wrote in *The Times*. Duncan started well enough, but missteps at the fifth and sixth holes rattled him so much that he fell apart, coming in with a fatal 83.

The road to victory was wide open for Braid, who again went out in the last group knowing what had to be done. Playing with relentless precision, he reached the turn in 38 and seized the lead by a stroke. Coming home, Braid played so beautifully, starting with two marvellous threes, that he could relax over his final holes. When he arrived at the 18th green, thousands of fans awaited him as he holed out for a third consecutive five that gave him a 76 and his fifth Open Championship.

'Braid was then carried off the green and up the steps in front of the clubhouse by a tumultuous crowd of his admirers,' Darwin wrote. 'There could be no question of the popularity of his victory.'

Braid had now moved to the front in the battle among what had by now become popularly known as The Great Triumvirate. He was the first among them to win five Opens, and his score of 299 that year made him the first player ever to come in below 300 over four rounds at St Andrews, which presented one of the toughest tests among the Championship venues.

'It was the last of our Open Championships that he was destined to win, though it would have been a very rash prophet who foretold any such thing at the time,' Darwin wrote years later in his biography of Braid. 'If James had known that this was to be his last victory I think he would have liked it to be won at St Andrews.'

In the years after that Championship, Braid was never as all-powerful as he had been during that decade. He began to have trouble with his eyes – not the ideal prescription for a man whose principal vulnerability was missing putts. Braid's eyes had been splashed with lime-laced plaster dust when he was young, and as he grew older his vision became more and more troublesome. It became so bad that in one Championship he ignored his doctor's advice to sit out and played wearing dark glasses.

Braid would experience only one more moment of major championship glory, winning his fourth and final News of the World title in 1911 on his home course at Walton Heath, defeating Ted Ray 1 up. His record of four wins in that championship would never be surpassed and equalled only twice – by Dai Rees in 1950 and Peter Thomson in 1967.

Braid's dominance during the first decade of the new century – winning nine major championships in a span of ten years – represented the greatest run of glory for Scottish golf since the days of Young Tom Morris. Between Braid, Herd and Jack White, Scotland had taken seven of the ten Opens played during the decade, and four of the eight News of the Worlds. With Duncan coming rapidly to the fore, there was also an emerging star on the horizon to carry the nation's banner in the years ahead.

Warning signs

In the flush of victory, it was easy to ignore the warning signs that had flashed after the Championships played in the years between Braid's remarkable string of Open victories. Those would be a portent of changes that the game would witness in years to come.

Without doubt, the most surprising Championship unfolded in the summer of 1907 at the links that had given birth to the English uprising, Royal Liverpool. Having racked up two consecutive Open victories,

Braid naturally entered as the favourite. But that changed in the qualifying rounds that had been instituted that season.

Frenchman Massy, who had already shown an affinity for Hoylake by finishing tenth in his Open debut five years earlier, turned in marvellous rounds of 73 and 75. He became a joint favourite with Taylor, who played nearly as well with 76 and 78. Braid had disappointing rounds of 82 and 85, which at least earned him a spot in the field.

Beautifully as Massy had played, British golfers remained confident that a nation whose empire spanned the globe was invulnerable to attack from countries like France that were relative newcomers to the game. 'Walter Travis had given our national complacency a shake by winning the Amateur Championship, but nobody had dreamed, least of all the professionals, that our Open Championship was in any danger from an invader,' as Darwin put it.

The opening rounds of that Championship were played in horrific weather, with a gale-force wind blowing from the west and rain coming down in torrents. Even Taylor described the conditions as 'heartbreaking'. If anyone was more likely than him to play well in such miserable weather, it was Massy. He had grown up in Biarritz, on the shores of the Bay of Biscay, where the wind can blow as mightily as it does at Hoylake.

Massy went out in that gale and played remarkable golf, coming in with a 76 that was easily the best score of the morning. Taylor was three strokes behind at 79. Braid and Vardon had, more or less, played themselves out of contention by coming in with 82 and 84, respectively.

Massy was not quite as marvellous in the afternoon, turning in an 81 that allowed Taylor to close the gap to a single stroke with another 79. English professionals dominated the rest of the leaderboard – among them Tom Ball, George Pulford and Tom Williamson – but no one expected an upset victory from one of them. The huge crowd that swarmed the links was anticipating a fight to the finish between the Frenchman and his dogged English adversary.

The weather for the final day did not look promising early on, with heavy wind and lowering skies. By noon, however, the sun was shining and a lovely afternoon was in store. Taylor went out and did exactly what every Englishman on the grounds expected him to do. He turned in twin nines of 38 for a tidy 76. That gave him a three-round total of 234.

Massy, on the other hand, got off to a ragged start. He made a six on Hoylake's claustrophobic opening hole and dropped another shot at the second. When he reached the turn in 42, Britain's confidence in its impregnability seemed justified. Massy found his stride on the home nine, however, playing brilliantly through that brutal finishing stretch to come in with 36. His 78 left him with a stroke to make up at 235.

The next closest players were four strokes behind Massy – among them Vardon, who finally found his game with a 74. Four strokes aren't easy to find on a course as testing as Hoylake, and when the deciding round began, Massy and Taylor split the crowd between them as they set off to battle it out.

Taylor's round had hardly begun when he stumbled badly. At the third hole, he hit a pop-up with his second shot and it plopped into a bunker. By the time he hacked it out, found the green and dropped his putt, it added up to a seven. Taylor fought bravely for the rest of the round, but could do no better than 80. That left him with a final score of 314.

With a huge crowd of fans in tow, Massy paraded merrily through his outward nine in 38. He played well enough coming home that by the time he approached Hoylake's fearsome finishing stretch it was obvious that only a collapse would prevent him from claiming the Claret Jug. When the Frenchman made a brilliant four at The Field, the Championship was all but over. He could finish with four fives now and still win. In the end, Massy's 77 that afternoon would give him a two-stroke victory.

The scene as the Frenchman approached the home hole provided a stark contrast to Royal St George's, where Travis had so demoralised Britain with his Amateur victory. 'The ropes were lined three or four deep,' wrote *The Glasgow Herald*. 'When the ball dropped into the hole a great cheer announced the first French victory in the greatest golfing event of the season. Massy was immediately surrounded and borne shoulder high to the clubhouse.'

One wonders what Travis must have thought when he read about Massy being carried off like a hero and begged by the Hoylake crowd to give a speech after he had been presented as the Champion Golfer of the Year. A smiling Massy said it made him proud to win for his native France, and drew massive applause when he shouted 'Vive L'Entente Cordiale,' referring to recently signed agreements that soothed the historically fractious relationship between the United Kingdom and its cross-Channel neighbour.

The stark difference between 1904 and 1907 came down to two things: Massy was a far more charming man than Travis, and he had honed his game on British soil, under the tutelage of Ben Sayers at North Berwick. Massy 'had a fine, rollicking, rapscallion way with him', Darwin wrote. 'He was admirable company and everybody was fond of him.'

The other reality was that a Frenchman winning seemed less shocking with so many golfers from Jersey, France's next-door neighbour, succeeding in golf. While players from Jersey competed as 'Englishman', the press was fond of noting that the Channel Islands could field a formidable side of its own in an international match. It would include Harry Vardon and his brothers, Tom and Fred, Ted Ray, Tommy Renouf, Willie and Jack Gaudin and Aubrey and Percy Boomer.

Fondness for Massy may have blinded Britain to the truth of what his victory suggested – that France would hardly be the last country to mount a challenge for supremacy in golf. Nations new to the game would set out to dethrone Britain in precisely the same way that England had taken the fight to the Scots for a generation now. In just over a dozen years, that painful lesson would be borne home.

Whatever threat Massy's victory posed, it seemed a distant one. The more immediate concern for Scots who believed Braid and his countrymen had turned back the English invasion were worrisome signs that arose in the 1909 Open and the 1907 and 1910 Amateur Championships.

Braid's victory in the 1908 Open left him and Vardon as the only golfers to equal the feat of the Scottish immortals who had four times been declared Champion Golfer – Willie Park Sr, Old Tom Morris and Young Tommy. That was not lost on Taylor, the combative man who had begun England's run of success in the Championship.

'My virile golfing days were mounting up and slipping past, and if I were to catch up on Vardon and Braid I had better see to it that they should not leave me permanently in the rear,' Taylor wrote. The Englishman must have smiled when Deal was announced as host of the 1909 Championship, a result of pressure from the PGA to bring the Open to England more often and to play the Championship at courses beyond Hoylake and Sandwich.

Taylor loved Deal. Hugging the shores of Pegwell Bay, he wrote it 'presented a picture that was pleasing and inspiring, reminding me of the flavour of my home in the West Country and of the imposing sweep of Bideford Bay and the Bristol Channel,' he wrote. Not to mention that Taylor's last memory of Deal was the glorious victory he and Vardon celebrated there in The International Foursome of 1905.

From the start, playing that windswept course as if he were right at home, Taylor dominated the Championship. It is true that two up-and-coming Englishmen beat Taylor's 74 in the opening round – Charles Johns with 72 and James Piper with 73. But no one at Deal believed for a moment that they would keep up that pace for four rounds.

Taylor shaved a stroke from his score the second time around to take the lead, and never looked back. Wielding his mashie like a magic wand, knocking down one flag after another in the stiff wind, Taylor posted two more scores of 74 for a total of 295 and the easiest of victories by six strokes. Only Tom Ball and Braid, who tied for second, managed to stay within shouting distance. Vardon was far down the list, a full 21 strokes behind.

'Without, I trust, being an egotistical fool, I may attribute my win at Deal to the pleasing recollection that for two days I appeared to be inspired in my shots up to the hole,' Taylor recalled. 'Those who have enjoyed this rare sensation of decorating the vicinity round about the pin with the ball from varying distances reachable with an iron club, need no reminding that such accuracy renders putting a simple proposition.'

The biggest surprise for Scotsmen may have come in the Amateur game, where they enjoyed unchallenged hegemony in the International Match and were neck and neck with England in Championships. James Robb's victory at Hoylake in 1906 brought Scotland within one win of evening the score in the Amateur, but the following year a sleeping giant awoke.

John Ball had not been a serious threat to win a Championship since he sailed for South Africa. That was hardly surprising. In the Transvaal, Ball had engaged in the kind of horrific fighting a man does not soon forget. When he came home in the summer of 1901, it was to a Royal Hotel made sadly empty by the passing of his mother. In July 1905, he endured another emotional blow, the death of his father, whose health had been in decline for years. Now the Royal must have seemed haunted by the old man's cries of, 'Me and my son will play any two!'

The cloud that descended on Ball had lifted by the time the 1907 Amateur came to St Andrews, a course the Englishman had never mastered. He unravelled its mysteries that year, however, beginning with a hard-fought first-round victory against his oldest adversary, John Laidlay. That was the eighth time the two had faced off in the Championship.

There was no stopping England's dour and bonny fighter after that. He mowed down his next six opponents and came into the final as the prohibitive favourite over Charles Palmer, a workmanlike golfer from the Midlands. Any chance Palmer had of winning disappeared when the morning of the final saw gales of wind and squalls of rain. Few men could fight through such conditions better than Ball. Had he not aggravated an old wrist injury during the morning 18, Palmer might not have lasted as long as he did. As it was, Ball sent him home on the 14th hole that afternoon.

The hero of Hoylake was back at it three years later – following another English win in 1908 by Edward Lassen at Sandwich and Scotsman Robert Maxwell's final moment of Amateur glory at Muirfield in 1909. Even though he was playing at Hoylake, Ball did not enjoy as smooth a path to the 1910 final as he had at St Andrews. One early match went to 18, and in the other he needed an extra hole to prevail.

In the semi-final, however, Ball returned to his all-powerful ways against long-driving Abe Mitchell of Sussex. He trailed Mitchell from nearly every tee but put him under relentless pressure with one gorgeous approach after another until Mitchell finally cracked, 5 and 4. Poor Colin Aylmer of Sidmouth was Ball's victim in the final. Aylmer played only 27 of the 36 holes before being brushed aside 10 and 9.

The resurgence of the two golfers who had first knocked Scotland off its Championship pedestal had to worry golfers north of the border, even as they carried Braid off in triumph after his fifth Open Championship at St Andrews later that season. Ball had not won in seven years before his victory in 1907. Taylor came into Deal having done no better than second for eight seasons, though he managed that four times.

If Harry Vardon and Harold Hilton were to awaken from their slumbers as well, there would be dark weather indeed on the horizon for Scotland. The two News of the World Championships that closed out the decade only raised fresh signs of trouble. England's Tom Ball and James Sherlock scored easy victories over rising Scottish star George Duncan and veteran Sandy Herd. The English assault may have been stalled to start the new century, but the southerners were by no means beaten.

Nineteen

CROWNING GLORIES

——————— • ● ◉ ● • ———————

T he years between 1910 and the outbreak of war unfolded as if some deity set out to prove that the old woman at Troon had been right all along. She had witnessed the eclipse of Scotland on that dismal afternoon at The International Foursome. James Braid's brave home stand – he won all five of his Opens on Scottish soil – had merely staved off the inevitable.

The championships remaining before the assassination of Archduke Franz Ferdinand set off 'the war to end all wars' amounted to a coronation march for the four Englishmen who had challenged Scotland's supremacy at its own game. The first to cross the stage was Harold Hilton. Since his last Amateur victory in 1901, Hilton's health had begun an inexorable decline. He suffered bouts of rheumatism and sciatica, and it showed in his game.

One of the few times Hilton made headlines during those years was in 1910, when he played a sensational match against 19-year-old Cecil Leitch at a time when the suffragette movement was gaining steam worldwide. Hilton had recently landed a job as editor of a new magazine called *Golf Monthly*, having previously made his living as a paid secretary for clubs across England. Three years later, he would become editor at *Golf Illustrated*.

Hilton had written often about how the best women golfers compared with men. He argued that any first-rate male amateur could spot a woman nine strokes a round and still win. *The Ladies Field* magazine took him up on it, challenging him to a match over two greens against Leitch, a powerful golfer from Silloth. That autumn they played 36 holes each at Walton Heath and Sunningdale. The match spawned tremendous hype and drew fervent crowds, 3,000 or more at both courses. Hilton prevailed at Walton Heath, despite being off form, and carried a 1-up lead into the final 36 holes.

He appeared set to run away from Leitch at Sunningdale. Hilton stretched his lead to four holes over the first 18, and when he won another early in the afternoon round he stood 5 up with 15 to play. Leitch was made of stern stuff, however. She may have been the only person on the links who did not consider her situation hopeless.

'In spite of this serious position, Miss Leitch was undismayed and played with unruffled confidence. She started to win hole after hole, until at the tenth the match stood all square,' wrote the *New York Times*, in a 'special cable' from across the Atlantic, filed by Bernard Darwin. 'Amid a great scene of enthusiasm, she took the lead at the 11th, and playing with all the coolness and determination of a veteran won the match on the 17th green.'

Cartoonists lampooned poor Hilton even as women celebrated her gritty victory. One cartoon showed a man wearing a placard that read: GREAT GOLF TEST. Man, twice Open and twice Amateur champion, DEFEATED by a mere girl. How about votes for women NOW?'

In the aftermath of that match, not even Hilton himself would have foreseen the season that was about to unfold for the 42-year-old Englishman. It began in late May at Prestwick, where the 1911 Amateur took on an international flavour.

Chick Evans, a rising star from Chicago, crossed the ocean to compete, as did four players from Australia, and one each from Singapore and Italy. Since Walter Travis's breakthrough in 1904 more and more Americans had come to test themselves in the Amateur, among them two-time US champion Jerome Travers in 1909. Arnaud Massy's Open victory at Hoylake no doubt inspired players worldwide to take on the British. These were early signs of the revolution that would follow the war.

The weeks leading up to the Championship had seen a hot, dry spell and record temperatures continued through the tournament. As it did so often, the weather had a determinative effect on the outcome. 'The ground was like a brick, and the rough at the sides of the course very thick,' as Darwin described it. It created a situation ideal for a golfer who had complete mastery over his ball – a player like Hilton.

Like so many golfers of that time, Hilton hit a draw to gain length by capitalising on the run of the ball when it landed. Early in the week at Prestwick, he realised his shots were simply running through the baked fairways and into the unmanageable rough. Hilton switched to hitting a fade, sacrificing distance for keeping the ball on the fairway.

The fade worked like a charm through the early rounds. Hilton breezed past his first five opponents, only twice having to play more than 14 holes, to earn his berth in the final. There he met Edward Lassen, a Yorkshire golfer who wasn't pretty to watch but was a dogged competitor not easily shaken off in a match.

In the first round of that final, perhaps fatigued by playing in suffocating heat, Hilton began to wobble like a prizefighter trying to survive a round. He started out well enough, and was 3 up by the turn. The rest of the morning, however, became a desperate struggle to find his swing. Hilton's fade became a slice into the rough; his approaches were feeble, and he missed an unforgivable number of short putts. By 17, he had fallen a hole behind, and it was all he could do to win the last and go to lunch all square.

The golf did not improve in the afternoon. When Hilton sorely needed to storm out of the gate, he putted miserably on the first two holes to lose one and halve the other. He went 2 down when Lassen took his turn to play the third brilliantly. Neither man, however, seemed able to shake off the scratchy golf that had prevailed all day. With success there for the taking, Lassen started knocking his shots into trouble and missing easy putts. By the turn Hilton was back to 1 up. From there it was he who made fewer mistakes – along with some brilliant shots – to claim his third Amateur 4 and 3.

Covering the tournament for *The Times*, Darwin could not avoid the painful truth. 'The golf was not very good on the whole, and was at times of an undeniably scrambling nature,' he wrote. 'One would have liked to see Mr Hilton keep up his brilliant form of the preceding days and win in a blaze of glory – and this he did not do.'

No one who watched that Amateur final would have bet a shilling that less than three weeks later Hilton would approach the 16th tee at the Open with a chance to make history.

The Championship returned that year to Sandwich, Harry Vardon's favourite course, and for the first three rounds he appeared destined to match James Braid by winning a fifth Open. Vardon's health had been improving, and for the first time in his career he had experimented with a training regimen before the Championship. It consisted of a light diet, plenty of rest and cutting back on smoking his beloved pipe.

At the end of the first two rounds, played on a windy day of intermittent sunshine and showers of rain, the young Scottish hope George Duncan had seized the lead with brilliant rounds of 73 and 71. Vardon, John Henry Taylor and Ted Ray were all four strokes back at 148, while Sandy Herd and Hilton sat two behind them.

The sky cleared for the final day, but the wind off Pegwell Bay picked up and blew harder as the afternoon wore on. Duncan fell away in the third round with an 83, while Vardon surged to the front with a 75. His total of 223 gave him a three-stroke lead over Herd and Taylor. Duncan, Ray, Braid and Arnaud Massy all had four strokes to make up. Hilton was five back.

Vardon was out first that afternoon, having abandoned his training regimen in favour of a hearty lunch. Whether that meal had any effect, and Vardon always believed it did, he was not the same player in the final round. He reached the turn in a steady 38, but stumbled on the way home. His score of 80, for a total of 303, left the door ajar for half a dozen competitors.

'The first real thrill of the afternoon – indeed the most thrilling moment of the whole meeting – arrived when the rumour flew across the links that Mr Hilton had reached the turn by magnificent golf in 33 strokes,' Darwin wrote. 'The glorious possibility of an amateur once again winning was enough to send the crowd scampering across the course in the wildest excitement.'

Hilton's outward nine had wiped out Vardon's five-stroke lead, and when he started home with two fours, *The Glasgow Herald* concluded that 'the amateur champion seemed destined to equal the feat accomplished by Mr John Ball, who won both Championships in 1890.'

The first sign of trouble appeared at the 12th. Hilton's tee shot looked perfectly placed, but it caught the corner of a hidden bunker and two shots were dropped. Years later, Darwin wrote that he never again passed that bunker 'without cursing it in my heart'. Still, all was not lost.

Hilton continued playing well and came to the 160-yard 16th with every chance to match Ball's Amateur–Open double. 'He had the Championship in the hollow of his hand – 13 strokes for the last three holes to beat Vardon and one of those holes a short one,' Darwin recalled. 'Alas! He was bunkered at that short hole and took five and two more fives completed the sad story.' Hilton finished a stroke behind Vardon at 304.

Herd was the next player with a legitimate chance to beat Vardon. The Scotsman went out in a brilliant 36, and came to the final hole needing a four to win and a five to tie. Tragically, he hooked his drive into the rough.

That left him facing a three-yard putt to force a play-off. Herd struck the putt beautifully. 'It went right into the hole, only to hop out again, and Vardon for the moment could breathe freely once more,' Darwin reported.

The thrill ride was not over yet. Reports poured in that Massy was on a tear, and 'the exhausted spectators rushed out once more to find the Frenchman left with 12 strokes for the last three holes to tie with Vardon,' Darwin wrote. On 16 Massy nearly holed his putt for a two, and he made a five on the difficult 17th, playing into a fierce wind. That left the Frenchman with a four on 18 to send the Championship into a play-off.

'A splendid tee shot left him with a rather nasty lie under the face of the hill,' Darwin reported. 'He took some lofted wooden club and hit a lovely shot straight on the green about 12 yards short of the hole. The putt was not a pleasant one, for the ball had to climb a hill, but he struck it perfectly, laid it stone dead, and holed out in four amid loud and well-deserved cheering.'

Vardon knew he had nearly thrown away his fifth Championship, and there was no holding him in the play-off the next day. He and Massy were neck and neck through the outward nine, but at 15 Vardon began to pull away. By the time he and Massy headed in for lunch, Vardon was five strokes ahead. Over the first 15 holes in the afternoon, his lead grew to an insurmountable 11 strokes. At the 17th, a weary Massy picked up his ball and conceded the Championship.

Vardon was a happy man, not only because he had tied Braid's five Open wins, but also because he had recaptured the form of his glory years. 'I can truthfully say my golf approached nearer to my old-time standard than it had for many years,' he wrote. It gave him every reason to look forward to more triumphs ahead.

Apawamis

Hilton apparently felt the same way about the revival of his game. He decided to cross the Atlantic that September and compete in the US Amateur at Apawamis Club in Rye, NY.

The Englishman's visit was treated as a major event by the American press. He was, after all, nearly as famous among British amateurs as Vardon was among professionals. Reporters dubbed the trip 'Childe Harold's Pilgrimage', the title of a poem by Lord Byron.

In those days, the US Amateur was ordinarily seen as a battle between rising stars from the eastern and western United States. That year, however, Americans approached it in the same way the British had seven years earlier when Walter Travis travelled to Sandwich to play in their Amateur. Every player's goal became to knock out the invader from overseas.

The dapper chain smoker from England, however, proved tough to beat. Hilton cruised to victory in the qualifying medal, winning by two strokes with scores of 76 and 74. He breezed past every opponent on his way to the Championship final, his closest encounter being a 3 and 2 victory over two-time US Amateur champion Jerome Travers.

In the final, Hilton nearly came up against his friend Evans, who was unexpectedly knocked out in the semis by a burly, long-ball hitter named Fred Herreshoff. He could be a tough customer when his drives were finding the fairway, much less so when they weren't.

Herreshoff was decidedly off form in the opening round of the 36-hole final. He sprayed tee shots everywhere, handing Hilton three holes on the outward nine. The Englishman added another to his lead before lunch by doing nothing more than keeping his ball in front of him.

The afternoon started the same way. Herreshoff's mistakes allowed Hilton to pocket two more holes early. At the fifth, he had a chance to go 7 up, but three-putted for a half. That breathed life into Herreshoff. He promptly won the sixth and claimed two more holes to reach the turn only 3 down despite his disastrous start.

It was a match now. By the 12th, Herreshoff had narrowed the lead to one. The closer he came, the more Hilton struggled. Herreshoff squared the match on 16 and had putts inside ten feet to win 17 and 18. He narrowly missed both, and the match went to a sudden-death play-off.

That first hole at Apawamis was a 377-yard, uphill par four. All the trouble was on the right, woods and a rocky slope beside the green. All 3,000 American fans lined the left side of the fairway as Herreshoff stepped up to his ball. He bombed his drive down the middle, and Hilton carved a fade into the fairway many yards behind. Then came a shot that would, indeed, be heard round the world.

Hilton took out a spoon, the club he trusted most, and let fly. 'When the ball left the club there was a gasp from the crowd as the ball with mischievous intent swerved to the right and headed for the trees beyond the rocks,' wrote historian H.B. Martin, who watched the fateful shot that afternoon.

As it neared the green the ball appeared destined to land amid the rocks and ricochet who knows where. 'But,' as Martin put it, 'the guiding hand of fate took care of Hilton's palpable mistake.' The ball landed in the grass short of the rocks and rolled down to the green, stopping ten feet from the hole.

Dumbfounded, Herreshoff topped his next and left it short. His approach was no better, stopping 20 feet from the pin. The American would have to hole it to keep the match alive. He didn't, and Hilton survived 1 up.

'Hilton's spoon to the 37th green became the most discussed single shot ever played in an American tournament,' Herbert Warren Wind wrote years later. Some eyewitnesses, like Martin, insisted it landed on grass, others that it deflected off a rock. 'In time, golf fans throughout the country, undoubtedly because the rock story made Hilton's victory seem less deserved, adopted this explanation,' Wind wrote.

However it happened, that lucky bounce gave Hilton a double to rival the one his childhood hero had earned in 1890 as he launched England's assault on its northern neighbour. It would stand as another of the epochal performances of that generation. Indeed, in all of history only three other men would win the Amateur Championships of both nations in a single season – Bobby Jones in 1930, Lawson Little in 1934 and 1935, and Bob Dickson in 1967.

There was no denying that Hilton's two wins had been scrappy affairs. It was equally undeniable, however, that his transatlantic double wrote another glorious chapter in the story of Hoylake. The Havemeyer Trophy would be proudly displayed in its clubhouse for a year. The gold medal that came with it would remain forever. Members honoured Hilton's accomplishment by subscribing £140 for a portrait of him that hangs on the clubhouse stairway next to the painting of John Ball.

Ageing warrior

Fittingly, it was Ball who followed Hilton in that pre-war procession for English golf. Even more appropriately, his moment would arrive at the very place where the game first took root south of the Tweed – Westward Ho!

The committee that ran the Amateur had been under pressure to add more English venues to the rota, just as the Open had done. It chose Royal North Devon as the site of the 1912 Amateur. Thirty-four years had passed since a 16-year-old Johnny Ball travelled north to Prestwick for his first taste of championship golf in the Open, and it was a reluctant 50-year-old warrior who turned up to compete at Westward Ho!

Before play began, fellow amateur Robert Harris teased Ball by saying he had heard that next year the committee was going to impose an age limit for competitors. 'I wish they'd done this before,' Ball replied. 'I didn't want to come here and play again.' He had only entered because his fellow members at Hoylake so desperately wanted to see him compete.

By 1912, Ball had taken to travelling by motorcycle. He loved it so much that he shaved off the moustache he had worn since he was old enough to grow one. On chilly winter mornings, his moustache tended to ice up as he travelled, and that was an inconvenience he could not bear.

Without his moustache, Ball looked gaunt and older, but he was still a fearsome competitor. He waltzed into the final of that Championship, running into trouble only once. A local player managed to get 2 up on him at 16, but the veteran pulled him back and won on the first extra hole.

In the final, Ball came up against a competitor he knew well from International Matches and the Amateur – Abe Mitchell, a member of the artisans' golf club at Ashdown Forest. Mitchell was half Ball's age, a tall, lean man who hit the ball forever. Their match in the final was played on a wet, stormy day at Westward Ho!, a decided advantage for Ball. It turned out to be eerily reminiscent of the breathtakingly close encounter at Prestwick in 1899 between Ball and Freddie Tait.

Neither man played brilliant golf on the first 18 holes. They traded mistakes all the way around, with Ball making most of them. Mitchell was 2 up by the turn and added another hole to his lead before lunch. If Ball was going to win, he would have to dig himself out of the same hole he'd been in 13 years ago in Ayrshire, when his friends anxiously telegraphed Hoylake reporting, 'Tait 3 up at end of first round.'

Ball would not lack motivation. Mitchell's presence in the final attracted a crowd of working-class men from Bideford who came out to cheer for the artisan player in the match. They viewed Ball as 'the typical capitalist, trampling on the honest workman,' Darwin wrote years later. When he missed putts, they cheered as raucously as if they were attending a football game.

'It was utterly repugnant to Mr Mitchell, whom they supported, and did him no good and probably a great deal of harm,' Darwin wrote. 'As to Mr Ball, if it had any effect on him at all, it was to harden his resolution and make him set his teeth even more tightly. To make him angry is the way to make him win.'

When the second round began, everyone on the grounds understood that the first two holes would be critical for Ball. 'The holes are of just such a length as to give Mr Mitchell a commanding advantage, and if he could win them, he would have such a lead as to be practically sure of victory,' Darwin wrote in *The Times*.

Mitchell did not win either of them, despite outdriving his opponent on both. Ball halved the first in five and won the second with a brilliant four. By the turn the lead had been whittled to 1 up, and it was anybody's match to win. Mitchell seemed to be staggering when he three-putted the 11th to hand Ball a half on a hole he had played horribly. Ball responded by stealing a long putt on 13 to square the match, and then poked his nose in front for the first time with another three on 14.

Everyone at North Devon expected Mitchell to falter, but he hit a lovely pitch on 15 to make honours even again. At 17, it was Ball who appeared to wilt under pressure. His second shot landed in a bunker and Mitchell went dormie, 1 up with one to play. With the match on the line, both men drove beautifully on 18 and played gorgeous seconds that stopped 30 feet from the hole.

Mitchell putted first and left himself a nerve-wracking five-footer. Ball laid his answer stone dead. Now Mitchell faced a short putt to win the Championship. 'Mr Mitchell had been putting very finely, but at the supreme moment he pushed the ball out two or three inches off line, and Mr Ball saved himself once more,' Darwin wrote.

On the first extra hole, both men found trouble with their seconds that must have reminded spectators of that tense moment in the Sahara Bunker at Prestwick in 1899. Ball's approach landed in a bunker right of the green. Mitchell's ball plunged into a puddle of water in a ditch. Ball played first and hit the middle of the green. Mitchell waded into the water, just as Tait had done, and played a magnificent shot that resulted in a half.

Years afterwards, Darwin recalled what he had done as he covered that match for *The Times*. He had raced down the second fairway, out of sight of the tee, to see where the critical shots landed. 'One came right down the middle of the course: that was Mr Ball's. There followed a long pause. No second ball came. What on earth had happened?'

In that moment of crisis, Mitchell topped his tee shot into a wet ditch. He managed to hack it out, but his third found another ditch, and in trying to extricate that one, Mitchell's shot rebounded off the lip and hit him. It was over. Ball had won the Amateur for the eighth and final time. Few records in sports – or in any pursuit – stand forever. Ball's eight victories over a span of 24 years seems destined to be one of them.

Hoylake had prepared, as always, to welcome its idol at the train station with blaring foghorns and blue-jerseyed fishermen waiting to bear him to the Royal Hotel in triumph. When the train pulled in, however, there was no Ball. The ageing warrior had had enough of hero worship by then. He had hopped off the train a stop early and walked home quietly along the beach.

The following season at St Andrews, Hilton would add the capstone to Hoylake's astounding generation of success by winning his fourth and final Amateur Championship. This time he would go out the way Darwin had hoped he would in 1911 – in a blaze of glory. Facing Carnoustie's Robert Harris in the final, Hilton was as merciless as his old nemesis Tait, trouncing poor Harris 6 and 5.

Conquering Hoylake

Royal Liverpool would be the scene of one more crowning glory before the war – the 1913 Open. Taylor came into that tournament as determined as he had been four years earlier at Deal. Braid and Vardon now had five Championships to his four, and he was once again intent on evening the score.

It also rankled Taylor that he had never conquered the pre-eminent venue in English golf. 'Ever since my caddie days at Westward Ho!,' he wrote. 'I had looked upon Hoylake as a second home – in those early days it was a next-door neighbour – the home of my other golfing hero, Johnnie Ball; and the thought that perhaps forever I should be thwarted from winning there not only disturbed my equanimity, but also injured my pride.'

Taylor nearly missed his chance to compete in that Championship by stumbling in the reinstated qualifying rounds. As he reached the last of those 36 holes, he asked Scotsman George Duncan the score required to get into the Open. Taylor was shocked to learn that he needed a five to earn a place in the field. It ought not to have been a difficult matter, but it became one when Taylor hit his approach into the front bunker. He got out, but the ball landed in the rough at the back of the green. His chip from there stopped six feet short. Now everything rode on a single putt.

'I remember saying to myself: "Well, Taylor my lad, there's only one place for this and that's the bottom of the hole,"' he wrote. 'The word relief is not sufficiently intense in its meaning to describe how I felt when I saw the ball disappear, dropping with a sickening wobble on the right-hand side.'

Bernard Darwin and a few other luminaries were watching as Taylor, always known as simply J.H. by his friends, stood over that six-footer. When it fell, 'those who knew him exclaimed in chorus, "It would be just like J.H. to win the whole thing now,"' Darwin wrote.

The defending champion that June at Hoylake was Ted Ray, who had won wire to wire the previous season at Muirfield, breaking 'the monotony of the Triumvirate's victories', as *The Glasgow Herald* put it. That Championship would be the first to see an international invasion of the sort that would become commonplace after the war. American Johnny McDermott came to compete after back-to-back victories in the US Open. Joining Arnaud Massy from France were Jean Gassiat and Louis Tellier.

It was an entirely different Taylor who showed up for the opening rounds of the Championship on a pleasant, breezy June afternoon along the Dee Estuary. He finally tamed Hoylake with scores of 73 and 75, placing him second, a stroke behind Ray. Vardon and McDermott were in the top ten, but well back.

When Taylor awoke the next morning at the Royal Hotel, he was stunned by what he saw from his window. 'During the night a gale of wind sprang up,' he remembered. 'I know something of what a gale of wind is like, but this visitation was much worse than I ever experienced. It was a full-throated hurricane, the wind blowing in intermittent gusts that were overwhelming, and it was accompanied with sheets of torrential rain.'

Taylor was to start at 9.25 a.m. and as he walked to the first tee he noticed that the tents erected for the Championship had been flattened, a sight 'depressing enough to crush every optimistic desire'. Nevertheless, no man was better equipped to brave a tempest than the pugnacious son of North Devon, with his flat-footed golf and three-quarter swing.

The sight of Taylor out in that hurricane remained etched forever on Darwin's memory. 'How he did stick his chin out and pull his cap down over his nose and bang that ball right through the gale!' he wrote. 'It was the greatest of all golfing victories of man over nature.'

Miraculously, Taylor fought his way around that narrow, testing course without a single score higher than five, coming in with a 77 that gave him a three-stroke lead. A devoted fan, probably with a serious wager riding on the outcome, had raided the lavatories at the Royal and made off with a bundle of towels, which he carried under his waterproofs and handed to Taylor as he played to help him keep his hands dry,

Like everyone else on the links, the big Jerseyman Ray had been battered about in the wind and could do no better than 81. McDermott and Vardon were seven and eight strokes back, respectively, and no man was making up that many shots in such a gale.

In the afternoon, the wind died down and the rain stopped, but conditions were still brutal enough that Taylor was the only contender to post a score in the 70s. His 79 was defined by a shot that lived forever in the memory of all who witnessed it. It came at the notoriously difficult sixth, the Briars. There, playing into the teeth of the wind, Taylor hit a driving mashie that 'nearly knocked the pin out of the hole and lay dead for a three', Darwin recalled. 'The glory of the Briars still dazzles my sight.'

Those two rounds gave Taylor a dominant eight-stroke victory, as Ray staggered in with 84, McDermott with 83 and Vardon with 80. Taylor was so proud of his performance – especially his 77 in a near-hurricane – that he framed his scorecards. 'I then considered, as I still do, that it was the finest round I ever played,' he wrote at the age of 72, when he sat down to compose a memoir of his storied career.

Curtain call

If fate had, indeed, orchestrated the coronation of English golf in the years before the war, it was never more evident than in the 1914 Open at Prestwick, the last one played before golf went dark.

It was not simply that Prestwick, birthplace of championship golf, should have the honour of staging the final Open of that glorious era. It was the way the tournament unfolded. No one would have been surprised to see Taylor and Vardon figure in the outcome, but who would have guessed that the luck of the draw would result in the two of them battling it out side by side in the final rounds?

Vardon came into that Open after another grand and lucrative tour of America in 1913, accompanied by his fellow Jerseyman Ray. Their trip ended, as every golfer knows, in one of the game's most storied moments – but not, alas, the victorious outcome Vardon and Ray had dreamed of when they set sail across the Atlantic.

The hero of that story was a 20-year-old caddie. Young Francis Ouimet, in one of sport's greatest upsets, miraculously defeated Vardon and Ray in a play-off – the most potent sign yet that America was taking aim at Britain. After that victory, Ouimet crossed the ocean to compete at Prestwick, where he found the going much tougher and finished far down the list.

Despite that shocking loss, Vardon remained one of the favourites to win at the course where he had claimed two of his five Open titles. His fellow members of The Great Triumvirate, Taylor and Braid, were also given a strong chance to claim a sixth Championship.

The tournament was played in gorgeous weather on a course that had been lengthened by 500 yards and toughened by the addition of bunkers strategically placed under the direction of Braid, who was increasingly earning a reputation as a gifted golf architect.

As punters had expected, the two professionals, who had led the southern assault on the Scottish game for a generation, were atop the leaderboard at the end of the first day's play. Vardon was in front at 150, with Taylor two strokes back. Fate showed its hand when they were drawn together for the final two rounds.

'The malignant goddess who rules over the draw had seen to it that their names came out of the hat together,' Darwin wrote, 'and that at Prestwick where the crowds were always large and impatient of discipline and the conformation of the course with its famous loop of the last four holes made the controlling of them a really desperate task.'

The pairing naturally attracted a multitude of fans, as train after train pulled in from Glasgow and beyond filled with fans clamouring to see the finale. Five thousand people lined the fairway as Vardon and Taylor began their round, and that number would nearly double as the afternoon wore on. It would be a long day for both men.

'With the huge excited crowd surging all around him, in their endeavour to be so placed as to have a view of the following stroke, it is only natural that the player should come in for a good deal of buffeting about,' Vardon wrote. 'It may come as a surprise to many people to know that after a big tournament my ankles and shins are black and blue. This is caused by the kicks received from those anxious to find a position in which to see some of the play.'

With all the attention on Vardon and Taylor the most brilliant round of the morning went mostly unnoticed. Glasgow's James Jenkins, a gentleman golfer who had claimed Scotland's final pre-war Amateur Championship earlier that year, went around in 73. It might easily have been a 71, a new record, had he not missed makeable putts on 17 and 18.

In the group every fan was following, Vardon struggled with either his game or the crowd. He started beautifully, adding a stroke to his lead before the turn. Beginning at the tenth, however, Vardon went through what Darwin described in *The Times* as 'a dismal series of disasters', allowing Taylor to take a two-stroke lead into lunch. Vardon seemed so frustrated that Taylor began to believe he might be the one destined to win a sixth Open.

'I sensed that Harry was sorely troubled at the way the game ran against him, and as it was so usual for him to hide his feelings under a cloak of apparent indifference, the revelation gave me hope that I should pull through with success,' Taylor wrote.

If Vardon's account of the day is any measure, Taylor was misreading his friend's emotions. 'I knew in my own mind I was playing well,' Vardon wrote. 'That I had been guilty of a few slips was only part and parcel of the game . . . I can truthfully say that I thought I was going to win the Championship even though I was two strokes behind.'

The outcome of that Open was decided at one of the holes Braid had altered most significantly – the fourth, where he had placed a bunker alongside the burn, leaving only a narrow passage for a drive to find the fairway. In the morning round, Taylor found a bunker on the left and made six. This time his drive landed in Braid's new bunker. Taylor got out, but chunked his next into the burn. The seven that resulted so rattled Taylor that he dropped two more shots at the short Himalayas, and the damage was done.

'Vardon now led by two strokes, and from this point the game was something in the nature of a procession,' Darwin wrote. 'Taylor went on trying as hard as he could – it is impossible to imagine him doing other- wise – but those two awful holes had broken just a little bit of that great heart of his and for some time he was distinctly unsteady. Vardon, on the other hand, settled down calmly and determinedly to take the gifts which the gods and his opponent had given him. Playing good golf – wonderfully good with that tumultuous crowd around him – he forged slowly ahead.'

In the end, Vardon beat Taylor by five strokes in that round – 78 to 83 – and won his sixth and final Open Championship by three, with a total of 306 to Taylor's 309. 'To admit disappointment is trite and impotent,' Taylor wrote of that final round, 'but this I do say: Harry Vardon deserved the high honour. He was the better player.'

Taylor was right about that. Peter Lewis, pre-eminent historian of that generation, dissected the results of every tournament conducted in Britain between Taylor's breakthrough Open victory in 1894 and the outbreak of world war. His conclusion? 'However one looks at it, Vardon was head and shoulders above any of his contemporaries.'

During those years, Vardon won 52 tournaments, followed by Braid at 34 and Taylor at 32. The proud son of Jersey won an astonishing 34 per cent of the tournaments he entered. Vardon also finished second 29 times, meaning he was in the top two more than half the time he took the field. That record, not to mention his otherworldly winning streak in 1898 and 1899, can stand up against any in history.

Interestingly, however, if viewed by the modern standard of who won the most major championships it is not Vardon whose name is at the top of the list. In those days, the majors consisted of the Open, the Amateur, their US counterparts and the British PGA Championship, known then as the News of the World. The honours for most victories in those championships are shared by the first hero of English golf and the last great Scotsman of that age – John Ball and James Braid. Both won nine majors. Vardon trailed them by one, with eight, followed by Taylor and Hilton with seven championships apiece.

In the generation-long battle between north and south, numbers made it undeniably clear that the English had vanquished the Scots. That remains true even if one includes the perspective of history, with Scotsman Allan Macfie's win in the first Amateur Championship of 1885 added to the north's total. England had 17 wins to 12 in the Amateur, and 15 Open victories to nine for Scotland.

Only at match play, their own true game, could Scots claim any edge, but even in that format results were decidedly mixed. Led by Braid, Scotland won the News of the World tournament six times to England's five. Scots dominated the Amateur International Match, nine to two, but that was offset by crushing defeats in its professional counterpart, which England won five times to one, with three matches halved.

Most tellingly, however, in both of the Great Matches between the two nations – the battles that would be remembered forever – Scotland had not simply lost; it had been humbled. That was true in single combat, Vardon vs Park, and it was true in The International Foursome. There was no denying, even after Braid's courageous last stand, that the rose had triumphed over the thistle.

Barely a month after Vardon won his final Open – on 28 June 1914 – came the Great War, and there would be no more championships to win in Britain for six long years. That marked the end of what Darwin described so eloquently as golf's 'long, golden afternoon'.

Scots may have been outnumbered and overrun on the battlefield, but they could, nevertheless, look back on that generation with a tremendous sense of national pride. In the 50 years since the first English club was formed at North Devon, Scots had seen the pastime they invented and nurtured for four centuries embraced by all the world, becoming one of those rare games played wherever the sun shines and the grass grows.

Not only that, the nation's premier club, the Royal and Ancient of St Andrews, had been anointed as the game's governing body and spiritual leader in every country except the United States. The ascendancy of the R&A and the emergence of St Andrews as the unquestioned Home of Golf ensured that for all time players from around the globe would make their reverent pilgrimages to the game's birthplace in Scotland, especially that ancient grey city by the sea and its famed Old Course.

The dramatic changes witnessed during that half-century, especially its final 25 years, have reverberated through the decades. The Professional Golfers' Association and the annual tour spawned by its News of the World and Sphere and Tatler qualifying tournaments has been replicated around the world, bringing untold riches to men once considered servants.

The quest to tame a devilishly difficult game, with balls that fly farther and clubs that are easier to hit, continues unabated, and the debate over technology's impact on golf remains as heated as it was when the R&A first took up the issue of the Haskell ball.

Golf literature continues to flourish. In every generation, descendants of Horace Hutchinson and Bernard Darwin have told the game's story with surpassing eloquence – from Grantland Rice and Pat Ward-Thomas through Henry Longhurst and Herbert Warren Wind to Dan Jenkins and Michael Bamberger.

The Golden Age of Golf Architecture is undergoing a modern revival with a new minimalist, strategic design movement that has seen the creation of gems from the sandhills of Nebraska to the shores of New Zealand.

The passionate rivalry between England and Scotland that defined pre-war golf has evolved, over time, into equally riveting battles between nations that are among the game's premier events – the Ryder, President's and Solheim Cups for professionals and the Walker and Curtis Cups for amateurs.

Indeed every aspect of the modern game can trace its origins to the moment that marked the dawn of golf's greatest generation – the autumn afternoon at Prestwick when John Ball became the first Englishman and the first amateur to be crowned Champion Golfer of the Year.

Epilogue

AFTER THE WAR

———————— •◦◉◦• ————————

B efore the war, Harry Vardon and Ted Ray had promised their American friends to return for another tour of the country. Their opportunity came in the summer of 1920, as championship golf resumed in Britain 18 months after hostilities ended in Europe.

When they returned home, this time with Ray carrying the US Open trophy, Vardon feared for British golf. Golf was now growing exponentially in the States. In 1913 the nation had a quarter of a million golfers. A decade later that number had exploded to two million, and with it the number of top-flight courses and players.

'It was apparent to me,' Vardon wrote, 'that the Americans would seriously have to be reckoned with in the near future. There could be no shadow of doubt, unless we were able to produce some fresh blood to take the place of the old-timers, Great Britain's supremacy in the Royal and Ancient game would be seriously challenged.'

It was not simply a matter of numbers. It was the approach Americans took to golf. They practised with an intensity unknown across the Atlantic, except by the Vardons and Hiltons of the world. They built facilities expressly for that purpose and honed their skills to a razor's edge. That was especially true of putting, where Americans developed what Vardon and Bernard Darwin both considered a decisive advantage.

Like the English before them, Americans considered stroke play a truer test of skill than a match, and were even more intently focused on making low scores. Their obsession with scoring all but ensured that the true Scottish game of thrust and parry would cease to be a central part of golf, as it had been for centuries.

Americans, too, brought their share of cultural changes to golf – notably the exclusivity of their country clubs. English and Scottish clubs also were private, but nearly all welcomed artisans' clubs and offered tee times to those who weren't members, a practice that continues today. American clubs, then and now, were strictly reserved for those wealthy enough to belong.

Fierce competitors that they were, Americans did precisely what Englishmen had done when the game began booming there in the 19th century. They set out to dethrone the reigning kings of golf – the British. Walter Travis had proven it was possible in 1904, and Americans had been coming after both the Amateur and Open ever since.

It would not be long after the war before Vardon was proven right. Fate graciously allowed George Duncan, the promising Scotsman who had been robbed of his prime by the six-year lay-off, to carry off the Claret Jug in the first Open Championship after the war at Deal.

The very next year, however, the shadow of what writers dubbed 'the American menace' began to spread across the kingdom, especially in the Open. That year Jock Hutchison returned to his birthplace in St Andrews to win his first and only Championship. Scotland could rightly claim him as a native son, but he was a proud American citizen by then and brought the game's most cherished trophy back home with him.

When Walter Hagen, the rising star of American golf, broke through the following season at Sandwich, there could be no more ambiguity. Britain would have but one more moment of glory – Englishman Arthur Havers's victory in 1923 at Troon – before the long, dark night descended.

For the next ten seasons, the Claret Jug sailed across the Atlantic in the hands of Hagen, Gene Sarazen, Bobby Jones and others as humbled Britons endured an unbroken string of American victories. The situation was not nearly as bleak in the Amateur, where the only Americans to carry off the trophy during those same ten years were Jones and Jess Sweetser.

It was clear by then, however, that professional golf was the future, and in that game the US would quickly emerge as the dominant force. The rest of the world would make its presence known after World War II, as South Africa, Australia and other nations racked up victories in the Open Championship. Never again would Britain reign supreme.

The old warriors of the nation's glory days – Ball, Hilton, Taylor, Vardon and Braid – did not go gently into that good night. They fought desperately to turn back the American tide, most of them well into their golden years. At times, one or the other would show a flash of the old brilliance, but to a man they were aware that the sun had set on their era and it was time for younger golfers to carry the banner for their country.

John Ball

After the war, Ball moved from the only home he'd ever known, the Royal Hotel at Hoylake, to a stately old house called Lygan-y-Wern at the foot of the Halkyn hills in North Wales. He had visited his sister and brother-in-law there for years, and came to love the tranquillity of the place. It did not hurt that with his binoculars Ball could spy on Hoylake across the Dee Estuary.

In 1920, aged 59, he became co-owner of Lygan-y-Wern, and a few years later his sister and brother-in-law moved out, leaving the house to him, his unmarried sister Elizabeth, their housekeeper Nellie Williams and the beloved donkeys Ball had brought with him from his farm.

Ball continued to turn up at Hoylake on medal days. Even as he aged, he never lost that lovely swing or the ability to deliver inspiring spurts of golf, even in the face of persistent betrayal by his putter. His name appears on the club's honours board as late as 1924, when he had reached the ripe old age of 63.

Ball played in his final Amateur three years later at Royal Liverpool in the hope of winning his 100th match in the Championship. He got a bye in the first round, and in the second fell hopelessly behind opponent J.R. Abercrombie, who went dormie with five holes to play. Then the relentless fighter in Ball surfaced, and for a moment a reverent Darwin thought the clock had been turned back to the early 1890s.

'Mr Ball began to fight with his back against the wall,' Darwin wrote. 'Two great shots gave him a putt for three at the Field (490 yards or so, and at 66 years old!) and one hole came back. His enemy made a mess of the Lake against the wind and a second hole came back. The years seemed to have rolled away; here was the irresistible spurt once again; once again we were to see the impossible achieved.

'To the Dun Mr Ball played two fine shots and was unkindly caught in the little bunker that comes jutting out on the left,' Darwin continued. 'Still, he got out; it seemed almost certain that he would have a putt to keep the match alive, and surely, surely he would hole it. But all our beautiful dreams were destroyed by Mr Abercrombie holing a long, long putt in the odd. And so the hero went down, glorious in defeat.'

Five years after that Championship, aged 71, Ball stunned his family and his friends by marrying the maid, Nellie Williams, who was nearly 30 years younger than him. Sadly, that decision led to a break with Elizabeth and the rest of his family. When Ball drafted his will the following year, beyond a small bequest to the woman who had taken over management of the Royal Hotel, Nellie was the sole beneficiary.

No other member of his family was mentioned beyond his one surviving donkey, Bessie. 'If my wife shall predecease me and my old donkey Bessie shall be still living,' Ball wrote, 'I direct the company to have my said donkey destroyed painlessly by a duly qualified veterinary surgeon.'

Ball rarely visited Hoylake after that, turning out only for championships and bemoaning how easy golf had become with newfangled clubs and balls, raked bunkers and manicured fairways and greens. His last days were darkened by the outbreak of the Second World War and the death in July 1940 of his friend and rival, Scotsman John Laidlay. That must have been a sad reminder of his own advancing age for Ball, whose time came six months later. The first hero of English golf died at his home in North Wales on 2 December 1940. He was weeks shy of his 79th birthday.

Harold Hilton

From his perch as editor of *Golf Illustrated*, Hilton continued after the war to be one of the most influential writers and thinkers in the game. It was the job he had been born to do. Until then he'd never found the perfect fit – not when he worked with his father in insurance, not during a stint at Kinnear Limited Cigarette and Tobacco Manufacturers, and not as the paid secretary of various golf clubs. The fishermen of Hoylake may have considered Hilton a 'toff', but life had never been easy for him.

It only became worse in later years as the physical decline that had begun after 1905 accelerated. Like the other leading golfers of his day, Hilton continued to compete into his old age. After 1913, however, he was rarely a factor in the Amateur, his best effort coming in 1922 at Prestwick, when he made it to the sixth round as a 53-year-old. Like Ball, Hilton's last Championship appearance would be at Hoylake in 1927, where he bowed out meekly, losing 4 and 2 to a 19-year-old artisan golfer.

Not long after that, Hilton's illness became so debilitating that he was forced to retire from golf and work. He and his wife, Frances, moved first to Cooden in East Sussex and later to Westcote in Gloucestershire. His fellow writer, Darwin, with whom Hilton maintained a lifelong friendship, came to visit him there in the waning years of his life.

'He was in bed, very ill and helpless, but he was cheerful and cour-ageous,' Darwin wrote, 'he still smoked one cigarette after another and he still liked to talk about golf. We talked in particular of his last round of 75 which brought him in the winner of his second Open Champion-ship at Hoylake in 1897, and I shall always remember the gentle chuckle with which he said: "I began with a three."'

Hilton died at his home in Westcote on 5 May 1942 at the age of 73. The cause of his death was listed as cardiac failure resulting from paralysis agitans, better known as Parkinson's disease. Darwin could not help but feel a sense of pathos about his friend's hardships. 'Harold's was in some ways rather a tragic life,' Darwin wrote. 'He might have fared better if he had applied his very astute mind to other things besides hitting a ball.'

The other golfer so closely associated with Ball and Hilton – John Graham, the third member of what Hoylake was fond of calling its Amateur Triumvirate – was among the game's most prominent tragedies during the Great War. Graham was killed on 16 June 1915 while leading a charge of the Liverpool Scottish at Hooge, Belgium, not far from Ypres. He would be remembered as the greatest amateur who never won a Championship – a man whose true preference was to be out on the Liverpool links of an evening with his beloved retriever and a few clubs under one arm.

John Henry Taylor

Taylor spent his post-war years exactly as one might expect, tirelessly promoting the game of golf through his work as a PGA committeeman and on the council of the Artisan Golfers' Association.

Taylor had played his first golf as a member of the artisans club at North Devon. It rankled him that most Scottish golf courses were public, while the vast majority in England were private. He felt compelled to change that situation. Taylor teamed up with *News of the World* proprietor George Riddell to push through plans for a public golf course near Richmond Park in London. It opened on 6 June 1922, and was such a roaring success that another 18 holes were added in 1925.

Four years later, the man who once worked as a bootblack had the pleasure of seeing his oldest son, also named John Henry, play for Oxford in the University Match at Burnham-on-Sea. 'When my reader recalls that Burnham was the scene of my first professional post he will understand the pride I felt at being a spectator there in 1926 at my son's debut,' Taylor wrote, and one can all but see him beaming.

Taylor was nearly 50 when golf resumed after the war, and he knew he had no more Championships in him. Still, it pained him to watch Americans take over the game. 'I am being, I hope, nothing but patriotic when confessing that the run of its successes inflicted a real hurt to my pride,' he wrote.

Taylor did his best to thwart the attack. He competed in the Open for nine more years, managing three top-ten finishes. In 1926 at St Annes, the year Bobby Jones won the first of his three Opens, Taylor dazzled the young American with the way he summoned the old magic.

'To me, John Henry Taylor, 56-year-old English professional, was the hero of St Anne's,' Jones wrote. 'John Henry shot a 71 in a hard wind in his third round, in his gallant effort to stave off the rush of the American invaders. It was better than I could do in any round . . . My hat is off to John Henry!'

The final great moment of Taylor's golf career came in 1933 when he was named non-playing captain of the British Ryder Cup team that would face Walter Hagen's American squad in Southport, England. The team gave Taylor the pleasure of leaving the field a winner, narrowly defeating the Americans by 6½ to 5½ and tying that fledgling series at two wins apiece.

In 1946, aged 75, he retired as the professional at Mid-Surrey, no doubt with a supreme sense of satisfaction. He had been golf's indispensable man. Along with Vardon and Braid, his mates in The Great Triumvirate, Taylor had risen to the occasion when professionals needed to stand up for themselves the way Young Tom Morris had ages ago in St Andrews, when he set his own terms for playing a match with gentlemen. Equally important, with their impeccable behaviour, the three superstars of the era had won the respect of the men who ran the game, just as Old Tom and Allan Robertson had done before them.

In his memoir, Andra Kirkaldy said he'd like to put his hand on Taylor's shoulder and say, 'You only have to look around you to see the good you've done. The whole army of professional golfers in this country, France and America, salutes you as the best friend and general they ever had. It is you they have to thank for their position today in the golfing world; and it is you they do thank.'

After leaving Richmond, Taylor returned to his birthplace at Westward Ho! He lived in a home not far from the cottage where he had been born, with a lovely view of the links and Bideford Bay beyond. Pat Ward-Thomas, golf writer for the *Manchester Guardian*, visited Taylor there in 1961 as he was approaching his 90th birthday.

'He was in excellent heart that morning,' Ward-Thomas wrote. 'Even the frailty of great age could never obscure the impression of strength there is about him; the sturdy frame, the splendid outlines of the head, the strong jaw and the sweetness of his smile. He came to the door to welcome us, shading his eyes from the sparkling light, and he was eager to talk. For an hour, the conversation never tired and he took us about the house while we admired the collection of sketches and paintings of himself, the Spy cartoon from *Vanity Fair*, a study in oils, and a beautiful line drawing from *Punch*, presented to him on his retirement from Mid-Surrey.'

Taylor died in his home at Northam on 10 February 1963, a bit more than a month from his 92nd birthday. Like Old Tom Morris, he had out-lived all his contemporaries, including his oldest friend, Kirkaldy, who died in St Andrews on 16 April 1934 at the age of 74. Indeed, Taylor very nearly lived to celebrate the 100th Anniversary of Royal North Devon Golf Club, the birthplace of the English game he had done so much to promote.

That other famous son of Westward Ho!, Horace Hutchinson, enjoyed no such peaceful sunset. In 1908, Hutchinson's place as a leading figure of his time – a writer and editor who became the voice of his generation, a member of virtually every influential golf committee and a two-time Amateur Champion – was recognised by his selection as captain of the Royal and Ancient Golf Club of St Andrews.

Sadly, the tall, handsome man who lashed at his ball with 'bombastic freedom' saw his always frail health decline severely after the war. For the last 18 years of his life, Hutchinson was incapacitated. He and his wife, Dorothy, moved from their home near Royal Ashdown Forest in Sussex to Lennox Gardens in the Chelsea area of London. There, on 27 July 1932, Horace ended his agony by taking his own life. He was 73 years old.

Harry Vardon

Among those too old to go off to fight in Europe, Vardon had the closest brush with death. Towards the end of the war a German airman dropped a bomb on Totteridge that exploded in the corner of his garden. It destroyed part of his home, flattened several others in the neighbourhood, and damaged the prized trophy he'd won as a boy in Jersey, thankfully not beyond repair. Miraculously, only one person was killed.

Since his childhood working as a gardener, Vardon had never lost his love of tilling the soil, and he kept a lovely garden at his home all his life. He was fond of telling a story about a neighbour who'd seen a newsreel featuring his golfing exploits. She told his wife, Jessie, she had known he was a Champion Gardener but not a Champion Golfer.

Fittingly, it was the greatest golfer of his age who came closest after the war to adding another major championship to his laurels. The focal point of Vardon's third tour of America in 1920 – one that saw him and Ted Ray play in a wearying 101 events – was the US Open, played in mid-August at Inverness Club in Toledo, Ohio.

Then 50 years old, Vardon was paired in the qualifying rounds with the young prodigy Bobby Jones, making his Open debut at the age of 18. In the tournament proper, Vardon seemed to sneer at Father Time, playing beautifully and putting as if he were a young man who had never been felled by tuberculosis. By the end of the third round, Vardon had a one-stroke lead. When he raced through the outward nine of the final 18 in 36 and played both ten and 11 brilliantly, it appeared the old man was destined to win.

At that moment, however, the sky became ominously dark. The wind began howling off Lake Erie, bringing with it squalls of rain. In Vardon's younger days, that would not have mattered a whit. But a tiring 50-year-old simply did not have the stamina to fight through it. Vardon dropped seven shots over the remaining holes and lost by a stroke.

His only consolation was that it was his fellow Jerseyman, Ray, who nipped him. That would be Vardon's last chance in a championship. He competed in the Open until 1929, never doing better than eighth and missing the cut in nearly half his appearances.

Through all of his years of championship glory, Vardon's life had been dogged by a singular sadness. Jessie had never overcome the depression that set in after the death of their firstborn son, and her sadness deepened after a miscarriage in 1896. In 1920, Vardon began a long-running affair with a woman named Tilly Howell, a Liverpool hotel worker and part-time dancer. In 1926, she gave birth to a son, Peter.

Vardon provided for Peter and his mother, and visited his son whenever he could, but as the boy became older Howell asked Vardon to stay away for fear of the scandal that would erupt if it became known that they had a child. The existence of his relationship with Howell and the birth of their son was not made public until 1991, when Peter's wife,

Audrey, published a book titled *Harry Vardon: The Revealing Story of a Champion Golfer.*

He may have been from Jersey, but Vardon remained for all his days the great symbol of English golf. In 1934, when Henry Cotton ended the nation's decade of darkness by winning the Open at Sandwich, his first thought was to bring the Claret Jug to Vardon's hotel room to share that glorious moment with the greatest champion the nation would ever know. Cotton and Vardon said little to one other, but both shed a tear.

Three years later, on 20 March 1937, Vardon died of pleurisy at his home in Totteridge. His funeral was attended by all the luminaries of his age – Herd, Taylor, Cotton and more – with Tilly Howell sitting quietly and unnoticed in a pew at the rear of St Andrew's Church.

James Braid

Braid lived out his golden years as the Grand Old Man of Walton Heath, where he and his family built a home he named Earlsferry as an homage to his birthplace. Like his mates in The Great Triumvirate, Braid continued to compete in the Open well past his prime, missing the cut in his final attempt as a 68-year-old and never finishing better than 16th.

At Walton Heath, he spent his days as he always had, giving lessons and playing golf with members, a healthy chunk of whom were politicians or royalty. Braid's students included Winston Churchill and the Duke of Windsor, a lifelong friend. Braid became so chummy with royals that his family called him once after being excited to learn that he had been invited to dinner with the Prince of Wales. Did he sit next to the Prince, they asked? 'No,' Braid replied slyly, 'he sat next to me.'

Long before his Championship days were behind him, Braid had begun to make a name for himself as a golf architect, just as his fellow professionals Old Tom Morris and Willie Park Jr had done. Park, in fact, had worked so feverishly at building his business, travelling back and forth across the Atlantic and taking daring financial risks which cost him dearly, that he all but worked himself to death in 1925 at the age of 61. Braid's design work was confined almost exclusively to Britain, as he suffered from motion sickness, especially on boats, and was reluctant even to cross the English Channel.

Over the years, Braid designed or refined 400 courses, demonstrating a gift for crafting holes that fit naturally into the landscape and feature spectacular views. He was also known for cleverly arranged bunkering that was beautifully shaped. Braid's lasting legacy is Gleneagles, where he built the King's and Queen's courses, but he also left behind gems like Boat of Garten and Brora, a wonderfully natural links course in the Scottish Highlands. Thanks to an admirer who happened also to be a five-time Open Champion, Australian Peter Thomson, since 1997 Brora has been home to the James Braid Golfing Society.

Braid remained robust as he aged, spending his last 11 years as a widower, following the death of his wife, Minnie, in 1939. He also outlived his partner in the famous International Foursome of 1905, the eternally young Sandy Herd, who made the cut in the Open at the age of 65. Herd died on 18 February 1944 in St Andrews of pneumonia resulting from a medical procedure. He was 75 years old.

On his 80th birthday, 6 February 1950, walking and carrying his own bag, Braid went around the notoriously difficult Walton Heath in the remarkable score of 81. Over the years, he had played every hole on the course in two strokes and amassed 18 holes in one.

In September of that year, Braid's status as a legend of Scottish golf was acknowledged when the Royal and Ancient made him an honorary member. Two months later, on 27 November 1950, Braid died at his home in Walton on the Hill. The R&A flew the Scottish saltire at half-mast that day, and Earlsferry later added a granite plaque to the town hall in memory of its illustrious native son.

Bernard Darwin

If Braid and his fellow golfers could jointly have expressed a wish, to a man they no doubt would have agreed with a parting plea Taylor shared in his memoir: 'I want nothing more,' he wrote, 'than to be remembered by posterity in the words of Bernard Darwin.'

Taylor and his contemporaries knew their era would be remembered forever for the transformative changes the game had undergone and for the astonishing performances witnessed on the links – among them half a dozen feats that remain unmatched or have rarely been repeated.

They knew, also, that Darwin shared their reverence for golf before the war and that no man would tell the story of their times with the same sense of romantic nostalgia. Since he was a boy, Darwin had been a passionate lover of games, which he never ceased to view as titanic struggles between heroes.

Taylor's wish would be granted to every luminary of his day, especially Braid. Darwin published a biography of Earlsferry's native son two years after his passing. In his books and columns, Darwin devoted himself to preserving the memories of pre-war legends – from Ball, Hilton and Tait to Taylor, Vardon and Herd.

Darwin covered golf into the age of Ben Hogan, writing for *The Times* until 1953 and *Country Life* nearly up to 1961, when he died aged 85 in a nursing home in Kent not far from his birthplace.

His work set a standard that has influenced writing about golf and other games ever since. Indeed, many consider him the greatest of all sportswriters, and some rank him among the greatest essayists on any topic. Darwin's pre-eminence was recognised by his election as Captain of the Royal and Ancient Golf Club in 1934 and, three years later, by his designation as a Commander of the British Empire in the Coronation Honours.

Even as he watched golf evolve into the modern, worldwide sport it has become, no new player who came to dominate the game – not even the immortal Bobby Jones – could eclipse the men Darwin once described as the gods of his youth.

His passion was always for golf before the Great War – at Hoylake, where John Ball could be seen chipping his way from the Royal Hotel to the links; at Sandwich where he believed the larks sang as they sang nowhere else; or on a northbound train where the sight of Leuchars Station would portend all the glories of St Andrews.

Darwin considered it his sacred mission to keep alive the memory of that greatest of generations lest, as he wrote, the deeds of its champions be forgotten, 'as the years go ruthlessly on and make dim the brightest of records'.

NOTES ON CHAPTERS

T his book, in keeping with its predecessor *Monarch of the Green*, is a narrative history. Its ambition is to tell the story of the transformative age when golf went global without straying from the documented record of the times. Below readers will find the source material that is the basis of quotations and critical statements of fact used in this book, as well as the scenes that unfold during the telling of this story. The only liberty I have taken is the historian's prerogative to interpret the meaning of events based on my extensive research, and to state my case with the voice of authority.

One

'TERRIBLE THINGS'

Horace Hutchinson's reflections on the 1890 Open Championship are from his memoir, *Fifty Years of Golf*.

Details of the 1890 Open Championship are drawn from reports in *The Scotsman* and *The Golfing Annual*, Vol. IX.

The story of Willie Campbell's misfortunes in the 1887 Open is drawn from the online history archives of the Royal and Ancient Golf Club of St Andrews.

Two

GOLF MOVES SOUTH

Details on the history of Royal North Devon Golf Club come from multiple sources, including a club history titled *The Royal North Devon Golf Club, 1864–1964*; *Tom Morris of St Andrews: The Colossus of Golf, 1821–1908*, by David Malcolm and Peter E. Crabtree; Hutchinson's memoir; and Robert Browning's *A History of Golf*.

The quotation from General Moncrieff that 'Providence obviously designed this for a golf links' is from the book *The Royal North Devon Golf Club, 1864–1964*.

Andra Kirkaldy's quote about the game spreading like 'Noah's flood' is from his memoir, *Fifty Years of Golf: My Memories*.

Details on the founding of Royal Liverpool Golf Club are from the club's first two histories – *The Royal Liverpool Golf Club*, by Guy B. Farrar, and *Mighty Winds . . . Mighty Champions: The Official History of Royal Liverpool Golf Club*, by Joe Pinnington. The detail about the Northern Lights streaking across the sky above Hoylake is from *Mighty Winds*.

Hutchinson's quote about English golf owing much to Royal Liverpool is from his book, *British Golf Links*.

Details of the Grand Tournament for Professionals are from the two Liverpool histories, contemporary newspaper accounts and the author's previous book, *Monarch of the Green: Young Tom Morris, Pioneer of Modern Golf*.

Details on the founding of the University Match are from Browning's *History of Golf* and Hutchinson's memoir.

The quotation by Hutchinson about the oddity of travelling with golf clubs in the 1870s is from his memoir.

The description of Hutchinson's swing is based on information in Bernard Darwin's *A History of Golf in Britain* and Malcolm and Crabtree's *Tom Morris of St Andrews*.

Details of the founding of the Amateur Championship are from multiple sources – Browning's *History*; John Behrend's *John Ball of Hoylake* and *The Amateur*; Hutchinson's memoir; Peter Lewis's *Why Are There Eighteen Holes?*; Royal Liverpool's two club histories; and the most recent history of the club, *A Hoylake Celebration*, by Blyth Bell and Roger Greenway.

Details on the playing of the first Amateur Championship are from the three Hoylake histories; Darwin's history of golf; Lewis's *Why Are There Eighteen*

Holes?; and Hutchinson's memoir, along with contemporary newspaper reports.

Three

A HERO FOR ENGLAND

Details about John Ball's early years at Royal Liverpool – including the winning of the Boys' Medal and his matches with club medal holder John Dunn – are from Behrend's *John Ball of Hoylake*, as well as from the three histories of the Royal Liverpool Golf Club and the *Oxford Dictionary of National Biography*.

Details of John's foursome match with Davie Strath are from Behrend's book on Ball and *The Golfing Annual*, Vol. I.

Bernard Darwin's quotations about the devotion of the Hoylake faithful are from his essay 'John Ball' in *Playing the Like*. That same essay is the source of the story about John hitting the ball just the height for a windy day, as well as Ball having told a newspaper reporter that he could not think of anything to say that his readers might find interesting.

Details about Ball's swing and approach to the game – including, with one exception, the quotations used – are from Hutchinson's *The Book of Golf and Golfers* and Bernard Darwin's essay 'John Ball'. Bobby Jones's comment on Ball's swing is from Robert Harris's book *Sixty Years of Golf*. The quotation from Hutchinson about sticking with Ball through the green is from Farrar's history of Hoylake.

Details of Ball's first appearance in the Open Championship in 1878 are from Behrend's *John Ball of Hoylake* and Peter Ryde's book *Royal and Ancient Championship Records*.

Details of Ball's match with Douglas Rolland are drawn from multiple sources, including *The Golfing Annual*, Vol. I, *John Ball of Hoylake*, *Tom Morris of St Andrews*, and Badminton Library's *Golf*, as well as contemporary newspaper reports.

The passage quoting Rolland as exclaiming, 'Awa' she sails with a dashing spray,' is from *The Book of the Links: A Symposium on Golf*, by Martin H.F. Sutton.

The specific quote about Rolland's court date involving an 'affair of gallantry' is from Behrend's *John Ball of Hoylake*, while the truth that it involved a paternity suit is from *Tom Morris of St Andrews*.

Harold Hilton's story about his wager for a shilling and the associated quotations are from his memoir, *My Golfing Reminiscences*.

Details about Bobby Jones's lean years are from *The Bobby Jones Story*, by O.B. Keeler.

Details of Ball's performance in the tournament at Carnoustie and his subsequent performance in the Open Championship are from Behrend's *John Ball of Hoylake* and Ryde's record book.

Details of the 1886 and 1887 Amateur Championships are from multiple sources, Behrend's *The Amateur* and *John Ball of Hoylake*; Hutchinson's memoir; Darwin's *The Darwin Sketchbook*; Ryde's record book and contemporary news reports.

Details of John Ball's record round of 73 at Lytham and St Annes are from *John Ball of Hoylake*.

The description of John Laidlay's swing – as well as the associated quotations – are from *The Book of Golf and Golfers* by Hutchinson.

Details about the life of John Laidlay's childhood and the lives of his parents are from an article titled 'John Laidlay', from the online site *Golf Bible*. Additional details on his parents were drawn from the *Biographical Index of Former Fellows of the Royal Society of Edinburgh, 1783–2002*.

The detail about John Laidlay providing photographs for Willie Park Jr's book, *The Game of Golf*, is from *Willie Park Junior: The Man who Brought Golf to the World*, by Walter Stephen.

Details of John Ball's victory in the 1888 Amateur Championship are from multiple sources, including Behrend's *John Ball of Hoylake* and *The Amateur*; *The Golfing Annual*, Vol. II; Ryde's record book and contemporary newspaper accounts.

Details of Ball's win in the inaugural St George's Grand Challenge Cup are from *A Course for Heroes: A History of the Royal St George's Golf Club*, edited by F.R. Furber.

Four

ROSE AND THISTLE

Details about the emergence of the rivalry between English and Scottish golfers are drawn from *Why Are There Eighteen Holes?*; *John Ball of Hoylake* and contemporary newspaper reports.

The letter written to *The Field* by 'St George' in 1882 is quoted from Lewis's book. In his letter, St George misspelled the last name of Horace Hutchinson, rendering it as Hutchesen. I've taken the liberty of correcting his spelling to make the quotation easier to read.

Hutchinson's recollections of evenings at Hoylake are from his memoir. The story of the ivory wand used by Thomas Owen Potter is from Farrar's history of Hoylake.

Details of the 1889 Amateur Championship are from *The Golfing Annual*, Vol. III; Behrend's *The Amateur* and *John Ball of Hoylake*; as well as Ryde's *Royal and Ancient Championship Records*.

Details about the growth of golf courses in Scotland and England are from Lewis's *Why Are There Eighteen Holes?*

Details of John Ball's victory in the 1890 Amateur Championship are from reports in *The Scotsman* and *The Golfing Annual*, Vol. IV; Behrend's *John Ball of Hoylake* and *The Amateuri* and Ryde's record book.

Details on the Great Match between Andra Kirkaldy and Willie Park Jr are drawn from *The Golfing Annual*, Vol. IV and *John Ball of Hoylake*.

Details of John Ball's breakthrough victory in the 1890 Open Championship are from reports in *The Scotsman*, *The Golfing Annual*, Vol. IV, Behrend's *John Ball of Hoylake*, and Hutchinson's memoir.

The story of the celebration that awaited John Ball at the Hoylake train station when he returned from the 1890 Open is from Farrar's history of Royal Liverpool and Behrend's *John Ball of Hoylake*.

Five

MINDS AT WORK

Details of the early developments in golf balls, clubs and equipment are from *Golf in the Making*, by Ian Henderson and David Stirk, as well as from Hutchinson's memoir.

Robert Harris's quote about the Bulger driver is from his memoir *Sixty Years of Golf*.

The statistics on golf patents are from *Why are There Eighteen Holes?*

The quotation about how golf promoted the core values of Victorian society is from an article by John Mallea titled 'The Victorian Sporting Legacy' that was published by McGill University.

Hutchinson's recollections about Badminton Library's hesitancy to devote a full volume to golf are from his memoir.

Details about the life of Arthur Balfour are from the *Oxford Dictionary of National Biography*, *A History of Golf*, and *The Golf Book of East Lothian*. The latter is the source of Balfour's remark about regretting that he had not taken up golf as a young man. Hutchinson's remarks about Balfour are from his memoir.

Details about the life of Charles Bauchope are from an obituary that appeared in Vol. II of *The Golfing Annual*. Details about the life of David Scott Duncan are from an online article published by Anent Scottish Running.

Details of the 1891 Amateur Championship are from Behrend's *John Ball of Hoylake* and *The Amateur*; Ryde's record book; *The Golfing Annual*, Vol. V, and reports in *The Scotsman*.

Details of the 1891 Open Championship are from *The Golfing Annual*, Vol. V.

GENTLEMAN'S DECADE

Details of Harold Hilton's childhood are from the *Oxford Dictionary of National Biography* and *Harold Hilton, His Golfing Life and Times* by John L.B. Garcia.

The descriptions of Hilton's swing are from Darwin's *Playing the Like* and Hutchinson's *The Book of Golf and Golfers*.

Details about Hilton's performances in the Boys' Medal at Hoylake are from his memoir, as well as the three histories of Royal Liverpool Golf Club. The detail about Hoylake patrons considering Harold a 'toff' is from *Mighty Winds*, the second history of Hoylake.

Hilton's quotes about his performances in medals and early championships are from his memoir.

Details of the meeting conducted by professional golfers in 1891, with Old Tom Morris acting as the chair, are from *Tom Morris of St Andrews*.

Details about the design of Royal St George's are from the club's history, *A Course for Heroes*. Darwin's description of the links is from his *Golf Course of the British Isles*. Hutchinson's remarks about the popularity of the St George's course are from his book *Famous Golf Links*.

Details about the Amateur Championship of 1892 are from *The Golfing Annual*, Vol. VI; Behrend's *The Amateur*, Garcia's *Harold Hilton*, and Ryde's record book.

Details about the controversy that erupted over the decision to move the Open to Muirfield are from *Tom Morris of St Andrews* and *The Golfing Annual*, Vol. VI.

Details about the 1892 Open Championship are from *The Golfing Annual*, Vol. VI, Ryde's record book and Hilton's memoir. His remarks at the presentation ceremony regarding winning as an amateur are drawn from Garcia's *Harold Hilton*.

Statistics about the performances of amateur golfers in the Open Championship between 1890 and 1899 were collated by the author from Ryde's record book and *The Majors of Golf*, by Morgan G. Brenner.

Details of the 1893 Amateur and Open championships are from *The Golfing Annual*, Vol. VII; Ryde's record book; Hilton's memoir; *The Amateur*; *F.G. Tait: A Record*, by J.L. Low; *Golf: My Life's Work*, by J.H. Taylor, and *My Golfing Life*, by Harry Vardon.

Seven

HOME-GROWN PROFESSIONALS

Details about Englishmen becoming professional golfers are from the memoirs of Vardon and Taylor; *Ted Ray: The Forgotten Man of Golf*, by Bill Williams, and Ryde's record book.

Details of Taylor's childhood and his early days at Royal North Devon are from the *Oxford Dictionary of National Biography*, as well as Taylor's memoir.

Darwin's quotes about Taylor's character and his swing are drawn from an essay titled 'J.H. Taylor' in *Playing the Like*. Taylor's quote about a man who can approach not needing to putt is from *The Parks of Musselburgh* by John Adams.

The salaries clubs paid professionals are based on multiple sources – principally Peter Lewis's *The Dawn of Professional Golf* and Williams's book on Ted Ray. Lewis's book includes a range of estimates for what professionals earned from their shop and lessons. They come from an article published in *Tit-Bits* in 1901, five years after the period discussed here. For that reason, the low end of the range has been used in an effort to paint the most accurate picture of earnings. Salaries based on these numbers are compared to those outlined in an article by Jeffrey G. Williamson, titled 'The Structure of Pay in Britain: 1710–1911', published in the journal *Research in Economic History*. In 1891, Williamson reported, an average police officer made £72 annually, a teacher £133 and an engineer £380.

Details about Taylor's home-and-home match against Andra Kirkaldy are from the memoirs of the two men.

Details of the 1894 Amateur are from *The Golfing Annual*, Vol. VIII, Behrend's *The Amateur*, and Hilton's memoir.

Details of the 1894 Open are from *The Times*, *The Golfing Annual*, Vol. VIII, and the memoirs of Taylor, Hilton and Hutchinson.

Details of the Gentlemen vs Players match at Sandwich are from *The Golfing Annual*, Vol. VIII, and the memoirs of Hilton and Taylor.

Eight

GOLF BOOM

The quotations from Dr Thomas Proudfoot about the aftermath of Ball's breakthrough in 1890 are from *The Golfing Annual*, Vol. IV. The quote from Willie Park Jr about being overwhelmed with work is from *The Parks of Musselburgh* by John Adams.

Statistics about the growth of golf in Britain are drawn from two works by Lewis – *The Dawn of Professional Golf* and *Why Are There Eighteen Holes?* Statistics about growth of clubs for women are from the former. Historian Michael Morrison also shared insight on his new research into the growth of golf clubs in Britain during the pre-war age.

Dates of the foundation of golf in various countries around the globe are from *The World Atlas of Golf*, supplemented by various volumes of *The Golfing Annual*.

The detail about a woman from Pau, France – whose name is, sadly, lost to history – spreading golf to Boston is from *Fifty Years of American Golf*, by H.B. Martin.

Robert Harris's remarks about the emigration of Scots from his home town of Carnoustie is from his memoir, *Sixty Years of Golf*.

Details about the formation of the Ladies Golf Union are from *The Golfing Annual*, Vol. VII and Browning's *A History of Golf*. Hutchinson's reply to Blanche Martin regarding the wisdom of founding a Union is quoted from an online article in the *Women's Golf Journal*.

Details about the life of Dr William Laidlaw Purves are from *A Course for Heroes*, the history of Royal St George's Golf Club.

Information about how golf took on a more English character as it grew is drawn from Browning's *A History of Golf* and a book by Hutchinson titled *Golfing: The Oval Series of Games*.

Details about the tumult over the rules of golf are drawn from *The Golfing Annual*, Vol. I, which included reprints of the series of letters that originally appeared in *The Field*, as well as from *Champions and Guardians*, the second volume of the history of the Royal and Ancient Golf Club, written by John Behrend, Peter N. Lewis and Keith Mackie. The specific detail about the stymie having been eliminated for one year by the Royal and Ancient is from Browning's *History*.

Details of the 1895 Amateur Championship are from *The Amateur*, *The Golfing Annual*, Vol. IX, Ryde's record book and Hilton's memoir.

Details of the 1895 Open Championship are from coverage in *The Times*, *The Golfing Annual*, Vol. IX, and the memoirs of Hilton, Hutchinson and Taylor.

Nine

'COCK OF THE NORTH'

Open and Amateur Championship results for England and Scotland were collated by the author from Ryde's record book and *The Majors of Golf*.

Ball's schedule in 1894 is drawn from Behrend's *John Ball of Hoylake*.

Details of Freddie Tait's childhood and schooling are from the *Oxford Dictionary of National Biography*, as well as John Low's biography *F.G. Tait: A Record*. The details about his father's career, including the quote from J.M. Barrie, are from the *DNB*.

The story of Freddie rescuing a boy from drowning is taken from Low's book, where it was first reported. The letters Freddie wrote home from Sedbergh and the Black Watch are also quoted from Low's book.

Hutchinson's recollections of Freddie playing as a boy at St Andrews and the way he never surrendered in a match are from his memoir. His description of Freddie's swing is from *The Book of Golf and Golfers*.

Darwin's descriptions of Freddie Tait are drawn from two of his books, *A History of Golf in Britain* and *Playing the Like*.

Coverage of the 1896 Amateur Championship is drawn from multiple sources – including Behrend's *The Amateur* and *John Ball of Hoylake*; articles from *The Scotsman* and *Golf* that are reprinted in Low's biography of Tait; *The Golfing Annual*, Vol. X; and Ryde's record book.

Hilton's quotes about the terrible weather in the 1896 Amateur and his loss to Freddie Tait are from his memoir.

Darwin's quotes about how Hilton never could beat Tait are from *Playing the Like.*

The story of Freddie Tait piping 'Cock of the North' at Sandwich the night before he played Hilton in the Amateur final is from Sandy Herd's memoir, *My Golfing Life.*

Details of the 1896 Open Championship are from *The Golfing Annual*, Vol. X, Hilton's memoir, and Garcia's book, *Harold Hilton.*

Ten

FINAL INNINGS

Details of the 1897 Amateur Championship are drawn from *The Golfing Annual*, Vol. XI and Hilton's memoir.

Information about the construction of the new clubhouse for the Royal Liverpool Golf Club is drawn from two of Hoylake's three histories – *Mighty Winds* and *A Hoylake Celebration.*

Information about the changes to the course – including its length in both 1890 and 1897 – was provided to the author by architectural historian and artist Joe McDonnell, who has conducted extensive research into the evolution of the course. Additional information was drawn from the Hoylake histories and the biographies of Ball and Hilton.

Details of the 1897 Amateur Championship are from *The Golfing Annual*, Vol. XI, Hilton's memoir, Garcia's *Harold Hilton*, and Behrend's *The Amateur.*

Details of the 1897 Open Championship are from *The Golfing Annual*, Vol. XI, coverage in *The Scotsman*, Hilton's memoir and Garcia's *Harold Hilton.*

The information about Hilton writing a weekly column for the *Sporting Chronicle* is from *The Golfing Annual*, Vol. XI.

Details of the 1898 Amateur Championship are from *The Scotsman*, Behrend's *The Amateur*; Low's *F.G. Tait: A Record*; Hilton's memoir, and *The Golfing Annual*, Vol. XII.

Tait's statement thanking the crowd for the way it accepted his 'fluky win' is from Behrend's *The Amateur.*

Darwin's recollection of watching the Hilton–Tait match at Hoylake is from his book, *Green Memories.*

Statistics about the performance of amateur golfers in the Open Championship between 1900 and 1914 were collated by the author from Brenner's *The Majors of Golf.*

Eleven

'RUTHLESS JUGGERNAUT'

Hutchinson's quote about how Vardon remained relatively unknown even after his victory in the 1896 Open Championship at Muirfield is from his memoir.

Details on Harry Vardon's childhood in Jersey, his marriage to Jessie Bryant, and the birth and death of his child, Clarence Henry, are drawn from multiple sources. These include the *Oxford Dictionary of National Biography*; Vardon's memoir; *Harry Vardon: A Career Record of a Champion Golfer*, by Bill Williams; and *The History of Ganton Golf Club*, by Ian McK. Douglas. The information about what an under-gardener earned is from *The Vardon Invasion*, by Bob Labbance, with Brian Siplo. That book puts Harry's salary at £16.

Hutchinson's description of Vardon's swing and his 'gay insouciance' on the links are from *The Book of Golf and Golfers*, while Darwin's comments are from an essay in *Playing the Like*.

Details of the early wagering in the 1898 Open Championship at Prestwick are drawn from *The Golfing Annual*, Vol. XII.

Information about the growth of Wm Park & Son is drawn from *The Parks of Musselburgh*. Willie Park's quotes about deciding to challenge Taylor and Fernie and to practise seriously for the 1898 Open are from the opening essay in his book, *The Art of Putting*. Details of those two matches are from Adams's book as well as Taylor's memoir.

Details of the 1898 Open Championship are from coverage in *The Scotsman*; *The Golfing Annual*, Vol. XII; the memoirs of Hilton, Taylor and Vardon; Low's Tait biography; and George Colville's *Five Open Champions and the Musselburgh Golf Story*.

Park's story about the missed putt on the final hole of the 1898 Open is from *The Art of Putting*. Taylor's doubts about the story are expressed in his memoir.

The details of Vardon's winning streak in 1898 and 1899 are from Bill Williams's *Harry Vardon: A Career Record of a Champion Golfer*, which painstakingly documents every professional appearance in Vardon's extraordinary career.

The quotation about Vardon marching up and down the country like a 'ruthless juggernaut' is from Darwin's *A History of Golf in Britain*, while the quote about Vardon being compared with Young Tom Morris is from Darwin's *Playing the Like*.

Details about negotiations on the challenge match between Vardon and Park are from Harry's memoir and Park's book on putting, as well as Adams's *The Parks of Musselburgh*. The details about Willie's home in North Berwick are from Adams's book.

Twelve

THE TRUE GAME

Darwin's quote about hopes that Tait and Ball would meet in the final of the 1899 Amateur Championship are from his book, *Green Memories*.

Details about the 1899 Amateur are drawn from multiple sources, including coverage in *The Scotsman*, *Golf Illustrated* and *The Golfing Annual*, Vol. XIII; Behrend's *The Amateur* and *John Ball of Hoylake*; Low's Tait biography; Hilton's memoir; and Darwin's *Green Memories* and *Playing the Like*.

The telegrams dispatched from Prestwick to Hoylake about John Ball's progress in the Amateur final are drawn from Behrend's *John Ball of Hoylake*.

The story of Ball receiving a putting lesson from Hilton during the lunch break at the final is from Darwin's *Green Memories*.

The story of Tait lying on the couch and complaining of feeling tired is from Low's biography.

The description of where players and caddies were standing on the 17th hole as Ball and Tait played from the water-filled bunker is based on a photograph printed in *F.G. Tait: A Record*.

Darwin's quotes about what happened as Freddie played his shot from the Sahara bunker are from *Playing the Like* and *Green Memories*.

Hilton's descriptions of crucial shots over the final three holes of the 1899 Amateur are from his memoir.

Darwin's quote about Hoylake fans retiring to the clubhouse and burying their heads in the sofa cushions is from *Playing the Like*. The same is true about his assertion that the 1899 final was the greatest golf match Darwin had ever witnessed.

The story about Ball, Tait and Low rooming together at Ganton is drawn from Low's biography.

Information about the painting of Ball's portrait, the installation of the turret clock and the gift of a watch is drawn from Behrend's *John Ball of Hoylake*, as is Tait's quote that he would rather be beaten by Ball than by any man alive.

Details of the 1899 Open Championship at Sandwich are drawn from *Golf Illustrated*, *The Golfing Annual*, Vol. XIII, and Vardon's memoir.

Harris's quote about the anticipation of the great match between Vardon and Park Jr is from his memoir, *Sixty Years of Golf*.

Details of the match between Vardon and Park are drawn from multiple sources – *Golf Illustrated*; *The Golfing Annual*, Vol. XIII; Adams's *The Parks of Musselburgh*; Park's *The Art of Putting*; and Vardon's memoir.

Robert Harris's quote about how Willie's loss was a blow to Scotland is from his memoir.

Details of Vardon's triumphal exhibition tour of Scotland to close out the 1899 season are from *Golf Illustrated* and *The Golfing Annual*, Vol. XIII.

The details of Vardon's invincible streak – 14 wins and three seconds in 17 tries – are from *Harry Vardon: A Career Record of a Champion Golfer*.

Information about Tait's preparations to get to the front in the South African War are from *F.G. Tait: A Record*. The letter to his brother Jack is quoted from the same book.

Information about Ball's plans to join the fighting, along with the gifts given to him by his three golf clubs, are from Behrend's *John Ball of Hoylake*.

Details of the final match at Lytham between Tait and Ball are from *Golf Illustrated* and Freddie's diary, portions of which are reprinted in *F.G. Tait: A Record*.

Thirteen

HEARTACHE AND TRIUMPH

Information about Tait's engagements in the South African War is from Low's biography, as are the letters by Freddie and his fellow soldiers.

The quotes from *The Golfing Annual* about the rumours of Tait's death are drawn from a profile of the late soldier that appeared in Vol. XIII.

Details of the 1900 Amateur Championship are from multiple sources, among them *The Golfing Annual*, Vol. XIV; *Golf Illustrated*; Behrend's *The Amateur*; Garcia's *Harold Hilton*; Hilton's memoir; and Ryde's record book.

Information about Vardon's voyage to America is drawn from his memoir; *Vardon in America*, by Bill Williams, and *The Vardon Invasion*, by Bob Labbance with Brian Siplo. Details of Vardon's record in America are from the extensive records compiled by Williams of Harry's performances throughout his tour of the United States.

Details of the 1900 Open Championship are drawn from multiple sources, among them *The Golfing Annual*, Vol. XIV; *Golf Illustrated*; the memoirs of Vardon, Taylor and Hilton; Ryde's record book; and *The Majors of Golf*.

Information about Taylor's trip to America is drawn from his memoir, as is his story about testing the new Haskell ball.

Details of the 1900 US Open are from multiple sources, including Williams's *Vardon in America*; Labbance and Siplo's *The Vardon Invasion*; *Golf Illustrated*; the memoirs of Taylor and Vardon; and *The Majors of Golf*.

Vardon's letter to a friend about being unhappy in America is quoted from *Golf Illustrated*.

Fourteen

SCOTLAND RESURGENT

Information about Walter J. Travis's golfing tour of England and Scotland is drawn from *The Old Man*, by Bob Labbance, as well as from reports in *Golf Illustrated*.

James Braid's record in exhibition matches during the 1900 golf season was compiled by Garden Smith, editor of *Golf Illustrated*.

The death of Robert Maxwell's brother in the South African War was reported in *Golf Illustrated*, as was the news that his sister had become gravely ill on the eve of the 1901 Amateur at St Andrews.

Coverage of the 1901 Amateur Championship is from *The Golfing Annual*, Vol. XV; *Golf Illustrated*; Behrend's *The Amateur*; Hilton's memoir; and Ryde's record book.

Hutchinson's quotes about Low's temperament and putting are from his *Book of Golf and Golfers*. Background about Low's life is from Daniel Wexler's *The Book of Golfers*.

The quote from a leading member of St Andrews about both Low and Hilton emerging as winners in the 1901 Amateur is from *Golf Illustrated*.

Information about Braid's childhood in Earlsferry is from multiple sources, principally a chapter titled 'Some Personal Matters' in Braid's book, *Advanced Golf*. It is supplemented by details from the *Oxford Dictionary of National*

Biography, Bob MacAlindin's book *James Braid: Champion Golfer*, and Darwin's biography, *James Braid*.

Details of the 1901 Open Championship – as well as the Musselburgh Open that same year are drawn from *Golf Illustrated*; *The Golfing Annual*, Vol. XV; MacAlindin's book; Ryde's record book; and *The Majors of Golf*.

Braid's reflections on his first Open victory are from his *Advanced Golf*, while the decision to name his son Harry Muirfield Braid is drawn from MacAlindin's biography.

Information about Ball's return from the Boer War – as well as his exploits while there – is drawn from Behrend's *John Ball of Hoylake*, as well as reports in *Golf Illustrated*.

Information about the formation of the Professional Golfers' Association comes from *Golf Illustrated* and Lewis's book *The Dawn of Professional Golf*.

Coverage of the first Amateur International Match at Hoylake is from *Golf Illustrated* and the first two histories of Royal Liverpool – *The Royal Liverpool Golf Club* and *Mighty Winds . . . Mighty Champions*. Low's toast after the match is from *Mighty Winds*.

The information about Walter Travis winning the 1901 US Amateur while playing with the new Haskell ball is drawn from Labbance's *The Old Man*.

Coverage of the 1902 Amateur Championship at Hoylake is from *Golf Illustrated*; Behrend's *The Amateur*; Ryde's record book; and Brenner's *The Majors of Golf*.

Darwin's story of learning about the Haskell ball while en route by train to Hoylake is from his biography of Braid.

Coverage of the 1902 Open Championship is from *Golf Illustrated*; Ryde's record book; Herd's memoir; and the memoirs of Vardon, Taylor and Hilton.

Information about the debate over the Haskell ball comes from multiple sources, principally *Golf Illustrated* and *Champions and Guardians: The Royal and Ancient Golf Club, 1884–1939*. Quotes from Low and Garden Smith related to the debate over the Haskell ball are from *Golf Illustrated*.

Fifteen

TWO ROADS

The motion submitted to the Rules of Golf Committee by Mure Fergusson and seconded by Low is quoted from *Champions and Guardians*, as is the outcome of the vote in late March 1903.

Vardon's lament about the passing of the gutty ball is from his memoir.

Information about B.F. Goodrich's unsuccessful lawsuit to protect its patent on the Haskell ball is drawn from *Golf Illustrated*, Hutchinson's memoir and *Golf in the Making*, by Stirk and Henderson.

Coverage of the 1903 Amateur Championship is drawn from *Golf Illustrated*, Behrend's *The Amateur*, Ryde's record book, and the memoirs of Hilton and Hutchinson.

Coverage of the International Amateur Match is drawn from *Golf Illustrated*, Behrend's *John Ball of Hoylake*, and Hutchinson's memoir.

Coverage of the International Professional Match is drawn from *Golf Illustrated*, Darwin's *James Braid* and Lewis's *The Dawn of Professional Golf*.

Coverage of the 1903 Open Championship is from *Golf Illustrated*, Vardon's memoir, Ryde's record book and *The Majors of Golf*.

Information about the onset of Vardon's illness is from his memoir, as well as reports in *Golf Illustrated*.

Information about the genesis of the News of the World golf tournaments is from Lewis's *The Dawn of Professional Golf*, *Golf Illustrated*, and MacAlindin's *James Braid, Champion Golfer*. Information about the subsequent creation of the Sphere and Tatler Cup is from Lewis's book, as are statistics on the growth of professional tournaments between 1894 and 1914.

Sixteen

AMERICAN INVADERS

Information on the life of Walter J. Travis, and his plans to compete in the Amateur Championship of 1904, is drawn principally from Labbance's *The Old Man*, with additional details from *Golf Illustrated*.

Coverage of the Amateur International Match is drawn from *The Scotsman*, as well as the club history of Royal St George's, *A Course for Heroes*.

Coverage of the 1904 Amateur Championship is from multiple sources – Labbance's biography; the memoirs of Hilton, Hutchinson and Taylor, and coverage in *The Times*. Quotes by Travis are from the Labbance biography. Hutchinson's quote is from his memoir.

Darwin's quote about the fear of Travis winning is from an essay titled 'Francis' in his collection *Out of the Rough*. In that essay, Darwin compares his feelings while watching Travis in 1904 to watching Francis Ouimet defeat Vardon and Ray in the 1913 US Open.

Hutchinson's quote about feeling spent after beating Robert Maxwell in a quarter-final match is from his memoir.

The quotes from Hutchinson and Taylor about the outcome of the 1904 Amateur Championship are from their respective memoirs. The quotes from Lord Northbourne and Travis at the prize ceremony are drawn from the Labbance biography.

Darwin's reflections on how the British treated Travis are from an essay in his *Out of the Rough* titled 'A Memory of Walter Travis'.

Coverage of the 1904 Open Championship is drawn from *The Times*; the memoirs of Hilton, Taylor and Vardon; Braid's *Advanced Golf*; Darwin's biography *James Braid*; Ryde's record book; and *The Majors of Golf*.

Information about the evolution of strategic golf course architecture is drawn from Low's book *Concerning Golf*; essays by architect Tom Simpson in Lonsdale Library's *The Game of Golf*; *The Evolution of Golf Course Design*, by Keith Cutten; and three articles by historian Robert Crosby published in *Through the Green*, the quarterly journal of the British Golf Collectors Society.

Simpson's quotes are all from the first of his three essays in Lonsdale's *The Game of Golf* – titled 'Golf Architecture'.

Coverage of the News of the World tournament is from *The Times*; Lewis's *Dawn of Professional Golf*; Darwin's biography of Braid; MacAlindin's *James Braid: Champion Golfer*; and Taylor's memoir.

Seventeen

SHOWDOWN AT TROON

Coverage of the 1905 Amateur International match is drawn from *The Times* of London.

Coverage of the Amateur Championship of 1905 is drawn from *The Golfing Annual*, Vol. XIX; *The Times*; Ryde's record book; Behrend's *The Amateur* and *John Ball of Hoylake*; and Garcia's biography of Hilton.

Discussion of the changes made to the Old Course in advance of the 1905 Open Championship is from *Golf Illustrated* and Robert Crosby's second instalment of the *Through the Green* series on Low, as well as from the new biography of Herbert Fowler, *A Matter of Course*, by Derek Markham.

Coverage of the 1905 Open Championship is from *The Times*; *The Golfing Annual*, Vol. XIX; *The Majors of Golf*; and the chapter of Braid's *Advanced Golf* in which he reflects on his career.

Information about the origins of The International Foursome of 1905 is drawn from *Golf Illustrated*; Lewis's *The Dawn of Professional Golf*; Darwin's biography of Braid; and the memoirs of Vardon and Taylor. The specific details about the foursome records of Braid and Herd vs Vardon and Taylor are drawn from Lewis's book.

Coverage of The International Foursome of 1905 is drawn from *The Times*, Lewis's book, and the memoirs of Herd, Taylor and Vardon.

Eighteen

HUMBLED BUT UNBOWED

Coverage of the 1905 News of the World Championship is drawn from multiple sources – Braid's *Advanced Golf*; Darwin's biography *James Braid*; MacAlindin's Braid biography; and Lewis's *The Dawn of Professional Golf*. The specific details about the testimonial from Walton Heath are from MacAlindin's book.

Information about the meeting of the Open Championship committee regarding limiting entries for the championship is drawn from Lewis's book, as well as Malcolm and Crabtree's *Tom Morris of St Andrews*. Lewis's book is also the source of information about the advent of The Sphere and Tatler Cup and the increasing opportunities for professional golfers in Europe.

Information about the International Amateur Match of 1906 is from *The Golfing Annual*, Vol. XX and Farrar's *The Royal Liverpool Golf Club*, while details about the Amateur Championship of 1906 are from *The Annual*, Behrend's *The Amateur* and Ryde's record book.

Information about the 1906 Open Championship is drawn from coverage in the *The Times*; *Glasgow Herald*; *Manchester Guardian*; *The Golfing Annual*, Vol. XX; Braid's *Advanced Golf*; Darwin's Braid biography; MacAlindin's Braid biography; *The Majors of Golf*; and Ryde's record book.

Information about the News of the World Championships of 1906, 1907, 1908 and 1911 is from Lewis's *The Dawn of Professional Golf*, supplemented by various editions of *The Golfing Annual*.

Coverage of the 1908 and 1910 Open Championships is from multiple sources, including *The Times* and *Manchester Guardian*; *Advanced Golf*; the Braid biographies by Darwin and MacAlindin; and the two championship record books.

Coverage of the 1907 Open is from *The Glasgow Herald*, Darwin's biography of Braid and the two championship record books.

Coverage of the 1909 Open Championship is from *The Glasgow Herald*, Taylor's memoir and the two championship record books. Information about the Amateur Championships of 1907 and 1910 is drawn from Behrend's biography of Ball and his history of the Amateur, along with Ryde's record book. The record of players from Jersey is drawn from Williams's *Ted Ray: The Forgotten Man of Golf*.

Nineteen

CROWNING GLORIES

Coverage of the 1910 matches between Harold Hilton and Cecil Leitch is drawn from reports in the *New York Times*, as well as Garcia's Hilton biography and Darwin's recollections in his book, *Golf in The Times*.

Coverage of the 1911 Amateur Championship is from reports in *The Times* of London, as well as Behrend's *The Amateur*, Garcia's biography of Hilton and Ryde's record book.

Coverage of the 1911 Open Championship is from reports in *The Times* and *The Glasgow Herald*, as well as Vardon's memoir and Darwin's Braid biography, which includes his recollections of Hilton's near miss in that year's Open.

Coverage of the 1911 US Amateur Championship is from *Fifty Years of American Golf*, by H.B. Martin; *The Story of American Golf*, by Herbert Warren Wind, as well as Garcia's biography of Hilton and the three histories of Royal Liverpool Golf Club.

Coverage of the 1912 Amateur Championship is from *The Times* and Behrend's two books, *The Amateur* and *John Ball of Hoylake*. Darwin's recollections of covering the match for *The Times* are from his book, *Green Memories*.

Coverage of the 1913 Open Championship is from *The Manchester Guardian*; the memoirs of Taylor and Vardon; Darwin's Braid biography, and his essay on Taylor in *Playing the Like*.

Coverage of the 1914 Open is from *The Times*, *The Glasgow Herald*, the memoirs of Taylor and Vardon, and Darwin's biography of Braid.

Details of the major championships won by leading players of the era are as follows: John Ball won eight Amateur Championships and one Open, for a total of nine. James Braid tied Ball with five Opens and four victories in the British PGA Championship, known in those days as the News of the World. Harry Vardon won six Opens, one US Open and one PGA Championship for a total of eight major victories. John Henry Taylor won five Opens and two News of the Worlds, while Harold Hilton won four Amateurs in Britain, one in the US and two Opens, giving those two men seven majors each.

Epilogue

AFTER THE WAR

Vardon's observations about the improvement in American golf are quoted from his memoir.

The numbers cited to support the growth of American golf are from Wind's *The Story of American Golf*.

Information about Ball's move to North Wales and his subsequent marriage to his maid, Nellie Williams, is drawn from Behrend's *John Ball of Hoylake*.

Ball's record in medal competitions at Hoylake is drawn from Farrar's history of the club, while his remaining finishes in the Amateur are from Ryde's record book.

Darwin's description of Ball's final match in the Amateur Championship is from his book *Green Memories*.

Darwin's remarks about Hilton's hardships are quoted from his collection of *Country Life* stories titled *Golfing By-Paths*, while his record in remaining Amateurs is from Ryde's record book.

The cause of Hilton's death is drawn from the *Oxford Dictionary of National Biography*.

Taylor's reflections on his life are drawn from his memoir, while the quotation from Pat Ward-Thomas is from *The Royal North Devon Golf Club, 1864–1964*.

Bobby Jones's quote about Taylor playing in the 1926 Open Championship is from his book, *Down the Fairway*, with O.B. Keeler. Taylor's finishes in remaining Opens are from *The Majors of Golf*.

Details about the final years of Hutchinson's life are from the *DNB*.

The story about a bomb dropping on Vardon's home towards the end of the Great War is from his memoir, as is the story about his neighbour considering him a Champion Gardener.

Information about Vardon's performance in the 1920 US Open is drawn from his memoir and Williams's *Vardon in America*. Vardon's record in his remaining Open Championships is from *The Majors of Golf*.

Information about Vardon's affair with Tilly Howell, the birth of his son and the cause of his death are all drawn from Williams's *Harry Vardon: The Career Record of a Champion Golfer.*

Information about Braid's work in golf architecture is from MacAlindin's biography; the *Evolution of Golf Course Architecture* by Keith Cutten; and *James Braid and his 400 Golf Courses*, by John F. Moreton and Iain Cumming.

Braid's record in his final Open Championship is from *The Majors of Golf.*

Information about Braid's final years at Walton Heath – including his quotation about sitting next to the Prince of Wales at dinner – is from MacAlindin's biography.

Taylor's wish to be remembered by the words of Bernard Darwin is quoted from his memoir, while the final quotation is from an essay on Hilton featured in Darwin's book *Playing the Like.*

BIBLIOGRAPHY

·•●•·

NEWSPAPERS/PERIODICALS

The Field
The Glasgow Herald
The Golfing Annual, volumes I to XX
Golf
Golf Illustrated
The Golfer
The Manchester Guardian
The Scotsman
The Times
Through the Green

ARTICLES

Crosby, Robert, 'John Low and Modern Golf Architecture: A Reassessment', *Through the Green* (June, 1910).

Crosby, Robert, 'John Low, Woking, and Modern Golf Architecture', *Through the Green* (September, 2009).

Crosby, Robert, 'A Thoroughly Modern Problem: Robert Crosby Talks Us Through the First Ball Rule and John Low's Forlorn Attempts to Curb the Distance of the Ball', *Through the Green* (December, 2020).

Ely, Mark, 'John Laidlay', online site *Golf Bible, The Home of Great Britain and Ireland Amateur Golf* (2014).

Everard, H.S.C., 'Mr H.H. Hilton, Champion Golfer 1897', *Badminton Magazine* (1897).

Knox, W.W., 'A History of the Scottish People: Poverty, Income and Wealth in Scotland, 1840–1940', *Scottish Cultural Resources Access Network* (1997).

Lewis, Peter N., 'Professional Golf 1819–1885', *British Golf Museum, Paper for De Montfort University* (1998).

Lowerson, John, 'Scottish Croquet: The English Golf Boom, 1880–1914', *History Today*, Vol. 33, No. 5 (1983).

Mair, Lewine, 'Gentlemen Only, Ladies Forbidden – A History', *Women's Golf Journal* (2015).

Mallea, John R., 'The Victorian Sporting Legacy', *McGill Journal of Education* (1975).

Millar, Neil, 'King Charles I and Early Golf in Scotland and England', *Through the Green*, (March, 2019).

Morrison, Michael, 'How Many Golfers? Part I: Men', *Through the Green* (June, 2021).

Murray, Roy, 'A Sporting Nation: Leslie M. Balfour-Melville', *British Broadcasting Corporation* (2014).

Williamson, Jeffrey, 'The Structure of Pay in Britain, 1710–1911', *Research in Economic History* (1982).

No author cited, 'Mr F.G. Tait Interviewed', *The Golfer* (1894).

No author cited, 'Mr John Laidlay Interviewed', (1894).

No author cited, 'Famous British Golf Courses: St. Andrews', *The American Golfer*, Vol. 1, No. 2, (1908) 79–91.

No author cited, 'Famous British Golf Courses: Prestwick,' *The American Golfer*, Vol. 1, No. 4, (1909), 209–220.

No author cited, David Scott Duncan, online site Anent Scottish Running (2013).

BOOKS: HISTORY

Balfour, James, *Reminiscences of Golf on St. Andrews Links* (Edinburgh, 1887).

Baxter, Peter, *Golf in Perth and Perthshire: Traditional, Historical and Modern* (Perth, 1899).

Behrend, John, *The Amateur: The Story of the Amateur Golf Championship, 1885–1995* (Worcestershire, England, 1995).

Brenner, Morgan G., *The Majors of Golf*, Vols. 1–3 (Jefferson, NC, 2009).

Browning, Robert, *A History of Golf* (London, 1955).

Clark, Robert, *Golf: A Royal and Ancient Game, Extracts from the Original 1875 Edition* (Midlothian, 1984).

Colville, George M., *Five Open Champions and the Musselburgh Golf Story* (Musselburgh, 1980).

Darwin, Bernard, *Golf Between Two Wars* (London, 1944).

Darwin, Bernard, ed., *A History of Golf in Britain* (London, 1952).

Geddes, Olive M., *A Swing Through Time: Golf in Scotland, 1457–1744* (Edinburgh, 2007).

Goodman, Ruth, *How To Be A Victorian* (London, 2013).

Hamilton, David, *Golf: Scotland's Game* (St Andrews, 1998).

Haultain, Arnold, *The Mystery of Golf* (New York, 1908).

Hilton, Harold H. and Smith, Garden G., *The Royal and Ancient Game of Golf* (London, 1912).

Hutchinson, Horace G. ed., *The Badminton Library: Golf* (London, 1890).

Hutchinson, Horace G., *The Book of Golf and Golfers* (London, 1899).

Hutchinson, Horace G., *Golf: A Complete History of the Game, Together with Directions for Selection of Implements, the Rules, and a Glossary of Golf Terms* (Philadelphia, 1900).

Hutchinson, Horace, *Golfing: The Oval Series of Games* (London, 1903).

Jackson, Alan F., *The British Professional Golfers: A Register* (Worcestershire, England, 1994).

Joy, David, compiled by, *The Scrapbook of Old Tom Morris* (Chelsea, MI, 2001).

Kerr, John, *The Golf Book of East Lothian* (Edinburgh, 1896).

Kirsch, George B., *Golf in America* (Chicago, 2009).

Labbance, Bob, *The Vardon Invasion* (Ann Arbor, MI, 2008).

Langston, Harry, *Thomas Hodge: The Golf Artist of St Andrews* (London, 2000).

Leach, Henry, ed., *Great Golfers in the Making* (London, 1907).

Lee, James P., *Golf in America* (New York, 1895).

Lewis, Peter N., *The Dawn of Professional Golf: The Genesis of the European Tour 1894–1914* (New Ridley, 1995).

Lewis, Peter N., *Why Are There Eighteen Holes?: St Andrews and the Evolution of Golf Courses, 1764–1890* (St Andrews, 2016).

Low, John, *Concerning Golf* (London, 1903).

Lowe, Stephen, *Sir Walter and Mr Jones* (Chelsea, MI, 2000).

Macdonald, Charles Blair, *Scotland's Gift: Golf* (New York, 1928).

Macdonald, Robert S. and Wind, Herbert Warren, *The Great Women Golfers* (Stamford, CT, 1994).

Martin, H.B., *Fifty Years of American Golf* (New York, 1936).

McPherson, J. Gordon, *Golf and Golfers Past and Present* (Edinburgh, 1891).

McStravick, Roger, *St Andrews in the Footsteps of Old Tom Morris* (St Andrews, 2014).

McStravick, Roger, *A History of Golf* (St Andrews, 2017).

Oliver, Neil, *A History of Scotland* (London, 2009).

Parker, Eric and The Right Hon. The Earl of Lonsdale, eds., *The Game of Golf* (Philadelphia, 1931).

Peper, George, *The Story of Golf* (New York, 1999).

Peter, H. Thomas, *Reminiscences of Golf and Golfers* (Edinburgh, 1890).

Robb, George, *Historical Gossip about Golf and Golfers* (Edinburgh, 1863).

Ryde, Peter, *Royal and Ancient Championship Records, 1860–1980* (St Andrews, 1981).

Smith, Garden G., *Golf* (New York, 1913).

Stirk, David, *Golf History and Traditions, 1500 to 1945* (Shropshire, England, 1998).

Sommers, Robert, *The U.S. Open: Golf's Ultimate Challenge* (New York, 1987).

Tombs, Robert, *The English & Their History* (London, 2014).

Wade, Don, ed., *The U.S. Open: One Week in June* (New York, 2010).

Waterston, C.D. and Macmillan, A. Shearer, 'Biographical Index of Former Fellows of the Royal Society of Edinburgh, 1783–2002', Vol. 2 (Edinburgh, 2003).

Wexler, Daniel, *The Book of Golfers: A Bibliographical History of the Royal and Ancient Game* (Ann Arbor, MI, 2005).

Williams, Bill, *Vardon in America* (Xlibris, 2016).

Wind, Herbert Warren, *The Story of American Golf: Its Champions and Its Championships* (New York, 1975).

BOOKS: BIOGRAPHIES/MEMOIRS

Adams, John, *The Parks of Musselburgh: Golfers, Architects, Clubmakers* (Worcestershire, England, 1991).

Adamson, Alistair Beaton, *Allan Robertson, Golfer: His Life and Times* (Worcestershire, England, 1985).

Behrend, John, *John Ball of Hoylake: Champion Golfer* (Worcestershire, England, 1989).

Crabtree, Peter and Malcolm, David, *Tom Morris of St Andrews: The Colossus of Golf, 1821–1908* (Royal Deeside, 2008).

Darwin, Bernard, *Green Memories* (London, 1928).

Darwin, Bernard, *James Braid* (London, 1952).

Darwin, Bernard, *The World that Fred Made* (London, 1955).

Garcia, John L.B., *Harold Hilton: His Life and Times* (Worcestershire, England, 1992).

Green, Robert, *Seve: Golf's Flawed Genius* (Fort Valley, GA, 2012).

Hagen, Walter, with Margaret Seaton, *The Walter Hagen Story: By The Haig Himself* (New York, 1956).

Harris, Robert, *Sixty Years of Golf* (Letchworth, England, 1953).

Herd, Sandy, *My Golfing Life* (London, 1923).

Hilton, Harold H., *My Golfing Reminiscences* (London, 1907).

Hutchinson, Horace G., *Fifty Years of Golf* (London, 1914).

Jones, Robert T. Jr and Keeler, O.B., *Down the Fairway* (New York, 1927).

Jones, Robert T. Jr, *Golf is My Game* (New York, 1960).

Keeler, O.B., *The Bobby Jones Story: The Authorized Biography* (Chicago, 2003).

Kirkaldy, Andra, *Fifty Years of Golf: My Memories* (New York, 1921).

Labbance, Bob, *The Old Man: The Biography of Walter J. Travis* (Chelsea, MI, 2000).

Low, J. L., *F.G. Tait: A Record* (London, 1900).

Moreton, John F., *James Braid: Champion Golfer* (Worcestershire, England, 2003).

Nicklaus, Jack, with Herbert Warren Wind, *The Greatest Game of All: My Life in Golf* (New York, 1969).

Ouimet, Francis, *A Game of Golf* (New York, 1932).

Sampson, Curt, *Hogan* (Nashville, 1996).

Sampson, Curt, *The Slam: Bobby Jones and the Price of Glory* (Emmaus, PA, 2005).

Sarazen, Gene, with Herbert Warren Wind, *Thirty Years of Championship Golf* (New York, 1950).

Stephen, Walter, *Willie Park, Junior: The Man Who Took Golf to the World* (Edinburgh, 2005).

Taylor, J.H., *Golf: My Life's Work* (London, 1943).

Tulloch, William W., *The Life of Tom Morris: With Glimpses of St Andrews and its Golfing Celebrities* (London, 1908).

Vardon, Harry, *My Golfing Life* (Plymouth, England, 1933).

Williams, Bill, *Harry Vardon: A Career Record of a Champion Golfer* (Xlibris, 2005).

Williams, Bill, *Ted Ray: The Forgotten Man of Golf* (Xlibris, 2018).

BOOKS: GOLF ARCHITECTURE/GREENKEEPING

Colt, H.S. and Alison, C.H., *Some Essays on Golf Course Architecture* (London, 1920).

Cornish, Geoffrey and Whitten, Ronald E., *The Golf Course* (New York, 1988).

Cutten, Keith, *The Evolution of Golf Course Design* (Victoria, Australia, 2018).

Darwin, Bernard, *The Golf Courses of the British Isles* (London, 1910).

Dickinson, Patric, *A Round of Golf Courses: A Selection of the Best Eighteen* (London, 1951).

Doak, Tom, *The Anatomy of a Golf Course* (New York, 1992).

Doak, Tom, *The Confidential Guide to Golf Courses* (Chelsea, MI, 1996).

Hunter, Robert, *The Links* (New York, 1926).

Hutchinson, Horace G., *Famous Golf Links* (London, 1891).

Hutchinson, Horace G., *British Golf Links* (London, 1897).

Hawtree, Fred, *Simpson & Co., Golf Architects* (Ballater, Scotland, 2016).

Klein, Bradley S., *Discovering Donald Ross* (Chelsea, MI, 2001).

Kroeger, Robert, *The Golf Courses of Old Tom Morris* (Cincinnati, OH, 1995).

MacKenzie, Dr Alister, *Golf Architecture: Economy in Course Construction and Greenkeeping* (London, 1920).

MacKenzie, Dr Alister, *The Spirit of St Andrews* (Chelsea, MI, 2001, 1995).

Markham, Derek, *A Matter of Course: The Life of William Herbert Fowler, 1856–1941* (Walton on the Hill, Surrey, 2021).

Moreton, John F. and Cummings, Ian, *James Braid and his Four Hundred Golf Courses* (Worcestershire, England, 2013).

Shackelford, Geoff, *Masters of the Links: Essays on the Art of Golf and Course Design* (Chelsea, MI, 1997).

Simpson, T. and Wethered, H.N., *The Architectural Side of Golf* (Stamford CT, 2005).

Sutton, Martin H.F., *A Symposium on Golf* (London, 1912).

Thomas, George C., Jr, *Golf Architecture in America. Its Strategy and Construction* (Los Angeles, 1927).

Ward-Thomas, Pat, et al., *The World Atlas of Golf: The Great Courses and How They are Played* (London, 2008).

BOOKS: GOLF INSTRUCTION/EQUIPMENT

Armour, Tommy, *How to Play Your Best Golf All the Time* (New York, 1953).

Aultman, Dick and Bowden, Ken, *The Methods of Golf's Masters: How They Played and What You Can Learn from Them* (New York, 1975).

BIBLIOGRAPHY

Beldam, George, *Great Golfers: Their Methods at a Glance* (New York, 1904).

Boomer, Percy, *On Learning Golf* (London, 1942).

Braid, James, *Advanced Golf* (London, 1908).

Henderson, Ian T. and Stirk, David I., *Golf in the Making* (Worcestershire, England, 1979).

Hilton, Harold, *Modern Golf* (New York, 1913).

Hutchinson, Horace G., *Hints on the Game of Golf* (Edinburgh, 1886).

Jones, Ernest, with Innis Brown, *Swinging into Golf* (New York, 1941).

Jones, Robert T. Jr, *The Basic Golf Swing* (Garden City, NY, 1969).

Miller, Johnny, *Breaking 90 with Johnny Miller* (New York, 2000).

Nelson, Byron, with Larry Dennis, *Shape Your Swing the Modern Way* (New York, 1976).

Olman, John M. and Olman, Morton W., *Olman's Guide to Golf Antiques and Other Treasures of the Game* (Cincinnati, 1991).

Park, William, Jr, *The Game of Golf* (London, 1896).

Park, William, Jr, *The Art of Putting* (Edinburgh, 1920).

Penick, Harvey, with Bud Shrake, *Harvey Penick's Little Red Book: Lessons and Teaching from a Lifetime in Golf* (New York, 1992).

Simpson, Walter G., Sir, *The Art of Golf* (Edinburgh, 1887).

Stirk, David, *Golf: The Great Club Makers* (London, 1991).

Taylor, J.H., *Taylor on Golf* (London, 1902).

Travis, Walter, J., *Practical Golf* (New York, 1901).

Vardon, Harry, *The Complete Golfer* (New York, 1905)

Vardon, Harry, *The Gist of Golf* (New York, 1922).

Vardon, Harry, compiled and edited by Herbert Warren Wind and Robert S. Macdonald, *Vardon on Golf* (Stamford, CT, 2002).

Venturi, Ken, with Al Barkow, *The Venturi Analysis: Learning Better Golf from the Champions* (New York, 1981).

Wethered, H.N., *The Perfect Golfer* (London, 1931).

Wethered, Joyce, *Golfing Memories and Methods* (London, 1934).

Woods, Tiger, *How I Play Golf* (New York, 2001).

BOOKS: GOLF LITERATURE

Bingham, Joan and Owen, David, *The Lure of the Links* (New York, 1997).

Campbell, Patrick, *How to Become a Scratch Golfer* (London, 1963).

Darwin, Bernard, *Out of the Rough* (London, 1932).

Darwin, Bernard, *Playing the Like* (London, 1934).

Darwin, Bernard, *Golf* (London, 1934).

Darwin, Bernard, *Golfing By-Paths* (London, 1946).

Darwin, Bernard, edited by Peter Ryde, *Mostly Golf* (London, 1976).

Darwin, Bernard, with editors Robert S. Macdonald and Ian R. Macdonald, *The Happy Golfer: A Collection of Articles from The American Golfer Magazine, 1922–1936* (Stamford, CT, 1997).

Dobereiner, Peter, *Golf a la Carte*, (Guilford, CT, 1991).

Dodson, James, *The American Triumvirate: Sam Snead, Byron Nelson, Ben Hogan and the Modern Age of Golf* (New York, 2012).

Feinstein, John, *The Majors: In Pursuit of Golf's Holy Grail* (Boston, 1999).

Frost, Mark, *The Greatest Game Ever Played* (New York, 2002).

Frost, Mark, *The Grand Slam: Bobby Jones, America and the Story of Golf* (New York, 2004).

Frost, Mark, *The Match: The Day the Game of Golf Changed Forever* (New York, 2007).

Jenkins, Dan, *At the Majors: Sixty Years of the World's Best Golf Writing from Hogan to Tiger* (New York, 2009).

Jenkins, Dan, *The Dogged Victims of Inexorable Fate* (Boston, 1970).

Keeler, O.B., *The Autobiography of an Average Golfer* (New York, 1925).

Laney, Al, *Following the Leaders: A Reminiscence by Al Laney* (Stamford, CT, 1991).

Leach, Henry, *The Spirit of the Links* (London, 1907).

Lema, Tony, with Gwilym S. Brown, *Golfer's Gold: An Inside View of the Pro Tour* (Boston, 1964).

McKinlay, S.L., *Scottish Golf and Golfers: A Collection of Weekly Columns from the Glasgow Herald, 1956–1980* (Stamford, CT, 1992).

Nash, George C., *Letters to the Secretary of a Golf Club* (London, 1935).

Noakes, Alistair, *Hoylake Hero* (Norfolk, England, 2018).

Plimpton, George, *The Bogey Man* (New York, 1967).

Price, Charles, ed., *The American Golfer* (New York, 1964).

Price, Charles, *Golfer-at-Large* (New York, 1982).

Rice, Grantland, with Claire Briggs, *The Duffer's Handbook of Golf* (New York, 1916).

Sagebiel, Neil, *The Longest Shot: Jack Fleck, Ben Hogan and Pro Golf's Greatest Upset at the 1955 U.S. Open* (New York, 2012).

Shaw, Joseph T., *Out of the Rough* (London, 1940).

Silverman, Jeff, ed., *Bernard Darwin on Golf* (Guilford, CT, 2003).

Ward-Thomas, Pat, *The Masters of Golf* (London, 1961).

Ward-Thomas, Pat, *The Long Green Fairway* (London, 1966).

Ward-Thomas, Pat, *The Lay of the Land* (Stamford, CT, 1990).

Wind, Herbert Warren, *America's Gift to Golf: Herbert Warren Wind on the Masters* (Greenwich, CT, 2011).

Wind, Herbert Warren, *On Tour with Harry Sprague* (New York, 1958).

Wind, Herbert Warren, *Herbert Warren Wind's Golf Book* (New York, 1973).

Wind, Herbert Warren, *Following Through: Writings on Golf* (New York, 1985).

Wind, Herbert Warren, *The Complete Golfer* (Stamford, CT, 1991).

Wind, Herbert Warren, *An Introduction to the Literature of Golf* (Stamford, CT, 1996).

Wodehouse, P.G., *Golf Without Tears*, originally published in Britain as *The Clicking of Cuthbert* (New York, 1919).

Wodehouse, P.G., *Divots*, originally published in Britain as *The Heart of a Goof* (New York, 1923).

BOOKS: CLUB HISTORIES

Bell, Blyth and Greenway, Roger, *A Hoylake Celebration: Royal Liverpool Golf Club, 1869–2019* (St Andrews, 2019).

Behrend, John and Lewis, Peter N., *Challenges and Champions: The Royal and Ancient Golf Club 1754–1883* (St Andrews, 1998).

Behrend, John, Lewis, Peter N. and Mackie, Keith, *Champions and Guardians: The Royal and Ancient Golf Club, 1884–1939* (St Andrews, 2001).

Clark, Eric P., *The 150 Years: A History of the St Andrews Golf Club, 1843–1993* (St Andrews, 1993).

Cruickshank, Charles, *The History of Royal Wimbledon Golf Club, 1865–1986* (London, 1986).

Douglas, Ian M.K., *The History of Ganton Golf Club, 1891–2006* (Ganton, England, 2006).

Everard, Harry Stirling Crawford, *History of the Royal and Ancient Golf Club from 1754–1900* (Edinburgh, 1907).

Farrar, Guy B., *The Royal Liverpool Golf Club* (Birkenhead, England, 1993).

Furber, F.R, ed., *A Course for Heroes: The History of the Royal St George's Golf Club,* (Sandwich, England, 1996).

Goodban, J.W.D., ed., *The Royal North Devon Golf Club: A Centenary Anthology, 1864–1964* (Bideford, England, 1964).

Henderson, Ian T. and Stirk, David I., *Royal Blackheath* (London, 1981).

Mackie, Keith, *One Hundred Years New: A History of the New Golf Club of St Andrews* (Haddington, Scotland, 2003).

Pinnington, Joe, *Mighty Winds . . . Mighty Champions: The Official History of the Royal Liverpool Golf Club* (Wirral, England, 2006).

Pottinger, George, *Muirfield and the Honourable Company* (Edinburgh, 1972).

Shaw, James E., *Prestwick Golf Club: A History and Some Records* (Glasgow, 1938).

Smail, David Cameron, ed., *Prestwick Golf Club: Birthplace of the Open, the Club, the Members, and the Championships, 1851 to 1989* (Prestwick, 1989).

Ward-Thomas, Pat, *The Royal and Ancient* (Edinburgh, 1980).

ACKNOWLEDGEMENTS

———————•◦●◦•———————

Writers who seek to tell the story of golf's history owe a debt of gratitude to the historians who've done the foundational research into the game, spending countless hours scouring archives to establish what can be known with relative certainty about golf's early years.

The pre-eminent historian of the era this book chronicles is Peter N. Lewis, former director of the British Golf Museum and historian emeritus of the Royal and Ancient Golf Club. Two of his books – *The Dawn of Professional Golf* and *Why Are There 18 Holes?* – are essential to any understanding of how golf grew and changed when the game spread to England.

Since I took up golf history, Peter has been unfailingly helpful and encouraging, for which I am eternally grateful. The same could be said of the entire community of St Andrews historians, among them Peter Crabtree, Roger McStravick, David Hamilton, and the members of the aptly named Literati of the Links.

I also wish to acknowledge the work of my late friend and fellow historian, Bill Williams, who passed away as this book was written. His *Harry Vardon: A Career Record of a Champion Golfer*, *Vardon in America*, and *Ted Ray: The Forgotten Man of Golf* contributed mightily to this project.

The two courses critical to the rise of English golf – Royal Liverpool and Royal St George's – have my gratitude for the warm welcome they extended to me, especially Hoylake's Chris Moore, who accompanied me on a round of its classic links and gave me a guided tour of its clubhouse.

No writer ever completes research on a book without the help of those unsung heroes, librarians. I spent many happy hours at the National Library of Scotland, and was inspired by how eager its staff was to help and the phenomenal skill those men and women bring to their jobs.

Historians I've met through social media also helped in various ways, among them Joe McDonnell, Sam Cooper, Jasper Miners, Lee Patterson, Alastair Noakes, and Paul Fowler. It also was through social media that I met Sandra Russell, the artist whose lovely watercolour of the 1899 Amateur Championship finale adorns both my writing room and this book.

I'd also like to thank those who read my first draft and offered suggestions for a rewrite, including Jim Blankenship, David Gormley, Frank Vega, Bob Proctor and Connor Lewis, who has steadfastly supported my work through his Society of Golf Historians. Jim Stokes, a personal friend, also provided moral support that has helped me more than he can know.

Illustrations for this book were kindly provided by collector David Low, Dick Verinder, Blyth Bell of Royal Liverpool Golf Club, and the Royal and Ancient Golf Club of St Andrews.

The person who deserves my utmost gratitude, however, is Lee Horwich, my friend and fellow journalist, who served as the first editor of this book. His careful reading and thoughtful suggestions improved it immeasurably, as did those of copy editor Ian Greensill, a man truly gifted at his job.

Finally, as always, I want to thank my family for its support – my son Bob, his wife, Hannah, and their son, Oscar Vincent; my daughter, Cori, and my wife of 38 years, Mara, without whom nothing I have ever accomplished would have been possible.

Stephen Proctor
Wittsend Farm
Malabar, FL

INDEX

INDEX

INDEX